AIRLINE NETWORK DEVELOPMENT IN EUROPE AND ITS IMPLICATIONS FOR AIRPORT PLANNING

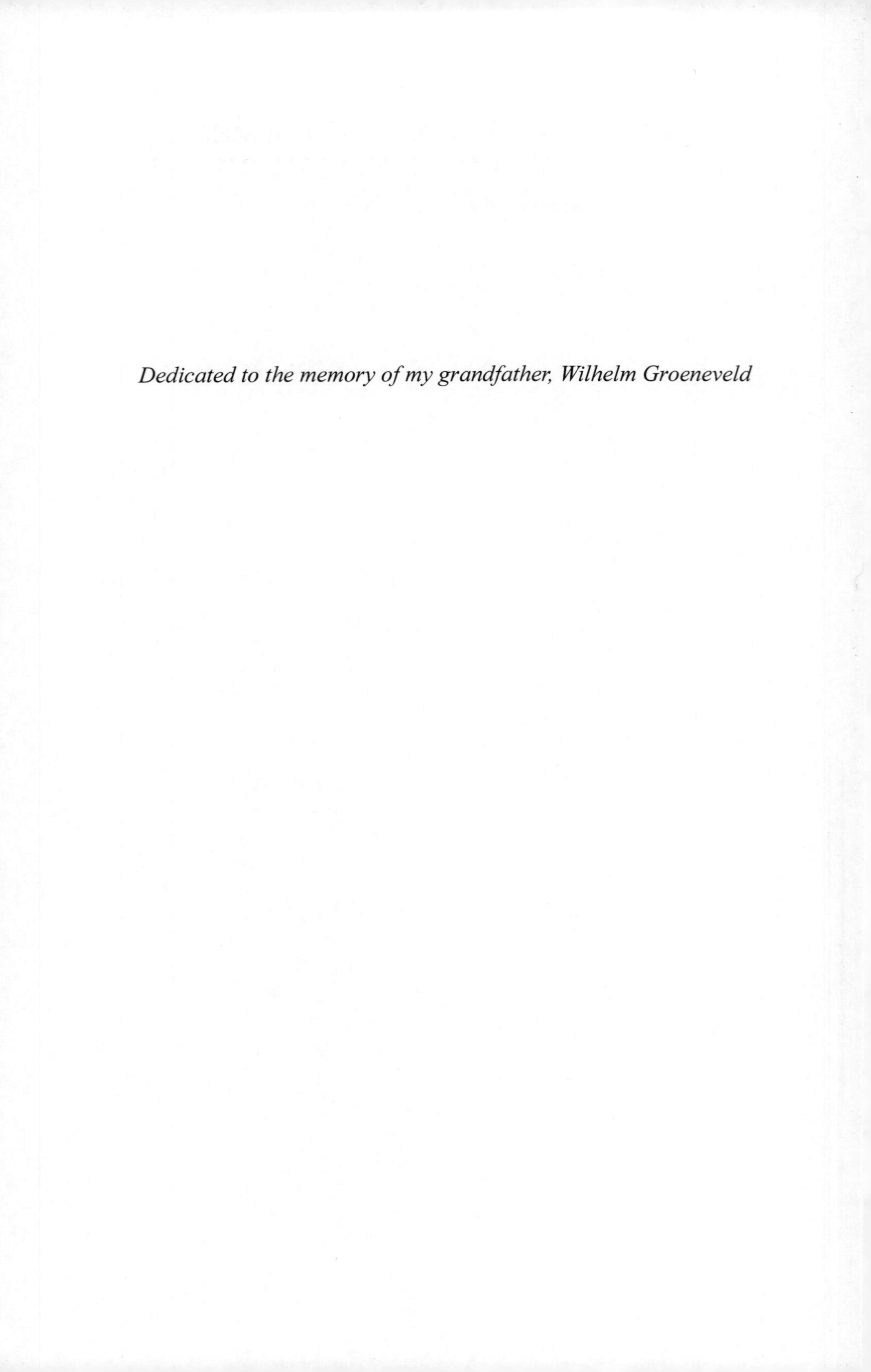

Dedicated to the memory of my grandfather, Wilhelm Groeneveld

Airline Network Development in Europe and its Implications for Airport Planning

GUILLAUME BURGHOUWT
Amsterdam Aviation Economics/SEO Economic Research, The Netherlands

LONDON AND NEW YORK

First published 2007 by Ashgate Publishing

Published 2016 by Routledge
2 Park Square, Milton Park, Abingdon, Oxfordshire OX14 4RN
711 Third Avenue, New York, NY 10017, USA

First issued in paperback 2016

Routledge is an imprint of the Taylor & Francis Group, an informa business

British Library Cataloguing in Publication Data
Burghouwt, Guillaume
Airline network development in Europe and its implications for airport planning
1. Airlines - Europe 2. Airlines - Deregulation - Europe
3. Airports - Europe - Planning
I. Title
387.7'2'094

Library of Congress Cataloging-in-Publication Data
Burghouwt, Guillaume.
Airline network development in Europe and its implications for airport planning / by Guillaume Burghouwt.
p. cm.
Includes bibliographical references and index.
ISBN: 978-0-7546-4506-1 1. Airports--Europe--Planning. 2. Airways--Europe--Planning. 3. Scheduling--Europe. 4. Airlines--Europe. 5. Aeronautics, Commercial--Europe--Forecasting. I. Title.

TL725.3.P5B87 2006
387.7'2094--dc22

2006031444

Figures and Cartography: Rien Rabbers, Ton Markus and Margriet Ganzeveld (GeoMedia, Faculty of Geosciences, Utrecht University)
English correction: Dr Anne Hawkins

ISBN 13: 978-1-138-24573-0 (pbk)
ISBN 13: 978-0-7546-4506-1 (hbk)

Contents

List of Figures

List of Tables

List of Boxes

Preface

To what extent have airlines reorganized their route networks following the deregulation of the European air transport market? What have been the implications of the changes in airline networks for European airports? How can airport planning deal with increasingly dynamic airline network behaviour and the related uncertainty concerning future airport traffic volumes? This book addresses these and other related questions, and will be of particular interest to air transport researchers, policymakers, and those working in the aviation industry.

The content of the book stems from PhD research carried out at the Faculty of Geosciences, Utrecht University between 2000 and 2005. I would like to take the opportunity to thank some of the people who have contributed to this research: Ton Kreukels (Utrecht University) and Jaap de Wit (University of Amsterdam) for their continuous guidance and support; Aisling Reynolds-Feighan of University College Dublin and Jacco Hakfoort of the Ministry of Economic Affairs were of great influence at the start of the research; Jan Ritsema van Eck was of help in configuring Flowmap for airline network visualization while Tom de Jong's programming skills enabled me to carry out the wave-structure analyses. My thanks should also go to Mark Dierikx, Nigel Dennis, Joop Krul and Maurits Schaafsma who opened doors for me that might otherwise have remained closed. Thanks also to Jan Veldhuis, Linda Heemskerk, Merith Pelger and Judith Wildbret at Amsterdam Aviation Economics for providing such a pleasant and reliable working environment. Thanks go to Guy Loft of Ashgate for his support and patience while preparing this text.

The collaboration of numerous professionals in the aviation industry contributed to the results presented in this book. Special thanks to the Airport Development Department of the Schiphol Group, NACO Netherlands Airport Consultants, KLM, British Airways, Lufthansa and Iberia.

I also thank my parents for their continuing interest in and support for the progress of this book. Finally, I must thank Yvette Bottenberg: for putting up with someone who gets excited when walking through the desolated terminals of Tempelhof, Florence and Düsseldorf-Weeze; and for her patience and good humour.

Financial support was provided by the Urban and Regional research centre Utrecht and SEO Economic Research.

Chapter 1

Introduction

This book explores airline network development and airport planning in the deregulated EU air transport market. Three issues are addressed: (1) How airlines in Europe have reconfigured their route networks after the deregulation of the EU air transport market; (2) how these changes affect the airport hierarchy as well as the network quality of individual airports; (3) how changes in airline networks affect the strategic planning of airport capacity. The study not only fills a gap in the current body of academic literature with respect to these issues, but also provides airports with information about ways of dealing with increasing uncertainty resulting from changing airline network behaviour.

Let us first address the regulation and deregulation of the EU air transport market and the potential consequences for airline networks, the airport hierarchy and airport planning, then consider the aim of this text.

Regime changes

At the Paris Convention of 1919, following the First World War, the allied countries decided that nation states would have full sovereignty over their own airspace. Since that time, national governments have been strongly involved in the development of national and international scheduled air transport networks.

International air carriers such as KLM and Lufthansa depended on a portfolio of bilateral air-service agreements between the governments of their country of registration and of the destination country. The bilateral air-service agreements specified, for example, the traffic rights given to the operating carriers (including the gateways accessible to each carrier), the number of carriers operating between the countries or points within these countries, and the flight frequencies. Sometimes the designated airlines pooled the revenue and/or costs on a certain route. In practice, the designated airlines were the national carriers or flag carriers of each country.

From 1947 on, the International Air Transport Association (IATA) (the umbrella organization of the international airlines) set the ticket prices charged by the international airlines at the worldwide IATA traffic conferences. Frequently governments owned their national airlines, or subsidized them heavily.

In short, the trinity of the national government, the national airline and the national airport dominated the international air transport markets. Little room was left for competition in the air transport regime of bilateralism.

Since the end of the 1970s the international air transport regime has been characterized by continuous deregulation of air transport markets. This trend started with the deregulation of the domestic US air transport market in 1978. Many bilateral air-service agreements were liberalized during the 1980s and 1990s. The United Kingdom–Netherlands agreement of 1984 and the United States–Netherlands agreement of 1992 were the first examples of these 'open skies' agreements between European countries and between the United States and other countries respectively. In 1988 a first 'package' of deregulation measures marked the beginning of the full, multilateral deregulation of the EU air transport market, which was eventually completed in 1997.

As a result, airlines are increasingly free to allocate resources in both space and time. The system of bilateral treaties no longer imposes a strict framework for intra-EU airline network development. Airlines can compete freely on ticket prices, frequencies, route networks and service levels. However, much of the extra-EU network is still regulated by means of bilateral air-service agreements.

The regime changes in aviation have resulted in significant changes for airlines and airports. Close examination of the consequences of deregulation of the US aviation market in 1978 reveals three important issues that existing studies have only addressed in a limited way with respect to the deregulated EU air transport market:

- the reconfiguration of EU airline route networks
- dynamics in the EU airport hierarchy
- the consequences for airport planning and development.

Let us briefly consider these issues in turn.

Airline network reconfiguration

Various studies have concluded that the deregulation of the domestic US aviation market in 1978 resulted in two major network strategies. The first of these was the adoption and intensification of hub-and-spoke-networks by major 'full-service' airlines such as American Airlines and Northwest Airlines. The second major strategy was the adoption or intensification of point-to-point networks by low-cost, no-frills airlines such as Southwest Airlines.

The adoption of hub-and-spoke networks by airlines has certainly been one of the most imaginative, surprising and radical effects of the deregulation of air transport markets. After US deregulation a number of major US airlines dropped their point-to-point route structures and introduced hub-and-spoke networks instead. These are concentrated spatially around one or more hub airports where passengers can transfer to their connecting flights within a limited time window. At the hub the airline operates a wave-system structure to maximize the number of connecting opportunities. In a highly competitive market, hub-and-spoke systems offer an airline the opportunity to benefit from certain cost and demand side advantages, to deter entry, and to exercise some bureaucratic control over the hub airport.

Low-cost, no-frills airlines followed an entirely different network strategy following US deregulation in 1978. Instead of the long-haul, high-yield and transfer markets, they concentrated on high-volume routes by using non-hub and secondary airports and offering very low priced, no-frills tickets. They preferred serving the origin-destination markets with a point-to-point network structure to serving the transfer markets with hub-and-spoke networks.

Dynamics in the airport hierarchy

Some studies have indicated that the adoption of spatially-concentrated hub-and-spoke networks by US airlines has resulted in more inequality in the US airport hierarchy. In other words, large airports, which are the home bases of major hub-and-spoke airlines, have acquired an increasingly large market share in total traffic (Goetz and Sutton 1997; Reynolds-Feighan 2000). The share in total departures of the largest 3 per cent of US airports increased from 25 per cent in 1978 to nearly 40 per cent in 1984 (Wojahn 2001, 36). In addition, hub-and-spoke networks and the freedom of entry and exit in deregulated markets are thought to have resulted in declining levels of air service at small community airports. Competition and network reorganization may focus on the larger airports, leaving the smaller airports with reduced air service or even a loss of air service altogether (Dempsey 1990; GAO 1997; Reynolds-Feighan 1995).

Other studies (Chou 1993a) have argued that hub-and-spoke networks have had the effect on the US airport hierarchy of reducing inequality. Traffic is in fact spread increasingly evenly over the US airports. The network economies of hub-and-spoke systems allow airlines to serve many more city-pairs than would have been the case in a point-to-point network without such network economies (Button 2002). Moreover, it is argued that the entrance of new airlines to the market induced the spread of traffic over more airports.

To what extent do different types of airlines have the effect of increasing or reducing inequality on the airport hierarchy? Such evidence is needed for the assessment of the potential inequality-increasing effects of EU deregulation as well as for the evaluation of the potential for future investments in airport infrastructure.

Flexible airport planning

The new air transport regime and the adoption of hub-and-spoke systems have changed the context of airport planning. A major element of this new context is the volatility (that is, the average year-to-year variation) of airport traffic.

The volatility of airport traffic tends to increase in deregulated markets. The freedom of route entry and exit, the footloose nature of transfer traffic, the rise of low-cost airlines and alliances have all led traffic volumes to become much more volatile and uncertain (de Neufville and Barber 1991). Examples in the United States show how airlines can build and abandon hub-airports (Charlotte and Raleigh-Durham, for example) in a relatively short period. Low-cost airlines can boost 'sleeping' regional airports, as Ryanair did at Brussels Charleroi. The bankruptcy of a hub carrier can reduce transfer traffic at the hub airport to virtually zero, as the bankruptcy of Sabena at Brussels has demonstrated.

At the same time, airport master planning needs reliable long-term traffic forecasts: investments in airport infrastructure are long-term issues and the planning of future developments needs estimations of capacity requirements. However, the growing dynamics in airline network behaviour and the resulting volatility and uncertainty have made airport traffic much more difficult to forecast and airports may face quickly changing market circumstances.

There is a tension between a volatile market environment and airport planning. The highly dynamic network development demands flexibility, whereas airport master planning demands reliable forecasts and certainty. The challenge for airport planning is, therefore, to be sufficiently flexible to be able to deal with an increasingly volatile network environment. Airports that are not able to deal with volatility and uncertainty in a flexible way face significant risks in terms of overbuilding, under-building and mismatches between infrastructure use and supply.

In this study, we have constructed a framework of flexible airport planning, and applied the framework to a real-world airport planning case.

Objective

In contrast with the United States, the research on airline network development and the consequences for the EU airport hierarchy and planning is still somewhat limited in scope. It is not clear to what extent European airlines have adopted hub-and-spoke network configurations or point-to-point networks against a background of an entirely different urban geography, system of regulations, ground access and history compared to the United States. Nor is it clear how changing route networks in the EU have affected the EU airport hierarchy. Neither has the issue of airport planning under a free EU market regime been addressed systematically in academic studies. These issues are highly relevant from a scientific and societal perspective.

Hence the objective of this text is to assess and describe to what extent airlines have reconfigured their route networks since the deregulation of the EU aviation market, how these network changes have affected the EU airport hierarchy, and how airport planning can deal with the changing context of airline network behaviour.

The first part of this book deals with the changing network behaviour of European airlines. Chapter 2 addresses the theory of airline network behaviour. Chapter 3 describes the changes in the geographical structure of European airline networks. Chapter 4 is focused on the changes in the temporal structure (wave-systems) of European airline networks. We bring together the spatial and temporal structure of airline networks in Chapter 5. In Chapter 6 we illustrate the changes in European airline networks by discussing a number of individual airline network cases, including KLM, Iberia, British Airways, Braathens and Air Berlin.

The second part of the book contains the analysis of the relationship between airline network behaviour and the network quality of European airports. Chapter 7 discusses the impact of the changes in airline network configuration on the distribution of seat capacity in the European airport hierarchy. In addition, we discuss the network quality of regional airports. The question is answered to what extent hub-and-spoke network development has been beneficial for the network quality of smaller airports at the downside of the European airport hierarchy.

The final part of this text addresses the issue of strategic airport planning in a highly dynamic air transport market. Chapter 8 surveys the requirements for a more flexible approach to airport planning. Based on these requirements, the strategic planning processed at Amsterdam Airport Schiphol is assessed in Chapter 9.

Chapter 2

Air Transport Networks

This is a study about airline network development and airport planning. In this chapter we provide a theoretical framework for such an analysis.

We begin by addressing the definition of an airline network. Next we ask, 'what are the decisive factors for airline network development?' Among other factors such as network economies, we put forward the international air transport regime as one of the key drivers of European airline network development. Lastly, we shift our focus from the airline to the airport level. We discuss the relationship between airport connectivity and airline networks. The final part of the theoretical framework, airport planning theory, can be found in Chapter 8.

Approaches to airline network analysis

How can we describe airline networks? There is no simple answer to this question, since airline networks are complex structures. We therefore begin this chapter by considering two approaches in the academic literature that aim to describe airline networks: the spatial approach and the temporal approach. The spatial approach can be found in graph theoretical studies, hub location models, and studies using concentration and dispersion measures. The temporal approach was only recently recognized in the academic air transport economic literature as an essential element for the description of airline networks.

Spatial approach

Graph theoretical approach The graph theoretical approach in geography was used extensively during the 1960s, 1970s and 1980s to study the spatial characteristics of networks (Gutiérrez Puebla 1987; James 2003; Tinkler 1977; 1979, for example). A graph represents an abstracted version of a network (Ivy 1993, 214). Tinkler (1979) defines a graph as 'a finite set of labels and a finite set of pairs of labels'. In relation to transport networks, the former is identified as a set of nodes and the latter as the connections (flows, linkages) between the nodes. Graph theory has brought forward a broad range of indices that describe various aspects of the structure of such graphs (James et al. 1970; Tinkler 1977).

In our view, graph theory has had a large but somewhat underestimated impact on the conceptualization and methodology of present-day airline network analysis. First, quite a large number of studies have actually applied graph theoretical measures to airline and aviation networks. In the 1970s graph theoretical measures were frequently used for the description of airline and aviation networks and transport networks in general (for example, James et al. 1970). But more recent studies have also applied measures originating from graph theory to airline network structures (Bania et al. 1998; Chou 1993a, 1993b; Ivy 1993; O'Connor 1997, 2003; Shaw 1993; Timberlake et al. 2000; Wojahn 2001). Graph theoretical measures were also used for the analysis of the effects of airline mergers on network structures (Shaw and Ivy 1994) and for the analysis of the relationship between air-service connectivity and employment (Irwin and Kasarda 1991; Ivy et al. 1995).

Second, graph theory has contributed to the conceptualization of airline networks. Several simple structures in graph theoretical studies were found so frequently that they have been recognized and named: the ring/Hamiltonian circuit, line, chain, star/radial, wheel, complete and tree graphs (James et al. 1970; Tinkler 1977). The fully-connected/complete and minimally connected graphs are generally considered the extreme types of graph. In recent literature on airline network economics and airline networks in general, the different graph structures listed have frequently been used to categorize airline networks: the line network (Hanlon 1996), the fully connected versus hub-and-spoke networks (Pels 2000; Schipper and Rietveld 1997; Shy 1997), the fully-connected/point-to-point versus the hub-and-spoke network (Bootsma 1997) and the linear versus the hub-and-spoke network (Oum et al. 1995; Reynolds-Feighan 2001; Williams 1994; Zhang 1996).

Insights from hub location-allocation models In contrast with graph theoretical studies, which have mainly described airline networks, hub location-allocation models aim to optimize spatially a special type of network: the hub-and-spoke. This approach has offered researchers a simple but important distinction between nodes and hubs. As O'Kelly (1998, 171) puts it: hubs are 'special nodes that are part of a network, located in such a way as to facilitate connectivity between interacting places'. O'Kelly distinguishes the hub from the service node. A service node is a point location from which only flows can originate and into which only flows which are destined for that location can enter. In contrast, a hub is a service node that also allows the passage or through-flow of transfer traffic. Corresponding with this, hub-and-spoke networks are 'networks where large numbers of direct connections are replaced with fewer, indirect connections' (O'Kelly and Miller 1994). Such hub-and-spoke networks have widespread application in transportation and are not unique for air transport networks.

Hub network design problems or hub location-allocation problems basically involve the modelling of the decisions on where to place the hub, how to assign non-hub origins and destinations to the hubs, how to determine the linkages between the hubs, and how to route the traffic between origins and destinations over the resulting network. The optimization is determined by internally minimizing the total transportation costs in a given network (O'Kelly 1998; O'Kelly and Miller 1994; O'Kelly and Bryan 1998; Kuby and Gray 1993).

Concentration and dispersion measures Another approach dealing with the description of the spatial aspects of networks is what we refer to as the 'network concentration' approach. In economics, sociology and industrial organization considerable attention has been paid to the measurement of concentration or dispersion in various types of populations, for example the distribution of income among individuals, or the distribution of market size among firms. Various measures have been developed to measure concentration or dispersion such as the C4 concentration ratio, Theil/Entropy index (T), variance of logarithms (L), herfindahl index (H), the coefficient of variation (V) and the Gini index (G) (Allison 1978; George et al. 1992; Sen 1976, for example).

Concentration and dispersion measures have been used frequently in air transport studies to evaluate market concentration in air transport markets or to analyze the relationship between airfares and market concentration in the context of antitrust issues (Borenstein 1989; DoT 1990a, 1990b; EURAFOR 2000; Frenken et al. 2004; Goetz 2002; Goetz and Sutton 1997; Lijesen 2004; Morrison and Winston 1995; Reynolds-Feighan 1998). More recently, Reynolds-Feighan (2001) and Wojahn (2001) applied concentration and dispersion indices to airline networks. The indices were used to measure the spatial distribution of air traffic over the population of airports in individual airline networks. High levels of concentration indicate a dominance of one or two central nodes in the network. Reynolds-Feighan (2001) and Wojahn (2001) argue that concentration measures are to be favoured over the more 'simple' (graph theoretical) measures. We return to the advantage of the network concentration measures in Chapter 3.

In conclusion, the three approaches discussed are all spatial approaches. The graph theoretical and concentration and dispersion measures aim to describe the spatial structure of networks. Central to the hub allocation-location models is the spatial optimization of hub-and-spoke networks. In other words, the three approaches consider the geographical variation of (airline) networks (nodes, linkages, flows) in space. All three approaches have offered researchers valuable tools and concepts for the analysis of airline networks. However, in none of these is the daily variation of a network in time considered. We argue that the temporal dimension of airline networks is an important characteristic of present-day airline networks.

Temporal approach

Why is the temporal dimension such an important feature of present-day airline networks? In 1955 (long before the deregulation of the US aviation market in 1978) Delta Airlines pioneered a hub-and-spoke strategy at their Atlanta hub in their efforts to entice passengers away from Eastern Airlines in the south-eastern part of the country (Delta 2004; Petzinger 1995; Toh and Higgins 1985). In June 1981 Robert Crandall's American Airlines adopted the hub-and-spoke network on an unprecedented scale, centring it on the Dallas hub.

Many US airlines followed the American Airlines example in a deregulated US aviation market. European airlines also embraced the hub-and-spoke network strategy after the deregulation of the market (see Chapter 3). Airlines adopt hub-and-spoke operations because they allow airlines to benefit from a number of cost and demand advantages. We deal with these advantages extensively later on.

From a spatial perspective, hub-and-spoke networks entail the concentration of traffic on one or two central hub airports where passengers can change planes on their way to their eventual destinations (Berry et al. 1996). Large numbers of direct connections are replaced by fewer indirect connections (O'Kelly and Miller 1994).

The definition of a hub-and-spoke network as a spatial concept would be indisputable if the passenger hub-and-spoke network were a delivery system: the same decision maker (the airline) positions the facilities (nodes and links) and determines the rules of allocation (passengers) to these facilities (O'Kelly and Bryan 1998). The airline would not have to worry about passengers who lose time because of a detour or a transfer at the hub. A detour is the ratio between the direct and indirect flight time. In a hub-and-spoke network many indirectly-connected city-pairs have a larger detour than would have been the case if these city pairs had been connected directly.

An example of a hub-and-spoke network as a delivery system is the air freight network. 'Air freight services may organize themselves without worrying about the travel itinerary of the individual packages' (O'Kelly and Bryan 1998, 172). Kuby and Gray (1993, 2) reported in a study on the air freight network of Federal Express: '[...] Detours are not a problem for cargo networks; as long as the package arrives on time, the customer doesn't care how it is routed.'

Air passengers, however, do care how they are routed and how much time they spend at the hub (Dennis 1994b). This difference derives from the fact that, in contrast with air freight networks, air passenger networks are not delivery systems but user attracting systems. In a user-attracting system 'the location of hubs and routing of aircraft is in the control of a single decision maker, but the impact of these decisions on air passenger acceptance of the carrier and the level of service/demand must be considered' (O'Kelly and Bryan 1998, 173). If an airline does not acknowledge the user-attracting nature of the passenger hub-and-spoke network, the costs associated with the possible detour of an indirect flight and the transfer time at the hub airport may result in a certain loss of passenger demand for indirect connections through the hub (Schipper 1999).

Assuming that the airline intends to operate a user-attracting hub-and-spoke network, how can the carrier minimize the loss of transfer passenger demand owing to detours and connecting time spent at the hub?

With respect to detours, the airline may resolve the loss of transfer passenger demand by choosing an optimal number of hubs, an optimal location of the hub(s) in space, and by designating suitable destinations to it so as to minimize the routing of passengers. The problem of finding such an optimal geographical location for hubs and designating suitable destinations to the hub was frequently addressed in various hub location-allocation models, econometric models (Berechman and de Wit 1996, for example) and empirical studies (Dennis 1994a; Dennis 1998, for example).

With regard to the loss of passenger demand through the transfer time at the hub, a temporal solution is needed: a wave-system structure (Bootsma 1997). This structure consists of a number of daily connection waves in the airline flight schedule for flights to and from the airline hub. 'A connection wave is a complex of incoming and outgoing flights, structured such that all incoming flights connect to all outgoing flights' (Bootsma 1997, 29). Waves are also known as banks, peaks or complexes. A wave maximizes the connection possibilities through a hub (given a certain number of direct flights); consequently it minimizes the waiting time for a transfer passenger. Without the synchronization of flight schedules, any method of connecting traffic succeeds 'by accident'. Only hubs with a very large number of direct flights per day would allow for large numbers of transfers within an acceptable time frame. These hubs are referred to as continuous hubs.

Corresponding with this, Bootsma (1997), Dennis (1994a; 1994b), Reynolds-Feighan (2000) and Wojahn (2001) explicitly underline the temporal dimension or scheduling as an essential element for the description of hub-and-spoke networks and present-day airline networks in general. The concentration of traffic in a number of daily waves of synchronized, incoming and outgoing flights can be considered a crucial aspect of the passenger hub-and-spoke networks in contrast with other air passenger network structures (a point-to-point network, for example).

Schedule coordination is not captured by graph theoretical or concentration measures (Wojahn 2001). As Bootsma (1997, 17) puts it, 'the schedule structure aspect is often neglected as a crucial aspect of the hub-and-spoke network structure.' The temporal dimension of the hub-and-spoke network and airline networks in general has not yet received much attention in the air transport economics literature. Annex 1 clearly demonstrates the focus on the spatial aspect of definitions of hub-and-spoke networks in the academic literature. Moreover, the definitions of the hub-and-spoke network in the literature vary substantially. There is no agreement on the definition of a hub-and-spoke network. Button (2002) articulated the same point: 'the lack of any universal accepted definition can be confusing in debate and, more importantly, can lead to a misunderstanding of what the role of any hub may be.'

These differences in hub-and-spoke definitions can be observed in four areas. First, most studies consider the hub-and-spoke network as an airline-oriented network. Some, however, consider the hub-and-spoke network as an airport-oriented network. Traditionally the United States Civil Aeronautics Board and later the Federal Aviation Administration have used the term hub to define any large airport (Dennis 1994a; Goetz and Sutton 1997; Ivy 1993; Reynolds-Feighan 1998).

Second, most studies see the spatial concentration strategy as the most important feature of the hub-and-spoke network. A hub is then a central node in the airline network and bears no reference to transfer traffic (Dennis 1994a, 221).

Third, only some studies explicitly acknowledge the temporal dimension of an airline network (see Annex 1). In these definitions the hub becomes associated with a high interconnectedness in both space and time where the hub carrier operates a number of daily waves of incoming and outgoing flights.

In our view, the present-day importance of airline hub-and-spoke network strategies requires not only an airline-oriented spatial approach, but also a temporal perspective.

In this section we have reviewed the various approaches to airline network analysis and the definitions of a special type of airline network: the hub-and-spoke system. Our conclusion is that the spatial approach in graph theory, hub location models and network concentration measures is a partial approach for the description of present-day airline network development. The adoption of hub-and-spoke network structures by US and European airlines requires the incorporation of a temporal dimension.

In this study we use an integrated approach; both the spatial and temporal dimensions of an airline network are used for the analyses performed in Chapters 3–5. Not only does the approach allow us to analyze the interconnectedness of networks in space, but also the interconnectedness of networks in time.

Defining airline networks

Given the wide range of definitions of a hub-and-spoke network and the different approaches to the description of airline networks in general, we have to make clear what we mean by an airline network and its different components. We therefore begin this section with a definition of an airline network. We present the airline network configuration as an analytical framework. We then turn to the roles different nodes may have in an airline network.

The time–space continuum of airline network configurations

Following the graph theoretical approach, we define a network as a set of interconnected nodes. We also argue that interconnectedness should be considered not only from a spatial, but also from a temporal perspective. To capture both dimensions, we introduce the airline network configuration as an analytical framework for the description of airline networks. We define an airline network configuration as the level of spatial and temporal concentration of an airline network. In other words, airline networks vary on a two-dimensional continuum of spatial concentration and temporal concentration.

Consequently, four extreme network configurations can be identified (Table 2.1). In fact, Figure 2.1 reveals that one may think of many 'intermediate' network configurations. The 'prototype' hub-and-spoke and point-to-point networks so frequently cited in the literature are just two network configurations among the many types possible. As Wojahn (2001, 23) puts it:

Table 2.1 The airline network configuration matrix

Level of spatial concentration	Level of temporal concentration at the hub	
	Co-ordinated	Random
Concentrated	Hub-and-spoke	Random radial
Deconcentrated	Co-ordinated/deconcentrated	Point-to-point

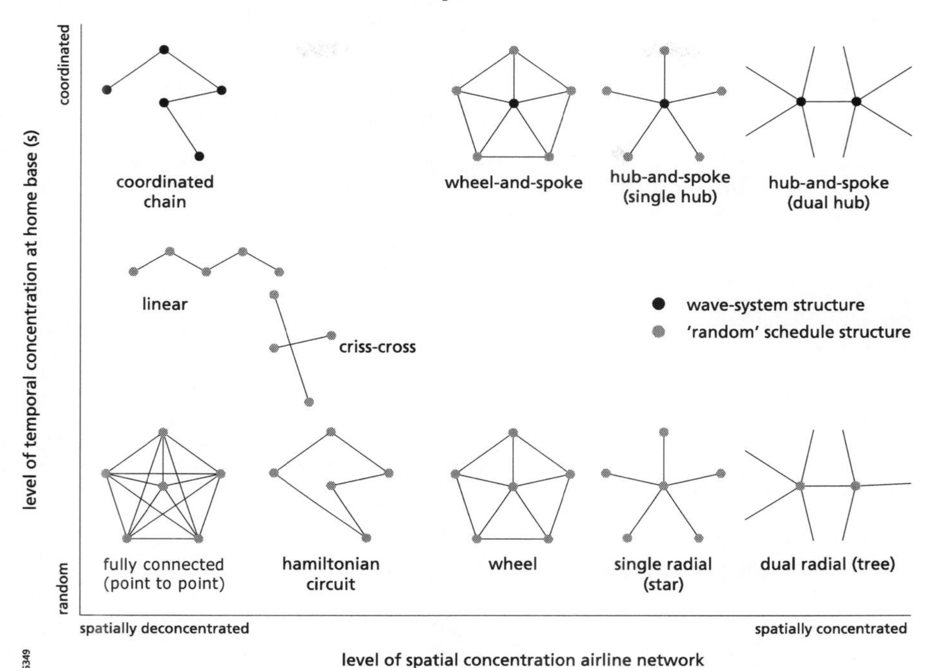

Figure 2.1 Time–space continuum of airline network configurations

> Real world airline networks [...] are a mixture between different forms, so that even in mainly hub-and-spoke type networks, some spoke cities have direct service between them, and even in mainly point-to-point type networks, some traffic is consolidated over transfer points.

In order to take into account both dimensions of airline network configurations, we use the time–space continuum of Figure 2.1 to describe airline networks empirically in Chapters 3–5.

We have no intention of presenting here an exhaustive review of airline network analysis. Spatial concentration and temporal concentration are not the only properties of an airline network. The complexity of airline network planning suggests that many other spatial and non-spatial properties of networks can be distinguished: network size (nodality), type of carrier operating the network (full service versus no-frills), average stage length, market share, type of equipment used, business model, and so forth (Dempsey and Gesell 1997). Given the current network behaviour of European airlines, we consider spatial concentration and temporal concentration the most important features with which to describe present-day airline networks.

Taxonomy of nodes in airline network configurations

As stated above, an airline network is a set of interconnected nodes. Within this concept we distinguish three basic types of node: station, traffic node and hub (Table

Table 2.2 Taxonomy of nodes in an airline network

		Spatial configuration of the node	
		Decentral	**Central**
Temporal configuration of the node	No wave-system structure in airline flight schedule	Airline station Feeder destination/spoke/ rim airport/non-hub	Traffic node Continuous hub
	Wave-system structure in airline flight schedule	(Intermediate node)	Hub Traffic hub, Hinterland hub, Directional/Hourglass hub, Allround hub, Eurohub, Specialized hub, Global hub, Hyper-hub, Mega-hub, Super-hub

2.2). According to our definition of an airline network configuration, nodes vary on a spatial and a temporal dimension.

Airline stations The simplest node is the airline station: it is not a temporal junction in the airline network, nor is it a spatial junction. It is a node from which only air passenger flows can originate and into which only flows which are destined for that node can enter. Special types of airline station are the feeder destination, spoke (airport) or non-hub airport. Spokes can only exist in relation to a (continuous) airline hub. They provide the hub with feeder traffic. Within a single airline network, spokes have a small direct, and no indirect connectivity, but a large onward connectivity through the hub(s).

Another specific type of airline station is the low-cost carrier node. The business model of the low-cost airline makes low-cost carrier networks less likely to be concentrated in time and space. The airline station is therefore an important feature of the low-cost airline network, characterized by short turn-around times and simple and efficient airport layouts.

Traffic nodes The traffic node is a central node in the airline network in the sense that it has a large share in the total airline network size.[1] Although the airline does not operate a wave-system structure, some indirect connections at the traffic node may be generated because of the spatial centrality of the node in the airline network (see Chapter 4). The continuous hub is a special kind of traffic node. Owing to the large origin-destination market, flights to the traffic node may be operated so frequently that large numbers of transfer passengers make use of the airport as a transfer node

1 In terms of seat capacity, number of flights, scope of the network or number of passengers.

(typically 20–30 per cent of the total number of passengers). A good example of such a continuous hub is London Heathrow (British Airways), as we see in Chapter 4. However, neither at the traffic node nor the continuous hub does the airline operate a deliberate schedule strategy in the form of a wave-system structure. The traffic node and continuous hub are not hubs in the strict sense, since it is not the aim of the scheduling strategy to maximize the number of journey possibilities.

In contrast, the 'rolling hub' (also known as the 'de-peaked' or 'peak-shaved' hub) resembles to some extent the continuous hub, but is the result of a deliberate scheduling strategy to deal with the complexity costs of the hub system or to ease congestion at the airport. Here, indirect connectivity is deliberately exchanged for better aircraft and infrastructure utilization by spreading and easing the waves in the schedule structure and allowing for more off-wave frequencies.

Hubs At a hub an airline concentrates its flights not only spatially, but also temporally. In other words, a hub is a traffic node at which the airline operates a wave-system structure to maximize indirect connectivity and minimize the waiting time for passengers. A literature review has revealed different types of hubs, although the criteria for the classification of different hub types are not always clear. In our opinion, we can classify hubs according to the size of the origin–destination market, the stage-length of the indirect connections offered, and the geographical specialization of the hubs. Let us consider these classifications.

First, we can classify hubs according to the size of the origin–destination market on which they rely. The origin–destination market consists of the passengers having the hub as their air-travel origin or destination. In generating direct and indirect connectivity, the traffic hub relies partly on a stable origin–destination market, and partly on the generation of transfer traffic by means of a wave-system structure (Figure 2.2). Hence a traffic hub is an airline hub making use of its potential for transfer traffic and its potential as an origin–destination node for local traffic. In contrast with the traffic hub, a wayport (de Wit and van Gent 1996, 307) relies heavily on transfer passengers (over 60 per cent). An airline may decide to operate a wayport because of its excellent geographical location with respect to traffic flows and large peak-hour capacity even in the absence of a significant origin–destination market. The wave-system structure is extremely important here to ensure maximal and seamless indirect connectivity. In 1991, for example, the transfer passengers at the wayport Charlotte (USAir) accounted for 74.1 per cent of total passenger numbers (Ivy 1993, 212).

Second, hubs can be classified according to the relative stage length of the segments of the indirect connections offered through that hub. In this context, Dennis (1994b) identifies the hinterland hub and directional hub. The hinterland hub links 'long-distance trunk or international routes with short-haul sectors' (Graham 1995, 113). In the European case, hinterland hubs concentrate on the connections between domestic/European feeder flights on the one hand and intercontinental flights on the other (Bootsma 1997, 15). In contrast with the hinterland hub, the directional or hourglass hub 'connects geographically separated regions' which 'broadly speaking, are located in the opposite direction' (Bootsma 1997) with the intention of minimizing unnecessary detours. The directional hub is concentrated mainly on the 'long-haul to long-haul' market. The typical hourglass hub is uni-directional. It may, for example, connect east–west or north–south flows. Delta Airlines operated an east–west uni-directional hub at Cincinnati for US domestic traffic, whereas Emirates connects Europe with Asia via Dubai (Airneth 2006). It can, however, also be multi-directional (east–west and north–south flows, for example). Obviously, such a multi-directional hourglass hub needs an excellent geographical position.

In a later paper, Dennis (1998) identified the regional hub. The regional hub mainly offers 'short-haul to short-haul' connections. Hubs offering all three kinds of connections (regional, hinterland, directional) are considered here as all-round hubs.

Third, one may classify hinterland hubs according to their geographic specialization within the total range of indirect connections offered. In the case of Europe, some hubs concentrate mainly on intra-European connections. These are referred to as eurohubs (Dennis 1994a). Other hubs may be specialized in a certain geographical market. Madrid is just such a specialized hub in the Europe-Latin America market. Finally, hubs covering the whole range of continental and intercontinental destinations can be considered as global hubs.

It is important to note that we have no intention of presenting here classifications that are commonly exhaustive or mutually exclusive. On the one hand, hubs can be classified along many more dimensions (size, efficiency, for example). On the other hand, a single airline hub can, at the same time, be a wayport and regional hub or a specialized directional hub and hinterland hub.

Consistently, the hyper-hub, mega-hub (Bootsma 1997) or super-hub (Ivy 1993, 216) may be considered the summum of 'hubness'. Not only is the hyper-hub an all-round hub: it is also a traffic hub and a global hub. The dual-hub of American Airlines and United at Chicago O'Hare is a good example of such a hyper-hub. The two carriers operate a wave-system structure here. Moreover, they can build on a large, stable origin–destination market and both hubs have an intercontinental and continental reach. However, in order to ease capacity shortages at Chicago O'Hare, both airlines started to 'de-peak' their wave-system structures. Apart from geographical location and origin–destination demand, abundant peak-hour capacity at the airport is certainly one of the most important requirements for an airline hub to reach the hyper-hub status.

Intermediate nodes There remains one last node to consider: the decentralized but temporally coordinated node in the airline network. Normally, spatial concentration is a precondition for temporal concentration. Without direct connectivity there can be no substantial indirect connectivity via the hub. Implementing a wave-system structure in the airline flight schedule becomes impossible. However, an airline may coordinate the flight schedule at a node for reasons other than improving indirect connectivity. An example is the intermediate node. At Gander International Airport (Canada), for example, many airlines made technical refuelling stops during the 1950s and 1960s. Aircraft flight range was not sufficient for non-stop transatlantic flights.

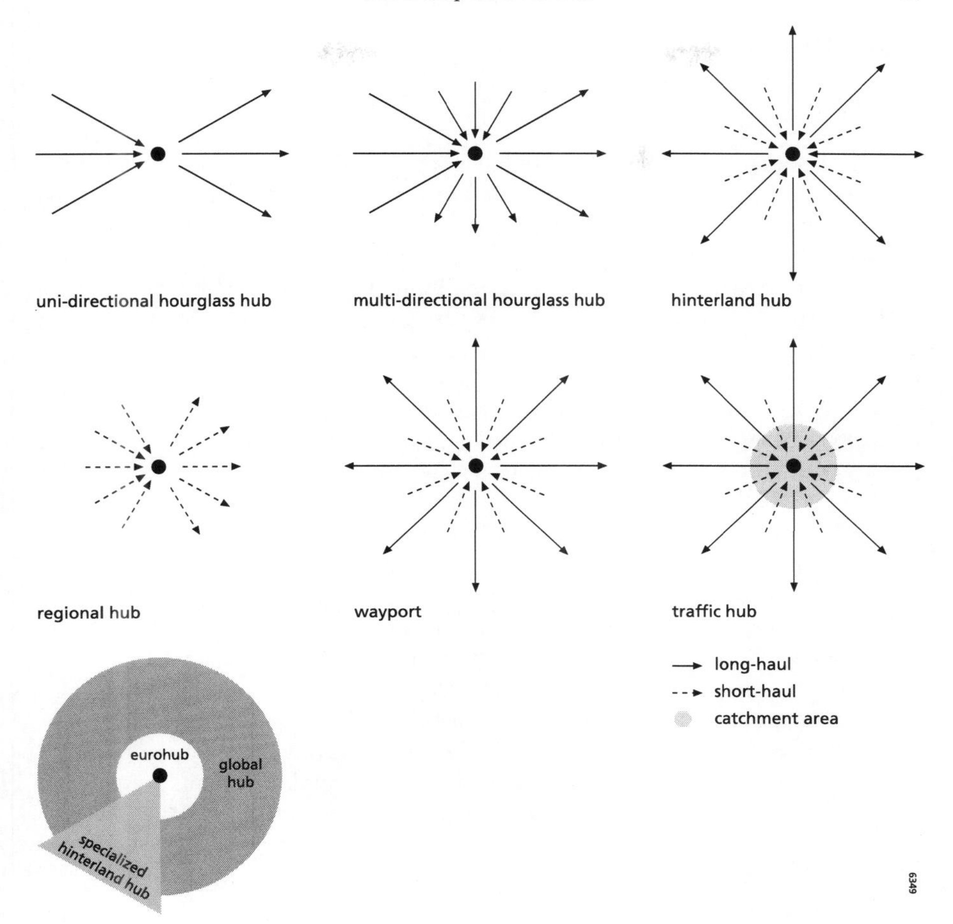

Figure 2.2 Different types of hub

After a short period of aircraft refuelling and stretching time for the passengers, the flight was resumed. The intermediate node is in fact a micro-scale directional hub with just a single connection. The intermediate node can still be found on ultra long-haul flights where aircraft range is not sufficient (the Europe–Australia market, for example) or to produce jointly two different markets when demand is not sufficient to serve them independently.

Up to this point we have concentrated on the description of airline networks and the role of nodes within such networks throughout this discussion. We now turn to the question of why airlines develop a certain network configuration, such as the hub-and-spoke or the point-to-point network.

Drivers for airline network development

Introduction

Why do airlines develop their networks in the way they do? This question is not easily answered, not only because of the numerous decision-making variables involved with respect to airline network planning, but also because airline network planning is based on the process of strategy formation within the airline. Strategy formation is not a fully analytical and rational process. Intuition, creativity (Mintzberg 1994), bounded rationality (Simon 1957), the organization's paradigm, luck, timing and political bargaining all play an important part in the formation of strategy within organizations. To provide a focus for the study and in line with our definition of the airline network configuration, we discuss here the most important factors influencing the spatial and temporal dimension of airline networks. In specific terms, we review the key drivers for (the development of):

- the extent to which an airline operates a spatially-concentrated or deconcentrated network
- the extent to which an airline operates a wave-system structure at the traffic nodes in the case of a spatially-concentrated network
- the interrelationship between the spatial and temporal dimensions.

Although it is not our primary objective in this study to explain airline network development empirically in relation to an airline's internal and external context, such a discussion is essential for a good understanding of the empirical results presented in this book. The key drivers for airline network configurations fall into four groups:

- the air transport regime
- network economies
- key drivers for airline nodes
- path dependency of airline network development.

The international air transport regime

An important variable affecting European airline network configurations is the international air transport regime. What is such a regime, and how does it affect airline network configurations?

The international regime concept Since the 1970s scholars of international relations have tried to conceptualize systems of international cooperation, which they refer to as international regimes (Zacher and Sutton 1996). According to Krasner, regimes are 'sets of implicit or explicit principles, norms, rules and decision-making procedures around which actors' expectations converge in a given area of international relations'.

We must clarify this. Principles are the most general standards of behaviour to which states/other actors in the regime attach varying degrees of importance (Zacher and Sutton 1996, 14). These principles often give rise to conflict. Examples include the principle of the free movement of commerce versus the principle of the internal political control of national air space in the international air transport regime.

Norms formulate the most general rights and obligations of states/other actors involved in a regime (Volten et al. 1999). Most states, for example, have accepted the innocent passage norm, which can be stated as: 'foreign commercial aircraft should have the right to pass through their sovereign air space in order to shorten the distance of a flight and to stop for technical assistance' (Zacher and Sutton 1996, 87).

Rules and decision-making procedures formally implement the norms of a regime (Zacher and Sutton 1996). Specifications of frequencies, capacity and tariff-setting procedures in bilateral air-service agreements are examples of such rules and procedures.

Here we use the regime concept for the explanation of the development of airline network configurations in Europe. We limit our discussion to the economic–jurisdictional part of an air transport regime, chosen because of its importance for airline network behaviour.[2] We refer to an economic–jurisdictional regime as a regime with respect on the one hand to the regulation of prices, market share, capacity and frequency and on the other to the level of state control over (access to) adjacent air space (which can be translated into the 'freedoms of the air', or traffic rights[3]) and the access to air space above the high seas.

European air transport regimes Between the Second World War and the end of the 1980s the European air transport regime[4] could be characterized as a regime of *quid-pro-quo* bilateralism (Wassenbergh 2003b). Until the end of the 1970s the international air transport regime was largely based on the principle of equity and internal political control. These principles were translated into norms of state control over adjacent air space and the equitable (*quid-pro-quo*) exchange of traffic rights through a framework of bilateral air-service agreements (ASA) between states (Wassenbergh 2003b; Zacher and Sutton 1996). Air service agreements in fact specified the rules and procedures of the regime. In general terms, an ASA specified frequency, tariffs, capacity, traffic rights,[5] the number of designated airlines and the

2 Damage-control regimes and regimes with respect to technical and procedural barriers remain outside the scope of this study (see Zacher and Sutton 1996).

3 See Annex 2 for an overview of traffic rights.

4 The 'European air transport regime' or 'EU air transport regime' is hereafter the regime covering all commercial, scheduled air services within the European Common Aviation Area (EU, Norway and Switzerland) and to third countries outside the European Common Aviation Area in 2003. EU air transport market contains all countries that are part of the European Common Aviation Area.

5 See Annex 2 for an overview of traffic rights. The first five of these are rooted in the Chicago Convention International Civil Aviation of 1944. States agreed upon the first

points/towns[6] served by each designated airline (Doganis 1991; Zacher and Sutton 1996). The designated airlines were mostly the flag carriers that operated from their national home bases. When the bilateral agreement did not regulate capacity, the designated airlines frequently agreed among themselves on an equitable sharing of capacity and/or revenue in inter-airline pooling agreements. Tariffs in an ASA were generally derived from the decisions of another important regime-actor: the International Air Transport Association (IATA), the organization of international airlines, founded in 1945. Participating airlines set the tariffs for air services at the yearly IATA regional conferences (Nayar 1995).

The ASAs differed in their regulatory restrictions, however, depending on the degree of importance the involved states attached to the principles of equity and political control versus the principles of efficiency and the free movement of commerce. In the view of Wassenbergh (2003b), the character of an ASA depends on the interpretation of the 'fair and equal' doctrine by the respective state: a balanced operation under equal circumstances (*quid-pro-quo*), or a level playing field (efficiency and competition).

A gradual transition of the international air transport regime took place during the 1970s and 1980s. After the deregulation of the US aviation market in 1978 the principle of efficiency and the free movement of commerce became increasingly important in the bilateral air-service negotiations of the United States with other countries (Doganis 1991, 2001; Nayar 1995). The result was a number of liberalized air-service agreements and open-skies agreements between the United States and a number of other countries. An open-skies agreement creates an open market between two countries in which carriers designated under the agreement can freely offer and operate air services between the two countries (Mendes de Leon 2002). The norm of competition prevails here. Restrictions remain, however, on the seventh, eighth and ninth freedom rights as well as the nationality of airlines (Annex 2). In other words the regime of *quid-pro-quo* bilateralism was replaced by a regime of limited competition, a regime of liberalism, a free-market regime or an open-skies regime (Toh 1998) in these markets.

The principles of free movement of commerce and efficiency became even more pronounced in the late 1980s. In 1987 the European Council decided to adopt a first Package of Deregulation Measures. A second (1990) and third Package (1992) further opened up the market for competition. The Packages apply to airlines of the European Common Aviation Area (ECAA) and the internal market (intra-ECAA air services). In 2000 the fifteen Member States of the European Union plus Iceland and Norway were part of the ECAA. In 2002 Switzerland entered the arena. Each package widened the opportunities for airlines to set airfares, frequency and capacity

---

two freedoms multilaterally. The multilateral exploitation of the other freedoms was rejected. These were left to the ASAs.

6 The points (towns/airports) that could be served by each designated airline were listed in the ASAs, or a more general right could be granted (all points in a specific country, for example) (Doganis 1991).

Box 2.1 Nationality of airlines

In theory, in a bilateral agreement between state A and B, state A can designate a non-national airline to operate air services. However, state B may refuse the designation of a non-national airline (Mendes de Leon 2002). A national airline is one that is 'substantially owned and effectively controlled by nationals of that state' (Doganis 2001, 83). Most states put restrictions on the foreign ownership and control of national airlines. The European Union's third Package of Deregulation Measures allows airlines within the EU to be owned by nationals or companies from any Member State. The level of ownership by non-EU nationals/companies is limited to 49.5 per cent.

(Annex 6). All restrictions on traffic rights were removed by 1997, including cabotage. State aid to national airlines was phased out, following a 'one time, last time principle' (Kinnock 1998). However, the European Commission has the right to intervene in order to prevent monopolistic or anti-competitive practices (Doganis 2001). Moreover, Council Regulation 2408/92 allows national governments to impose a Public Service Obligation on routes or groups of routes that are considered 'vital for the economic development of a region' (Williams 2002, 135), but where a commercially viable operation is not possible (CEC 1999; Reynolds-Feighan

Table 2.3 Development of Netherlands–US aviation relationship

	Netherlands–USA air service agreements and amendments			
	Bilateral air-service agreement of 1957	**Protocol of 1978 (amendment of the 1957 agreement)**	**Memorandum of Consultation of 1992 (open-skies agreement)**	**EU Third Package of deregulation measures (1992)**
Nationality requirements	Applicable	Applicable	Applicable	Community requirements
Designation	Multiple	Multiple	Multiple	Unlimited
Traffic rights	I–V	I–VI	I–VI	I–IX
Pricing	Subject to conditions	Country of origin rules	Free	Free
Capacity	Subject to conditions	Closely related to traffic demand	Free	Free
Code sharing	Not mentioned	Not mentioned	Allowed	Allowed
Change of gauge	Not permitted	Not permitted	Allowed	Allowed
Routes	2 designated points in USA for Dutch carriers operating out of Amsterdam	4 designated points and 1 additional point	Unlimited	Unlimited
Regime	*Quid-pro-quo* bilateralism	Liberalism	Open-skies	Free-market

Source: *Adapted from Mendes de Leon (2002)*
Note: *See Annex 2 for traffic rights.*

1999). National governments then provide the subvention for the operation of Public Service Obligation routes by air carriers following a tendering process.

Nowadays the European airlines that operate extra-European air services (air service between an EU country and a non-EU country) face different bilateral regimes. Mendes de Leon (2002) encapsulated this issue by listing the characteristics of the Netherlands–USA aviation relationship between 1957 and 1992 (Table 2.3) in contrast with the EU 1992 Third Package of Deregulation Measures. The table may serve as an illustration of the wide range of bilateral air-service agreements between EU states and third countries. Some of these arrangements are open-skies or liberalized bilateral air-service agreements, but 'most of the existing arrangements are quite protectionist and traditional' (Doganis 2001).

Though much more could be written about the background, content and future of the intra-European air transport regime, the main point is that the principles of efficiency and the free movement of commerce dominate this free-market regime. The norm of competition is dominant.

Regimes and airline network configurations International air transport regimes are important explanatory variables of the present-day network behaviour of European airlines. Let us explain why.

The regime of *quid-pro-quo* bilateralism in the post-War period was responsible for the formation of star-shaped networks of 'flag carriers' centred at the national airports of the European states. The listing in the bilateral agreements of points (airports/towns) that could be served by each designated carrier induced the spatial concentration of international traffic on a limited number of nodes.

When transfer traffic was considered in the air-service agreements as a combination of third and fourth freedom rights (Annex 2), the restricted third and fourth freedom rights could constrain the opportunities of carriers to optimize network coverage and frequencies to build a temporally concentrated airline hub (with a wave-system structure).

Some countries considered transfer traffic as a special form of the fifth freedom right: the sixth freedom right (Wassenbergh 1996). This view was frequently held by those countries originating or attracting large volumes of traffic, but which were not located centrally enough on the global traffic flows to benefit from transfer traffic (Hanlon 1984). Hence some of the air-service agreements limited the designated airlines to market transfer connections or carry transfer passengers (Hanlon 1984). For example, country A (the grantor state) might put a restriction in the bilateral air-service agreement with country H (the home state) to carry traffic between country A and country C via country H.

The regime of *quid-pro-quo* bilateralism still applies to many intercontinental services today. It therefore continues to pin designated intercontinental carriers to national gateways or airports within the national territory. Bilateralism basically prohibits non-designated carriers from operating these services. The success of bilateral negotiations between states defines where airlines can operate air services as well as the specifications of these services.

Even with regard to liberalized, open-skies bilateral air-service agreements, carriers are still bound to their country of origin. Nationality clauses in the ASAs prevent third-country carriers from using the respective traffic rights (Mendes de Leon 2002), although this is about to change (see also Box 2.2).

Some of the bilateral agreements between countries A and B allow a carrier from country A to operate a hub in country B, which is then referred to as the change-of-gauge hub (Dennis 1994b). Fifth freedom rights in combination with change-of-gauge rights (change of aircraft type) give the carrier from country A the right to build a hub in country B (Dennis 1994b), assuming that the third countries involved have agreed the fifth freedom rights. The problem with such an operation is that it is not very commercially attractive. Where 'a dedicated change-of-gauge fleet is maintained [...] utilization of the short-haul aircraft will be very poor' (Dennis 1994b, 141). Moreover, owing to the lack of cabotage rights and seventh freedom rights, effective online feedering is difficult. Not surprisingly, the change-of-gauge hubs of US carriers in Europe (TWA at Paris Charles de Gaulle, Pan Am/United Airlines at London Heathrow) were gradually dismantled during the 1990s when alliances became a more attractive alternative.

The free-market regime refers to the current intra-European air transport market. Airlines operating within this market are free to configure their networks as they wish since all traffic rights, including cabotage (eighth and ninth freedoms), were agreed upon multilaterally. Such carriers are, assuming that airport slots are available, in fact footloose companies (Klapwijk 1996), which governments cannot directly control (Rosenau 1992). Moreover, airlines are free to set fares, capacity, routes and frequency. Such a free-market regime thus implies less network stability for those airlines operating at the European or regional level. In contrast, airlines with an intercontinental network are still bound to the country of registration, although this is about to change as Box 2.2 shows.

What this discussion on air transport regimes shows is that European airlines that operate on a supra-European level face different coexisting, asymmetric (Oum et al. 2001), or even conflicting regimes. On the one hand, they operate under a free-market regime based on the principles of efficiency and free movement of commerce. On the other hand, they operate under a myriad of bilateral agreements for extra-EU services. Among other things, the bilateral regimes curtail the opportunities of airlines in building optimal, multi-hub, world-embracing networks because they limit an airline's field of action in a spatial and temporal sense. In answer to the hybridity, airlines may circumvent the asymmetry by engaging in global alliances with other carriers to create larger online networks (Oum et al. 2001; Wassenbergh 2003b). The alliance partner offers the carrier access to markets where the regulatory barriers of current bilateral regimes impede the carrier from entering fully into that market[7] (Doganis 2001). As Oum and colleagues (Oum et al. 2001, 62) put it: 'The

7 The KLM–Northwest alliance, for example, gives KLM access to the entire domestic US market, which it cannot itself serve economically in the absence of seventh freedom and cabotage rights (see Annex 2).

Box 2.2 The future of the European air transport regimes

The European air transport regimes continue to change. In November 2002 the European Court of Justice ruled that the open-skies agreements between eight European countries and the United States were illegal, since they discriminated against the airlines of other EU countries. Moreover, the Court decided that the European Commission should take bilateral negotiations over from the individual Member States (Mendes de Leon 2002). Furthermore, carriers from any EU Member State should be able to exercise traffic rights from any EU Member State other than the one in whose territory they are licensed (the so-called 'national treatment' of EU carriers).

Finally, the initiatives of the Association of European Airlines in 1999 and the European Transport Commissioner Loyola de Palacio regarding a Transatlantic Common Aviation Area between Europe and the United States and the subsequent negotiations between the EU and the US may be considered as steps towards the further strengthening of the principles of efficiency and free movement of commerce in the European aviation regimes (Airwise 2004; Moselle et al. 2002). These steps 'beyond open skies' will further increase the unconstrained field of action of airlines with respect to the configuration of their networks and may eventually give rise to a significant network restructuring of European carriers operating at a supra-European level. For further discussions on the future of the European air transport regime, we refer to Doganis (2001), Mendes de Leon (2002; 2003), Wassenbergh (2003a), for example.

immunized alliance is one limited way of dealing with the restrictions inherent to the bilateral system.' An immunized global airline alliance is in fact an example of governance of an air transport market without government (Rosenau 1992).

Our conclusion is that, through their particular norms, rules and procedures, the European aviation regimes have a considerable impact on the way in which airlines configure their networks. In fact, the air transport regimes define the field of action of an airline to configure its network. In particular, the different regimes that carriers face for operating intra- and extra-European service restrict the opportunities to optimize their networks spatially and, to a lesser extent, temporally.

Let us now turn to another factor that drives airline network development: the network economies of spatial and temporal concentration.

Network economies of spatial and temporal concentration

Let us assume that an airline with a certain cost structure operates under a perfect free-market regime. The airline, together with other airlines in the market, will have unlimited traffic rights and there will be no restrictions on capacity, frequency, entry, exit or price setting. Demand is sensitive to price, in-flight time and waiting time. All other things being equal, how would the airline configure its network spatially and temporally? This question has been discussed in various studies. We briefly review some of the insights from these studies and make some specifications according to the objectives of this book. We start with the need for the spatial concentration of an airline network. We then turn to the advantages and disadvantages of the temporal concentration at hubs.

Economies of density, aircraft size and scope Let us start with the spatial dimension. The airline industry is said not to be characterized by economies of scale at the firm level. Economies of scale exist if an increase in the size of the network in terms of the network size (number of nodes served) results in lower average costs per passenger (Braeutigam 1999; Wojahn 2001), regardless of the network configuration and traffic density. But, according to White (1979, quoted in de Wit 1995a) 'economies of scale are negligible or non-existent at the overall firm level'. We refer to Caves et al. (1984), for example, for empirical evidence on constant returns to scale in the airline industry.

At the isolated route level, however, scale economies do exist. Economies of aircraft size arise because average costs on a route fall as aircraft capacity increases (Berry et al. 1996; de Wit 1995b; Pels 2000). And given an aircraft's capacity, average costs fall as the length of the route increases (de Wit 1995b). Also, given route length and capacity, average costs fall as the average load factor increases. In the context of this study, it is important to note that these declining unit costs of service do not depend on the spatial configuration of the network, or its size as such. It is the traffic density on the individual routes that is important (Caves et al. 1984). Hence economies of traffic density arise because increasing traffic density in a network of a given size leads to lower average costs per passenger, given the scale economies at the route level (Braeutigam 1999; Brueckner and Spiller 1994; Caves et al. 1984; Keaton 1993).

With respect to the US airline networks, Reynolds-Feighan (2001) asserted that most US airlines operate a spatially-concentrated network with one or two central nodes. Only a few airlines – such as Southwest Airlines – operate a spatially-deconcentrated network (Reynolds-Feighan 2001). But even in such an airline network, some nodes are placed higher in the network hierarchy than others (Dallas Love Field, for example). Why do airlines concentrate their networks spatially if scale economies do not depend on the size (number of nodes) and spatial configuration of the network, but on the density of isolated routes?

First, spatial concentration is a phenomenon driven by the unequal spread of traffic demand. To a large extent, the geography of demand sets the limits for the development of airline nodes and airports in general (Graham 1998).

Second, even in a network that is not temporally concentrated and where there is no joint production of different air services on a single route (see below), there are some economies of scope associated with spatial concentration. Economies of scope exist when there are cost advantages for a firm concerned with providing a large number of diversified products rather than specializing in the production of a single output (Bailey and Friedländer 1982).

In the case of spatial concentration, economies of scope arise because certain inputs such as aircraft, maintenance and crew are imperfectly divisible, so that the provision of deconcentrated air services would leave excess capacity in the utilization of these inputs (Bailey and Friedländer 1982). According to Reynolds-Feighan, the concentration of a network around focal points is always more attractive than operating a fully deconcentrated (such as a linear, chain or fully connected) network, even in the absence of transfer passengers who travel through these focal points. The tendency to concentrate a network depends on a variety of cost reasons. These include (1) the ease of crew and aircraft rotations, (2) the sharing of fixed airport costs (check-in, maintenance, and so forth) over more passengers, and (3) the more intensive use of capital (Reynolds-Feighan 2001).

Economies of scope and temporal concentration Now let us consider a single hub network that is concentrated not only spatially, but also temporally: the airline operates a fully developed wave-system structure at the hub. Why would an airline concentrate its network in time? Because besides the economies of density, such a network configuration may be attractive for an airline, since it may benefit from economies of scope, demand advantages, entry deterrence and bureaucratic control.

Scope economies in a hub-and-spoke network are associated with the joint production of heterogeneous products (different origin–destination markets) on a single air service. On the Stavanger–Amsterdam service, KLM carries not only point-to-point passengers between Stavanger and Amsterdam, but also the transfer passengers who travel beyond Amsterdam to New York, Nairobi, Detroit, and so forth. The economies of scope arise because the density on the spokes is higher (Pels 2000) compared to a point-to-point network. These economies of density in turn imply economies of scale at the individual route level owing to the use of larger aircraft, higher load factors, and so forth.

One should note that an airline does not necessarily need a wave-system structure to benefit from the cost advantages discussed here. In other words, its network does not have to be temporally concentrated. An airline may offer indirect connections through a traffic node (Southwest at Dallas Love Field, British Airways at London Heathrow, for example).

However, passenger air transport networks are user-attracting systems. Hence, waiting time at the hub and large detours result in a certain loss of passenger demand (Schipper 1999). The loss of demand through excessive waiting time at a hub can be minimized by adopting a wave-system structure in the flight schedule. A wave structure maximizes the number of indirect connections given a certain number of direct flights within a limited time frame. Adopting a wave-system structure in the airline flight schedule thus stimulates the cost and demand side advantages of hub-and-spoke operations. The wave-system structure increases the scope of city-pairs offered within the maximum perceived waiting time for the passenger and increases density and scale economies.

Box 2.3 'Self-help hubbing'

Interestingly, if an airline is able to increase the maximum acceptable waiting time of passengers (by lowering prices for price-sensitive passenger segments in order to decrease the generalized costs of the passenger journey, for example) and at the same time is able to increase frequencies, a wave-system structure may not be needed to benefit from extensive network economies. Low-cost, 'self-help' hubbing becomes possible at almost no extra cost for the airline (Franke 2004). Such a system is comparable to the transfer process between different lines in a metropolitan subway or bus system. High frequencies and low prices are the drivers for such a hub-and-spoke system.

Transfer passengers of Southwest (a low-fare, low-cost US airline with a random schedule structure and a spatially deconcentrated network) accounted for 10–15 per cent of total passenger numbers in the 1990s (Dempsey & Gesell 1997). Franke (2004, 19) even argues that such an extended low-cost business model could be an example for full-service hub-and-spoke carriers to ease the drawbacks of hubbing operations and 'to break free of the vicious cycle of connectivity and complexity'. We refer to the October/November issue of the Journal of Air Transport Management (2004) for extensive discussions on the drawbacks of the full-service versus the low-cost airline model.

Demand advantages Hub-and-spoke networks also lead to certain advantages in relation to passenger demand. Through the economies of scope and densities a hubbing airline can offer the consumer a wider range of (indirect) destinations at higher frequencies than would have been the case in an alternative network configuration with the same number of links (Lijesen et al. 2000; Oum et al. 1995; Pels 2001). In a network with one hub and n spokes, the hubbing carrier offers n direct and n(n-1)/2 indirect markets. Obviously, the multiplier-effect of hub-and-spoke networks makes the network much more attractive for consumers.

Various authors (Berry et al. 1996; Borenstein 1989; Lijesen et al. 2000; Oum et al. 1995) state that consumers may be willing to pay a higher price (the hub premium or mark-up) for the local (spoke) services of the dominant hubbing airline. The airline offers them a wider network, greater flight frequencies and better frequent-flyer programmes. The airline still loses some traffic, however, because for some passengers the generalized costs for the indirect trip via the hub are too high compared with a direct trip. In this respect, the quality of the wave-system structure is extremely important in ensuring minimum connecting times. On the other hand, being a dominant hub airline at an airport also gives the carrier the opportunity to exploit its market power and raise fares (Lijesen 2004).

Entry deterrence Airlines can use the hub-and-spoke system to deter the entry of new airlines. First, when an entrant wants to take indirect traffic from the incumbent, some kind of arrangement between incumbent and entrant in schedules and fares for the connecting passengers is required. This arrangement would involve costs that neither the incumbent airline nor the entrant may want to face.

Second, when the entrant has no access to the incumbent's connecting traffic, the entrant will only have a small market share (Oum et al. 1995; Zhang 1996). Moreover, the incumbent high-density hub carrier will be able to offer a much broader network to the consumer, and may benefit from lower unit costs and other advantages over the new entrant, such as frequent-flyer programmes and control over scarce airport facilities. Entering the hub–spoke market of the incumbent carrier would be a costly and risky undertaking for a new entrant (Zhang 1996). The market dominance on the spoke markets allows an incumbent to set higher prices (Lijesen et al. 2000). On the basis of an empirical study, Berry and colleagues (1996) conclude that raising prices for non-business, price-elastic passengers may be disconcerting, while for business passengers who are less price sensitive the strategy may be acceptable.

Bureaucratic control A less-frequently cited factor for an airline's choice of a hub-and-spoke network is the fact that being a home carrier with a large market share and network at a nearly congested hub may give this airline some bureaucratic control over airport operations and development and so serve its needs better. In many cases airline operations are still the main source of revenue for airports (Lijesen et al. 2000).

Alliances Alliances and mergers between airlines can be vehicles for the further exploitation of the advantages of hub-and-spoke networks. Alliances and mergers allow airlines to create multiple-hub networks. The networks of the (alliance) partners can be linked through the respective hubs (Pels 2001). Many alliance arrangements are possible (Rhoades and Lush 1997), but the only alliances which can be further exploited are those where the partners have complementary networks and are able to blend their flights through the hubs in order to achieve a seamless service (in contrast to the parallel alliance, where the alliance networks largely overlap).[8]

Some remarks Hub-and-spoke networks do not come without drawbacks for the carrier. Hub-and-spoke networks have not proven to be necessarily the most profitable (Button 2002; Toh and Higgins 1985; Tretheway 2004). We refer to such drawbacks as network duplication and complexity costs. Network duplication may appear when an airline ends up competing with itself across duplicated hubs (Graham 1995). Such duplications are mainly caused by airline alliances or mergers that are not fully complementary in terms of network coverage. The downsizing or closing of unprofitable hubs ('de-hubbing') may then be a solution. USAir, for example, closed

8 We refer to Bissessur and Alamdari (1998), Chen and Chen (2003), Dresner et al. (1995), Gudmundsson and Rhoades (2001), Morrish and Hamilton (2002), Oum et al. (2000), Park et al. (2003) and Pels (2001) for further discussions on the advantages of airline alliances.

its Dayton hub and downsized Baltimore operations in 1991, because these hubs were competing with Pittsburgh and Philadelphia after the merger with Piedmont.

Complexity costs arise when increasing traffic density leads to higher average costs per passenger in a network of constant size (number of nodes). In relation to a wave-system structure, complexity costs are associated with the relatively low aircraft utilization and reduced utilization of resources (Bootsma 1997; Franke 2004). First, gates and other resources are only utilized for a limited period during the day. Second, a limited number of connection waves results in long aircraft turn-around times at the spokes. Finally, a wave-system structure is a highly time-critical operation. Significant recuperation costs may occur when flights are delayed or when baggage is lost. An airline can de-peak or randomize its schedule to contain the complexity costs of the hub operation (Back 2002). According to Franke (2004, 20), airlines best de-peak their schedules by prioritizing indirect connections according to the yield of the traffic carried. This phenomenon is also known as the 'rolling hub' concept, a 'peak-shaved' hub or a 'de-peaked' hub.

Unit costs versus passenger demand Furthermore, the hub-and-spoke network is not equally attractive for every airline. Much depends on the cost structure of the airline in relation to passenger demand. Shy (1997) and Pels (2000) find that the hub-and-spoke network (with the joint production of different origin–destination markets in a single air service) is more profitable when unit costs associated with maintaining a route are large compared with passenger demand on that route. Alternatively, when demand is large compared with the unit costs for maintaining a route, point-to-point operations (without the joint production of different origin–destination markets in a single air service) are more profitable. Hence, the cost structure of an airline is an important factor for its network configuration. In this regard, a distinction can be drawn between the high-cost, full-service hub-and-spoke (network) airline business model on the one hand and the low-cost, low-fare, no-frills airline business model on the other.

Consistently, high-cost, full-service carriers such as KLM and Lufthansa are likely to operate spatially and temporally concentrated hub-and-spoke networks in particularly low-density markets (KLM 2002). In contrast, carriers with a low-cost, low-fare business model (Southwest, Ryanair, for example) can be expected to (1) operate in medium/high-density origin–destination markets, (2) focus on origin–destination passengers rather than transfer passengers (point-to-point operations), and (3) operate a random flight schedule without a wave-system structure.

Low-cost carriers offer low fares, thereby alienating regular passengers from full-service carriers, capturing latent passenger demand (Franke 2004) and enlarging the catchment area. Some medium-size markets, which previously needed a hub-and-spoke system to be profitable, can now be served relying only on origin–destination markets.

In addition, low-cost airlines have relatively low unit costs. These are mainly the result of operating medium/high-density routes with high aircraft-load factors, high-density seating, the standardization of aircraft types, electronic ticketing, low levels of on-board service, use of under-utilized secondary airports and flexible labour contracts (Dempsey and Gesell 1997; Doganis 2001; Reynolds-Feighan 2001; Williams 2001). In other words, the cost advantages of low-cost carriers do not stem as much from the network economies of hub operations as from overall lower unit costs. In fact, the absence of hubbing operations is in itself a cost advantage for low-cost carriers. These do not suffer from any of the complexity costs associated with operating a temporally-concentrated wave-system structure.

Besides being temporally deconcentrated, their networks are likely to be less concentrated in space. Spatial concentration is a condition for a hub-and-spoke network configuration. Hence, spatial concentration is less important for low-cost carriers than for full-service carriers. Moreover, a more deconcentrated network configuration may be chosen to prevent head-to-head competition with full-service carriers. Nevertheless, some level of spatial concentration is still needed in order to avoid excessive costs for aircraft maintenance, crew rotation, and so forth. But these costs are in any case lower for low-cost carriers, because they tend to use secondary airports with low airport charges, outsource aircraft maintenance and airport handling, and provide no facilities for connecting passengers (Doganis 2001).

A new low-cost carrier is therefore likely to start operations from a central home base, preferably a secondary airport close to a major city. Larger low-cost carriers may have a more deconcentrated network pattern, although other low-cost network configurations exist, as we see in Chapters 3–5. The deconcentrated low-cost network is still centred on a multiple central traffic node (home bases) (de Wit 2004). These home bases do not dominate the network as much as the hubs of the full-service airlines. As discussed earlier, central traffic nodes are still needed for technical, operational and scheduling reasons.

In conclusion, the air transport regime mainly sets the unlimited field of action of airlines to configure their networks. In the hypothetical situation of a perfect free-market regime, economies at the node level would stimulate the spatial concentration of airline networks, regardless of the joint production of different origin–destination markets in a single air service in that network. Airlines can further increase cost- and demand-side advantages by jointly producing different origin–destination markets in a single air service through the central traffic node(s). Hub operations, characterized by a wave-system structure in the airline flights schedule, minimize the loss of passenger demand resulting from transfer time at the hub. However, hub-and-spoke networks do not come without drawbacks. Airlines with low unit costs may in any case prefer alternative network configurations.

We have concentrated here on the air transport regime and network economies. The development of real-world airline networks is, however, much more complex. We therefore discuss below a number of intervening factors at the level of the individual nodes.

Table 2.4 Key drivers for nodes in airline networks

	Airline station	Traffic node	Hub
Airport	• Safety of the airport and destination • Efficiency of ground (turn-around times), baggage and terminal handling • Airport charges and other airport related costs (visit costs)	• Capacity • Airport amenities according to airport size • Efficient airport lay-out that minimizes taxi-times • Opportunities for future growth • Opportunities for aircraft maintenance	• Peak-hour capacity of airport • Transfer facilities minimizing minimum connecting time • Facilities for connecting passengers • Gate-positions hub carrier • Opportunities for operating dedicated airline terminal(s)
Airport context	• Size of a solid origin–destination market, which is determined by: ◦ Population size and growth ◦ Personal disposable income in catchment area ◦ Level and nature of economic activity in catchment area ◦ Social environment (length of holidays, attitudes to travel) ◦ Level of tourist attraction ◦ Historical/cultural links ◦ Earlier population movements ◦ Migrant labour flows • Travel restrictions • Landside accessibility in relation to airport size • Reliability of runway system in various weather conditions • Flying (sector) time to hub(s) (in case of a spoke) • Competitive position: degree of market dominance that is likely to be achieved in direct and onward markets • Level of competition of other transport modes	• Degree of market dominance that is likely to be achieved by the hub-carrier in both direct and to a lesser extent indirect markets • Location with respect to global time zones and night curfews	• Geographical location of hub with respect to the major traffic flows • Existence of commuter feeder

Key drivers for airline nodes

Although it is unlikely for an airline to 'pick up and drop' its hub or traffic node in order to continue its operation at an alternative location (Bootsma 1997), it may still be useful to identify the criteria for choosing a location for a hub or traffic node. Doing so may give some insight into the question why certain airlines adopt a wave-system structure in their airline flight schedule and others do not. Second, key drivers reveal why some traffic nodes or hubs show higher growth rates than others and hence are located more centrally in space than others (Dennis 1998). Third, the identification of key drivers is useful when considering a strategic alliance or merger with the aim of building a multiple-hub network (Bootsma 1997). Finally, such an overview may be useful in assessing the future potential of hubs and traffic nodes (Dennis 1998). What key drivers can be distinguished for airline nodes?

A survey of the relevant scientific literature and interviews with airline and airport managers reveals a large number of key drivers. We have listed them in Table 2.4. The taxonomy is cumulative. In other words, the drivers distinguished for airline stations also apply to traffic nodes and hubs, and the drivers for traffic nodes also apply to hubs. Hence some basic drivers, such as a safe and reliable airport infrastructure, are relevant for all types of node. Others, such as short minimum connecting times and peak-hour capacity, are only important for hubs.

In addition, Barrett (2004, 37) identified a number of distinctive key drivers for nodes served by low-cost airlines. These key drivers include:

- low or no airport charges
- quick 25-minute turn-around times
- single-storey airport terminals
- quick check-in
- good catering and shopping at the airport
- good facilities for ground transport
- no executive/business-class lounges.

Path dependency

The development of airline network configurations is rooted in history. Airline networks are, in a way, path dependent. In evolutionary economics, path dependency refers to the dependence of the economic behaviour of a firm on its specific history. Firms tend to build on past experience and the resources they already have (Boschma et al. 2002, 42). Political bargaining within an organization stimulates further building on the current situation in strategy formation. This is likely to be incremental rather than radical (Mintzberg 1994). If a strategy is successful, firms tend to consolidate their behaviour. If proven unsuccessful, firms may adapt according to the resources, routines and knowledge they already have. Eventually there may be a lock-in situation: historical and random events can lead to an outcome that is not necessarily the most desirable (Arthur 1989; Boschma et al. 2002).

In the airline industry, the development of large-scale hub-and-spoke networks in particular is characterized by path dependency and lock-in for several reasons.

First, the very nature of hub-and-spoke networks favours the addition of frequencies and destinations to the existing hubs, all other things being equal. Obviously this approach is associated with network economies. Every frequency added to the network creates network economies for the airline and a multitude of new origin–destination markets offered to the consumer. The cumulative causation of hub connectivity thus favours large nodes over smaller nodes in the development of the hub-and-spoke network (Barabasi 1999; Barabasi et al. 2000). In contrast, the networks of low-cost airlines, which do not depend on network economies but on overall lower unit costs, imply a different type of path dependency, including more short-term network dynamics.

Second, the investments and risks associated with building new hubs or large-scale traffic nodes are enormous. An airline may wish to relocate or add hubs because its current hub operation is not optimal. Further, an airline may have to build a multiple-hub network when detours become too large to serve a larger geographical market, (KLM, for example, would need a secondary hub to serve [transfer] markets within Southern Europe). But, according to Bootsma (1997, 9), 'it is hardly possible for an airline to pick up its operation and continue at another location'. The huge investments in resources (labour, equipment, infrastructure, advertising, and so forth) and the limited knowledge of the local market make it risky to build an additional hub outside the home market(s) or choose another location for the present hub operation(s) (Jagersma 2003; Oum et al. 1993). Moreover, hub relocation is associated with divestment in the present hub location.

We have no intention of suggesting that hub building and discontinuous network change is impossible. However, in general terms, network change is an incremental rather than a radical process. Hub building favours existing hubs/traffic nodes over greenfield locations. In accordance with this, alliances, acquisitions and mergers can be more suitable for building a multiple-hub network, since vulnerable greenfield investments are not needed (de Wit 1995a). Discontinuous network change is possible (such as the implementation of wave-system structures, as in the case of Air France at Paris CDG, or the hub building of Lufthansa at Munich), but is much less frequent.

Finally, the location of European hubs is seldom the result of a rational choice made by an airline in an economic sense. Seemingly trivial historical events were often much more important. Furthermore, the historical accumulation of traffic rights associated with certain airports favours the continuous development of an airport from one or a number of central nodes.

In the course of time a hub location may result in being suboptimal in an economic sense, but the hub carrier may be locked in at the hub because of regulatory barriers in the air transport regime, the lack of slots at other airports and the huge investments associated with choosing another hub location.

In conclusion, we have reviewed the drivers for (the development) of airline network configurations. Insights from the international regime theory, transport economics, economic geography and evolutionary economics have been used to discuss these drivers. We argue that international regimes, network economies, key drivers at the nodal level and path dependency are important determinants for the development of airline network configurations in Europe. This overview will facilitate understanding of the empirical results presented in the following chapters.

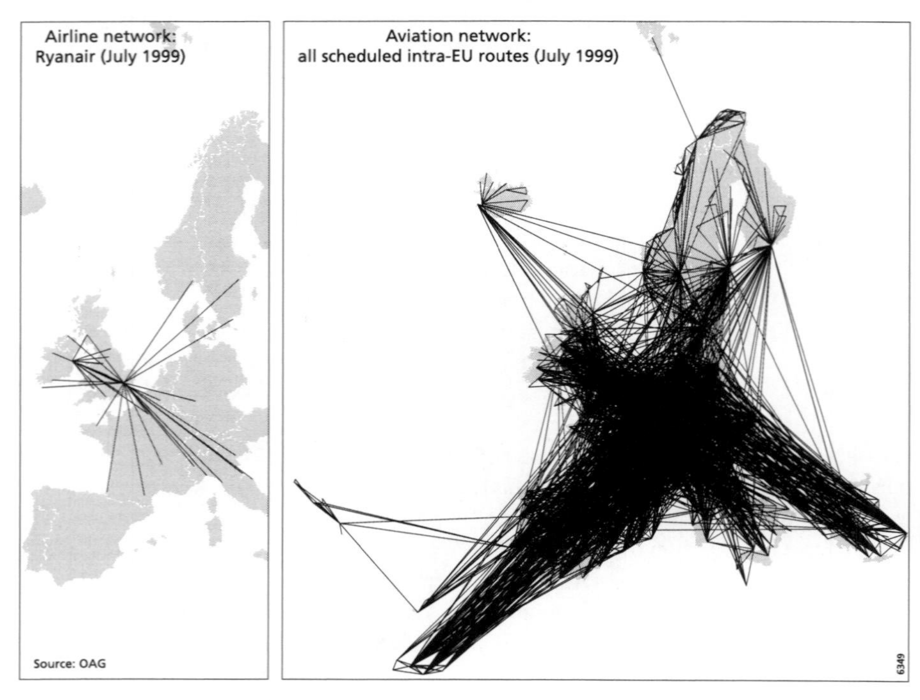

Figure 2.3 The airline network versus the aviation network

Airline network configurations and airports

In this study we use airline network behaviour as the starting point. We assume that the position of an airport in the aviation network is the sum of the output of the different airlines on an airport in terms of destinations, number of connections, or seat capacity. Figure 2.3 illustrates the difference between an individual airline network and the aviation network, which is in fact the aggregation of all individual airline networks.

In this study an airport it is not a node at the airline network level, but a node at the level of the aviation network. The airport acts as a forum in which the network activities of different airlines are brought together to facilitate the interchange between airside and surface transport (Doganis 1992). More specifically, we consider the connectivity of an airport to be the result of the aggregated airline network behaviour at a particular airport.

The airline viewpoint (Chapters 3–5) can be justified in different ways. First, an airport has the role of network-service provider in contrast with the role of an airline as an air-service provider (Stout 2001). The airport enables the air-service provider to make safe and efficient use of the airport infrastructure. An airport can only facilitate connectivity, but can never determine it directly, unless of course the airport engages in airline operations. Second, the airline viewpoint is important because of the high degree of dominance by one or two airlines or alliances at Europe's major airports (de Wit et al. 1999; Frenken et al. 2004).

What the airline viewpoint suggests is that the network decisions of individual airlines or alliances may have severe consequences for the connectivity of an airport as well as traffic demand. We discuss the effects of airline network behaviour on European airport connectivity in Chapter 7. In other words, we provide an answer to the question, to what extent have the network strategies of European airlines since the deregulation of the European aviation market resulted in spatial concentration or deconcentration of seat capacity among the European airport population. Moreover, the impact of airline network strategies on airport planning is analyzed (Chapters 8–9).

On the basis of the insights from this chapter, we can now analyze airline network development in the EU. Let us therefore turn to the first empirical chapter of this study: the changes in the spatial configuration of airline networks in Europe between 1990 and 2003.

Chapter 3

The Spatial Configuration of Airline Networks in Europe[1]

To what extent have European airlines changed their network behaviour following the deregulation of the European air transport market? In Chapter 3 and Chapter 4 we look at the changes in network configurations of European airlines in answer to the first research question of the study.

The time–space continuum of airline network configurations discussed in Chapter 2 defined an airline network configuration as the level of spatial and temporal concentration of that network. Within this continuum configurations of airline networks range from simple linear systems to radial networks and from point-to-point to hub-and-spoke networks.

The ongoing regime changes in European aviation and increased competition are likely to underlie the changes in European airline network configurations. Two issues deserve special attention here: first, the adoption and intensification of hub-and-spoke operations among large airlines; second, the development of point-to-point operations among low-cost airlines. The underlying theoretical assumptions and experiences in the deregulated US aviation market support the hypotheses of increased hub-and-spoke and point-to-point operations among certain categories of airlines (see Chapter 2). The question addressed here is: To what extent have European airlines in fact reconfigured their route networks?

In this chapter we describe our analysis of the developments in the spatial dimension of airline network configurations between 1990 and 2003. We then consider the changes in the temporal dimension of airline network configurations in Chapter 4. Lastly, in Chapter 5 we provide a synthesis of both the spatial and temporal dimension of airline network configurations, and support our synthesis with a number of airline network cases.

We begin this chapter by reviewing the relevant empirical studies in which the spatial and temporal dimensions of airline network configurations in both Europe and the United States have been analyzed. Then, the Gini methodology and the data used to measure the spatial concentration of an airline network configuration are described. Lastly, the empirical results are discussed.

---

1 In relation to this chapter, the following article has previously been published: Burghouwt, G., Hakfoort, J.R. and Ritsema van Eck, J. (2003), 'The spatial configuration of airline networks in Europe', *Journal of Air Transport Management* 9:5, 309–23.

Literature review

To what extent have researchers analyzed the spatial and temporal dimensions of airline network configurations in both Europe and the United States? Let us consider some important studies describing US and European airline networks.

United States

The developments in graph theory during the 1960s and 1970s resulted in a number of geographical studies that applied graph theoretical measures to various types of transport networks, including air transport networks (James et al. 1970, for example) Yet in most of these studies the application and usefulness of the newly-developed graph theoretical measures to real-world transport networks prevailed over the analysis of air transport networks itself.

Geographers' interest in airline network development was renewed by the deregulation of the US air transport market in 1978 and the subsequent adoption and intensification of hub-and-spoke networks. Geographers showed particular interest in the description of the spatial structure of US airline networks, together with the accessibility of nodes within these networks. Ghobrial's (1983) dissertation entitled *Analysis of air network structure: the hubbing phenomenon* was one of the first academic studies to consider the spatial structure of US hub-and-spoke networks in the deregulated market. Simple (graph theoretical) measures were subsequently used to analyze the spatial structure of US airline networks. These measures include the percentage of transfer passengers (DoT 1990a; Kanafani and Ghobrial 1985; Morrison and Winston, 1995), the percentage of traffic at the three busiest airports in an airline's network (McShan and Windle 1989), the number of outlying cities served from pre-defined hubs divided by the number of spokes radiating from it (Toh and Higgins 1985), and the actual number of connections in a network compared with the maximum number of connections (Wojahn 2001). Morrison and Winston (1995) demonstrated clearly the intensification of hub-and-spoke operations of US carriers after deregulation in 1978. The increase in hubbing operations translated into a strong growth of the percentage of passengers who needed to make on-line connecting flights.

Later, Shaw (1993) and Bania et al. (1998) classified the US airline stations according to their position in the airline network at a particular point in time. Both studies criticize former analyses (especially those featuring the hub/non-hub dichotomy in the hub location/allocation models) as too simplistic for describing airline hubbing. Moreover, Bania, Bauer and Zlatoper (1998) argue that it is difficult to 'capture a complex, multidimensional activity with a single scalar measure'. Using various (graph theoretical) measures, they classify a number of airline stations as hubs offering different levels of connectivity.

Whereas Shaw (1993) and Bania and colleagues (1998) looked at the hub-and-spoke operations at the level of individual airline stations using graph theoretical measures, Reynolds-Feighan (2001) shifted the level of analysis to the airline network level. She did not, however, use graph theoretical indices to measure spatial concentration of airline traffic. Instead, she used economic concentration and dispersion measures, in particular the Gini index. In Reynold-Feighan's view 'other measures [...] take little or no account of the number of airports served, they are scale independent, and they are insensitive to almost all the variations in traffic distributions, other than those at the extremes.' The advantages of the use of the Gini index are discussed in detail in Reynolds-Feighan (1998). In her 2001 study she showed that US airline networks had already been concentrated spatially before deregulation for reasons of cost and scheduling. After deregulation US carriers increased the extent to which their traffic flows were concentrated at a small number of key nodes (or hubs). This pattern is consistent for all the carriers examined, except for the low-cost, no-frills carrier Southwest Airlines, which operated a spatially deconcentrated network.

In his thesis, Wojahn (2001) applies the consolidated hubbing index to a large number of airline networks for the year 1999. The consolidated hubbing index is the average value of the normalized Gini, Theil, McShan-Windle index and the Coefficient of Variation. He finds that, in general, EU and US airline networks are highly concentrated in space, except for some low-cost airlines such as Southwest. However, Wojahn did not perform a time-series analysis with the consolidated hubbing index, making it impossible to draw any conclusions about the changing spatial configurations of EU airline networks.

Our conclusion is that most of the US studies have provided a snapshot picture of airline network development. Only a few studies actually empirically demonstrated the increased level of spatial concentration as a result of airline hub-and-spoke strategies at a few key nodes in the network.

It is interesting to note that very few studies in the academic literature describing US airline and aviation networks have paid attention to the temporal dimension of the airline network. As we saw earlier, a hub-and-spoke network needs a wave-system structure at the central hub(s) to maximize the number of transfer opportunities and minimize the waiting time for passengers. The emphasis in the US studies has clearly been on the spatial dimension of airline network configurations. The temporal dimension was at best demonstrated indirectly through the percentage of transfer passengers at central airports (Morrison and Winston 1995; Wojahn 2001).

Europe

Network developments in the deregulated US air transport market resulted in a flurry of research. The number of studies concerning European airline networks is considerably smaller. One reason is that European regulatory reform is obviously much more recent. Furthermore, the data needed to analyze European airline network development is scarce. A database like the T-100, which gives monthly passenger and freight traffic data for the US domestic and international route markets, or a 10 per cent ticket sample, is not available for Europe. Then again, the flow data of Eurostat and IATA are not comprehensive or up-to-date. An alternative is the use of OAG flight schedules, which provide information about the structure of airline networks, but not about the realized flows in that network. OAG flight schedules list all scheduled flights from certain airports broken down by destination, airline, flight number, flight time, aircraft type, weekly frequency, and so forth.

Dennis (1994a; 1994b) was one of the first academics to address airline network developments in the deregulated European aviation market. Using OAG flight schedules he analyzed the connecting opportunities in various geographical markets at major European airports in 1992 given minimum and maximum connecting times. In essence, Dennis used both a spatial and a temporal perspective to describe the hubbing phenomenon in Europe. Later, Bootsma (1997), Veldhuis (1997) and Veldhuis and Kroes (2002) further elaborated the concept of indirect connectivity at major airports. Veldhuis and Kroes found a significant increase in indirect connectivity at the major European airports, indicating an intensification of the hub-and-spoke operations of European airlines.

Dennis (1994b) made a further valuable contribution. He developed a connectivity ratio to facilitate the evaluation of the relative quality of the schedule structure in generating indirect connections compared with a random schedule structure. He was able to classify European airline hubs in terms of the efficiency of their wave-system structures. An entirely different approach to evaluating the schedule structure was developed by Bootsma (1997). He visualized the schedule structure by means of a wave-structure analysis. Using a similar, but much simpler approach, Stratagem Amsterdam (1997) and De Wit and colleagues (1999) found evidence that European airline hubs had adopted or intensified wave-system structures after the deregulation of the market (see also Chapter 4).

In our opinion, the analysis of EU airline networks concentrated more on their temporal dimension (the schedule structure, indirect connectivity given minimum and maximum connecting times, for example) than on their spatial dimension. In particular, no graph theoretical applications similar to those frequently found in the US literature were encountered. Most studies carried out during the 1990s dealing with the spatial distribution of traffic flows within European airline networks or airport hierarchies were based on comparisons with the United States and anecdotal evidence rather than comprehensive empirical research (Caves 1997; Caves and Gosling 1999; de Wit 1995b; Nijkamp 1996, for example). Some exceptions, however, have given some useful insights into small community and regional air services (Graham 1997b; 1998; Reynolds-Feighan 1995), network developments in relation to the introduction of regional jets (Dennis 2001b), the impact of the EU Public Service Obligations on air services (Williams 2002; Williams and Pagliari 2004), and the development of the aviation networks in certain regions of the EU (for example, Thompson 2002).

Airline networks have a spatial and a temporal dimension. The evidence on the dynamics of the spatial and temporal dimensions of airline network configurations in Europe is far from complete. This chapter adds to the evidence by considering the spatial dimension of airline networks in Europe. Chapter 4 deals with the temporal dimension. Chapter 5 integrates the two.

Measures of spatial concentration

Various graph theoretical indices and economic concentration or dispersion measures are available to measure the level of spatial concentration of a network. Examples of the graph theoretical measures include Chou's (1993a; 1993b) beta index of spatial concentration, the Shimbel index, the valued-graph index (Shaw, 1993), the topological hubbing index (Wojahn, 2001) and gross vertex connectivity (Ivy 1993). Examples of economic concentration measures include the coefficient of variance, the herfindahl index, Theil's entropy measure, the C4-firm concentration ratio and the Gini index.

Reynolds-Feighan recommends the Gini index as the most appropriate concentration measure for airline networks (Reynolds-Feighan 2001) or airline traffic distributions at airports (Reynolds-Feighan 1998). Allison (1978) and Sen (1976) examined the properties of income inequality measures and proposed a series of characteristics that indices should possess. The C4 index only reacts to changes in the traffic distribution in an airport population when the four biggest airports are involved. Moreover, the herfindahl index is only sensitive to changes in the extremes of the population. The coefficient of variance, on the other hand, reacts well to changes in the population, but is extremely sensitive to the underlying distribution.

The Gini index was the only index to satisfy all the criteria. The Gini index is not sensitive to the distribution of the population and reacts quite well to changes in all parts of a given population.

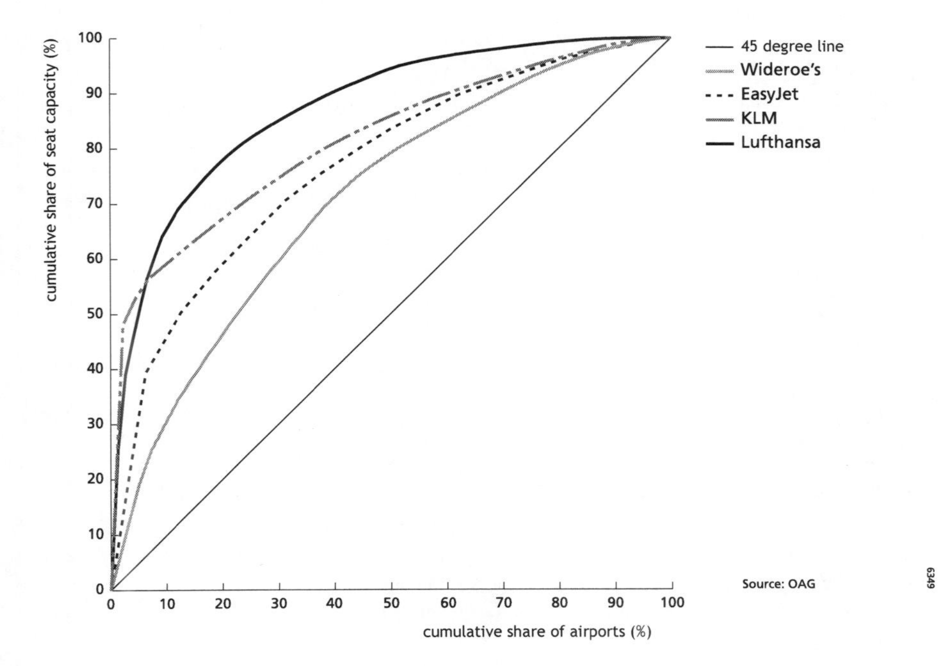

Figure 3.1 Lorenz curves for selected airline networks, 1999

With regard to the spatial concentration, the Gini index can be defined as:

$$G = \frac{1}{2n^2 \bar{y}} \cdot \Sigma_i \Sigma_j \mid y_i - y_j \mid \quad (1)$$

where y is the air traffic at airport i or j, defined as the total number of supplied seats per week, and n is the number of airports in the airline network. The Gini index is based on the absolute difference in seat capacity between every possible airport pair in the airline network scaled to the number of airports in that network and the average seat capacity per airport. The Gini index can be illustrated graphically with a Lorenz curve. The 45-degree line represents the case where all traffic is equally distributed over all nodes in the airline network and the Gini index has a value of 0. The greater the Gini index, the larger the area between the 45-degree line and the Lorenz curve. Figure 3.1 presents the Lorenz curves for various airlines.

If we assume that the total incoming air traffic at each airport is approximately equal to the total outgoing air traffic at the same airport, it is obvious that no airport will have more than half the total air traffic. Therefore, the Gini index cannot reach its theoretical maximum value of 1. The maximum Gini score increases with the number of airports in an airline's network (n) and can be computed as follows:

$$G_{max} = 1 - \frac{2}{n} \quad (2)$$

This maximum Gini index can be observed in a single-hub network where traffic flows are concentrated on one route (see Figure 3.2). Theoretically, this makes sense, since a single-hub system is most efficient from the airline viewpoint (Dennis 2001a; O'Kelly and Bryan 1998) and the concentration of traffic on one route obviously allows for further scale economies.

In this study we have corrected for the size of the airline network (number of airports) whenever we have measured network concentration. We define NC (the level of network concentration) as:

$$NC = \frac{G}{G_{max}} \quad (3)$$

where G is the observed Gini-index in a network and G_{max} is the maximum Gini-index given the number of airports in the network.

Let us turn to some examples of different network configurations and corresponding NC values (Figure 3.2). An NC varies between 0 and 1. An NC of 1 corresponds to a single radial network where traffic flows are concentrated on one route. A decline in NC indicates a more even spread of seat capacity over the airport population, whereas an increase in NC indicates a more unequal spread of seat capacity over the airport population. Any network where all the airports command equal shares of the total traffic will result in an NC of 0. This situation includes many different configurations, ranging from fully connected networks at one extreme to collections of isolated routes at the other.[2]

Extensive visual inspection of large, real-world network configurations (>20 nodes) reveals that NC values of dual- or triple-radial networks range between 0.71 and 0.80. A single-radial network with traffic fairly equally distributed over all routes would show an NC value of 0.61 to 0.70. In other words, according to the NC index, a dual- or triple-radial network is spatially more concentrated than a single-radial network. NC values of 0.49 and lower are associated with deconcentrated, criss-cross networks. Radial networks with a large number of 'bypass' routes between smaller airports generally have NC values of between 0.50 and 0.60. When discussing the NC values, we label airline networks as described in Table 3.1.

Data and classification of carriers

Our dataset consists of OAG (Official Airline Guide) data for the years 1990 –99 and the year 2003. Unfortunately, the years 2000–2002 were not available for analysis.

---

2 In essence, an increase in the NC index in a network of a certain seat-capacity size could be the result of any of these three components:

- route network effect: a more equal distribution of destinations (routes) over the airport population, while holding seat capacity per flight (aircraft size) and flight frequency per route constant. This effect is related to the morphology of the route network and indicates whether a network has a radial, non-radial or intermediate structure
- frequency effect: a more equal distribution of flights over the airport population, while holding the number of routes per airport and the seat capacity per flight constant
- capacity effect: a more equal distribution of seat capacity over the airport population, while holding the number of routes per airport and flight frequencies per route constant.

In theory, each effect can be measured separately by using different inputs for the NC index. The NCdestinations measures the route network effect. The difference between NCfrequency and NCdestinations measures the frequency effect. The difference between NCfrequency and NCcapacity measures the capacity effect. Hence, the NCcapacity is the combined expression of the route network effect, the frequency effect and the capacity effect. For the sake of comparability with the results obtained by Reynolds-Feighan (2001) and to reduce the complexity of the analysis, we have only used seat capacity as an input for the NC index (NCcapacity). NCcapacity captures all the effects mentioned above quite well where the larger airline networks (>20 nodes) are concerned. In other words, a high NC index in terms of seat capacity also implies a radial network morphology (high NCdestinations). For smaller networks, however, the NCcapacity can deviate markedly from the NCdestinations (route network morphology) or NCfrequency. For example, in smaller networks a high NCcapacity can be caused by a single, highly-frequent connection with a large-capacity aircraft, while at the same time the network morphology is of a non-radial type (low NCdestinations). Hence, for smaller networks, we only use the NC index in terms of seat capacity for drawing conclusions about the distribution of seat capacity over the airport population. It is advisable to compute the NC index in terms of the number of destinations/ frequency when drawing conclusions about network morphology for smaller networks.

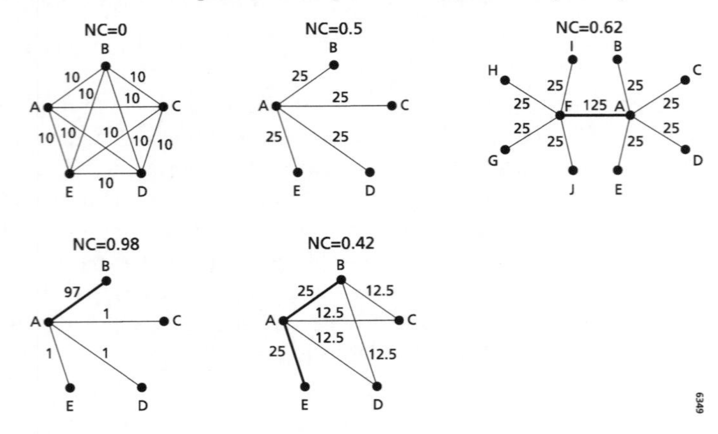

Figure 3.2 Network types and NC values

The OAG dataset contains variables based on published information on scheduled flights. Variables include departure airport, destination airport, flight frequency, aircraft type and seat capacity for each flight, and the number of stops made during the flight. The data are based on a week in July of each year.

The OAG data suffer from several limitations. First, OAG data provide insight only into scheduled flights and not into realized demand or supply. Load factors, weather conditions, technical problems and congestion lead to differences between the two. Given that we are interested in the structure of the aviation network, we did not consider this discrepancy to be a problem.

Second, the OAG data only register scheduled services. We have deleted full freight flights from the dataset and have only considered passenger flights (including 'combi' flights). Alliance relationships were not included in the analysis. This limitation is a drawback to the value of the results presented here, given the current importance of alliances. The complex and highly dynamic alliance relationships make the inclusion of every alliance in the analysis of the spatial configuration of airline networks an extremely time-consuming task, as the yearly survey on airline

Table 3.1 NC values and categorization of airline networks

NC value	Spatial distribution of seat capacity		Morphology of the route network	
	Large network (>20 nodes)	Small network (<=20 nodes)	Large network (>20 nodes)	Small network (<=20 nodes)
<0.49	Deconcentrated	Deconcentrated	Non-radial	–
0.49–0.60	Moderately concentrated	Moderately concentrated	Non-radial/radial	–
0.61–0.70	Concentrated	Concentrated	Radial	–
0.71–0.82	Very concentrated	Very concentrated	Multi-radial	–

Note: – *cannot be defined by NC value alone.*

alliances in Airline Business illustrates. Future research should take alliances into account. Yet, we did include closely integrated regional affiliates for some of the, in particular national, airline networks. Finally, the dataset that is available to us only lists direct flights. We deal with indirect flights in the following chapter.

In order to analyze the changing network configurations of different types of European carriers, the European airlines were categorized into three groups:

- National airlines: carriers (formerly) designated as the flag carriers of member states of the Common European Aviation Area[3] (KLM, Air France, and so forth). For 2003, SN Brussels and Swiss are regarded as the national carriers of Belgium and Switzerland respectively. They replace Sabena and Swissair as the national carriers in our database.
- Low-cost, no-frills airlines: all European-based carriers operating on a low-cost scheduled or mixed (low-cost scheduled/charter) basis (Ryanair, easyJet, for example). Our database included 21 low-cost airlines in 2003.[4]
- Regional airlines: all other airlines registered in the EU. Our database included 115 regional carriers in 2003 (British Midland, Wideroe's Flyveselkap, Air Littoral, for example).
- Extra-EU airlines: all airlines with intra-EU services but registered in a non-EU country (TWA, Cathay Pacific).

The classification of carriers is listed in Annex 3. The categorization of low-cost airlines was based on Williams (2001) and the low-cost airline survey of Airliner World (Airliner World 2003).

Seat capacity developments according to carrier type

Between 1990 and 2003 the European airline networks grew considerably. The total seat capacity of the European aviation network increased by 86 per cent between 1990 and 2003 (Table 3.2). This growth must be related to the recovery of the European economy after the recession and the Gulf War at the beginning of the 1990s (CAA 1998) and lower ticket prices. After 1993 most European economies recovered quickly and the doubled fuel prices quickly fell back to their normal levels. The result was

3 European Union+ Norway, Iceland and Switzerland. The Common European Aviation Area, Single European Aviation Market and European Union/EU have been used in this study without any distinction being drawn between them, unless otherwise indicated.

4 Most of the low-cost airlines distinguished here adopted some kind of low-cost model during the second half of the 1990s or even later. In the early 1990s we classified a few airlines (Ryanair, Transavia) as low-cost airlines, which would be important low-cost airlines by 2003. Yet the extent to which these carriers could be considered as low-cost airlines in the early 1990s is doubtful. Ryanair, for example, is known to have adopted fully the low-cost model in 1992 (Creaton 2004), while Transavia was mixed charter/scheduled airline. Therefore one should be careful drawing conclusions about the NC values of low-cost airlines in the early 1990s.

an increase in the demand for air travel. September 11th, SARS and the economic recession, however, slowed down the growth in the demand and supply of air travel from 2000/2001 on.

There are, however, significant differences between different types of airline, as Table 3.2 reveals. Low-cost carriers such as easyJet and Ryanair have enjoyed remarkable growth levels since 1995. Seat capacity tripled between 1995 and 1999 and tripled again between 1999 and 2003. The no-frills airlines took advantage of the freedom of entry, capacity and price-setting in the deregulated aviation market. These carriers managed to increase market share by offering lower ticket prices and higher frequencies than the national carriers. Nevertheless, one should remember that these carriers all started from a relatively low traffic base in comparison with the national and regional carriers. Most of the low-cost carriers considered here only entered the market in the second half of the 1990s or even later. From 2000 onwards low-cost carriers continued to show very high growth levels, while the number of low-cost airlines increased strongly, even after September 11th. In 2003 the low-cost carriers accounted for 23 per cent of total intra-EU seat capacity.

National airlines also experienced above-average growth levels until 1999. Because of this growth and the ongoing process of strategic alliances with intercontinental and regional partners, the 'flag carriers' still dominated the intra-EU market (Table 3.2). From 2000 on, however, the growth levels of national carriers decreased considerably. Most carriers rationalized their networks in reaction to the economic recession, the events of September 11th and SARS. Two flag carriers, Sabena and Swissair, went bankrupt, resulting in a significant loss of market share for the flag carriers.

Table 3.2 Evolution of intra-EU seat capacity since 1990

	Low-cost	National	Regional	Extra-EU	Total
'90	100	100	100	100	100
'91	128	106	107	68	104
'92	156	112	110	72	109
'93	176	113	115	79	112
'94	480	113	131	35	116
'95	1001	115	131	60	121
'96	1361	137	143	25	138
'97	2504	144	138	20	146
'98	2682	167	121	18	155
'99	3132	180	142	15	172
'03	9408	143	170	9	186
share '90	0	62	31	6	100
share '99	8	65	26	1	100
share '03	23	48	29	0	100

Source: *OAG*

Note: *Index of evolution of intra-EU seat capacity (1990=100); share is the percentage of carrier type in total intra-European seat capacity.*

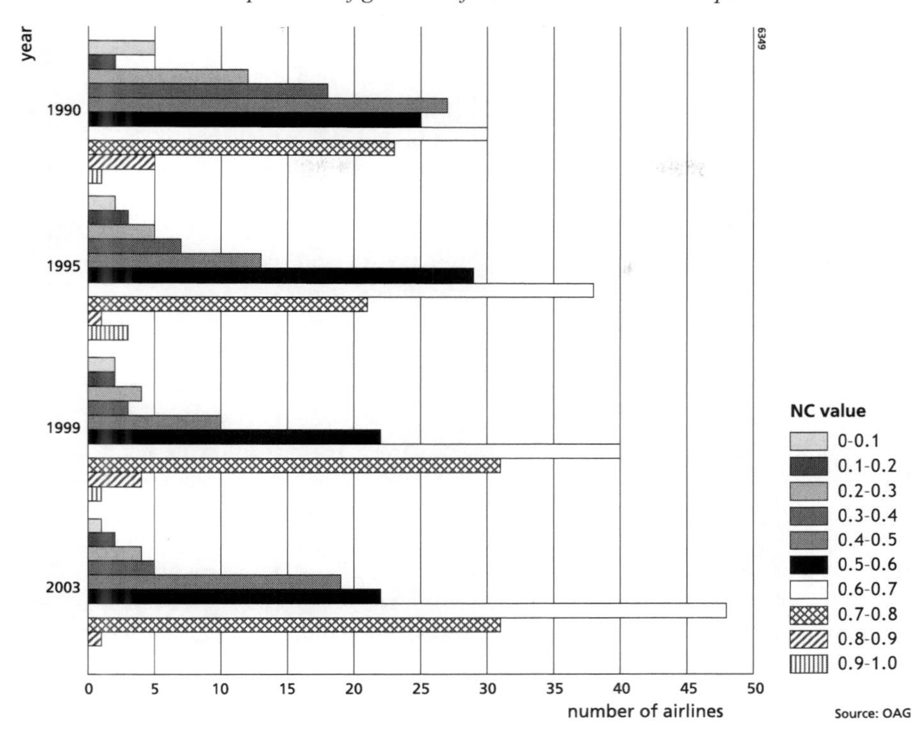

Figure 3.3 Frequency distribution of NC values

Airlines from third countries with fifth freedom rights to operate services within Europe have gradually retreated. Amongst other things, global airline alliances offer a substitute for the traffic of non-EU carriers within Europe (Weber and Dinwoodie 2000). By 2003 their market share had decreased to 0.3 per cent.

Analysis of airline network configurations

A first impression

The network concentration scores (NC) and Gini indices of all carriers operating on intra-EU routes have been computed in order to evaluate the spatial dimension of European airline network configurations. Figure 3.3 shows the frequency distributions of NC in 1990 and 2003. At first sight it seems that more airlines adopted concentrated network configurations during the period of analysis: the mean moved towards a higher network concentration rate. However, the higher average NC values were primarily caused by the retreat of extra-EU airlines from the EU aviation market at the beginning of the 1990s and the entrance of many low-cost airlines with relatively high NC values at the end of the 1990s. In contrast with 1990, non-radial networks with low NC values were almost nonexistent in 2003.

Figure 3.4 shows the evolution of NC between 1990 and 2003 according to carrier type. The national carrier network configurations had overall higher NC-indices than other airline types. This outcome is plausible. It reflects the national carriers' orientation towards their national hubs. Because of the partial deregulation of the European aviation market, carriers are still bound to their country of registration for their intercontinental services. These intercontinental 'chains' resulted in quite stable NC values between 1990 and 2003.

Regional carriers had, on average, lower NC values that the national carriers. Yet there was a wide variation in the spatial distribution of seat capacity in the regional-airline networks as Figure 3.5 indicates. Regional-airline networks ranged from deconcentrated, criss/cross networks to highly concentrated networks.

Extra-EU airlines showed the lowest NC scores. These result from the nature of the air services of these carriers within Europe: when they operate intra-EU services, their network is linear, based on fifth freedom rights (Weber and Dinwoodie 2000). Only a few extra-EU airlines operated concentrated intra-EU networks at the beginning of the 1990s. These networks were based on the extensive use of fifth freedom rights. Pan Am, for example, used fifth freedom rights for its hub operation at London Heathrow. However, all of the significant fifth freedom hub-operations were suspended during the 1990s.

National airlines

National-airline networks can be characterized as concentrated to very concentrated networks with respect to the spatial distribution of seat capacity, implicating a radial

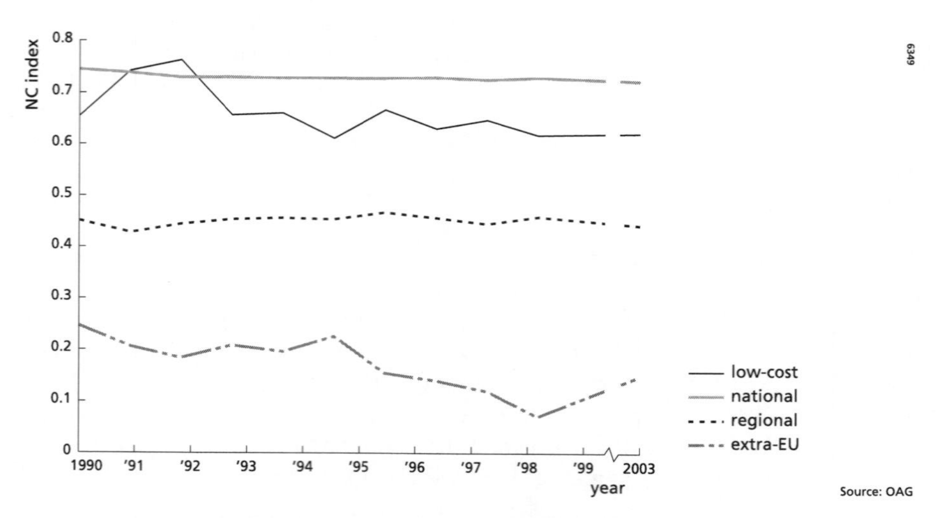

Figure 3.4 Evolution of Network Concentration values

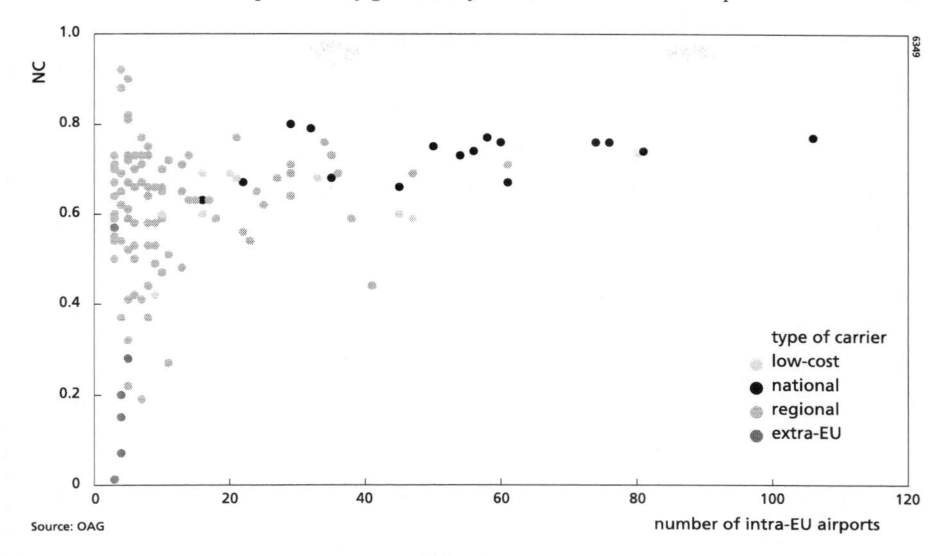

Figure 3.5 Number of airports and NC values

Note: *FlyBe: formerly British European/Jersey European; Régional Airlines: formerly Air Vendée, acquired by and integrated into Air France in 2000–2001; Eurowings: formerly NFD; Braathens was categorized as being part of SAS in 2003 (SAS Braathens); KLM UK was categorized as being part of KLM in 2003 (KLM Cityhopper); Air Liberté: formerly TAT European Airlines, bankruptcy in 2001.*

or multi-radial route network structure. The differences between the national carriers in terms of concentration indices for intra-EU traffic were small during the entire period of analysis. They varied between 0.66 (Icelandair) and 0.82 (Lufthansa) in 1990, 0.63 (Austrian) and 0.80 (Aer Lingus) in 1999, 0.65 (SN Brussels) and 0.79 (Lufthansa) in 2003.

The underlying Gini indices represent the typical US hubbing carrier network configurations after deregulation, as found by Reynolds-Feighan (2001). Nevertheless, because the European national airlines were already operating their networks from one of two central (national) airports before deregulation, the Gini values for the European national airlines had already reached this level by the beginning of the 1990s (Table 3.3, Figure 3.6). This level reflects the fact that the bilateral regime pinned the national airlines to their national home bases.

These results are clearly in contrast with the domestic network concentration in the United States immediately following the Airline Deregulation Act of 1978. Then, the Gini indices of major US airlines ranged between 0.5 and 0.6 (Reynolds-Feighan 2001), although some degree of concentration was also present in the US domestic-airline networks.

Hence, the network concentration levels of national European carriers remained quite stable between 1990 and 2003. The stability of the networks of the national airlines was primarily caused by the fact that they were bound to certain key airports

Table 3.3 Network characteristics of national airlines

	Number of airlines	Network concentration (NC)	Gini index	Number of* nodes	Capacity %**
1990	16	0.744	0.705	44.8	3.1
1991	16	0.739	0.702	46.4	3.2
1992	16	0.730	0.694	46.4	3.4
1993	16	0.730	0.695	46.6	3.5
1994	16	0.729	0.693	45.9	3.5
1995	16	0.728	0.693	47.1	3.5
1996	16	0.728	0.694	48.8	4.2
1997	16	0.730	0.695	49.1	4.4
1998	16	0.726	0.691	51.6	5.1
1999	16	0.729	0.695	53.4	5.5
2003	16	0.723	0.697	56.0	3.4

Source: *OAG*

Note: *Network concentration and Gini index are average values.*

* *Average number of intra-European nodes per airline.*

** *Average percentage of airline in total intra-European seat capacity.*

in their country of registration through bilateral air-service agreements. These reduced the opportunities for flag carriers to optimize their networks on a pan-European scale. Moreover, building the network on an existing home base has cost advantages.

Yet we can observe some important differences between the individual national carriers. As we stated before, NC values between 0.61 and 0.70 generally indicate a radial route network structure with a single central node, whereas NC values of 0.70 and higher imply a radial network with two or more central nodes. All of the national carrier networks could be considered as single- or multi-radial networks during the period of analysis. The NC index indicates that carriers such as Air France, Alitalia, Finnair, British Airways, Iberia, Lufthansa, Olympic, SAS and TAP Air Portugal operate multi-radial networks. The NC indices of Luxair and Aer Lingus also indicate a multi-radial route network structure. Yet this is merely caused by a capacity effect: for Aer Lingus, the NC value captures the high-density route between Dublin and London Heathrow, resulting in Heathrow being the second node for Aer Lingus in terms of seat capacity behind Dublin. The same holds true for Luxair (Frankfurt) and KLM in 1990 (London Heathrow). Yet the networks of these carriers were single-radial. The networks of the other carriers are characterized as 'pure' single-radial networks, including KLM after 1992, Austrian, Sabena and SN Brussels.

During the period of analysis the network of TAP Air Portugal changed from a multi-radial to a single-radial network due to a concentration of seat capacity growth on Lisbon. Also the network of Swissair evolved from a multi-radial network (Zurich, Geneva, Basle) to a single-radial network, concentrated primarily at Zurich.

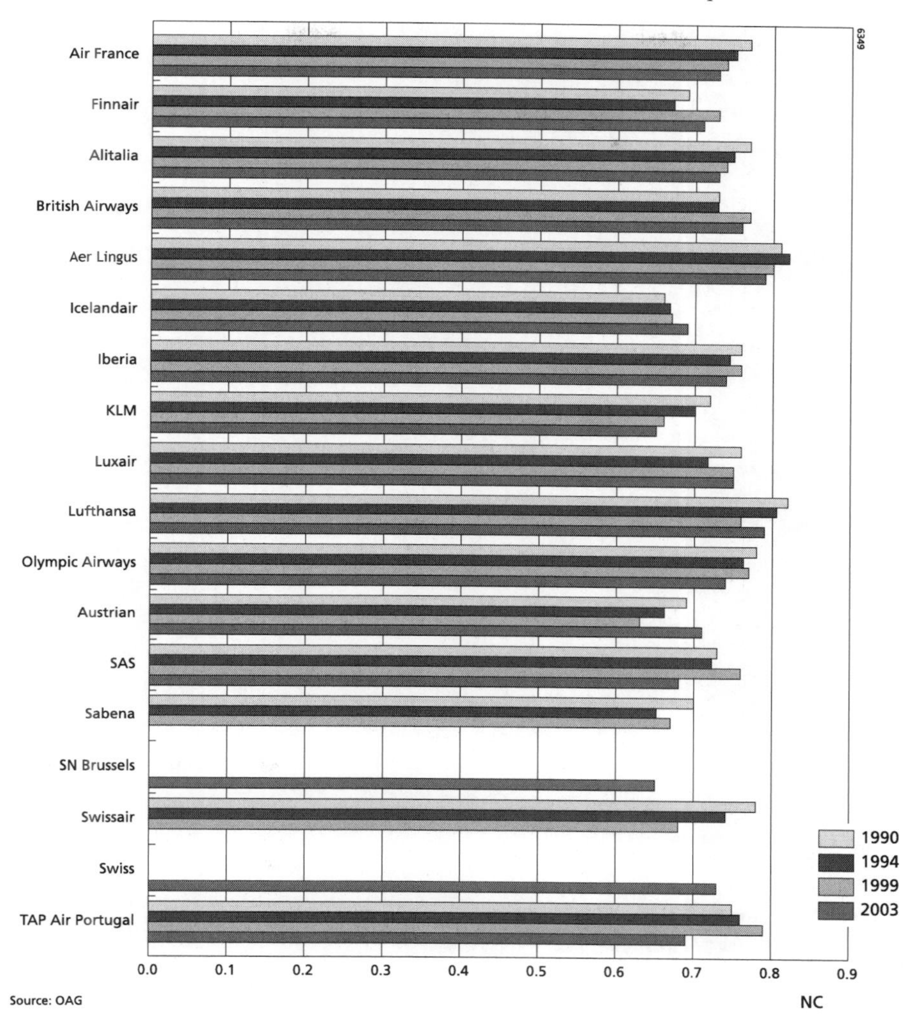

Figure 3.6 NC values for national airlines

Regional airlines

The group of regional carriers is heterogeneous: it ranges from single city-pair carriers to regional carriers operating at the pan-European level. Most of the regional carriers had much smaller networks and lower concentration rates (NC) than the national carriers during the period of analysis (see Figure 3.5, Table 3.4). The Swiss airline Crossair, for example, served more intra-EU destinations in 1999 than most of the flag carriers (Figure 3.9). In that year most of the regional carriers had less concentrated networks than the nationals.

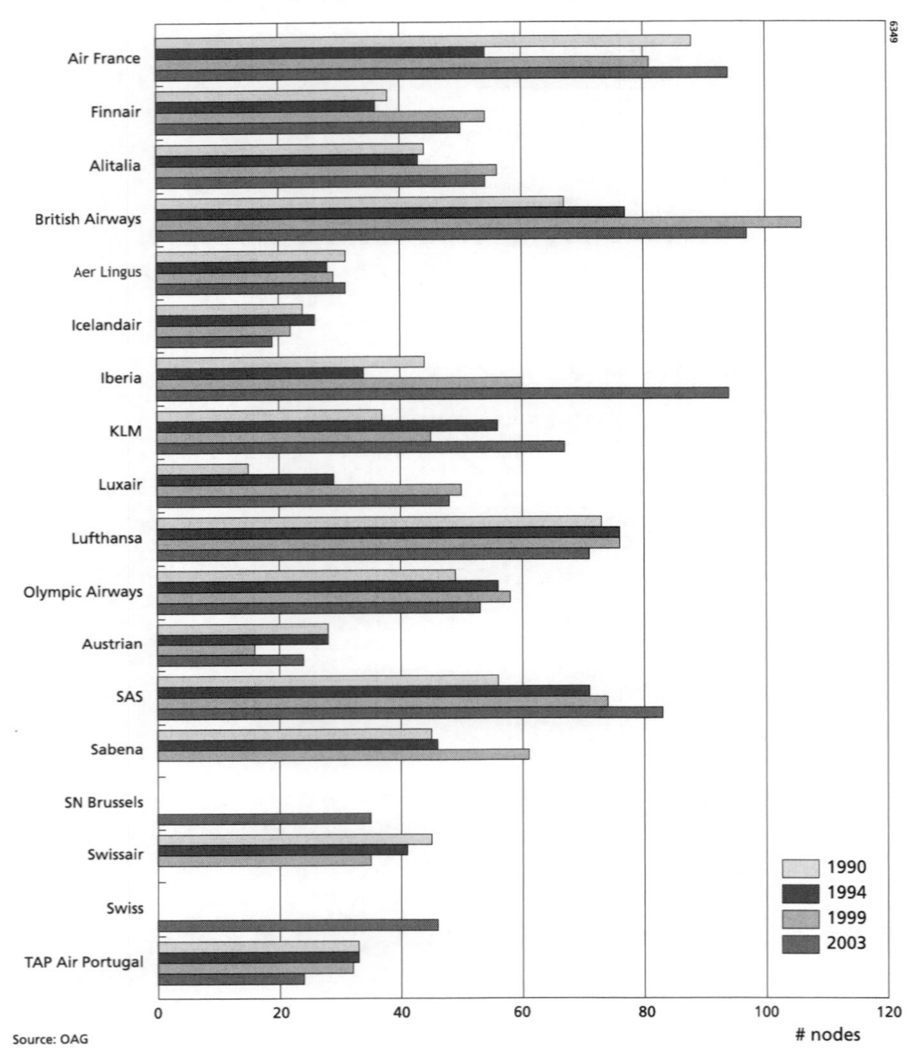

Figure 3.7 Number of EU nodes served, national airlines

A large variation in traffic distributions can also be observed, however, with respect to spatial distribution of seat capacity (Figure 3.8): the regional network configurations ranged from deconcentrated networks (Wideroe's Flyveselkap, Suckling Airways[5]) to moderately concentrated networks (Skyways, Régional Airlines) to very concentrated radial networks (Crossair, Air Littoral, Braathens). Yet

5 In 1999 Suckling Airways was renamed Scot Airways.

Table 3.4 Network characteristics of regional airlines

	Number of airlines	Network concentration (NC)	Gini index	No. nodes*	Capacity %**
1990	124	0.451	0.299	8.3	0.2
1991	110	0.428	0.284	8.4	0.2
1992	120	0.445	0.296	8.5	0.2
1993	116	0.454	0.298	8.5	0.3
1994	121	0.457	0.306	8.4	0.3
1995	120	0.454	0.305	8.7	0.3
1996	116	0.468	0.322	9.4	0.3
1997	112	0.457	0.322	9.7	0.3
1998	116	0.445	0.307	9.3	0.3
1999	124	0.459	0.321	9.3	0.3
2003	115	0.442	0.336	10.4	0.2

Source: *OAG*

Note: *Network concentration and Gini index are average values.*

**Average number of intra-European nodes per airline.*

***Average percentage of airline in total intra-European seat capacity.*

if we do not consider the two- and three-node networks with very low NC values, the concentrated network dominated the scene in 2003.

Between 1990 and 2003, the regional carrier network configurations remained less stable than those of the national carriers in terms of both the network size and the level of concentration. While changes in the NC of national carriers did not exceed 0.1 points between 1990 and 1999, the network concentration levels of several regional carriers changed dramatically (Figure 3.8). In contrast with the national airlines, regional airlines have had many more opportunities to reconfigure their networks. They operated largely on a European or national scale and were not dependent on restrictions in the bilateral air service agreements. Moreover, the addition of a single-capacity unit has a larger impact on the NC value of a small network than on the NC value of a large network.

Most of the regional airlines concentrated their networks to some extent around one or two central hub airports. This strategy can be an independent, mini-hub expansion, as in the case of the French carrier Régional Airlines at Clermont-Ferrand, Crossair at Basle or Air Littoral at Nice. But this could also be the consequence of alliances between national and regional carriers, in which the regional carriers play a hub-feeding role (Graham 1997b). For example, Eurowings, Braathens and KLM/ Air UK centred their network on KLM's hub Amsterdam Schiphol between 1990 and 1999.

Non-radial strategies among larger regional carriers are rare in Europe. Even the Norwegian carrier Wideroe's – probably the best example of (partly PSO-subsidized) linear carrier in Europe – became somewhat more concentrated on Oslo during the period of analysis. Their scarcity exemplifies the earlier conclusion that the spatial

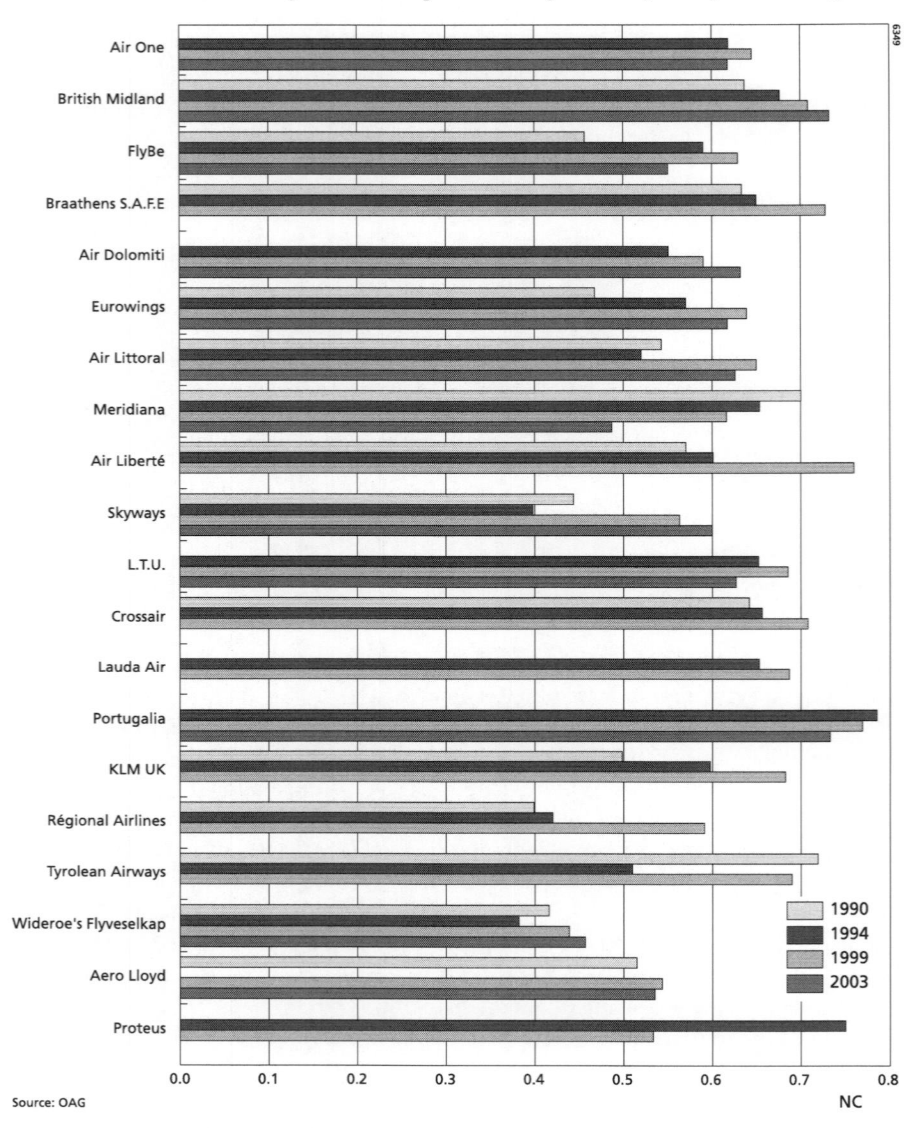

Figure 3.8 NC values for selected regional airlines

concentration of traffic at a limited number of airports has cost advantages, even without the transfer of passengers from one flight to another. These cost advantages include the spread of fixed costs over more passengers as well as more straightforward crew rotation and aircraft maintenance.

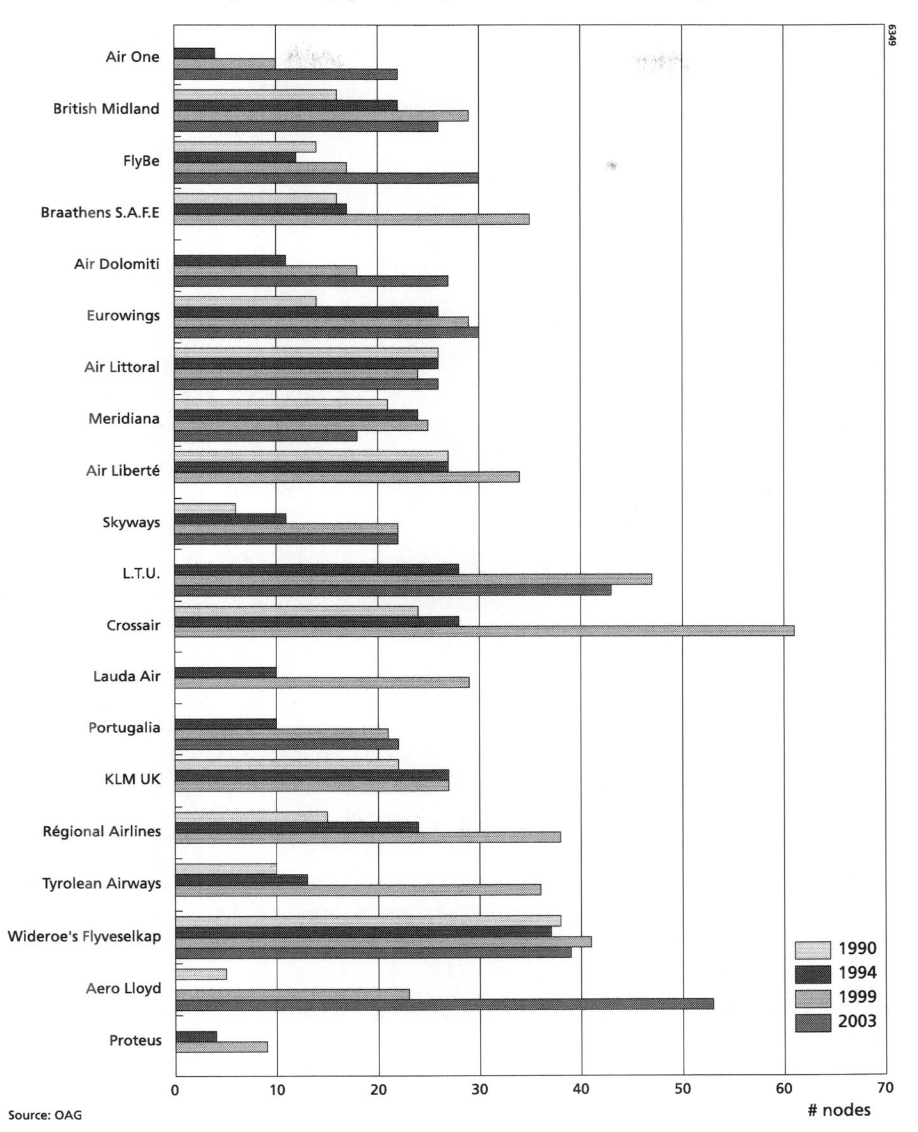

Figure 3.9 Number of EU nodes served, regional airlines

Low-cost airlines

The entrance of low-cost carriers onto the European aviation market during the 1990s marked a most profound deregulation effect. In the United States some low-cost carriers, such as Southwest, operate networks with low levels of network concentration, while others show a much more concentrated network pattern,

Table 3.5 Network characteristics of low-cost carriers

	Number of airlines	Network concentration (NC)	Gini index	No. nodes	Capacity %
1990	2	0.654	0.280	8.0	0.2
1991	2	0.742	0.389	6.5	0.2
1992	3	0.763	0.566	8.5	0.3
1993	3	0.657	0.498	9.3	0.2
1994	5	0.660	0.524	15.2	0.3
1995	6	0.611	0.484	13.7	0.6
1996	8	0.667	0.518	13.5	0.6
1997	9	0.630	0.543	19.9	1.0
1998	9	0.647	0.561	21.3	1.1
1999	9	0.617	0.551	24.1	1.3
2003	21	0.625	0.532	24.2	1.1

Source: *OAG*

Note: *Network concentration and Gini index are average values.*

**Average number of intra-European nodes per airline.*

***Average percentage of airline in total intra-European seat capacity.*

according to the 1999 data of Reynolds-Feighan (2001). Besides, low-cost airlines are known to operate from smaller, secondary airports so as to cut airport charges and reduce head-to-head competition with major carriers. How did EU low-cost airlines configures their networks during the period of analysis?

In Europe low-cost carrier growth started to gain momentum after 1999, as Table 3.5 reveals. On average, the EU low-cost carrier networks were not as concentrated as the national carriers' networks in 2003 (Table 3.5, Figure 3.10 and Figure 3.12).

Some important differences can be observed with respect to the size of their networks, the spatial distribution of seat capacity and the type of airports served. With respect to the spatial distribution of seat capacity, we can distinguish low-cost airlines with concentrated and more deconcentrated network patterns. On the one hand, 14 of the 21 low-cost airlines with scheduled services in 2003 had concentrated to very concentrated networks (Figure 3.10). This included Ryanair, the airline modelled after US carrier Southwest airlines. In 2003 Ryanair was by far the largest low-cost carrier in terms of the number of airports served. Although serving mainly secondary, smaller airports (Figure 3.12), the carrier's network was still centred around multiple home-bases in 2003 (London Stansted, Charleroi and Frankfurt Hahn, for example). In contrast, the network of the US low-cost carrier Southwest had a NC index of 0.47 in 1999, indicating a very deconcentrated network structure. Similarly, Virgin Express had its network centred at Brussels, Germanwings was operating a radial network from Cologne, and Spanair's seat capacity was concentrated at Madrid, Barcelona and Malaga, while BMIBaby operated mainly out of East Midlands, Cardiff and Manchester in 2003.

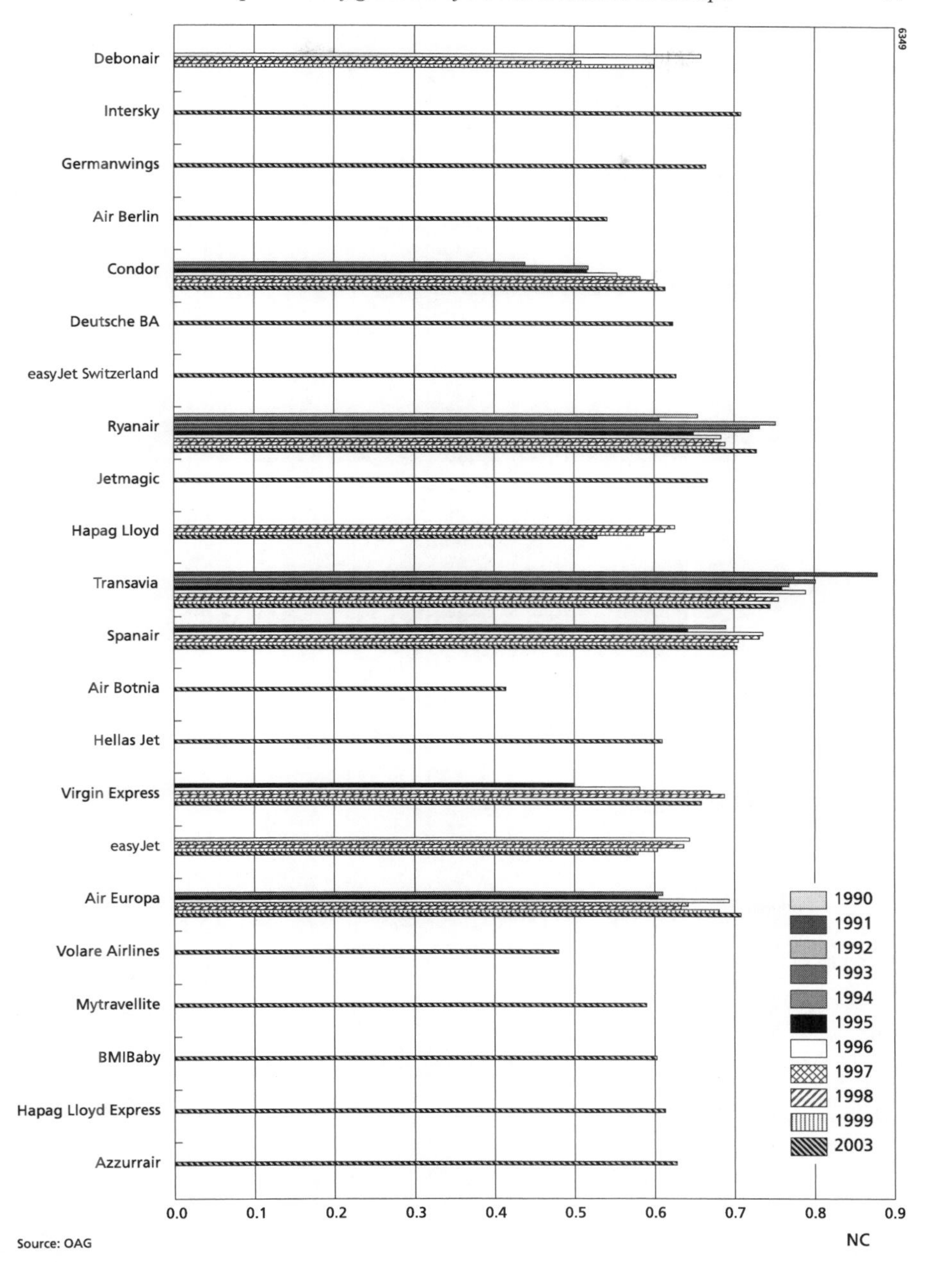

Source: OAG

Figure 3.10 NC values for low-cost airlines

On the other hand, some low-cost airline networks were much more deconcentrated in terms of the spatial distribution of seat capacity. Most of the larger deconcentrated

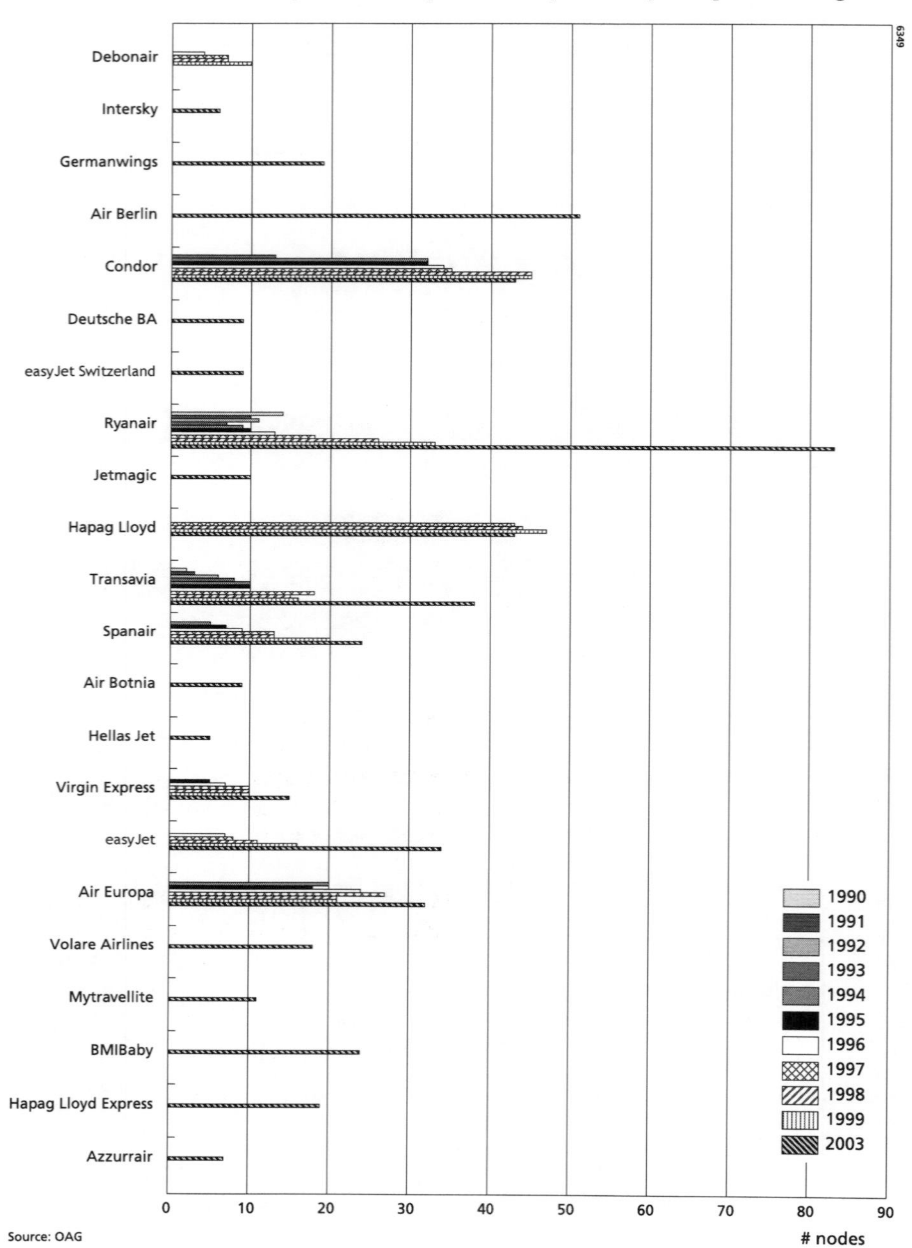

Figure 3.11 Number of EU nodes served, low-cost airlines

networks belonged to (former) German charter airlines, such as Air Berlin, Hapag Lloyd. These networks exhibit a strong north–south pattern, connecting German

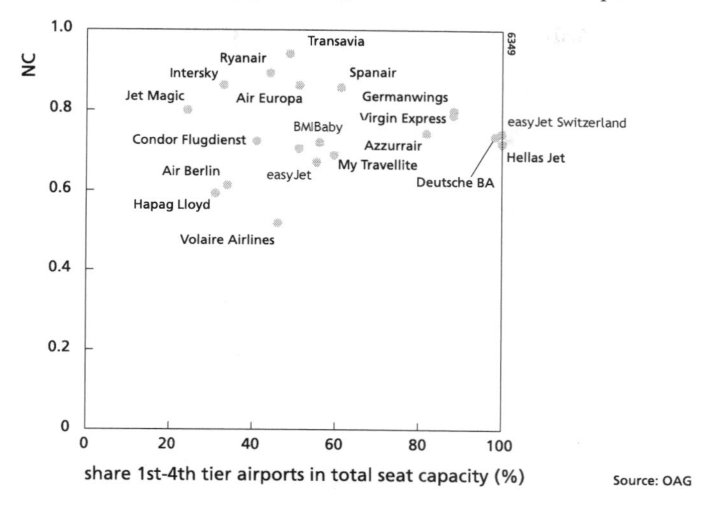

Figure 3.12 NC value and type of airport served, 2003
Note: *Low-cost carriers only.*

cities with holiday destinations in the Mediterranean region. These former charter airlines increasingly engaged in selling seat-only tickets in addition to the seats selled to tour operators as part of a holiday package. Moreover, the network of easyJet evolved from a concentrated to a more deconcentrated network in 2003.

Also with respect to the type of airports served, there are major differences between the low-cost airlines. It is generally expected that low-cost airlines serve smaller, secondary airports for cost and competitive reasons. Figure 3.12 shows the relationship between the type of airports served by each carrier and the network concentration level in 2003.

The 5th tier airports are the non-hub airports. We discuss the classification of the EU airports in detail in Chapter 6. The 1st–4th tier airports are the 49 largest EU airports in 1999, including London Stansted and London Luton. Given the lower unit operating cost strategy of the low-cost carriers, one would expect low-cost airlines to have a small share of 1st–4th tier airports in the total seat capacity they supply.

Yet this hypothesis is only true for a limited number of low-cost airlines. In essence, there seem to be three groups of low-cost airlines. The first consists of those operating concentrated networks but serving mainly non-hub airports. Examples are Ryanair, Air Europa and Jetmagic. A second group consists of low-cost carriers such as Virgin Express, Germanwings and Deustche BA. These airlines also operated concentrated networks but served mainly the larger airports in the hierarchy. A third group consists of carriers serving the primarily non-hub airports (5th tier airports), but with a more deconcentrated or only moderately concentrated network pattern. This group includes Air Berlin, Hapag Lloyd, easyJet, BMIBaby and MyTravellite.

In short, the beginning of the new millennium saw a new wave of carriers, which started to offer services on a low-cost basis. Yet the low-cost carriers distinguished

Table 3.6 Network characteristics of extra-EU airlines

	Number of airlines	Network Concentration (NC)	Gini index	No. nodes	Capacity %
1990	72	0.246	0.159	5	0.08
1991	66	0.206	0.136	5	0.06
1992	67	0.184	0.123	5	0.06
1993	68	0.208	0.131	5	0.06
1994	37	0.196	0.108	4	0.05
1995	30	0.226	0.118	4	0.06
1996	41	0.155	0.079	3	0.03
1997	34	0.141	0.078	3	0.02
1998	31	0.120	0.064	3	0.02
1999	34	0.071	0.034	2	0.02
2003	21	0.149	0.078	2	0.00

Source: *OAG*

Note: *Network concentration and Gini index are average, unweighted values.*

**Average number of intra-European nodes per airline.*

***Average percentage of airline in total intra-European seat capacity.*

here showed a wide range of NC values, type of airports served and network size. In 2003 there did not seem to be a dominant low-cost network model.

Extra-EU airlines

For a long time, apart from the IATA interlining system, the use of fifth freedom rights provided an international airline with the only opportunity to create a world-embracing network (Weber and Dinwoodie 2000). The fifth freedom is 'the right of an airline of one country to carry traffic between countries outside of its own country of registry as long as the flight originates or terminates in its own country of registry' (Button and Taylor 2000, 210). This traffic right was defined at the Chicago Conference of 1944 and could be agreed upon in air-service agreements drawn up between states. The right enables international airlines to operate routes that would not be economically viable as non-stop destinations.

Overall, the fifth-freedom networks of extra-EU airlines were deconcentrated networks with a linear character. However, during the period of analysis, a significant decline of NC values together with a decline in capacity share/number of airports served/number of extra-EU airlines operating took place (Table 3.6).

This development is in line with the study by Weber and Dinwoodie (2000) on fifth-freedom traffic operations. They assert that, in the early 1990s fifth-freedom traffic provided the only opportunity for extra-EU airlines, apart from interlining, to develop a European network with destinations that would not be viable as non-stop routes. Some airlines, such as Pan Am, Delta, TWA and United Airlines, even set up mini-hub operations for intra-EU traffic. Hence, they were the only extra-EU carriers with considerable intra-EU networks with high levels of network concentration. Operations of this kind resulted in higher NC values in 1990 compared with 1999.

Pan Am was probably the most intensive user of fifth freedom rights in the early 1990s. First it operated a small hub at London Heathrow in 1990 to connect the North American flights with the European operations. In addition, Pan Am operated domestic services between Berlin Tegel and German airports. The services from Berlin Tegel could not be called fifth-freedom operations, however, since Pan Am was operating from West Berlin, which was formally still under sovereignty of the United States, Britain and France. Lufthansa was not allowed to operate from Berlin before the German reunifaction: its first services to Berlin started in October 1990. Pan Am withdrew from Berlin in 1991 and faced bankruptcy in the same year.

During the second half of the 1990s the number of extra-EU airlines with intra-EU services and the number of these services gradually decreased, with only a small upsurge in 1996, when a number of airlines from Asia and the former USSR started operating intra-EU services. Weber and Dinwoodie identify a number of factors that limited the intra-EU operations of extra-EU carriers during the period of analysis:

- Global airline alliances: alliances form a substitute, or even a refinement of fifth-freedom traffic: European partner airlines can offer better connectivity to more destinations.
- Technological developments: the introduction of the Airbus A330/340 and Boeing 767/777 has enabled airlines to operate somewhat thinner long-haul routes economically from their own home bases.
- Product life cycle of international routes: several fifth-freedom routes have reached maturity and have generated sufficient demand to justify a non-stop service.
- Competition: the competition of European carriers with higher corporate strength in the markets served makes the operation of fifth-freedom traffic less attractive.

These developments resulted in a decline in market share of extra-EU airlines, a declining number of extra-EU airlines and lower NC values. A number of US and Asian carriers have given up most of their fifth-freedom operations.

Conclusions

To what extent have airlines in Europe reconfigured their networks since the deregulation of the European air transport market? We have used the concept of the airline network configuration to analyze this question. Both the level of spatial concentration of seat capacity on a limited number of hubs and the temporal concentration of flights around a number of synchronized waves of flights per day are essential features of an airline network configuration. This chapter has presented an overview of the changes in the spatial concentration of airline networks in Europe during the period between 1990 and 2003.

The national carrier networks can be characterized as concentrated, radial networks. Changes in the network concentration level of national carriers were very small during the period of analysis. No radical geographical restructuring of the networks of major carriers, as occurred in the United States after deregulation, can be observed in Europe. The ongoing bilateral regulation of intercontinental services still binds the flag carriers to their national airports; this implies the operation of radial network structures. The cumulative causation of hub connectivity networks as well as a general lack of large scale airport capacity is likely to further contribute to the stability of the spatial dimension of major-airline networks.

Nevertheless, on a smaller scale, spatial concentration strategies can be observed more frequently among the regional carriers. Taking advantage of the liberalized market, some of the regional airlines restructured their networks from deconcentrated to concentrated networks. Others started from a small traffic base at a central airport and, through alliances with national carriers, benefited from traffic feed from large intercontinental carriers. In Chapter 4 we consider whether these concentration strategies are real hub-and-spoke strategies or just represent a concentration on central airports as a result of other, more general cost and demand considerations. Large, deconcentrated networks were an exceptional phenomenon in Europe at the end of the 1990s. The PSO-subsidized Norwegian carrier Wideroe's is probably the best example of a large, deconcentrated non-radial network.

Low-cost entrants show a variety of spatial network configurations. There is no dominant low-cost network model. Three groups of low-cost carriers were identified in terms of the spatial distribution of seat capacity and the type of airports served. The Ryanair-type network is a concentrated network, serving non-hub airports. The Virgin Express model serves mainly the larger EU hub airports and is also fairly concentrated. A third group of carriers, including easyJet, has a much more deconcentrated network pattern and serves non-hub and hub airports.

Finally, extra-EU airlines operated primarily deconcentrated networks. The bilateral framework gave them virtually no other opportunity, except from a few change-of-gauge hubs. However, since the beginning of the 1990s most of the carriers have retreated from intra-EU routes. This retreat is remarkable given the fact that since 1990 more open-skies agreements have been drawn up between EU and non-EU countries. Many of these open-skies agreements gave extra-EU carriers more freedom to operate routes within Europe on the basis of fifth freedom rights. We have, however, listed a number of reasons that caused extra-EU carriers to withdraw from intra-EU routes. Because of the deconcentrated intra-EU network configurations, their retreat contributed to a large extent to the overall increase in the level of network concentration.

A concentrated, radial network is not the equivalent of a hub-and-spoke network as long as flight schedule coordination is lacking. We have therefore added the temporal dimension in the next chapter by introducing the concept of the wave-system structure and indirect connectivity. The empirical elaboration of the concept enables us to provide a full answer to the question of to what extent European airlines have changed their network behaviour following the deregulation of the European air transport market.

Chapter 4

The Temporal Configuration of Airline Networks in Europe[1]

In the previous chapter the changes in the spatial dimension of airline network configurations were described. Based on the time–space continuum of airline network configurations (Chapter 2), we argued that not only the spatial, but also the temporal dimension of airline network configurations is essential for the understanding of airline network behaviour.

Hence this chapter reports our investigation of the extent to which a temporal concentration trend can be observed among the European airline networks under the hybrid regimes of the free market (intra-EU) and bilateralism (extra-EU). We have analyzed the presence and configuration of wave-system structures at European airline home bases together with the resulting transfer opportunities. We have used OAG data (1990–2003) for all European carriers with scheduled services.

The chapter is structured as follows. First, the specific theoretical background of the chapter is considered in relation to the relevant empirical and methodological literature. Next, the methodology used is elaborated. Then the empirical results are discussed with respect to the indirect connectivity at the home bases of Europe's major airlines and the wave-system structure analysis.

Theoretical framework and literature review

Theoretical considerations on the temporal configuration of an airline network

What is the temporal configuration of an airline network? We define it as a certain organization of the airline flight schedule at an airline station resulting in a certain number and quality of indirect connections offered through that airline station. The number and quality of indirect connections through an airline station can be enhanced by concentrating the flight schedule in time: or, in other words, by adopting a wave-system structure in the airline flight schedule.

A wave-system structure consists of the number of waves, their timing and the structure of the individual waves. According to Bootsma (1997, 53) a connection

1 In relation to this chapter, the following article has been published: Burghouwt, G. and de Wit, J.G. (2005), 'Temporal configurations of airline networks in Europe', *Journal of Air Transport Management* 11:3, 185–98.

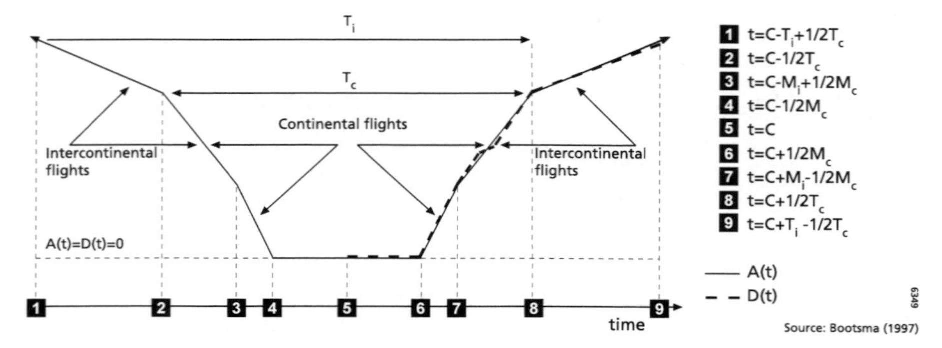

Figure 4.1 Theoretical connection wave of a European hinterland hub

Note: *A(t)=number of flights that still have to arrive at the hub at time t; D(t)=number of flights that still have to depart from the hub at time t; C=wave centre; Mi=minimum connection time for intercontinental flights; Mc=minimum connection time for continental flights; Ti=maximum connection time for intercontinental flights; Tc=maximum connection time for continental flights.*

wave is 'a complex of incoming and outgoing flights, structured such that all incoming flights connect to all outgoing flights [...]'.

Three elements determine the structure of such a connection wave:

- the minimum connecting time for continental and intercontinental flights
- the maximum connecting times
- the maximum number of flights that can be scheduled per time period (peak-hour capacity).

Figure 4.1 presents an ideal type of connection wave for a hinterland hub. Connections have to meet the minimum connecting times (M). Then, a trade-off has to be made between the maximum acceptable connecting time (T) for the airline and the maximum number of flights that can be scheduled in a time period (A(t)+D(t)). The hub-and-spoke concept stimulates the addition of an extra connection to the same wave. Since, however, no airport has unlimited peak capacity, new flights can only be scheduled at the edges of the wave. These flights might be subject to longer waiting times that transfer passengers may not find acceptable (Dennis 2001a).

However, in reality, such an ideal picture is not very likely to occur. Bootsma (1997) puts forward a number of disturbing factors:

- some spokes may be located too close, or too far away from the hub to fit into the wave-system structure. these flights will be located off wave
- strict scheduling may jeopardize fleet utilization
- environmental constraints and/or capacity constraints may prevent airlines from fitting all flights into the wave-system

- in strong origin–destination markets, scheduling a number of flights off-wave may be attractive
- the incoming and outgoing european waves may overlap, since not all connections are feasible, because of the detour/routing factor[2]
- we can add to this list the fact that an airline may simply not have chosen to adopt, or may not be capable of adopting, a wave-system structure.

Bootsma (1997) draws a clear distinction between on the one hand the actual temporal configuration of an airline flight schedule (the wave-system structure) and on the other the effects of the airline flight schedule on the number and quality of the indirect connections generated by the flight schedule. In other words, on the one hand one can describe the actual temporal configuration of the airline flight schedule, while on the other the effects of a certain temporal configuration on indirect connectivity can be determined.

The resulting indirect connectivity of a wave-system structure at the hub depends on a number of elements in the airline flight schedule (Bootsma 1997; Dennis 1998; Veldhuis 1997). First, the number of direct flights (frequency) to and from the hub determines the maximum number of indirect connections following the formula n(n-1)/2, where n denotes the number of spoke-airports in the network. Second, the number of indirect flights will depend on the minimum connecting time (mct) at the airline hub. The mct-window is necessary for the transfer of passengers and baggage between two flights as well as for the aircraft itself to be turned around. An indirect connection that fails to meet the mct-criterion cannot be considered a viable connection.

However, not every connection will be equally attractive. An indirect flight with a waiting time of five hours would not be as attractive as a similar indirect flight with a transfer time of only 45 minutes.

The attractiveness of an indirect connection depends on the (Bootsma 1997; Dennis 1994b, 1998; Veldhuis 1997; Veldhuis and Kroes 2002):

- waiting time at the hub: attractiveness declines as waiting time increases
- routing factor: the in-flight time for an indirect flight compared with the direct-flight time. Some indirect connections (such as Hamburg–Oslo–Nice) are not attractive for the average air traveller, because the detour factor is too large
- perception: passengers perceive transfer time as longer than in-flight time
- fares: lower fares may compensate for longer transfer and in-flight times
- flights of a certain airline may be attractive, because the air traveller participates in the loyalty programme of the airline
- amenities of the hub-airport involved in the transfer.

When quantifying the effects of the configuration of the airline flight schedule in terms of indirect connectivity, account should be taken of the difference in attractivity of a certain connection. However, since data on fares, airport quality and loyalty

2 The ratio between indirect and direct flight times/distances.

programmes are scarce and unreliable, we have concentrated on the roles of waiting time and in-flight time.

Based on these theoretical considerations, we have used the characteristics of the ideal type connection wave as the benchmark for our analysis. We have:

- Evaluated the indirect connectivity of the airline flight schedule, given the presence or absence of a wave-system structure. We define indirect connectivity as the number and quality of the indirect connections generated by the existing flight schedule.
- Analyzed the presence of a wave-system structure empirically and determined the number of waves at the airline hub, based on the definition of a theoretical connection wave.
- Assessed the effects of the presence of a wave-system structure on indirect connectivity.

Methodology

This chapter has a threefold aim: first, to provide a description of the presence of a wave-system structure and the number of waves at an airline hub; second, to present the analysis of the indirect connectivity generated by the wave-system structure; third, to assess the effects of a wave-system structure on the number of indirect connections. The first purpose has been fulfilled by using the theoretical wave-system structure developed by Bootsma (1997). To fulfil the second purpose, a simplified connectivity measure has been used. The third purpose has been fulfilled by combining both methodologies. For all types of analysis, OAG data for the period 1990–1999 and the year 2003 were used.

A methodology for the identification of the wave-system structure

Recalling Figure 4.1 and Bootsma (1997, 61), the time windows for departing and arriving intercontinental (ICA) and departing and arriving European (EUR) flights can be determined:

- ICA arriving window: $[C\text{-}T_i\text{+}0.5T_c, C\text{-}M_i\text{+}0.5M_c]$ (1)
- ICA departing window: $[C\text{+}M_i\text{-}0.5M_c, C\text{+}T_i\text{-}0.5T_c]$ (2)
- EUR arriving window: $[C\text{-}0.5T_c, C\text{-}0.5M_c]$ (3)
- EUR departing: $[C\text{+}0.5M_c, C\text{+}0.5T_c]$ (4)

where:

T_i is the maximum connecting time involving intercontinental flights;
T_c is the maximum connecting time for connecting European flights;
M_i is the minimum connecting time involving intercontinental flights;

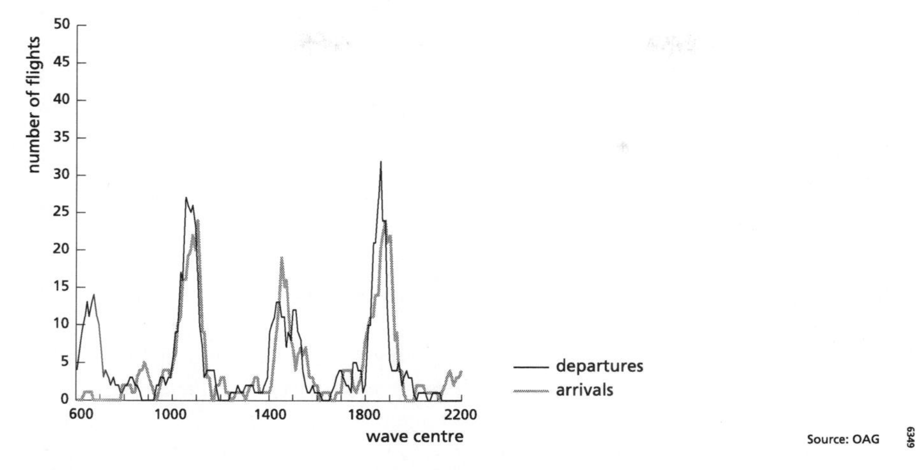

Figure 4.2 Wave-system analysis, Lufthansa, Munich

Note: The minutes of the wave centres were converted to the decimal system. For example, 1050 equals 10.30h, 2040 equals 20.24h.

M_c is the minimum connecting time for connecting European flights;
C is the wave centre.

Bootsma (1997) has defined standard maximum connecting times for different types of connections: the quality thresholds. Minimum connecting times are unique for every hub airport and can be derived from the Official Airline Guide (OAG). For the sake of simplicity, for all flights in the wave-system analysis performed we have chosen a minimum connecting time of 40 minutes and a maximum connecting time of 90 minutes; this standard is high compared with the thresholds chosen by Bootsma (1997).

Given the theoretical definition of an ideal connection wave, the actual wave-system structure can be identified. This can be done by creating progressing 'virtual' wave centres in steps of x minutes. Whether an airline actually operates a wave structure for that hypothesized wave-centre is determined by counting the number of flights within the departure and arrival windows for that specific wave-centre.

We have illustrated the procedure for the network of Lufthansa at Munich (Figure 4.2). Artificial wave centres are allocated in steps of 6 minutes. The maximum and minimum connecting times are 90 minutes and 40 minutes respectively. Hence flights have to arrive between t=C-45 and t=C-20 and depart between t=C+20 and t=C+45 to fit into the hypothesized wave. This statement actually implies the application of a time window that moves forward in steps of 6 minutes and within which the number of departing flights and arriving flights are counted respectively. An actual wave-centre can be identified when the maxima of the waves for incoming and outgoing flights (almost completely) coincide. At Lufthansa's Munich hub we can identify a clear wave-system structure with three connection waves: morning, afternoon and evening.

This methodology is helpful in identifying the presence of a wave-system structure, the number of waves, and the timing of the waves. For a large number of airline hubs, the identification of wave-system structures becomes very time consuming. We therefore first evaluate the effects of airline flight schedules on indirect connectivity. Only airline hubs with a significant indirect connectivity have been analyzed to identify the characteristics of the wave-system structure. Airports without any significant indirect connectivity are not expected to be competitive hubs in the transfer market.

Evaluation airline flight schedule effects: Indirect connectivity

Earlier we concluded that the number of direct frequencies, the minimum connecting times and the quality of the connection determine indirect connectivity.

Building on insights from connectivity measures developed by Bania et al. (1998), Bootsma (1997), Dennis (1994b), Veldhuis (1997), we therefore define a weighted indirect connection[3] as:

$$WI = \frac{2.4 * TI + RI}{3.4} \tag{5}$$

where

$$TI = 1 - \frac{1}{T_j} T_h \tag{6}$$

where $T_h > M_{ij}$ and $TI = 0$ when $T_h > T$

$$RI = 1 - (2\frac{1}{2} R - 2\frac{1}{2}) \tag{7}$$

and

$$R = \frac{IDT}{DTT} \tag{8}$$

where $1 <= R <= 1.4$ and $RI = 0$ when $R > 1.4$.

Where:

WI = weighted indirect connection
TI = transfer index (linear function of transfer time)
RI = routing index (linear function of the routing factor)
M_{ij} = minimum connection time for connection j at airport i
T_j = maximum connection time for connection j
T_h = transfer time at the hub
IDT = actual in-flight time, indirect connection

3 Only on-line, one-stop, same-day-transfer connections (on a Wednesday in July) were considered in this paper.

DTT = estimated in-flight time, direct connection based on Great Circle Distance[4]

R = routing factor (ratio between estimated direct and actual indirect in-flight time).

The weighted connectivity of an indirect connection depends on both the quality of the connection at the hub (TI) and the quality of the indirect flight compared with the direct flight (RI). We take the weighted average of TI and RI to compute WI, assuming that passengers value transfer time 2.4 times as long as in-flight time (Lijesen 2003). Both TI and RI are defined as being a linear function of the flight time and transfer time respectively.

The transfer index (TI) equals 1 if the transfer time T_h equals 0. The transfer index (TI) equals zero when the transfer time T_h exceeds the maximum connection quality threshold.[5] The TI index cannot reach its theoretical maximum of 1 because $T_h > M_{ij}$ in order to include differences in minimum connecting times between airports.

The routing or circuity index (RI) equals zero when the routing factor exceeds a certain limit. The maximum routing factor for distance is typically 1.25 (Bootsma 1997). However, since we take in-flight time as the input for the routing factor instead of Great Circle Distance, we should allow some time for take-off and landing. We have therefore added 0.15 points to the maximum routing factor. This results in a maximum routing factor of 1.4. Connections with a routing factor $R>1.4$ are not considered to be viable connections and are left out of the analysis. The routing or circuity index (RI) equals 1 if the total actual in-flight time for an indirect connection equals the estimated in-flight time for the direct connection.

The WI index can be aggregated in various ways. We have used:

$$WNX = \Sigma\,(WI) \tag{9}$$

where WNX = Total number or weighted indirect connections.

Airline flight schedule effects: Indirect connectivity

Indirect connectivity

Figure 4.3 shows the WNX index for the top 54 European hubs in terms of indirect connections in 2003. The distribution of indirect connectivity is highly skewed. In 2003 the top 10 airline hubs out of 105 airline stations with more than 10 indirect connections per day accounted for 81 per cent of all indirect connections. The distribution of indirect connectivity yielded a Gini index of 0.86, indicating a very concentrated distribution.

---

4 Great Circle Distance: the shortest distance between two locations (as the crow flies).

5 These values correspond to the poor T_j values proposed by Bootsma (1997) ranging from 180 minutes for European transfers to 720 minutes for intercontinental transfers.

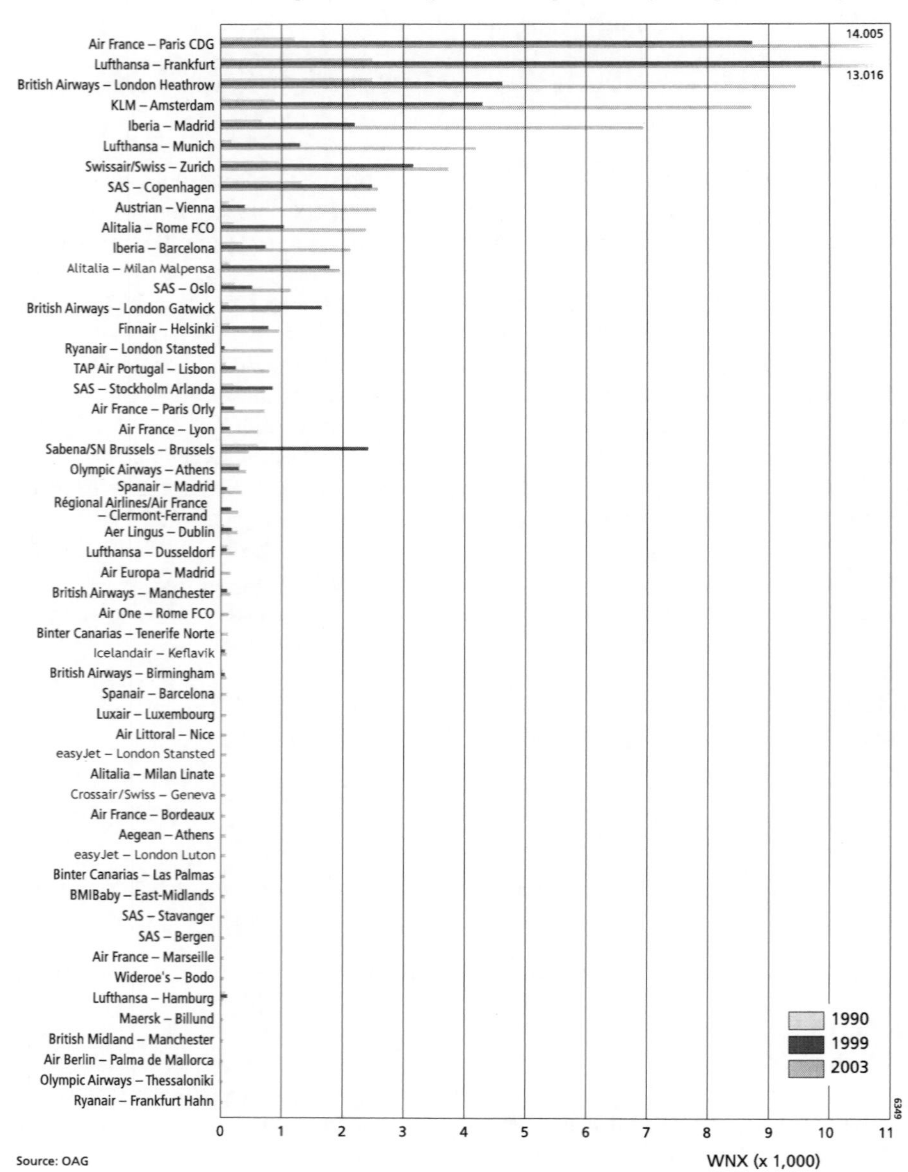

Figure 4.3 Weighted indirect connectivity via primary hubs

Note: *WNX value for Alitalia at Milan are values for Malpensa in 1999 and Linate in 1990. WNX values for Oslo are for Fornebu in 1990 and Gardemoen in 1999 and 2003.*

In 2003 Frankfurt, Paris CDG, London Heathrow and Amsterdam dominated the market for indirect connections. Together the four hubs accounted for 57 per cent of

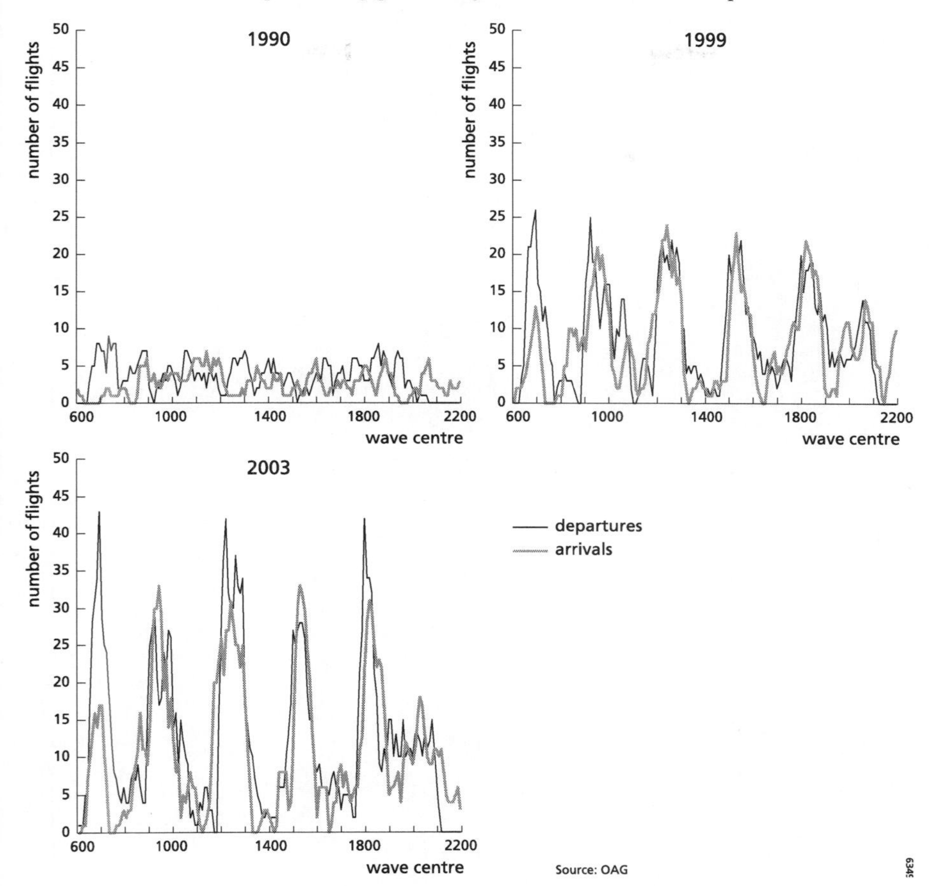

Figure 4.4 The rise of an airline hub: Air France at Paris CDG

all indirect connections generated by the airline stations with more than 10 indirect connections per day.

KLM at Amsterdam significantly improved its position as a hubbing carrier during the period of the analysis. Between 1990 and 1999 the carrier added extra waves to the wave-system structure, achieving a much more competitive frequency in many transfer markets. Air France started hub operations at Paris Charles de Gaulle in March 1996 with five waves a day (Dennis 2001a). A sixth wave had been added by 1999 (Figure 4.3). Lufthansa's hub at Frankfurt was already an important hub in 1990, with four daily waves. The intensification of its wave-system, in terms of a growth in the capacity per wave, resulted in sharp increases in the number of indirect connections.

In contrast, British Airways at London Heathrow faced a relative decline in its competitive position for transfer traffic compared with the other major hubs. From first position in 1990, British Airways at London Heathrow fell to third position in 1999 and 2003. The end of the split-hub strategy of British Airways at Heathrow

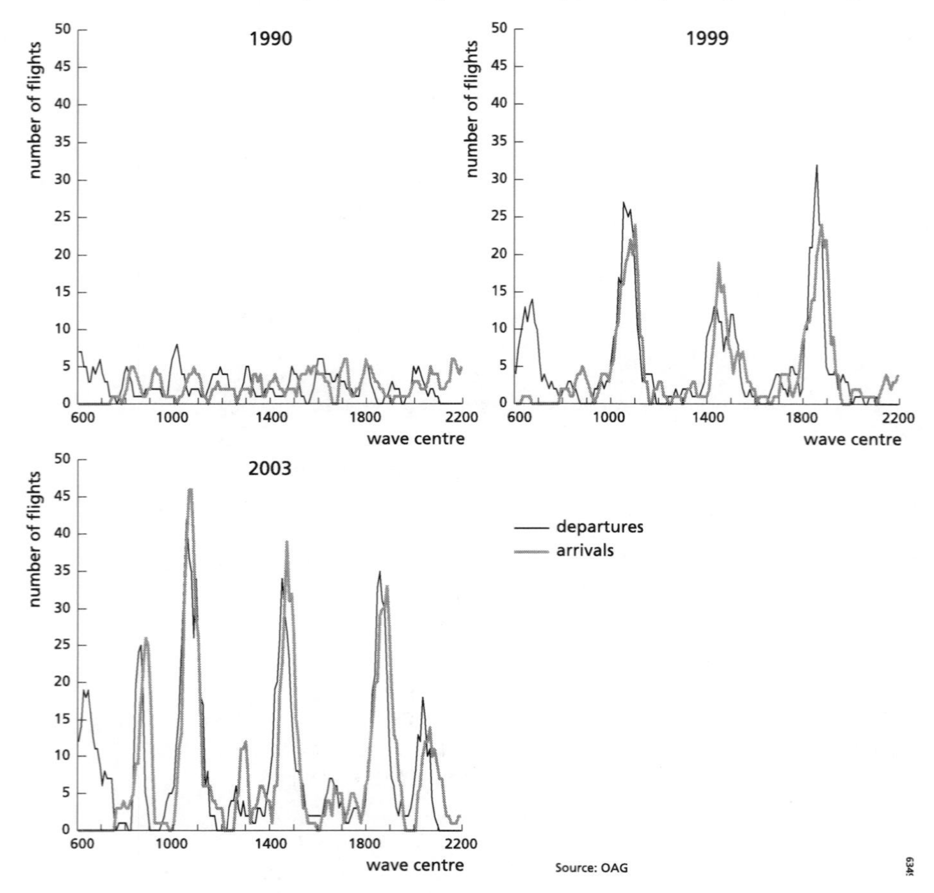

Figure 4.5 The rise of an airline hub: Lufthansa at Munich

and Gatwick in 2000 meant the transfer of intercontinental services from Gatwick back to Heathrow. The end of the split-hub strategy was one of the reasons for the significant increase in indirect connectivity between 1990 and 2003.

We can observe some new hubbing strategies among the national carriers. In this respect, Munich was definitely the rising star in the deregulated era. Munich saw its indirect connectivity increase by a factor of seven as a result of Lufthansa's dual-hub strategy and the opening of the new Munich airport in 1992 (Figure 4.5). In terms of the number of indirect connections, Munich moved from 14th position to 6th position in 2003. Lufthansa developed Munich as a strong hub in the intra-EU market and the market between the EU and Eastern Europe.

Another very fast growing hub was Vienna, where Austrian Airlines and its subsidiary Tyrolean developed a highly efficient wave-system structure. Vienna moved from 17th position in 1990 to 9th position in 2003. The hub is specialized in the Eastern European, Asian and directional transfer markets.

Alitalia started hub operations at the new airport Milan Malpensa. Malpensa had taken over Rome Fiumicino's position as the primary hub for Alitalia in 1999, but lost its position again to Rome in 2003.

British Airways started to build up hub operations at London Gatwick during the 1990s, because capacity problems at Heathrow prevented the carrier from implementing a wave structure at that airport. BA reorganized the flight schedule to and from Gatwick in order to allow for connections to be made within 26 minutes in Gatwick's North Terminal (Caves 1997). British Airways abandoned the Gatwick hub-strategy again in 2000.

Sabena intensified its hub operations at Brussels Zaventem, mainly in the intra-European and African transfer markets. Yet, because of the bankruptcy of Sabena in 2001, Brussels saw its indirect connectivity decrease dramatically. The successor of Sabena, SN Brussels, still operated a wave-system structure of three waves in 2003, but it had been scaled down significantly compared to the three-wave system of Sabena in 1999. In contrast, the bankruptcy of Swissair did not have such a dramatic impact on the hub operations at Zurich: the number of connections at Zurich even increased slightly between 1999 and 2003.

SAS was an early hubbing airline at Copenhagen. It already operated a wave-system structure at the airport in 1990. The carrier needed transfer passengers to compensate for its relatively small origin–destination market. Yet growth of indirect connectivity slowed down between 1999 and 2003. There was almost no increase at the airport. One of the reasons might be the fact that Copenhagen was given a role as a European hub within the Star alliance, whereas Frankfurt, the hub of Star alliance partner Lufthansa, was given the role as the primary intercontinental hub.

At smaller airports regional hub strategies have evolved. Dennis (Dennis 2001b) argues that the introduction of regional jets facilitates the growth of these niche hubs. Régional Airlines implemented a wave-system structure at Clermont-Ferrand. The carrier and its hub were taken over by Air France in 2000. The hub was served by a mix of turboprop and regional jet aircraft (Thompson 2002). Air France started regional hub operations at Lyon during the 1990s. Crossair established a mini-hub at Basle (now operated by Swiss) and Air Littoral initiated hub operations at Nice.

However, the weighted number of indirect connections generated by these carriers remains small in comparison with the large hubs. It is likely that these regional mini-hubs can only be successful if they serve a niche market not covered by major hubs.

Geographical submarkets

Substantial differences can be observed in the parts played by the various hubs in each geographical market segment. For the main European airline hubs we analyzed the competitive strength in terms of the number of weighted indirect connections in eight geographical sub-markets for the year 1990, 1999 and 2003:

1. intra-EU
2. from EU to other European destinations

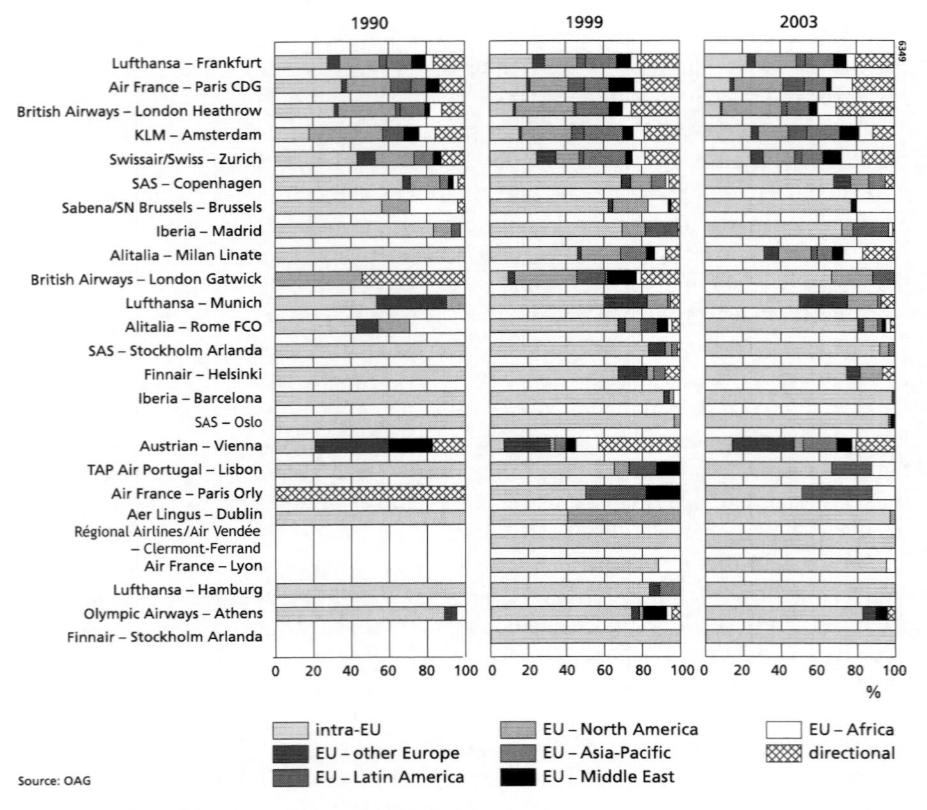

Figure 4.6 Geographical specialization of hubs

Note: *Share of different geographical submarkets in total WNX values for primary European airline hubs. Only submarkets with WNX>10 have been included.*

3. from EU to North America
4. from EU to Latin America
5. from EU to Asia and the Pacific
6. from EU to Africa
7. from EU to Middle East
8. between non-European submarkets (directional).

Figure 4.6 shows the break-down of indirect connections according to geographical segment. Note that only outbound EU connections (EU to North America, for example) have been taken into account for computational reasons. If the inbound EU connections (North America to EU, for example) would have been taken into account, the percentages of directional and intra-EU traffic would be lower. However, including the inbound connections would not alter our overall conclusions.

Let us now recall our classification of airline nodes in Chapter 2. On the basis of the average stage length, we distinguished several different hub types: all-

Table 4.1 Categorization of airline hubs by market orientation

Airline	Hub	1990	1999	2003
Aegean	Athens	–	regional	regional
Aer Lingus	Dublin	regional	specialized	regional
Air Berlin	Palma de Mallorca	–	–	regional
Air Europa	Madrid	–	regional	regional
Air France	Bordeaux	regional	regional	regional
Air France	Clermont-Ferrand	–	–	regional
Air France	Lyon	–	regional	regional
Air France	Marseille	regional	regional	regional
Air France	Paris CDG	global all-round	global all-round	global all-round
Air France	Paris Orly	directional	specialized	specialized
Air Littoral	Nice	–	regional	regional
Air One	Rome FCO	–	–	regional
Alitalia	Milan Linate	regional	regional	regional
Alitalia	Milan Malpensa	–	specialized	global all-round
Alitalia	Rome FCO	specialized	regional	regional
Austrian	Vienna	directional/specialized	directional	directional/specialized
Binter Canarias	Las Palmas	regional	regional	regional
Binter Canarias	Tenerife Norte	regional	regional	regional
BMIBaby	East Midlands	–	–	regional
British Airways	Brimingham	regional	regional	regional
British Airways	London Gatwick	directional/specialized	specialized	regional/specialized
British Airways	London Heathrow	global all-round	global all-round	global all-round
British Airways	Manchester	regional	regional	regional
British Midland	Manchester	regional	regional	regional
easyJet	London Luton	–	regional	regional
easyJet	London Stansted	–	regional	regional
Finnair	Helsinki	regional	regional	regional
Iberia	Barcelona	regional	regional	regional
Iberia	Madrid	regional	specialized	regional/specialized
Icelandair	Keflavik	regional	regional	regional
KLM	Amsterdam	specialized	global all-round	global all-round
Lufthansa	Dusseldorf	regional	regional	regional
Lufthansa	Frankfurt	global all-round	global all-round	global all-round
Lufthansa	Hamburg	regional	regional	regional
Lufthansa	Munich	regional	specialized	specialized
Luxair	Luxembourg	regional	regional	regional
Maersk	Billund	–	regional	regional
Olympic Airways	Athens	regional	regional	regional
Olympic Airways	Thessaloniki	regional	regional	regional
Régional Airlines	Clermont-Ferrand	–	regional	–
Ryanair	Frankfurt/Hahn	–	–	regional
Ryanair	London Stansted	–	regional	regional
Sabena	Brussels	specialized	specialized	–
SAS	Bergen	–	–	regional
SAS	Copenhagen	regional	regional	regional
SAS	Oslo	regional	regional	regional
SAS	Stavanger	–	–	regional
SAS	Stockholm Arlanda	regional	regional	regional
SN Brussels	Brussels	–	–	regional
Spanair	Barcelona	–	regional	regional
Swiss	Geneva	–	–	regional
Swiss	Zurich	–	–	global all-round
Swissair	Geneva	specialized	regional	–
Swissair	Zurich	global all-round	global all-round	global all-round
TAP Air Portugal	Lisbon	regional	regional	specialized
Wideroe's	Bodo	regional	regional	regional

Source: *OAG*

Note: *– indicates less than 10 indirect connections per day.*

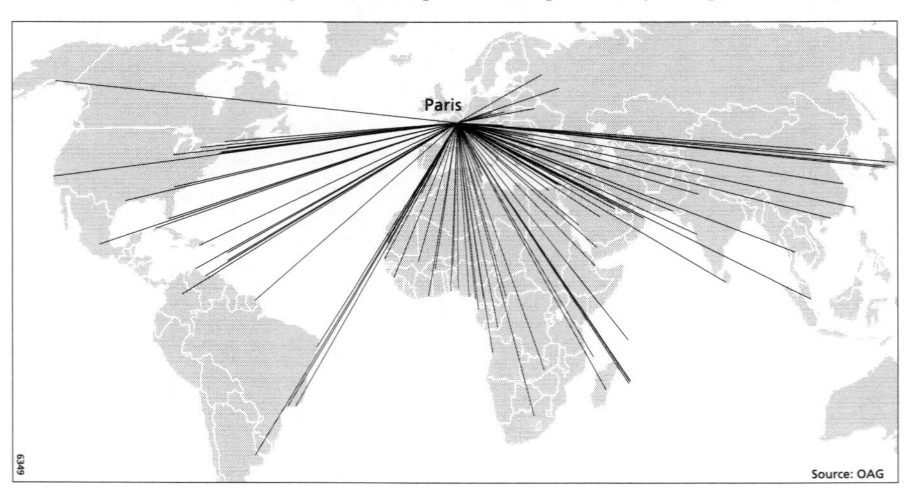

Figure 4.7 The Paris CDG hub of Air France
Note: Only extra-EU destinations are shown (1999).

round hubs, directional hubs, hinterland hubs and regional hubs. On the basis of the geographical orientation, we distinguished the global, the specialized and the regional hub (eurohub/mini-hub).

When analyzing the sub-markets, we can divide the EU airline hubs into four broad categories:

- Global all-round hubs that serve long-haul to long-haul hub traffic (directional hubbing), short-haul to long-haul (hinterland hubbing) and short-haul to short-haul (regional hubbing). Short-haul is considered to be intra-EU traffic. Long-haul is considered to be extra-EU traffic.
- Specialized hinterland hubs serving a specific segment of the hinterland hub market between the EU and extra-EU destinations.
- Directional hubs serving the long-haul to long-haul market (extra-EU to extra-EU).
- Regional hubs mainly serving short-haul to short-haul connections between intra-EU destinations (more than 65 per cent intra-EU). From a geographical perspective, these connections can be EU-wide (Euro-hub) or truly regional (mini-hubs).

Table 4.1 shows the categorization of selected airline hubs.

The all-round hubs Only a few all-round hubs can be distinguished (Figure 4.6 and Table 4.1). All-round hubs are hinterland hubs: hubs with a high degree of indirect connectivity from hinterland Europe to all geographical sub-markets outside the EU. All-round hubs are also directional or hourglass hubs. They can offer not only hinterland connections, but also hourglass connections between major economic

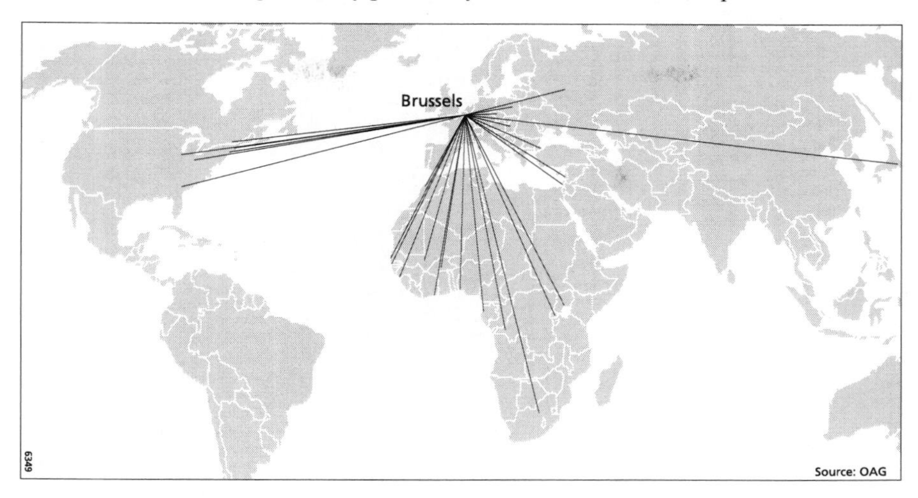

Figure 4.8 Brussels: A specialized hinterland hub for Africa
Note: Only extra-EU destinations of Sabena are shown (1999).

regions in the world because of their central geographical position and extensive extra-EU network.

In 2003 the European all-round hubs were Frankfurt (Lufthansa), London Heathrow (British Airways), Amsterdam (KLM), Paris CDG (Air France), Milan Malpensa (Alitalia) and Zürich (SR).

In 2003 London Heathrow performed poorly in the Eastern European and South American market. Paris Charles de Gaulle had a poor position in the EU to Middle East market, while Frankfurt lagged behind in the African market, and Amsterdam offered considerably fewer directional connections.

In 1999 London Gatwick could be considered an all-round hub, although its Asia-Pacific network was very poorly developed. Yet Gatwick lost its strong position in the African and Latin American markets after the decision of British Airways to close down the Gatwick hub from 2000 on (see also Chapter 6).

Milan Malpensa joined the group of all-round hubs in 2003. Alitalia offered connections in all of the geographical submarkets. Yet the absolute number of connections offered is small compared to the other all-round hubs.

Specialized hinterland hubs Certain hubs have a specialization in one or more extra-EU sub-markets. Moreover, they provide neither a significant service to all the sub-markets, nor large numbers of hourglass connections. These hubs can be defined as specialized hinterland hubs.

Until 1999 Madrid, Brussels, Paris Orly and Munich were perhaps the best examples of specialized hubs. Madrid and Paris Orly focused on the Latin America market, Brussels (Figure 4.8) and Paris Orly on the African market and Munich on the Eastern European market. Dublin was a smaller specialized hub for the Europe to North America market.

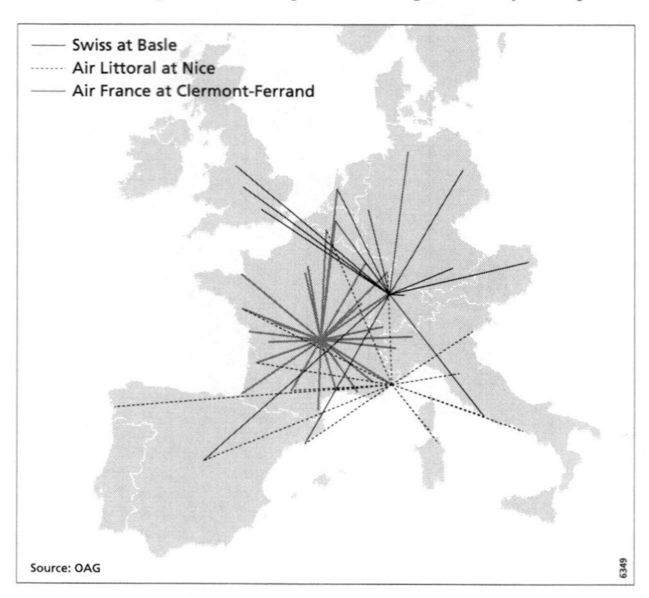

Figure 4.9 Examples of regional mini-hubs, 2003

In 2003 Brussels had lost its strong position as a specialized hub because of the bankruptcy of Sabena in 2001. In the same year Austrian was a strong player in the market between the EU and Eastern Europe, while Air Portugal at Lisbon focused on the Europe–Brazil and the Europe to Mozambique/Senegal market.

Iberia's hub at Madrid was categorized as a regional/specialized hub in 2003. The connectivity portfolio of Madrid mainly concerned domestic-EU connections and connections to Latin America in 2003 (Chapter 6). About 10 per cent of the domestic-EU connections involved a Madrid–Barcelona route, on which Iberia operates a flight every 15 minutes at peak-hours. The air bridge between Barcelona and Madrid stimulates the number of connections enormously since every incoming flight at Madrid (or Barcelona) connects to a multitude of flights to Barcelona (or Madrid).

Most of the geographical specialization seems to be related to social, economic and historical relations with the area considered (Brussels to Africa and Madrid to Latin America, for example). Others are based on geographical proximity, like the orientation of Munich and Vienna towards the Eastern European market.

Regional hubs/Eurohubs Airline hubs such as Oslo (SAS), Barcelona (Iberia), Rome Fiumicino (Alitalia), Helsinki (Finnair), Manchester (British Airways) and Birmingham (British Airways) offer a number of indirect connections, but these are mainly intra-EU (over 65 per cent).

Regional/mini-hubs Regional mini-hubs also concentrate on intra-EU connections, but the average distances of the route network are much smaller in the case of the

Table 4.2 Presence and quality of wave-system structures

Presence and quality of wave-system structure	Number of airline stations 1990	1999	2003
Absent	94	79	81
Very poor	6	9	5
Poor	1	2	4
Limited	3	5	5
Good	1	10	10
Total	105	105	105
% of airline stations with wave-system structures	10%	25%	23%

Source: *OAG*

Note: *Based on a sample of 105 airline stations.*

Euro-hubs. Clermont-Ferrand (Air France), Lyon (Air France), Basle (Swiss) and Nice (Air Littoral) are examples of regional mini-hubs (Figure 4.9).

Regional mini-hub transfer traffic seems to be the most vulnerable category. On the one hand more and more indirect intra-European services will be replaced by point-to-point services, because of the introduction of more efficient regional aircraft, the growth of low-cost carriers and the extension of the high-speed rail network. On the other hand European hubs suffer from larger routing factors, because of the short in-flight time compared with the direct flight time and the transfer time at the hub.

Directional or hourglass hubs Directional hubs offer long-haul to long-haul indirect connections between two major economic areas as a result of their attractive geographical position. Austrian's hub at Vienna was the only hourglass hub in Europe. With regard to the directional connections, Vienna mainly offered connections between Eastern Europe on the one hand, and Asia-Pacific, North America and the Middle East on the other hand. However, the absolute number of these connections is small in comparison with the directional component of the all-round hubs.

The above conclusions about 'hubness' need to be treated with caution. As we stated in Chapters 2 and 3, we only consider an airline node to be a real hub when a schedule structure is present at the airline station to maximize the number of connection opportunities: the wave-system structure. Without analyzing the flight schedule structure, the airline nodes can only be categorized as traffic nodes, but not as hubs in a strict sense. For example, the flight schedule of Ryanair at Stansted in 2003 generated as much indirect connections in 2003 as hub carrier KLM at Amsterdam in 1990. However, Ryanair did not operate a wave-system structure at Stansted, nor is serving the transfer market part of its business strategy. Let us therefore turn to the analysis of wave-system structures in airline flight schedules.

Wave-system structures

Only a small part of the European airport ranking offers significant numbers of indirect connections. Therefore, in the analysis of the airline flight schedule itself

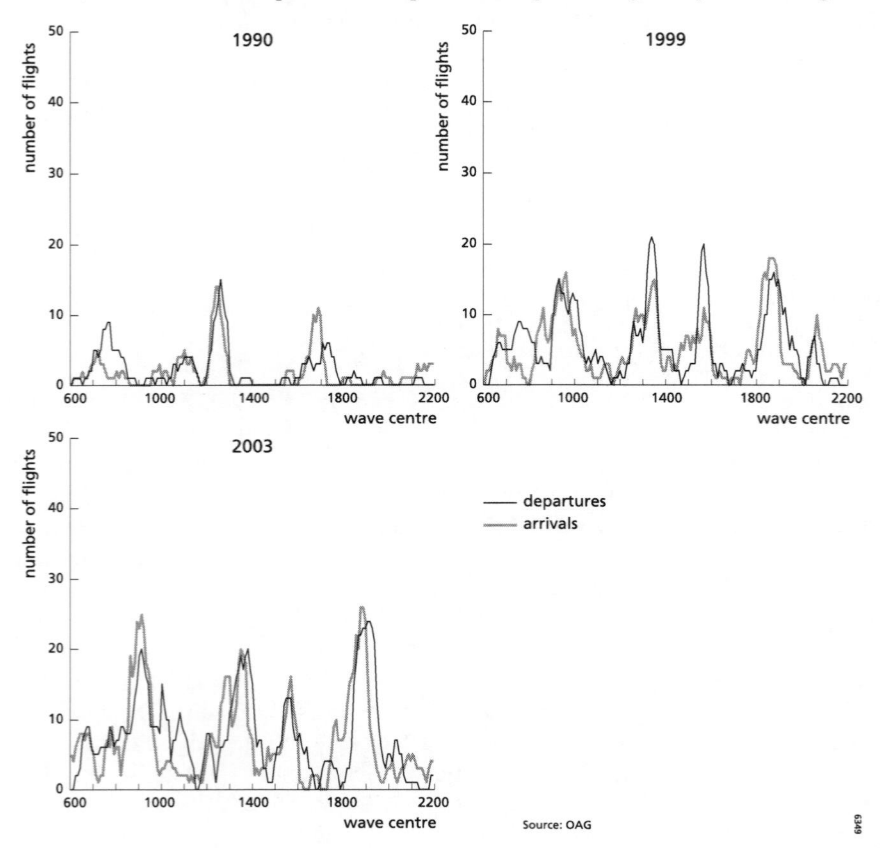

Figure 4.10 Wave-system structure, KLM at Amsterdam

we have only considered airline hubs with a WNX value of 10 or higher in 1999 or 2003 as competitors in the indirect market. This condition resulted in a sample of 105 airline stations. Subsequently we analyzed the sample for the presence of a wave-system structure using the methodology described earlier.

The presence of wave-system structures in airline flight schedules

On the basis of the sample of 105 airline stations we can conclude that European airlines increasingly adopted wave-system structures or intensified the existing structures during the period of analysis (Table 4.2). The number of airline hubs with a wave-system structure doubled during the period of analysis. Several airlines intensified the wave-system structure by adding more waves, or increasing the quality of the wave-system structure (Table 4.2).

Air France adopted a six-wave system at Paris CDG, reconfiguring the airport in a real traffic pump (Figure 4.4). Alitalia did the same at Milan Malpensa with a four-wave

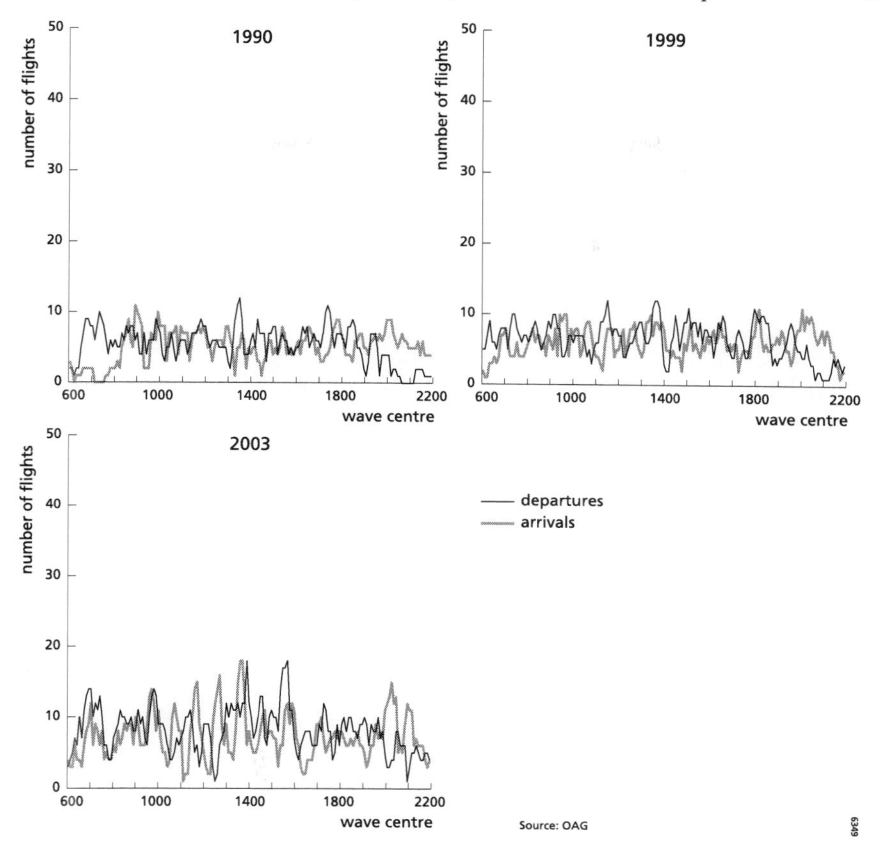

Figure 4.11 Schedule structure, British Airways at London Heathrow

system. Lufthansa built up its Munich hub. The three waves at Munich fit exactly into the wave-system structure at Frankfurt, thereby allowing temporal complementarity between the two hubs to be achieved. Régional Airlines, Air France and Iberia set up wave-system structures at Clermont-Ferrand, Lyon and Barcelona respectively. Crossair implemented a wave-system structure at Basle and Air Littoral at Nice.

Some airlines intensified their hub operations during the period of analysis. KLM added more waves to its three-wave system of 1990 and expanded the capacity per wave (Figure 4.10). Swissair consolidated its intercontinental operations at Zurich and added waves to its hub operations at this airport. Austrian Airlines made its wave operations at Vienna more efficient and effective.

There are four major exceptions to the temporal concentration trend among the major airline home bases. First, the British home bases lack flight-schedule coordination. British Airways was not able to implement a significant wave-system structure successfully at either Heathrow or Gatwick (Figure 4.11). British Airways intended to implement such a structure at Gatwick during the second half of the

Table 4.3 Wave-system structures at primary European hubs

Airline code	Airline name	Primary nodes	Wave-system structure 1990	Wave-system structure 1999	Wave-system structure 2003	Number of waves 1990	Number of waves 1999	Number of waves 2003	Number of weighted indirect connections per day 1990	Number of weighted indirect connections per day 1999	Number of weighted indirect connections per day 2003
4U	Germanwings	Cologne			absent						26
A3	Aegean Airlines	Athens		absent	absent						74
A3		Thessaloniki		absent	absent						16
AB	Air Berlin	Palma de Mallorca		absent	poor			2			39
AB		Alicante		absent	absent						14
AF	Air France	Paris CDG	absent	good	good		6	5–6	1205	8727	14005
AF		Paris Orly	absent	very poor	very poor		3–4	3–4	38	214	709
AF		Lyon	absent	good	good		3	3	20	142	594
AF		Clermont-Ferrand	absent	absent	good			4		169	283
AF		Bordeaux	absent	absent	absent						74
AF		Marseille	absent	absent	absent						51
AF		Nantes	absent	absent	absent						37
AF		Toulouse	absent	absent	absent						19
AP	Air One	Rome FCO	absent	absent	absent						119
AY	Finnair	Helsinki	absent	very poor	very poor		2–3	2–3	144	770	957
AY		Stockholm Arlanda	absent	absent	absent					109	16
AY		Turku	absent	absent	absent					14	
AZ	Alitalia	Rome FCO	very poor	poor	good	2	5	5	201	1028	2384
AZ		Milan Malpensa	absent	limited	limited		4	4		1782	1946
AZ		Milan Linate	absent	absent	absent				145	58	78
BA	British Airways	London Heathrow	absent	absent	absent				2480	4623	9439
BA		London Gatwick	absent	very poor	absent		1–2		126	1647	979
BA		Manchester	absent	absent	absent				23	99	150
BA		Birmingham	absent	absent	absent				32	64	93
BA		Johannesburg	absent	absent	absent					15	63
BA		Inverness	absent	absent	absent						13
BD	British Midland	Manchester	absent	absent	absent						40
BD		London Heathrow	absent	poor	absent					29	20
BD		East Midlands	absent	absent	absent				4	18	

Table 4.3 Continued

Airline code	Airline name	Primary nodes	Wave-system structure 1990	Wave-system structure 1999	Wave-system structure 2003	Number of waves 1990	Number of waves 1999	Number of waves 2003	Number of weighted indirect connections per day 1990	Number of weighted indirect connections per day 1999	Number of weighted indirect connections per day 2003
BU	Braathens	Oslo (Fornebu/ Gardemoen)	absent	absent					33	170	
BU		Bergen	absent	absent					14	59	
BU		Stavanger	absent	absent						58	
BU		Trondheim	absent	absent						18	
DE	Condor Flugdienst	Frankfurt		absent	absent						12
DM	Maersk	Billund	absent	absent	absent					30	48
DM		Copenhagen	absent	absent	absent					18	17
DY	Norwegian Air Shuttle	Oslo (Gardemoen)			absent						19
EI	Aer Lingus	Dublin	absent	absent	absent				46	172	267
EI		Shannon	absent	absent	absent				17	21	28
FI	Icelandair	Reykjavik/Keflavik	very poor	very poor	poor	2	2	2	22	70	96
FR	Ryanair	London Stansted	absent	absent	absent					60	849
FR		Frankfurt Hahn		absent	absent						38
FR		Brussels Charleroi		absent	absent						21
FR		Stockholm Skvasta		absent	absent						15
FU	Air Littoral	Nice	absent	very poor	poor		4	4		18	89
GR	Aurigny Air Services	Guernsey	absent	absent	absent						18
IB	Iberia	Barcelona	absent	limited	limited	2	2	2	344	729	2128
IB		Madrid	very poor	limited	limited	3	3–4	3–4	669	2193	6941
IB		Miami	absent	good	good		2	2			14
IB		Palma de Mallorca	absent	absent	absent						12
IG	Meridiana	Rome FCO	absent	absent	absent						10
IJ	Air Liberté	Paris Orly	absent	very poor			2			13	
IW	AOM	Paris Orly		absent						68	
JK	Spanair	Madrid	absent	absent	very poor			2–3		96	336
JK		Barcelona	absent	absent	absent					10	91
JK		Malaga	absent	absent	absent						11
JZ	Skyways	Stockholm Arlanda	absent	absent	absent						14
KL	KLM	Amsterdam	limited	good	good	3	5	5	890	4296	8713

Table 4.3 Continued

Airline code	Airline name	Primary nodes	Wave-system structure			Number of waves			Number of weighted indirect connections per day		
			1990	1999	2003	1990	1999	2003	1990	1999	2003
LG	Luxair	Luxembourg	absent	absent	absent					96	90
LH	Lufthansa	Frankfurt	good	good	good	4	4	4	2480	9859	13616
LH		Munich	absent	good	good		3	5	167	1297	4184
LH		Dusseldorf	absent	absent	absent				112	95	214
LH		Hamburg	absent	absent	absent				80	110	52
LH		Stuttgart	absent	absent	absent				14	20	26
LH		Cologne	very poor	absent	absent	2			28	40	11
LH		Berlin Tegel	absent	absent	absent					20	
LT	LTU	Dusseldorf	absent	absent	absent					38	
LX	Crossair	Basle	absent	good			4			30	
LX		Zurich	absent	absent						18	
LX(2)	Swiss	Zurich			good			6–7			3734
LX(2)		Geneva			absent						78
LX(2)		Basle			very poor			2			20
NB	Sterling Airways	Copenhagen	absent	absent	absent						37
NG	Lauda	Vienna	absent	absent						24	
NI	Portugalia	Oporto		absent	absent						11
NT	Binter Canarias	Tenerife	absent	absent	absent						110
NT		Las Palmas	absent	absent	absent						73
OA	Olympic	Athens	very poor	very poor	poor	2	3	2	295	307	408
OA		Thessaloniki	absent	absent	absent				38	30	40
OS	Austrian	Vienna	poor	good	good	2	5	5	133	388	2553
OS		Linz	absent	absent	absent						11
QI	Cimber Air	Copenhagen	absent	absent	absent						13
SK	SAS	Copenhagen	limited	limited	limited	4–5	5–6	5–6	1323	2481	2576
SK		Oslo (OSL)	absent	absent	absent				217	511	1139
SK		Stockholm Arlanda	absent	absent	absent				199	846	727
SK		Stavanger	absent	absent	absent					13	63
SK		Bergen	absent	absent	absent						59
SK		Trondheim	absent	absent	absent						33

Table 4.3 Continued

Airline code	Airline name	Primary nodes	Wave-system structure			Number of waves			Number of weighted indirect connections per day		
			1990	1999	2003	1990	1999	2003	1990	1999	2003
SK		Bodo	absent	absent	absent						21
SK		Gothenbrug	absent	absent	absent						15
SK		Tromso	absent	absent	absent				20	21	15
SN	Sabena	Brussels	limited	good		4	4		592	2417	
SNB	SNBrussels	Brussels			limited			3			452
SR	Swissair	Zurich	very poor	good		3	7		961	3161	
SR		Geneva	very poor	absent		1			206	40	
TP	TAP Air Portugal	Lisbon	absent	very poor	very poor		2	2–3	74	242	792
TP		Oporto	absent	absent	absent					16	17
TV	Virgin Express	Brussels		absent	absent						17
U2	easyJet	London Stansted			absent						88
U2		London Luton		absent	absent					13	73
U2		Bristol			absent						29
U2		Liverpool		absent	absent						18
UX	Air Europa	Madrid		absent	absent					29	154
UX		Barcelona		absent	absent						15
VM	Régional Airlines	Clermont-Ferrand	absent	good			4			169	
VO	Tyrolean	Vienna	absent	very poor						46	
VS	Virgin Atlantic	London Heathrow	absent	absent	absent						19
VZ	MyTravellite	Birmingham			absent						12
WF	Wideroe's	Bodo	absent	absent	absent				14	23	52
WF		Trondheim	absent	absent	absent						22
WF		Tromso	absent	absent	absent						19
WF		Hammerfest	absent	absent	absent						11
WW	BMIBaby	East-Midlands			absent						71
X3	Hapag Lloyd Express	Cologne			absent						27

Source: *OAG*

Note: *Only nodes with WNX>10 in 1999 or 2003 have been analyzed. Presence and quality of wave-system structures and number of waves, 1990, 1999 and 2003 for primary European hubs (WNX>10 in 1999 or 2003).*

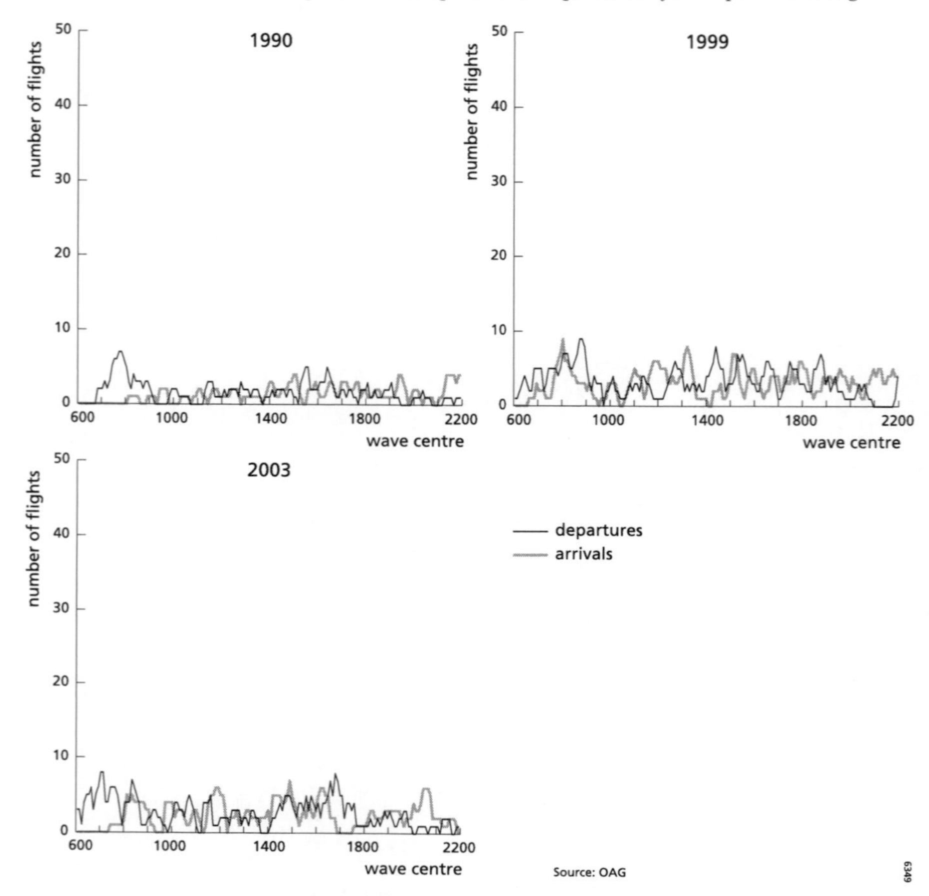

Figure 4.12 Schedule structure, SAS at Stockholm Arlanda

1990s. Yet the Gatwick-strategy failed and from 2000 on British Airways 'de-hubbed' Gatwick (Chapter 6). Shortages in peak-hour capacity at these two airports make it extremely difficult for the airline to implement a wave-system structure. However, the high frequencies still generated a very large number of connections at Heathrow in 2003. Hence, Heathrow can be considered a continuous hub.

Second, most of the Southern European airports only show at best limited wave-structures. Their geographical position makes it difficult to compete with the traffic flows into northern Europe (Bootsma 1997). Instead, the home carriers of Southern European airlines seem to concentrate on origin–destination traffic and some indirect connections in the domestic-EU markets and some intercontinental niche markets. Iberia successfully applied such a strategy at Madrid and to a lesser extent Barcelona (Chapter 6). Network strategies to establish hubs outside the home market (such as Iberia at Hamburg and Finnair at Stockholm Arlanda) were short-lived.

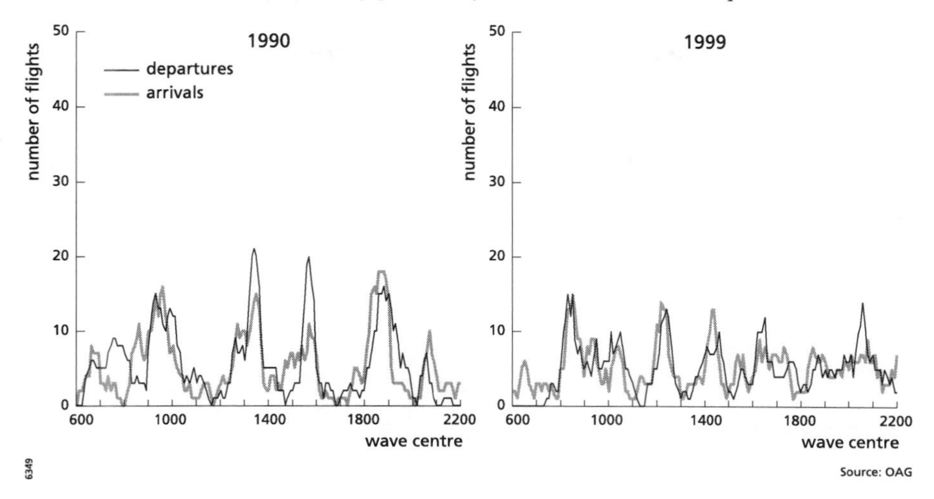

Figure 4.13 Wave-system structures at Amsterdam (left) and Rome Fiumicino (right)

Note: *Wave-system structure of KLM at Amsterdam and Alitalia at Rome Fiumicino.*

Third, a number of smaller nodes such as Oslo (SAS), Stockholm Arlanda (SAS) (Figure 4.12), Helsinki (Finnair), London Stansted (Ryanair) and Dublin (Aer Lingus) are not hub airports in a strict sense. The network of the home carriers is to some extent centred on these airports, but a clear schedule structure is lacking. The carriers have no specific schedules to facilitate transfers, although some connections are generated 'by accident'. The carriers concentrate on origin–destination traffic and/or traffic feed to the major hubs.

Fourth, the vast majority of the smaller airline nodes in Europe had no wave-system structure at all in 2003. These airports concentrate on the local origin–destination market and/or hub-feed to the network of a major alliance partner.

The impact of wave-system structures on indirect connectivity

We found that a number of European airlines adopted wave-system structures in their flight schedules. Another group of carriers did not implement such a structure in the flight schedule, or did not implement one fully. If airlines implement a wave-system structure, do these structures significantly improve the total weighted indirect connectivity of a hub airport? Let us consider the effect of a wave-system structure on the number of indirect connections generated.

The objective of a wave-system structure is to maximize the number of connecting opportunities within a limited time-frame, given the number of direct flights. Hence the ratio between a given number of direct connections on the one hand and the number of indirect connections at the airline hub on the other should theoretically be larger for airports with a wave-system structure than for airports without such a structure.

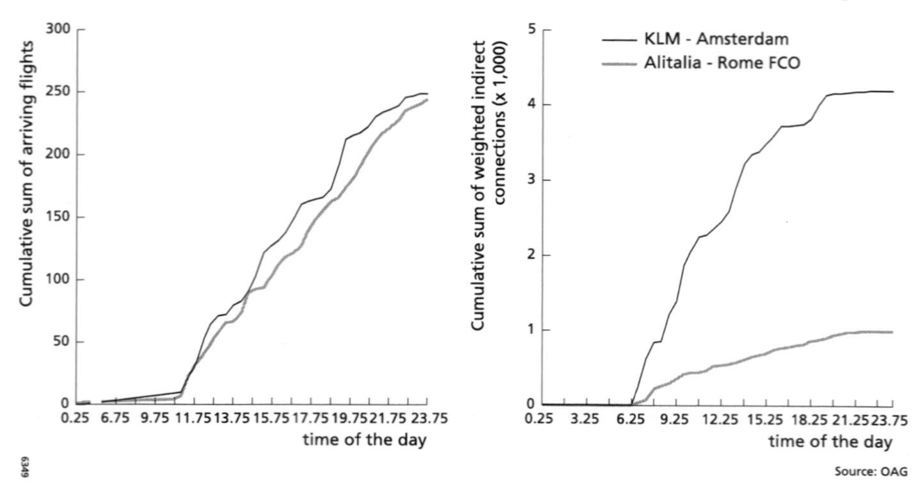

Figure 4.14 The impact of a wave-system structure: Amsterdam and Rome

Note: *Cumulative number of daily direct flights for Alitalia at Rome Fiumicino and KLM at Amsterdam in 1999 per time unit (left) and the cumulative number of weighted indirect connections for Alitalia at Rome Fiumicino and KLM at Amsterdam in 1999 per time unit (right).*

Wave-system structures indeed seem to have a positive impact on the total indirect connectivity of a hub airport. This impact can be illustrated by comparing KLM's hub at Amsterdam Schiphol with Alitalia's hub at Rome Fiumicino. Amsterdam is comparable to Alitalia at Rome in terms of the number of direct flights (Figure 4.14). However, KLM is able to offer many more indirect connections per direct flight than Alitalia (Figure 4.14). KLM operates a well-developed wave-system structure at Amsterdam. The wave-system structure of Alitalia at Rome is less efficient, because of the smaller waves and many off-wave frequencies (Figure 4.13). Moreover, the minimum connecting times are shorter in Amsterdam than in Rome, resulting in more possible connections for every arriving flight. In addition, Rome has a less favourable geographical position as a hub.

The result of the less-pronounced wave-structure system at Rome is the slow increase of the cumulative number of weighted indirect connections (WNX) during the day (Figure 4.14). The well-developed wave-system structure at Amsterdam enables KLM to increase substantially the cumulative number of weighted indirect connections stepwise in every single wave.

SAS at Copenhagen may similarly be compared with British Airways at London Gatwick. SAS operated a full wave-system structure at Copenhagen in 1999, whereas British Airways at Gatwick only operated a very poor wave-system structure. The two airports were comparable in terms of the number of direct daily flights; however the number of weighted indirect connections was much higher for Copenhagen than for Gatwick as a result of the wave-system structure (Figure 4.15). The same advantage holds true for the hub of Régional Airlines at Clermont Ferrand (with

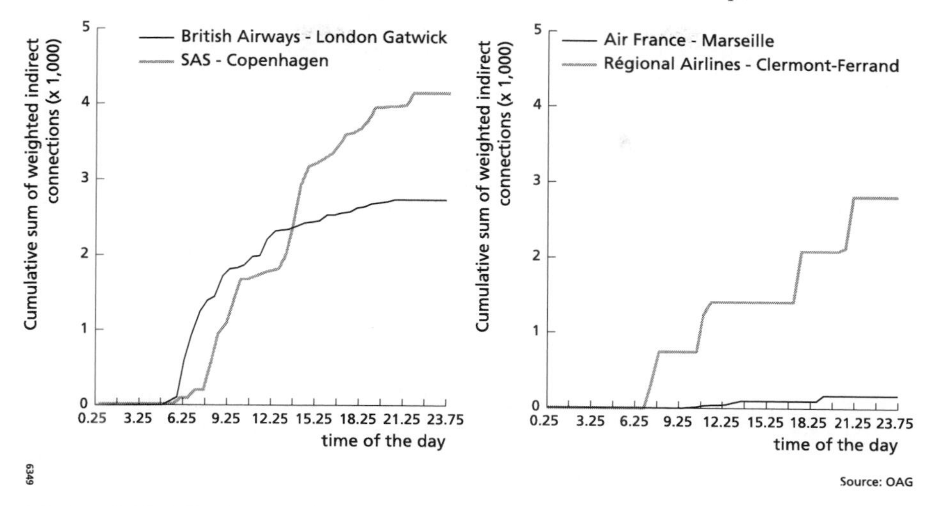

Figure 4.15 The impact of a wave-system structure

Note: *Cumulative number of weighted indirect connections for British Airways at London Gatwick and SAS at Copenhagen (left) and the cumulative number of weighted indirect connections for Régional Airlines at Clermont Ferrand and Air France at Marseille (right) (1999).*

a wave-system structure) with respect to Air France at Marseille (without such a wave-system structure) (Figure 4.15).

In summary, the presence of a wave-system structure indeed has a significant effect on the number of indirect connections generated by the airline flight schedule, given a certain number of direct connections.

Conclusions

After the deregulation of the US aviation market airlines adopted hub-and-spoke networks to benefit from cost- and demand-side economies as well as to deter entry. These networks are characterized by spatial and temporal concentration. The question which arises is whether European airlines followed the same network strategy after the deregulation of the EU aviation market.

In the previous chapter it was shown that the networks of major European airlines were already concentrated in space around a limited number of central airports at the beginning of deregulation.

What about the temporal configuration of airline networks in Europe? A trend towards increasing temporal concentration can indeed be identified. Major European airlines implemented or intensified their wave-system structures at the major hubs during the period of analysis (1990–2003). The major airlines and some niche carriers in particular have followed this hub-and-spoke strategy. This finding is in line with our expectations of airline network development in deregulated markets: temporal concentration by means of a wave-system structure may increase the competitive position of an airline network in the deregulated market, because of certain cost and demand advantages.

Most of the smaller airlines as well as the newly-entering low-cost airlines concentrate on origin–destination traffic and do not play a significant part in the market for transfer traffic. The difference between large and small carriers might be explained by the fact that large hub-and-spoke networks have a very large demand and cost advantage in terms of the number of city pairs served compared with smaller airline hubs. According to Oum and colleagues (1995), a new entrant has to compete with the entire hub-and-spoke network of the incumbent hub carrier. Such an undertaking would be both costly and risky. Therefore, small airlines concentrate on origin–destination and hub-hub markets or fulfil a hub-feeding role, unless their hubs are sufficiently separated from the major hubs, as is the case for Régional Airlines and Air Littoral.

The increase in wave-system structures has stimulated the number of connecting opportunities at hub airports. We have shown that, in general, airports with wave-system structures offer more indirect connections than airports without a wave-system structure, given a certain number of direct flights. In the next chapter we provide a synthesis of the spatial and temporal configuration of airline networks in Europe. In Chapter 6 we illustrate our findings with a number of cases on airline network development.

Chapter 5

Intermezzo: The Spatial-Temporal Configuration of Airline Networks

So far we have analyzed the spatial and temporal configuration of EU airline networks separately. To understand the dynamics in airline network configurations fully, we must bring both dimensions together. In this chapter, therefore, we provide a synthesis of the spatial and temporal dimension of airline network configurations.

The spatial and temporal configuration of airline networks in Europe

To what extent have airlines in the EU reconfigured their networks following EU deregulation? We showed that EU airline networks are organized in a multitude of spatial-temporal configurations, ranging from deconcentrated criss-cross networks to highly-concentrated multi-hub networks with wave-system structures at a few key nodes. Can we identify a trend of intensified hub-and-spoke networks and point-to-point operations among certain groups of carriers during the period of analysis? Table 5.1 summarizes the spatial and temporal characteristics. Only those airlines that generated more than 10 indirect connections per day in 1999 or 2003 at one of its nodes were included.

Hub-and-spoke networks

With respect to hub-and-spoke operations, we can indeed identify the adoption and intensification of hub-and-spoke operations. Defining a hub-and-spoke network as a spatially and temporally concentrated network, we demonstrated that a number of airlines adopted or intensified a wave-system structure at key nodes in their networks between 1990 and 2003.

The number of nodes with wave-system structures increased during the period of analysis. Air France adopted wave-system structures at Paris Charles de Gaulle and Lyon, Lufthansa at Munich, Régional Airlines at Clermont-Ferrand, Alitalia at Milan Malpensa, Crossair at Basle, Air Berlin at Palma de Mallorca, Iberia at Madrid, Barcelona and Miami, Air Littoral at Nice, and so forth. KLM intensified its wave-system structure at Amsterdam, as did Austrian at Vienna, Swissair at Zurich and Alitalia at Rome Fiumicino. SAS and Lufthansa maintained their wave-system structures at Copenhagen and Frankfurt respectively. The number of connecting opportunities at the 'wave-system structured' airline nodes grew much more rapidly than would have been the case with a non-coordinated flight schedule.

Some nodes were de-hubbed too, although this development was of a more recent date. Sabena's efficient European hub at Brussels was closed down and only to a limited extent continued by SN Brussels. Swissair's hub at Zurich was continued on a full scale by Swiss following Swissair's bankruptcy (see Chapter 6). However, Swiss scaled down the hub operations of Crossair at Basle significantly. The very limited wave-system structure of British Airways at London Gatwick was dismantled in 2003. Recently Iberia announced its intention to de-hub its Miami-hub (see Chapter 6). Air France announced its intention to scale down Clermont-Ferrand, a hub it took on after the acquisition of Régional Airlines (see Chapter 6). The regional mini-hub of Air Littoral at Nice ceased to exist after the bankruptcy of the carrier in 2004.

In contrast with the development of airline networks in the domestic US market, the temporal concentration of flights into wave-system structures was not accompanied by any radical restructuring from deconcentrated route networks into concentrated route networks. Only for smaller airline networks such as the networks of Air Littoral and Régional Airlines could we observe the temporal concentration of the network accompanied by spatial concentration.

What are the major reasons for the stability in the spatial dimension of large-scale airline networks in Europe? First, the relocation or building of hubs brings significant costs in terms of marketing, and so forth. Second, building a hub from scratch is risky, particularly in the absence of a significant origin–destination market. Transfer traffic is highly volatile since transfer passengers can easily divert to other hub airports. In many cases wayports, or desert hubs, (with a very large percentage of transfer traffic) have not proven successful. Various wayports in the United States, such as Charlotte and Nashville Tennessee were torn down by the home carriers. The same seems to hold true for Europe. Basle was scaled down, the Nice hub disappeared following the bankruptcy of Air Littoral, and Air France announced the intention to de-hub Clermont-Ferrand. Nevertheless, in the case of a large, established origin–destination market, hubbing may prove to be successful. In this respect, the hubbing initiatives of Air Berlin at Palma de Mallorca are interesting, since the operation relies on a large origin–destination market between Germany and Palma (see case study on Air Berlin).

Third, the carriers with an intercontinental network depended on their portfolio of traffic rights during the period of analysis, which pinned them down to the airports in their country of registration. A Transatlantic Common Aviation area between Europe and the United States and the negotiation of air-service agreements by the European Union may lift the barriers for the spatial restructuring of large-scale airline networks in Europe.

Table 5.1 The spatial and temporal configuration of EU airline networks

	Spatial distribution of intra-EU seat capacity				Wave-system structure			Number of waves			Number of weighted indirect connections per day		
Airline name	**1990**	**1999**	**2003**	**Primary nodes**	**1990**	**1999**	**2003**	**1990**	**1999**	**2003**	**1990**	**1999**	**2003**
Germanwings	n.o.	n.o.	concentrated	Cologne			absent						26
Aegean Airlines	n.o.	moderately concentrated	concentrated	Athens		absent	absent						74
				Thessaloniki		absent	absent						16
Air Berlin		moderately concentrated	moderately concentrated	Palma de Mallorca		absent	limited			2			39
				Alicante		absent	absent						14
Air France	very concentrated	very concentrated	very concentrated	Paris CDG	absent	good	good		6	5–6	1205	8727	14005
				Paris Orly	absent	very poor	very poor		3–4	3–4	38	214	709
				Lyon	absent	good	good		3	3	20	142	594
				Clermont-Ferrand	absent	absent	good			4		169	283
				Bordeaux	absent	absent	absent						74
				Marseille	absent	absent	absent						51
				Nantes	absent	absent	absent						37
				Toulouse	absent	absent	absent						19
Air One	n.o.	concentrated	concentrated	Rome FCO	absent	absent	absent						119
Finnair	concentrated	very concentrated	very concentrated	Helsinki	absent	very poor	very poor		2–3	2–3	144	770	957
				Stockholm Arlanda	absent	absent	absent					109	16
				Turku	absent	absent	absent					14	
Alitalia	very concentrated	very concentrated	very concentrated	Rome FCO	very poor	poor	good	2	5	5	201	1028	2384
				Milan Malpensa	absent	limited	limited		4	4		1782	1946
				Milan Linate	absent	absent	absent				145	58	78
British Airways	very concentrated	very concentrated	very concentrated	London Heathrow	absent	absent	absent				2480	4623	9439
				London Gatwick	absent	very poor	absent		1–2		126	1647	979
				Manchester	absent	absent	absent				23	99	150
				Birmingham	absent	absent	absent				32	64	93
				Johannesburg	absent	absent	absent					15	63

Table 5.1 Continued

Airline name	Spatial distribution of intra-EU seat capacity 1990	1999	2003	Primary nodes	Wave-system structure 1990	1999	2003	Number of waves 1990	1999	2003	Number of weighted indirect connections per day 1990	1999	2003
				Inverness	absent	absent	absent						13
				Manchester	absent	absent	absent						40
				London Heathrow	absent	poor	absent					29	20
British Midland	concentrated	very concentrated	very concentrated	East Midlands	absent	absent	absent					18	
Braathens	moderately concentrated	very concentrated	n.o. *(SK)*	Oslo (Fornebu/ Gardemoen)	absent	absent					33	170	
				Bergen	absent	absent					14	59	
				Stavanger	absent	absent						58	
				Trondheim	absent	absent						18	
Condor Flugdienst	n.o.	moderately concentrated	moderately concentrated	Frankfurt		absent	absent						12
Maersk	concentrated	concentrated	concentrated	Billund	absent	absent	absent					30	48
				Copenhagen	absent	absent	absent					18	17
Norwegian Air Shuttle	n.o.	n.o.	concentrated	Oslo (Fornebu/ Gardemoen)			absent						19
Aer Lingus	very concentrated	very concentrated	very concentrated	Dublin	absent	absent	absent				46	172	267
				Shannon	absent	absent	absent				17	21	28
Icelandair	concentrated	concentrated	concentrated	Reykjavik-Keflavik	very poor	very poor	poor	2	2	2	22	70	96
Ryanair	concentrated	concentrated	very concentrated	London Stansted	absent	absent	absent					60	849
				Frankfurt Hahn		absent	absent						38
				Brussel Charleroi		absent	absent						21
				Stockholm Skvasta		absent	absent						15
Air Littoral	moderately concentrated	concentrated	concentrated	Nice	absent	very poor	poor		4	4		18	89
Aurigny Air Services	concentrated	concentrated	concentrated	Guernsey	absent	absent	absent						18

Table 5.1 Continued

Airline name	Spatial distribution of intra-EU seat capacity 1990	1999	2003	Primary nodes	Wave-system structure 1990	1999	2003	Number of waves 1990	1999	2003	Number of weighted indirect connections per day 1990	1999	2003
Iberia	very concentrated	very concentrated	very concentrated	Barcelona	absent	limited	limited	2	2	2	344	729	2128
				Madrid	very poor	limited	limited	3	3–4	3–4	669	2193	6941
				Miami	absent	good	good		2	2			14
				Palma de Mallorca	absent	absent	absent						12
Meridiana	very concentrated	concentrated	moderately concentrated	Rome FCO	absent	absent	absent						10
Air Liberté	moderately concentrated	moderately concentrated	n.o.	Paris Orly	absent	very poor			2			13	
AOM	n.o.	very concentrated	n.o.	Paris Orly		absent						68	
Spanair	n.o.	concentrated	very concentrated	Madrid	absent	absent	very poor			2–3		96	336
				Barcelona	absent	absent	absent					10	91
				Malaga	absent	absent	absent						11
Skyways	deconcentrated	moderately concentrated	moderately concentrated	Stockholm Arlanda	absent	absent	absent						14
KLM	very concentrated	concentrated	concentrated	Amsterdam	limited	good	good	3	5	5	890	4296	8713
Luxair	very concentrated	very concentrated	very concentrated	Luxembourg	absent	absent	absent					96	90
Lufthansa	very concentrated	very concentrated	very concentrated	Frankfurt	good	good	good	4	4	4	2480	9859	13616
				Munich	absent	good	good		3	5	167	1297	4184
				Dusseldorf	absent	absent	absent				112	95	214
				Hamburg	absent	absent	absent				80	110	52
				Stuttgart	absent	absent	absent				14	20	26
				Cologne	very poor	absent	absent	2			28	40	11
				Berlin Tegel	absent	absent	absent					20	
LTU	n.o.	concentrated	concentrated	Dusseldorf	absent	absent	absent					38	

Table 5.1 Continued

Airline name	Spatial distribution of intra-EU seat capacity 1990	1999	2003	Primary nodes	Wave-system structure 1990	1999	2003	Number of waves 1990	1999	2003	Number of weighted indirect connections per day 1990	1999	2003
Crossair	concentrated	very concentrated	n.o. *(LX(2))*	Basle	absent	good			4			30	
				Zurich	absent	absent						18	
Swiss	n.o.	n.o.	very concentrated	Zurich			good			6–7			3734
				Geneva			absent						78
				Basle			very poor			2			20
Sterling Airways	deconcentrated	n.o.	moderately concentrated	Copenhagen	absent	absent	absent						37
Lauda	n.o.	concentrated	*(OS)*	Vienna	absent	absent						24	
Portugalia	n.o.	very concentrated	very concentrated	Porto		absent	absent						11
Binter Canarias	very concentrated	moderately concentrated	concentrated	Tenerife Norte	absent	absent	absent						110
				Las Palmas	absent	absent	absent						73
Olympic	very concentrated	very concentrated	very concentrated	Athens	very poor	very poor	poor	2	3	2	295	30	408
				Thessaloniki	absent	absent	absent				38	30	40
Austrian	concentrated	concentrated	very concentrated	Vienna	poor	good	good	2	5	5	133	388	2553
				Linz	absent	absent	absent						11
Cimber Air	deconcentrated	concentrated	moderately concentrated	Copenhagen	absent	absent	absent						13
SAS	very concentrated	very concentrated	very concentrated	Copenhagen	limited	limited	limited	4–5	5–6	5–6	1323	2481	2576
				Oslo (Fornebu/ Gardemoen)	absent	absent	absent				217	511	1139
				Stockholm Arlanda	absent	absent	absent				199	846	727
				Stavanger	absent	absent	absent					13	63
				Bergen	absent	absent	absent						59
				Trondheim	absent	absent	absent						33

Table 5.1 Continued

Airline name	Spatial distribution of intra-EU seat capacity 1990	1999	2003	Primary nodes	Wave-system structure 1990	1999	2003	Number of waves 1990	1999	2003	Number of weighted indirect connections per day 1990	1999	2003
				Bodo	absent	absent	absent						21
				Gothenburg	absent	absent	absent						15
				Tromso	absent	absent	absent				20	21	15
Sabena	concentrated	concentrated	n.o.	Brussels	limited	good		4	4		592	2417	
SNBrussels	n.o.	n.o.	concentrated	Brussels			limited			3			452
Swissair	very concentrated	concentrated	n.o.	Zurich	very poor	good		3	7		961	3161	
				Geneva	very poor	absent		1			206	40	
TAP Air Portugal	very concentrated	very concentrated	concentrated	Lisbon	absent	very poor	very poor		2	2–3	74	242	792
				Porto	absent	absent	absent					16	17
Virgin Express	n.o.	concentrated	concentrated	Brussels		absent	absent						17
easyJet	n.o.	moderately concentrated	moderately concentrated	London Stansted		n.o.	absent						88
				London Luton		absent	absent					13	73
				Brussels		n.o.	absent						29
				Liverpool		absent	absent						18
Air Europa	n.o.	concentrated	very concentrated	Madrid		absent	absent					29	154
				Barcelona		absent	absent						15
Régional Airlines	deconcentrated	moderately concentrated	n.o. *(AF)*	Clermont-Ferrand	absent	good			4			169	
Tyrolean	very concentrated	concentrated	n.o. *(OS)*	Vienna	absent	very poor						46	
Virgin Atlantic	n.o.	moderately concentrated	deconcentrated (ICA conc.)	London Heathrow	absent	absent	absent						19
MyTravellite	n.o.	n.o.	moderately concentrated	Birmingham			absent						12
Wideroe's	deconcentrated	deconcentrated	deconcentrated	Bodo	absent	absent	absent				14	23	52
				Trondheim	absent	absent	absent						22
				Tromso	absent	absent	absent						19

Table 5.1 Continued

Airline name	Spatial distribution of intra-EU seat capacity 1990	1999	2003	Primary nodes	Wave-system structure 1990	1999	2003	Number of waves 1990	1999	2003	Number of weighted indirect connections per day 1990	1999	2003
				Hammerfest	absent	absent	absent						11
BMIBaby	n.o.	n.o.	concentrated	East Midlands			absent						71
Hapag Lloyd Express	n.o.	n.o.	moderately concentrated	Cologne			absent						27

Source: *OAG*

Note: *n.o.: airline not operating; –: airline not operating services to node; if the number of indirect connections is blank, the number of indirect connections is zero or less than 10.*

Non-hub networks

However, only a limited number of national airlines and a few niche-carriers at a limited number of key nodes in these airline networks adopted, intensified, maintained a wave-system structure. Most of the EU airlines in our database did not operate a wave-system structure and they did not offer any indirect connections through their central nodes, or at best generated some indirect connectivity 'by accident'.

It is important to note that we did not include alliance groups as such in our network analyses. Many regional airline services may fit perfectly well into the wave-system structure of hub-and-spoke carriers. In code-share partnership with these carriers they can generate additional indirect connections through the hubs. Since we have only included highly-integrated regional affiliates as part of the hub-and-spoke carrier networks (KLM Cityhopper, Lufthansa CityLine, Alitalia Express, for example), future research should also include other partnerships, in order to obtain a more accurate picture.

The spatially-concentrated network is clearly the preferred network configuration not only of the hub-carriers, but also of the majority of the non-hub carriers. Spatial concentration has advantages, even in the absence of any network economies associated with the hub-and-spoke network. These advantages include aircraft maintenance, aircraft utilization, crew rotation and marketing. Our results confirm the general advantages of spatial concentration (Chapter 2).

Low-cost carrier networks

Even most of the low-cost carrier networks were quite concentrated in space. The deconcentrated Southwest-model is the exception rather than the rule among Europe's low-cost airlines, although some deconcentrated network patterns were found. Even the network of the largest low-cost carrier, Ryanair, was spatially concentrated around multiple home bases in 2003. Only the easyJet network could be considered to be deconcentrated in terms of the spatial distribution of seat capacity. In addition, the networks of low-cost airlines with origins in the leisure market, such as Air Berlin and Hapag Lloyd, showed a more deconcentrated network pattern. However their networks were still rooted in the charter networks that had been established before deregulation. Among these carriers we see a gradual shift towards more concentration now they have entered the scheduled low-cost market. In essence, the latter type of low-cost network is path-dependent on the charter networks: their network structure can only be understood when taking into account the fact that the current scheduled network of these carriers grew out of a charter network.

What then can be said about the general expectation, which frequently circulates in the media, aviation magazines and journals, that low-cost airlines generally operate point-to-point networks?

In Chapter 2 we defined a point-to-point network as a deconcentrated network without a wave-system structure at any of the nodes. In this respect, low-cost airline networks in Europe can only be labelled as point-to-point networks to a certain extent. We concluded that most low-cost airlines operated concentrated networks centred on certain key nodes. In this respect, low-cost airline networks are not point-to-point networks from a spatial point of view. It is true, however, that virtually all low-cost airlines focused on the origin–destination market, taking into account the structure of their flight schedule. Only two low-cost airlines (Air Berlin and Spanair) operated a very small wave-system structure at one of their home bases (Palma de Mallorca and Madrid respectively), with the intention of stimulating connecting traffic. Similar developments of low-cost hubbing are taking place in the United States, where the low-cost airline Frontier, for example, operates a wave-system structure at Denver International Airport. By 2003, however, almost all EU low-cost airlines could be classified as non-coordinated/random networks from a temporal perspective.

The hypothesis that low-cost airlines primarily serve secondary airports for cost considerations and the absence of head-to-head competition with the major airlines cannot be confirmed either. In Chapter 3 we revealed the large variation in the types of airport served by the low-cost carriers. Airlines such as Ryanair and Air Berlin indeed concentrated on the smaller airports. Others such as Virgin Express and Germanwings mainly concentrated on the larger EU airports.

Deconcentrated networks

Although the concentrated network pattern prevails, deconcentrated network patterns also existed during the period of analysis. One of the most extreme examples of such a deconcentrated network pattern is Wideroe's Flyveselkap, now part of the SAS group. The carrier operated a deconcentrated network along the coast of Norway between 1990 and 2003. However, its network must be seen in relation to the financial support of the Public Service Obligation to connect the remoter regions of Norway with the rest of the country (Williams 2002). Most of the deconcentrated networks concerned very small networks in terms of the airports served, some of them only covering a single route. The deconcentrated networks also included the networks of most of the extra-EU carriers within Europe. Only a few carriers such as TWA and Pan Am operated small hubs with high levels of spatial concentration at the beginning of the 1990s. Most of the extra-EU carriers retreated from the EU market during the 1990s, however, owing to the emergence of airline alliances, the use of new aircraft equipment and intensified competition on intra-EU routes. All the significant fifth-freedom hubs within the EU were dismantled.

In short, airlines reconfigured their networks following EU deregulation. The adoption and intensification of wave-system structures, the disappearance of extra-EU carrier networks and the rapid growth of low-cost carrier networks were among the most important network developments in the deregulated EU air transport market. There is a wide variation of network configurations and network evolutions. Identification of the network developments needs a careful, network-wide and longitudinal analysis that covers both the spatial and temporal dimension of airline networks, analogous to the analyses performed in Chapters 3 and 4.

Chapter 6

Airline Cases

In the previous chapters the development of airline network configurations was described. The question remains why airline networks developed in the way that they did. The airline case studies in this chapter shed some light on this issue. They illustrate the changes in the spatial and temporal dimension in the networks of a number of national carriers, regional airlines and low-cost carriers in detail. The network developments of KLM, British Airways and Iberia are described most extensively, followed by nine minor case studies of regional and low-cost networks.[1]

KLM Royal Dutch Airlines

Background: 1945–1980

KLM was founded in 1919 by a group of Dutch investors. KLM acknowledged early in its history that its national market would not have sufficient demand to maintain a worldwide network. During the 1950s the airline began to target the transfer market actively. The carrier developed its home base, Amsterdam Airport Schiphol, as a sixth-freedom hub by marketing indirect connections between European and intercontinental destinations via Amsterdam (Dierikx 1999). In particular, the London–Amsterdam and Germany–Amsterdam routes were important feeder routes for KLM's intercontinental routes to Asia, Africa, the Middle East and North America during the 1950s (Figure 6.1). Carrying traffic to and from Germany was especially attractive because the allied forces had forbidden German air carriers to undertake such transport. Only in 1955 did Lufthansa start operating scheduled air services in Germany.

However, there was still no efficient structure to optimize the number of transfer connections at that time. The flight schedule structure at Amsterdam could be characterized as random (Figure 6.2) and remained so until the 1980s, when a more pronounced wave-system structure was developed.

The hub strategy of KLM did not come without its problems, however. The early hub-and-spoke operations of KLM hindered bilateral negotiations with the United States (Dierikx 1999). Since the United States had returned to a protectionist aviation policy after the failure of the Chicago Conference, the United States based their

1 The case studies are based on interviews with airline and airport representatives, aviation experts, document and data analysis and literature review.

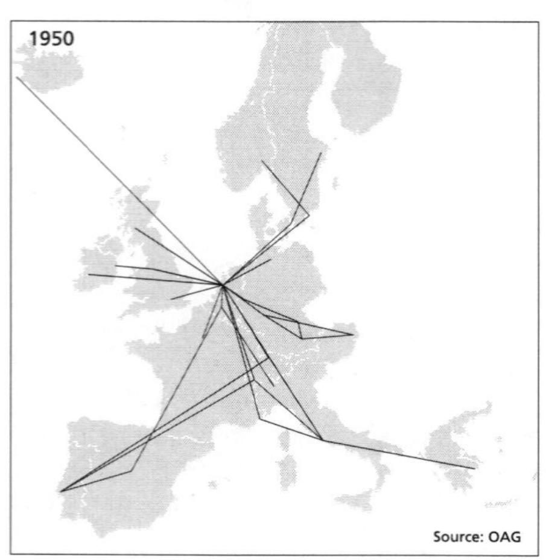

Figure 6.1 KLM intra-EU route network,n 1950 and 1980

negotiations on traffic rights on the principle of the equitable exchange of economic benefits. In practice, this principle meant that the US only wanted to agree on the exchange of traffic rights (destinations, frequencies, capacity) on the basis of KLM's home market, but not on the basis of its transfer traffic beyond the Dutch market (sixth-freedom traffic).

The United States suspected KLM of carrying large numbers of passengers from Europe via Amsterdam Schiphol to the United States. KLM, however, asserted that they did not know where their departing passengers came from. The Dutch government and the carrier asserted that this type of traffic was just a combination of third- and fourth-freedom traffic. According to an academic expert on the history of KLM:

> You can see this strategy in the administration of traffic flows. KLM was eager to separate the traffic flows. The carrier administered the traffic flows Amsterdam–Helsinki, but never the data for Helsinki–New York via Amsterdam. If KLM were to administer these traffic flows, there would be the risk of a country saying 'this wasn't part of the deal'. KLM would not have been able to grow to its current size if the carrier had not carried transfer traffic.

In fact, KLM operated a 'hidden' intercontinental hub at Schiphol from the 1950s until the 1970s. It was difficult for the US to 'prove' KLM's transfer strategy. KLM did not publish any origin–destination traffic statistics on this matter. Moreover, neither was there a pronounced wave-system structure at Amsterdam (Figure 6.2). The dispute between the United States and the Netherlands made it impossible to reach a bilateral air-service agreement until 1957. As a result, KLM could not serve any US destinations other than New York. Other European carriers that did not engage in so much transfer traffic because they had a large home market, and/or were given ample financial state support, were gradually given more points in

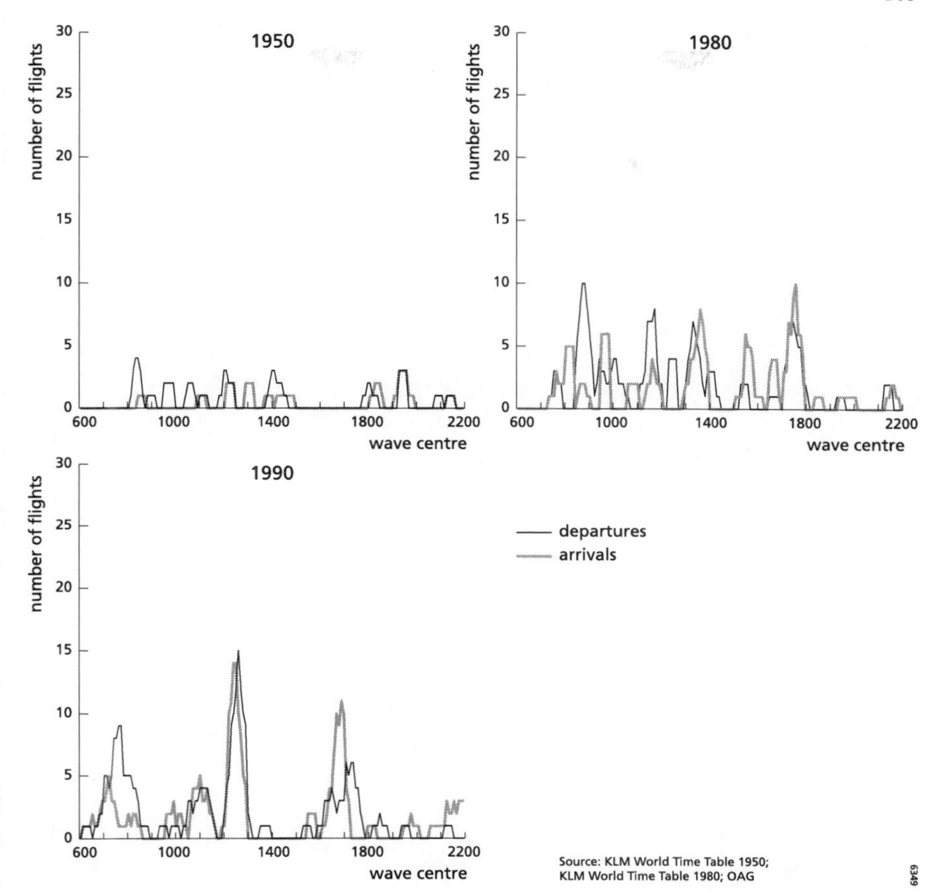

Figure 6.2 Flight schedule structure of KLM at Amsterdam, 1950, 1980, 1999

the United States. Finally, in the bilateral air-service agreement of 1957, KLM was given the rights to operate to New York and Houston, but not the most desired routes to the US west coast.

In addition to its sixth-freedom hub strategy, KLM could maintain a worldwide network through the extensive operation of low-frequency, multi-stop routes. Various destinations were served with a single flight, making stops at intermediate nodes. Apart from the network coverage objective, intermediate stops were also needed for technical reasons, since in the 1950s aircraft range was still limited. The extensive operation of intercontinental multi-stop routes continued throughout the 1980s.

Change came about for KLM in 1978 when the US domestic air transport market was deregulated. Following domestic deregulation, the United States started to renegotiate a number of bilateral air-service agreements in order to reduce regulatory control on routes to and from the United States. The revised bilateral air-service agreement of 1978 between the United States and the Netherlands was the first in a series of less restrictive air-service agreements (Doganis 1991). Among other things, capacity and frequency restrictions were removed and the number of US points that could be served by Dutch airlines increased. In addition, there was no restriction on sixth-freedom traffic.

The unrestricted right to carry sixth-freedom traffic gave KLM the opportunity to grasp the benefits of the transfer market to the United States. The opportunities of doing so were further enhanced by the open-skies agreement between the Netherlands and the United Kingdom in 1984 and the gradual deregulation of the intra-EU market from 1988 on. During the 1980s KLM developed a more pronounced wave-system structure at Amsterdam. Feeding from the United Kingdom was organized via the partner airline Air UK (later to become KLM UK). As a historian put it:

> In practice, KLM operated a hub in Amsterdam, but legally, the hub did not exist. Transfer flows existed, but they had to be invisible for political reasons. Only since deregulation has KLM had the opportunity to coordinate its flight schedules in an efficient way. Gradually, the coordination of arrivals and departures has improved. Since deregulation there has no longer been any need to disguise the origin of the passenger flows.

1990–1997: Hubbing and rationalization

Hubbing In 1990 the KLM network could be characterized as a single-radial, concentrated network. In 1990 the Network Concentration index of the carrier's network was fairly high (0.72 in 1990 against 0.65 in 2003). The high NC index in 1990, such as is normally found in multi-hub networks, reflects the high density/capacity route of KLM to London Heathrow, with a weekly frequency of 55 flights, served by Airbus A310 and Boeing 737 aircraft. The high capacity offered on the routes to and from London Heathrow made the airport the second most important in the KLM network at that time. The capacity offered at Heathrow was so large in relative terms, the Network Concentration index captures Heathrow as a secondary home base. During the 1990s, however, its European network became much better balanced as KLM gained the freedom to set capacity and frequency on the intra-EU routes. The relative dominance of London Heathrow in terms of seat capacity declined and, as a result, the Network Concentration index decreased.

From a temporal point of view, KLM operated a rudimentary wave-system structure at Amsterdam (Figure 6.2). The structure consisted of an early-morning wave and afternoon and late-afternoon waves.

We discuss here two important developments in the spatial and temporal developments for the period 1990–1997: hubbing and the rationalization of the intercontinental network.

The hubbing strategy of KLM in the early 1990s needs to be viewed against the background of the deregulation of the intra-EU air transport market, the alliance with Northwest Airlines and the size of KLM's origin–destination market. First, as a reaction to the new market environment and economic downturn in the beginning of the 1990s, in 1991 Pieter Bouw, the CEO of KLM, adopted the cost reduction plan 'Concurrerend Kostenniveau' to cope with increasing competition on the European market and the downward pressure on ticket prices (Dierikx 1999). One of the goals of the business plan was to reorganize the KLM network into an efficient hub-and-spoke system. The existing structure was characterized by poor utilization of the short-haul fleet and poorly timed connections for business passengers (Dennis 1994a). A more efficient wave-system structure would enhance the load factors on the KLM flights because of the economies of scope, density and aircraft size generated by hub-and-spoke operations.

Second, in 1992 the Dutch and US government drew up an Open Skies agreement liberalizing the market between the United States and the Netherlands. The agreement gave KLM full access to all destinations in the United States. Moreover, the Open Skies agreement was '*conditio sine qua non*' to receive anti-trust immunity from the US Department of Transport for the KLM's alliance with Northwest Airlines (Mendes de Leon 2002). The alliance with Northwest Airlines demanded better coordination of the KLM flight schedule at Amsterdam in order to integrate both networks via their respective hubs Amsterdam, Minneapolis/St. Paul, Detroit and Memphis.

Finally, KLM came to realize that its world-embracing network could not be justified by its origin–destination market alone. The only way to operate as a leading intercontinental carrier was to feed its network with traffic from all over Europe. As one KLM manager put it:

> KLM is a carrier with a very small home market. In fact, KLM is too big an airline for the Netherlands and too small for Europe. We have to make sure that we optimize our connections and collect our passengers from all over Europe to fill the intercontinental network. A wave-system structure was crucial for us to be able to do this.

Hence, in the winter of 1992–1993 a wave-system structure of three waves was implemented at Schiphol (Figure 6.4). Part of the short-haul fleet was now stabled at the spokes overnight. The aircraft would fly into Schiphol in the morning, making effective feeding to the departing intercontinental flights possible. The frequency of European flights increased as a result of the introduction of the system (Figure 6.5). The system proved to be highly successful. KLM was growing at a rate of 10 per cent per year in terms of traffic volumes, whereas the market was growing at a rate of 6 per cent per year. KLM made the transition from being the largest of the small airlines to being the smallest of the four largest EU airlines.

During the 1990s KLM allied with partner airlines such as Air UK, NLM Cityhopper, Netherlines, Braathens SAFE, Eurowings,[2] Air Engiadina and Air Exel in order to feed the hub system (Figure 6.3). NLM Cityhopper and Netherlines, both daughter companies of KLM, merged and were renamed KLM Cityhopper in 1991.

2 The partnerships with Eurowings and Braathens SAFE came to an end in 2000 and 2001 respectively. Eurowings became a partner of the Lufthansa group, whereas SAS took up a stake in Braathens.

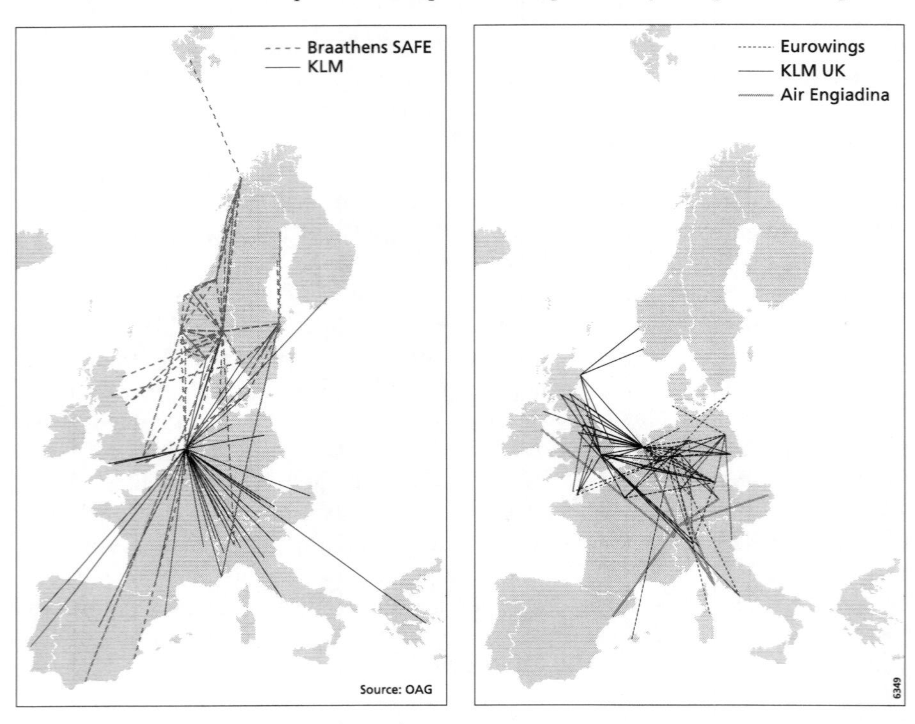

Figure 6.3 European network of KLM and partners, 1999

As part of KLM's 'brand visibility' strategy, at the end of the 1990s Air UK, Air Exel Commuter and Air Engiadina were renamed KLM UK, KLM Exel and KLM Alps respectively. The aircraft changed to the KLM livery. Carriers such as Tyrolean, Cyprus Airways, Aer Lingus and Régional Airlines had code-share agreements with KLM on specific feeder routes.

However, Bootsma's PhD research (1997) showed that the 3-wave structure was suboptimal in terms of the balancing of intercontinental traffic over the various waves. Moreover, there was an overlap of incoming and outgoing waves that resulted in lost connections. Apart from the desire to increase European frequencies to a more competitive level, the sub-optimality of the 1993 system was one of the causes of the reorganization and expansion of the system in 1997 based on Bootsma's design (see Chapter 4).

In 1997 a new generation wave-system structure consisting of five waves was implemented. Although the new structure was called a 5-wave system structure, in fact it was a 4-wave structure with a split fifth wave. The first half of the split wave could be found in the late evening, when incoming European flights connected with intercontinental departures. However, the second half of the wave was to be found in the early morning of the next day, when intercontinental arrivals connected with European departures. The other four were fully-fledged waves according to the

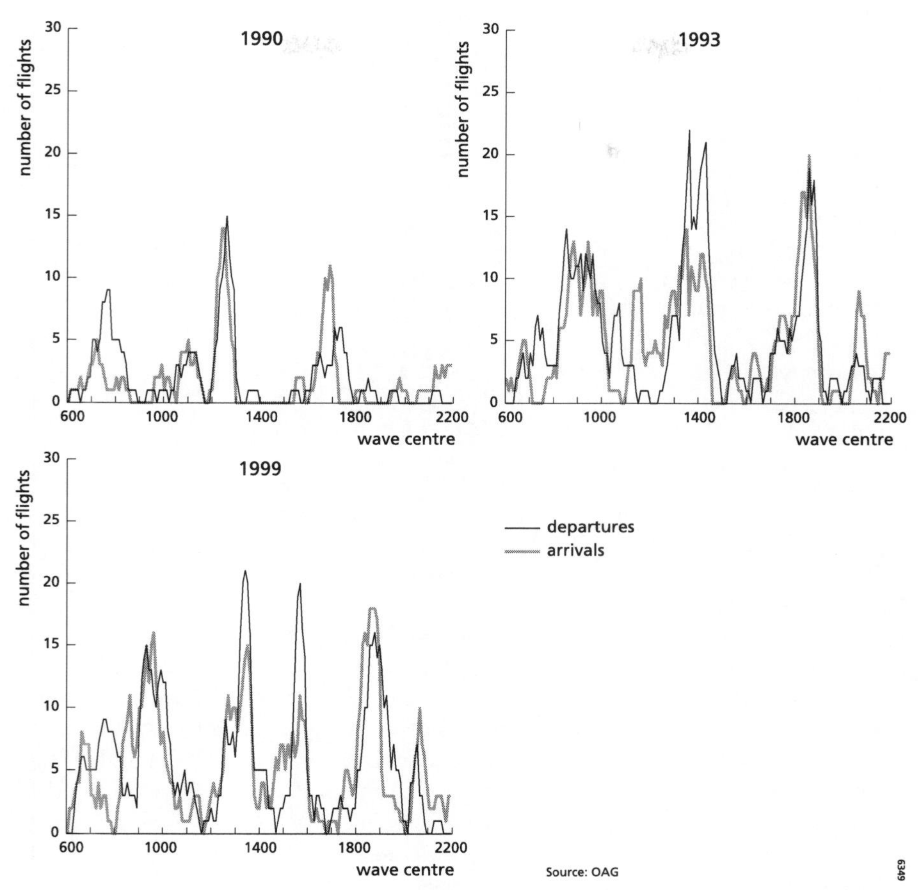

Figure 6.4 KLM wave-system, 1990, 1993 and 1999

theoretical connection wave of Chapter 4: intercontinental arrivals and European arrivals followed by European departures and intercontinental departures. In 2004 KLM was still operating basically the same wave-system structure.

The number of indirect connections was boosted by the introduction of the 1993 and 1997 wave-system structures (Chapter 4). As a result of the introduction of the 1997 system, the frequency of European flights was raised significantly: many European destinations were served 4–5 times per day to connect with the European and intercontinental flights in each wave (Figure 6.5). The alliance with Northwest airlines even enabled some of the intercontinental destinations to be served frequently on a daily basis. In 1999, for example, the Detroit–Amsterdam route was served four times a day by KLM and Northwest, although local demand between the Netherlands and the Detroit region did not justify such a service. Similarly, by 1999 the Amsterdam to Nairobi route was served twice daily as a result of the alliance agreement drawn up between KLM and Kenya Airways in 1996.

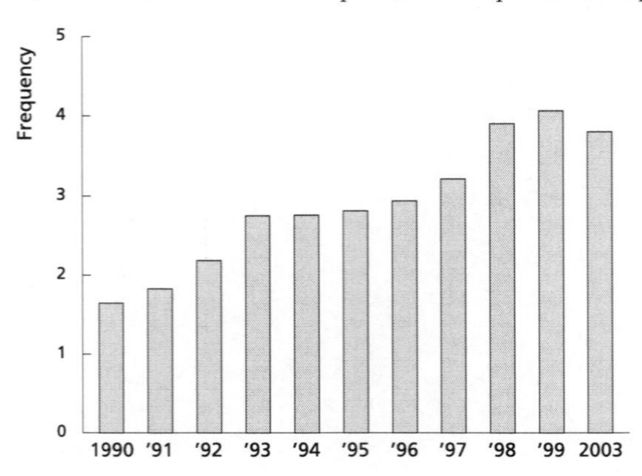

Figure 6.5 Average daily intra-EU KLM frequency at Amsterdam

Rationalization The influence of Northwest on the network strategy of KLM was present not only in the intensification of the wave-system structure, but also in another dimension of the KLM network: its fifth-freedom traffic. In 1990 KLM still operated a large number of low-frequency, multi-stop intercontinental routes based on fifth-freedom rights. The aim of such routes was network coverage, but the frequency of many of those intercontinental routes was rather low.

KLM's partner Northwest Airlines argued that these multi-stop routes were not effective from either a cost or a competitive point of view. From a cost perspective, making in-between stops with a large aircraft generates a lot of extra expenditure. The rise in costs results in an increase in the break-even load factor of each flight. From a competitive point of view, a carrier can only be an effective competitor when it has significant market presence in terms of flight frequencies. The high-yield business passengers in particular demand at least a daily non-stop frequency. Operating low-frequency, multi-stop services therefore makes little sense. As a result, during the 1990s there was a rationalization of the KLM network: a focus on the routes the airline could operate profitably at least once a day with a non-stop service if that was possible from a technical point of view. According to one KLM manager:

> You can operate effectively in a market when you have a strong position in that market. If you fly, for example, twice a week to Buenos Aires, while Aerolineas Argentinas and Iberia fly daily to Europe, you do not have a strong position. You will not be able to attract high-yield business traffic. [...] In fact, Northwest said to us: if you don't operate routes on a daily, non-stop basis, then cut them. Hence, on the intercontinental side, we went through a process of network focusing.

1997–2003: Optimization

Following the introduction of the 5-wave system in 1997, the KLM network remained relatively stable from a spatial and temporal perspective. The Network Concentration index stabilized during the second half of the 1990s at 0.65: a value

Table 6.1 Potential size of origin–destination markets

Hub	1hr by car	2hrs by car	1hr by train	2hrs by train
Amsterdam	8.2	21.8	6.4	13.8
London Heathrow	14.8	24.4	11.4	21.5
Frankfurt	7.6	24.7	6.0	25.5
Paris Charles de Gaulle	12.2	20.6	11.1	23.4

Source: *RPB 2005*
Note: *Potential OD-market in number of passengers (x mln). Numbers for 2003.*

that is characteristic of a single-hub network. The wave-system structure of five waves was not altered. Nevertheless, the number of flights in each wave was increased, doubling the number of indirect connections. First, this increase was caused by a composition effect in our connectivity analysis: in 2003 we considered KLM UK to be part of the core network of KLM, since it was to be fully integrated into KLM Cityhopper in 2004 and was no longer operating under its own flight code. Second, part of the growth was caused by a growth in the number of direct KLM flights.

The observation of the expansion of the existing waves instead of adding new waves fits in with the vision of KLM with respect to the expansion of the hub system. As a strategist of KLM put it:

> You can extend the wave-system structure in two ways. You can either quickly add new waves, as the US carriers do, or expand the existing waves. Our choice is the latter: we enlarge the waves first before adding new ones. In one way or another you will end up with a wave-system structure with many large waves. The end of the story is to use the peak-hour capacity of the runway system at its maximum.

One of the major problems of the KLM network in this period was, however, the relatively small amount of origin–destination traffic owing to the relatively small local catchment area compared with carriers such as Air France (Paris) and British Airways (London Heathrow). Lufthansa at Frankfurt and Munich was suffering from the same problem, but enlarging its catchment area was made possible by the expanding German high-speed rail network (Table 6.1). Because of the small origin–destination market, KLM depended heavily on the transfer market. According to a study by AAE (KLM 2002), KLM would lose 60–70 per cent of its passengers if it were to concentrate on carrying origin–destination traffic only. Its intercontinental network would be reduced to a single daily connection to New York (Veldhuis and Kroes 2002). Hence, the hub-and-spoke network of KLM was crucial for the existence of intercontinental connections.

However, KLM was also experiencing intensified competition from the low-cost airlines in the larger intra-EU origin–destination markets to and from Schiphol. The developments at its home base Schiphol are illustrative: in 2003 easyJet was the third carrier at Schiphol in terms of seat capacity.

In answer to the small origin–destination market, which could not be enlarged by KLM, the main feature of the network strategy was to optimize the wave-system structure. One solution was the further expansion of the number of transfer markets on city-pairs with low to medium density origin–destination markets. These markets can only be served profitably by hub-carriers via their hubs, since they do not have enough origin–destination demand to be served directly by low-cost airlines. On monopolized transfer routes, the hub carrier can raise ticket prices and improve yields. The same strategy can, however, be applied by other hub-carriers that cover the same market area (KLM 2002).

Another solution was to improve KLM's hub operation at the home base Schiphol itself. In Chapter 2 we discussed a number of key drivers for hub airports. According to KLM, improvements could be made by the Amsterdam Airport Schiphol in terms of gate position and peak-hour capacity. With respect to the gate positions, KLM had to share its European D-pier with a number of other airlines such as British Airways and easyJet. If KLM were to be able to use the entire D-pier, reductions in minimum connecting times could be achieved and more connections could be made. With respect to the peak-hour capacity, new runways were considered necessary to increase the peak-hour capacity and reliability of the runway system. KLM would then be able to further increase the number of flights per wave and the number of waves.

As a KLM strategist stated:

> When you perform badly in the local market, you have to compensate in the transfer market by means of a superior connection system. This means that you need peak-hour capacity at Schiphol. You cannot perform badly on all key success factors. That would be the end of the story.

Finally, KLM was searching for a strong partner airline in Europe. One reason among many was the idea that a strong partner airline would increase the connectivity of the KLM network.[3] Eventually the various initiatives to merge with British Airways and Alitalia all failed.

In September 2003 KLM and Air France announced a merger of the two airlines. In the short run, the merger will not affect the shape and size of the KLM network significantly. The Dutch government agreed with Air France/KLM that the new airline would at least continue to serve 42 intercontinental key destinations from Amsterdam for the next five years. A fairly equal development of Amsterdam Schiphol and Paris Charles de Gaulle seems to be guaranteed for the short term. In the long run, however, network optimization may be expected (Burghouwt and De Wit 2005b).

Conclusions

In short, KLM was one of the first European airlines to focus on the transfer or sixth-freedom market. Throughout its history, the small size of its origin–destination

---

3 For a detailed overview of the alliance and merger strategies of KLM see Jagersma (2003), for example.

market was one of the main reasons for carrying sixth-freedom traffic. As a result, Amsterdam was already a sixth-freedom hub before deregulation took place. Only during the 1980s, when deregulation was introduced on a limited scale, was a first, more pronounced wave-system structure developed at Schiphol. During the 1990s the carrier took major steps to optimize the hub operation at Schiphol. In 1993 and 1997 the 3- and 5-wave-system structures were implemented. Feeder traffic was organized through partnerships with regional carriers. In 2003 the carrier was Europe's fourth hub airline in terms of the number of indirect connections. KLM merged with Air France in September of the same year.

British Airways

British Airways (BA) was formed in 1974 out of a merger between the British Overseas Airways Cooperation (BOAC) and British European Airways (BEA). The merger resulted in the combined operations of BOAC's long-haul operations and BEA's European and domestic services. In 1987 the government-owned carrier was privatized. Freed from government ownership, BA and British Caledonian merged later that year.

1990–1995: Geographic expansion

In 1990 British Airways, Europe's largest carrier, operated a very concentrated network with associated high Network Concentration values centred on London Heathrow. This was by far the most dominant node with respect to intra-EU and extra-EU seat capacity. Secondary nodes could be found at London Gatwick, Birmingham, Manchester and Berlin Tegel and, to a lesser extent, Aberdeen, Edinburgh, Glasgow, and Inverness (Figure 6.6). London Gatwick was the only significant node for extra-EU connections other than London Heathrow. The BA operations from Berlin Tegel were merely a relic from the Cold War/Second Word War. Lufthansa was not allowed to operate services to Berlin, owing to the formal British, French, US and Russian sovereignty of the city. Instead, Pan Am and BA in particular operated the domestic and international routes from Berlin Tegel.

The airline did not operate a wave-system structure at Heathrow, Gatwick or any of the other central nodes in its network. Shortages in peak-hour capacity at Heathrow hindered the development of a wave-system structure. But because of the size of the London Heathrow operation, BA at Heathrow offered the most indirect connections of all EU airline nodes in 1990.

In the early 1990s the strategic reaction of BA to the deregulation of the intra-EU market in terms of its network development was geographic network expansion through investment in or acquisition of local and non-local airlines. The configuration and size of the core network of British Airways remained largely the same during the early 1990s, an observation reported earlier by the CAA (CAA 1995).

Figure 6.6 Intra-EU route network of British Airways, 1990

British Airways foresaw the effects of the Third Package of Deregulation Measures, which would give airlines the freedom to purchase the ownership of other EU carriers (Chang and Williams 2002). Hence, at the beginning of the 1990s BA started to buy into local UK and other EU carriers. As a BA network manager put it:

> The primary consequence of deregulation as we observed it was to open up new opportunities for strong carriers like ourselves to expand into new markets. So we decided that we should target the main, the biggest markets in Europe, and actually plan and run our business in France and Germany. […] Deregulation allowed us to operate within Europe.

In 1992 BA acquired stakes in foreign airlines for the first time, entering in particular the French and German domestic markets. BA acquired a 49.9 per cent share in Delta Air, which was later renamed Deutsche BA. In the same year, 49.9 per cent of TAT European Airlines of France was purchased. Later TAT was merged into Air Liberté, a French airline acquired by BA in 1996.

Local airlines that were (partly) acquired in the early 1990s were Dan-Air, GB Airways, Brymon Aviation and CityFlyer Express. Franchise arrangements were

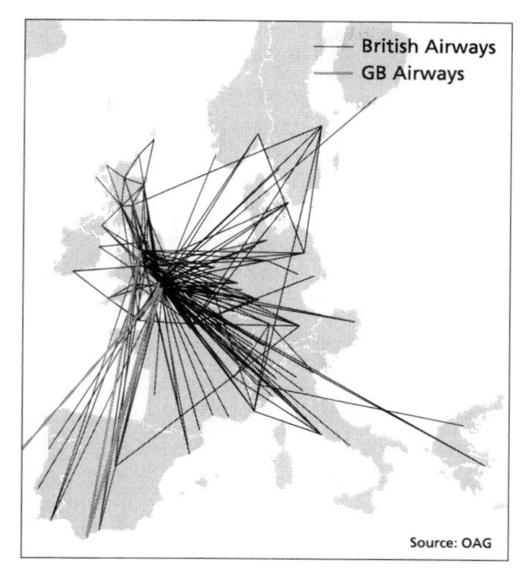

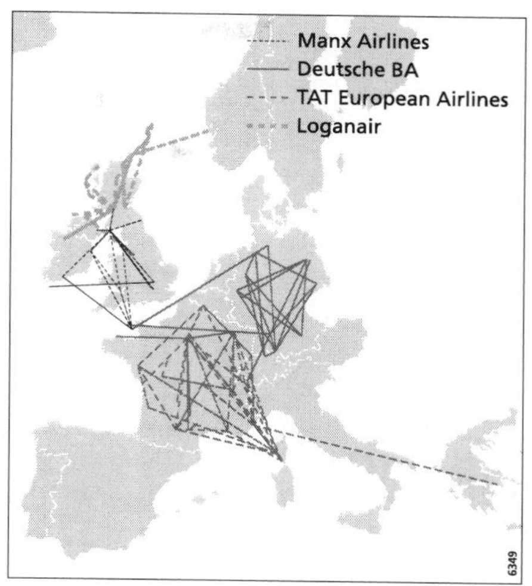

Figure 6.7 Selected BA franchise and subsidiary networks, 1994
Note: Data Manx Airlines for 1995

made with Loganair from Scotland and Manx Airlines. Maersk from Denmark started to fly under the British Airways banner in 1995.

On a global scale, BA bought a 25 per cent stake in Australia's Qantas in 1993 and invested in USAir in 1992. Figure 6.7 illustrates the expansion strategy with selected subsidiaries and franchise partners.

1995–2000: Building the Gatwick hub

Although BA did not operate a wave-system structure at London Heathrow, its extensive network (in particular to North America, Asia and Europe) generated a considerable amount of indirect connectivity through Heathrow. As a result, about 28 per cent of passengers at Heathrow were making connections. This percentage was quite high in those days, in comparison with Amsterdam (27 per cent), Paris Charles de Gaulle (10 per cent), Vienna (15 per cent) and Brussels (5 per cent). Only Zurich (29 per cent), Frankfurt (44 per cent) and Copenhagen (30 per cent) ranked higher in terms of the percentage of connecting passengers in 1990 (EURAFOR 2000).

However, as we have demonstrated in the preceding chapters, the airlines engaged increasingly in the hub-and-spoke operations during the 1990s, drawing transfer traffic away from the inefficiently organized transfer node of BA at Heathrow. BA concluded that if the carrier wanted to continue its role in the transfer market, a second hub would be needed. The opportunities to increase the indirect connectivity at Heathrow were limited, because slot constraints and the small market share of BA at Heathrow hindered the establishment of a wave-system structure and frequency growth in general.

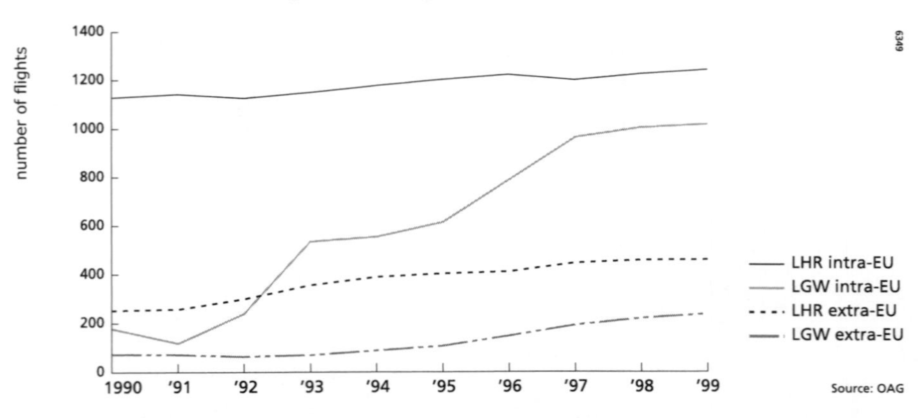

Figure 6.8 Number of weekly BA flights from Heathrow and Gatwick

Various options were considered in the early 1990s, such as mergers with KLM and Sabena to gain access to Amsterdam or Brussels. The attempts to merge were not fruitful, however. The European Commission objected to the shareholding of Sabena in 1990 (British Airways 2003b). Operation Sahara – the merger plan between KLM and BA – ended following disputes about the shareholding in the new company and financial aid to the distressed KLM partner Northwest Airlines. Moreover, difficulties were expected with regard to the portfolio of traffic rights of both companies, which were tied to the country of registration (Jagersma 2003). Instead, BA decided to set up a hub operation at London Gatwick in addition to its operations at London Heathrow.

From the outset it was clear that this solution was not optimal either, given the limited peak-hour capacity of the single-runway system at London Gatwick. As a manager from BA stated:

> So we turned Gatwick into a hub. And it basically worked. But it is a single-runway operation, so we were never able to establish an efficient wave structure. In terms of local markets it is too close to Heathrow, so Gatwick gets the overspill rather than the first choice market [...].

Nevertheless, it was considered to be the 'least worst' solution:

> Even at that time, it was recognized that this was far from ideal. The logic was: It is critical for us to continue to grow at something like market growth. It was taken as an act of faith: one must grow at a rate of 6 or 7 per cent a year. By this time, the geographical expansion pieces were losing a lot of money [...]. That was clearly not a platform for growing a new operation organically if you like. We had a look at the acquisition-led or merger-led geographical expansion in terms of acquiring another hub, that of KLM or Sabena. But we have not been able to bring that off. We still have to grow at six per cent a year. We can't do that at Heathrow any more. Therefore, the only answer left is Gatwick.

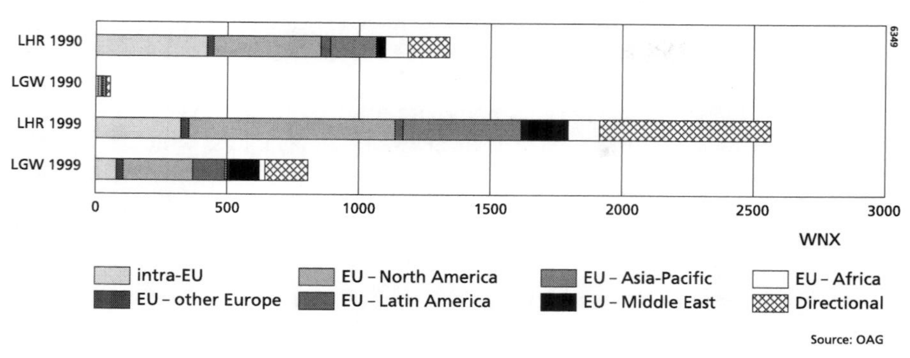

Figure 6.9 Geographical specialization of Heathrow and Gatwick
Note: Breakdown of indirect connections of BA at London Heathrow and Gatwick according to geographical market.

In 1995 BA started to build its hub operations at Gatwick. The long-haul destinations to South America and Africa were transferred from Heathrow to Gatwick. Part of the short-haul feeder network to Heathrow was duplicated at Gatwick to ensure sufficient feeder services. Figure 6.8 shows that the number of flights departing from London Gatwick increased significantly from 1995 on, in particular with respect to intra-EU flights and to a lesser extent to extra-EU flights as a result of the hubbing strategy.[4] In 1996 the services to Africa were transferred from Heathrow to Gatwick. The services to South America followed in 1997. In addition, by 1997 many services to North America operated out of Gatwick.

However, owing to the lack of runway capacity at Gatwick, BA was never able to implement an effective wave-system structure there. We described the flight schedule structure at Gatwick in 1999 as very limited. According to our wave-structure analysis methodology (Chapter 4), two widely spread-out waves could be distinguished in 1999: one European–intercontinental wave in the morning and a mainly intra-European wave in the afternoon. The increase in services to and from Gatwick and the implementation of a – though very limited – wave-system structure resulted in an impressive increase in the number of marketable indirect connections between 1990 and 1999 (Chapter 4). Figure 6.9 shows the breakdown of indirect connections according to market region[5] for London Heathrow and London Gatwick. Gatwick became particularly important to BA in providing connections between the EU and North/South America.

With regard to the spatial distribution of seat capacity, the Gatwick strategy translated into a slight increase in the Network Concentration index from 1995 on, reflecting the evolution to a multi-radial network centred on two primary nodes.

4 The increase in 1992 was caused by BA's takeover of Dan-Air, which operated an extensive intra-EU network centred at Gatwick.

5 Note that the hinterland component (indirect connections between the EU and non-EU destinations) is uni-directional: it only includes connections from the EU to other world regions. For the directional component, all possible connections were counted.

The transfer strategy was continued at London Heathrow after 1995, although without a wave-system structure. Because frequency building at the airport was not possible, growth in (transfer) passenger volume was sought in providing more seats per departure and hence using larger aircraft. In 1999 the average number of seats per scheduled BA departure at Heathrow was 224 compared with 180 in 1990. Only 14 per cent of the departing aircraft movements at Heathrow were operated with equipment smaller than a Boeing 757 (180 seats). In contrast, the average seat capacity per departure for KLM at Amsterdam was 131 seats, for Lufthansa at Frankfurt 152 seats, and for Air France at Paris CDG 149 seats (1999).

BA focused primarily on the densest transfer markets (Frankfurt–Heathrow–New York, for example) in contrast with carriers such as KLM, which concentrated on the low-density markets that could only be served with a hub-and-spoke network (Stavanger–Amsterdam–Detroit, for example). Hence the Boeing 747 aircraft on the long-haul flights from Heathrow were fed by Boeing 767 and 757 on short-haul flights.

In addition to the Heathrow and Gatwick strategy, BA became involved in other alliances and code-share agreements with major airlines around the world in order to increase geographical market coverage, benefit from network economies, and create a larger market base. The global expansion strategy had started in the early 1990s with the participation in and cooperation with Qantas on the Europe to Australia market. In 1996, after BA ended its cooperation with and participation in USAir, BA and American Airlines announced their plans for a broad alliance, including extensive code-sharing across each other's networks. In September 1998 BA, American Airlines, Cathay Pacific, Canadian Airlines and Qantas announced that the airlines would cooperate in the Oneworld alliance. This alliance was later extended with Finnair (1998), Iberia (1999), LAN chile (1999) and Aer Lingus (1999), while Canadian withdrew in 2000 following its acquisition by Air Canada.

2000–2003: Rationalization

The year 2000 marked a new strategy for BA in response to the changing market circumstances. BA had tried to answer the increasing hub competition from other hub carriers by developing a secondary hub at London Gatwick, since Heathrow's infrastructure was insufficient. However, the split-hub operation in combination with an awkward airport layout at Gatwick did not prove to be a successful strategy and was commercially not very profitable. According to a BA manager speaking with respect to the Gatwick hub:

> It was never a very good hub. It was never a sort of Schiphol, a 70 per cent transfer type.

Moreover, the focus on dense markets from Heathrow meant that BA did not have a monopoly on its indirect routes via that airport. The indirect connections offered by BA could easily be attacked by other hub carriers, driving down yields. In addition, most intra-EU transfer flows could not be served competitively from London because

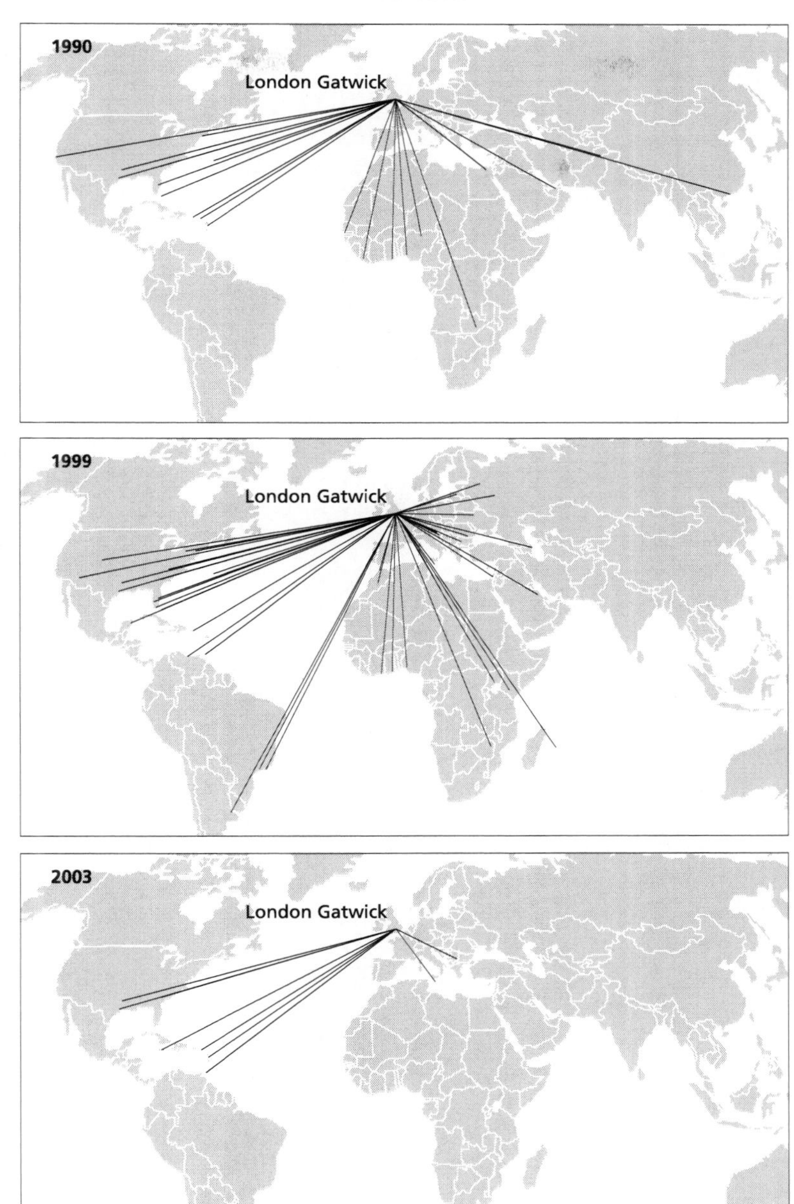

Figure 6.10 The rise and fall of an intercontinental hub: Gatwick
Note: Extra-EU routes of BA from London Gatwick, 1990, 1999 and 2003.

of large detour factors. Besides, low-cost airlines operating out of London Stansted and Luton were drawing traffic away from BA at Heathrow and Gatwick, while the economic downturn had a negative impact on air travel demand.

Hence, BA reviewed its strategy and came to the conclusion that, on the one hand, it would have to reduce its 'exposure to unprofitable market segments' (British Airways 2003b, 63), specifically the short-haul passengers and connecting leisure passengers. And on the other hand, it would have to strengthen its position in the high-yield, business market. In essence, the new strategy entailed the rationalization of the transfer and short-haul segment. Let us consider a few network developments that were part of this strategy.

First, in November 2000 BA announced its intention to dehub London Gatwick and to focus more on the high-yield, point-to-point market. BA reduced seat capacity at Gatwick by 40 per cent and the number of long-haul destinations was reduced from 43 to 25 between 1999 and 2002 (Eddington 2002). Some of the services were cut; others were transferred to London Heathrow. The dehubbing of Gatwick was also reflected in a decrease in the number of indirect connections offered at Gatwick (Chapter 4) and a slight decrease in the Network Concentration index (Chapter 3).

Gatwick concentrated increasingly on the point-to-point market. The number of duplicated routes operating out of Gatwick and Heathrow was reduced significantly. Nevertheless, Gatwick still offered some long-haul services in the leisure market (to the Caribbean and Florida). In addition, in 2003 Gatwick still hosted some long-haul services that could not be allocated to London Heathrow owing to bilateral constraints (the Gatwick–Dallas service, for example).

Secondly, rationalization was also achieved by a shift towards the use of smaller aircraft (Boyle 2002, 3), a strategy that had already been started at the end of the 1990s. The concentration on the origin–destination market meant that somewhat smaller aircraft could be used. A large number of Boeing 767 and Boeing 757 aircraft on the short-haul routes was retired or transferred to the long-haul segment. Smaller aircraft (mainly A319 and A320) were increasingly used for short-haul operations. Some of Gatwick's 767 aircraft were moved to Heathrow to serve the long-haul market. The somewhat smaller Boeing 777 aircraft were gradually replacing the old Boeing 747 equipment at Heathrow.

Finally, part of BA's geographical expansion strategy of the 1990s came to an end. In 2000 BA sold its stake in the French carrier Air Liberté because of the carrier's continuing losses. Deutsche BA was sold in 2003, while BA's low-cost subsidiary Go was sold to easyJet in 2002.

Conclusions

The large origin–destination market enabled BA to develop an extensive worldwide network, which was also attractive for transfer passengers. In 1990 BA already offered a substantial number of indirect connections through Heathrow. However, the slot constraints at Heathrow hindered the development of a fully-fledged hub with a wave-system structure. Hence a hub operation at Gatwick with a very limited wave-system structure was established during the second half of the 1990s. In addition, BA intended to grow by acquiring domestic and international airlines.

The Gatwick strategy did not prove to be successful. Gatwick was dehubbed from 2000 on. Stakes in a number of other airlines were eventually sold. Concentration was directed to the high-yield business point-to-point market at Heathrow. In fact, BA returned to its single primary home-base operation at the beginning of the 1990s. In contrast with most other EU airlines, BA eventually dehubbed its network, focusing on high-yielding point-to-point and transfer markets instead.

As a BA manager put it:

> Deregulation is about new opportunities. After a while you discover that some operations are unprofitable. [...] We are now where we were at the beginning of the 1990s. Deregulation is more about rationalizing capacity now and reducing costs than opening up new markets. You discover in the end that deregulation is about restructuring, rationalizing and focusing. We retrenched to the core.

Iberia

The history of modern Iberia began in 1940 as the Spanish flag-carrier, with a large interest from Deutsche Luft Hansa. Iberia was the first airline to fly from Europe to South America via the Spanish Sahara, reflecting its longstanding economic, social and historical links with South America.

1990–1995: A distressed flag carrier

For a long time Iberia was considered one of the most financially troubled and inefficient airlines in Europe. Year after year between 1989 and 1995, the carrier reported substantial losses. In 1995 the carrier was on the brink of bankruptcy. On several occasions the European Commission allowed the Spanish government to rescue the troubled carrier with state aid (Spaeth 2002). One of the reasons for Iberia's awkward financial position was its interest in the loss-making airlines Aerolineas Argentinas and VIASA from Venezuela. Moreover, the airline's load factor was low and the operating costs per seat high (Comité des Sages 1994). Finally, Iberia was left competing with itself because of the operations of the regional carrier Aviaco, which was fully owned by Iberia. Aviaco offered point-to-point routes between most Spanish airports. Iberia also served many of these routes either directly or indirectly via Madrid or Barcelona (Table 6.2). From a supply point of view, this situation was not very efficient. However, there was no price competition at the time since Aviaco and Iberia were the only domestic scheduled airlines until 1994.

The international network of Iberia in this period could be characterized as multi-radial, with two primary home bases in Madrid and Barcelona and secondary nodes at Palma de Mallorca, Valencia and Bilbao. The spatial distribution of seat capacity was heavily concentrated on Madrid and Barcelona owing to the requirements in bilateral air-service agreements and the economic, demographic and political

Table 6.2 Network duplication, Iberia and Aviaco

Airline code	Departure airport	Arrival airport	Frequency per week
AO	Lanzarote	Las Palmas	21
IB	Lanzarote	Las Palmas	42
AO	Lanzarote	Tenerife Norte	7
IB	Lanzarote	Tenerife Norte	11
AO	Malaga	Madrid	8
IB	Malaga	Madrid	52
AO	Alicante	Barcelona	7
IB	Alicante	Barcelona	14
AO	Alicante	Palma de Mallorca	10
IB	Alicante	Palma de Mallorca	7
AO	Barcelona	Alicante	7
IB	Barcelona	Alicante	14
AO	Barcelona	Ibiza	35
IB	Barcelona	Ibiza	4
AO	Barcelona	Palma de Mallorca	34
IB	Barcelona	Palma de Mallorca	53
AO	Ibiza	Barcelona	35
IB	Ibiza	Barcelona	4
AO	Las Palmas	Lanzarote	21
IB	Las Palmas	Lanzarote	42
AO	Las Palmas	Madrid	7
IB	Las Palmas	Madrid	42
AO	Las Palmas	Tenerife Norte	7
IB	Las Palmas	Tenerife Norte	7
AO	Madrid	Malaga	8
IB	Madrid	Malaga	52
AO	Madrid	Las Palmas	7
IB	Madrid	Las Palmas	47
AO	Madrid	Palma de Mallorca	21
IB	Madrid	Palma de Mallorca	31
AO	Madrid	Seville	4
IB	Madrid	Seville	52
AO	Palma de Mallorca	Alicante	10
IB	Palma de Mallorca	Alicante	7
AO	Palma de Mallorca	Barcelona	34
IB	Palma de Mallorca	Barcelona	57
AO	Palma de Mallorca	Madrid	21
IB	Palma de Mallorca	Madrid	31
AO	Seville	Madrid	4
IB	Seville	Madrid	52
AO	Tenerife Norte	Lanzarote	7
IB	Tenerife Norte	Lanzarote	4
AO	Tenerife Norte	Las Palmas	7
IB	Tenerife Norte	Las Palmas	7

Source: *OAG*

Note: *Duplicated routes of Iberia (IB) and Aviaco (AO) in 1990 on the domestic Spanish market.*

Figure 6.11 Domestic route network of Iberia, 1990

importance of both cities. The other nodes only played a minor part in terms of the share in total intra-EU, let alone extra-EU, seat capacity. The domestic network was much more internally connected than the international network, with many point-to-point connections between the Spanish airports (Figure 6.11).

Between 1990 and 1995 neither Madrid nor Barcelona could be called a hub in the strict sense of the term. The number of indirect connections generated was very small. Moreover, there was no substantial wave-system structure at the Iberia home bases. Instead, there was a focus on origin–destination traffic. What were the major reasons for the national airline's concentration on origin–destination traffic instead of developing a fully-fledged hub-and-spoke network?

First, there was a lack of understanding of the ability of hub-and-spoke operations to increase profitability within the organization. According to an Iberia manager who had studied hub-and-spoke operations among US carriers at MIT on behalf of Iberia, there was considerable resistance within the organization to the adoption of a new network structure:

> You become an expert on some topic and you have a message that is really good for the company. You should be able to deliver that message, especially when you were sent to university by that company in the first place. But it doesn't work like that, because large companies are complex human organizations. And even if someone has a very clear

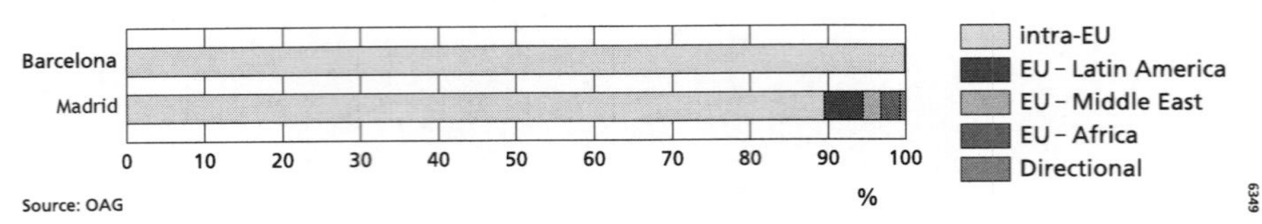

Figure 6.12 Geographical specialization of Madrid and Barcelona

Note: Percentage of weighted indirect connections through Madrid and Barcelona by Iberia in 1990.

> strategic idea of where to go, it may take a long time for that idea to translate into a practical solution. I tried to convince Iberia that we should do that, but I didn't succeed until the middle of the 1990s, because then we had such a huge crisis. The lesson we have to learn is that large companies are more likely to take action when they are under heavy pressure. [...] This is sad in a way. If we had done this in 1989, we would have been a different player now.

Second, Madrid and Barcelona are not centrally located with respect to the 'natural traffic flows'. In 1994, Dennis (1994b) demonstrated empirically that Barcelona and Madrid were indeed very peripherally located. Only for the market between Spain and the rest of Europe did both nodes generate some indirect connectivity (Bootsma 1997). Moreover, Madrid offered some indirect connections between Europe/Spain and South America. But even this market did not seem to be fully exploited, however, given the relatively small number of indirect connections offered (see Figure 6.12).

Third, a further restriction was the limited peak-hour capacity at Madrid and Barcelona (Iberia 1996). There were constraints at both airports in terms of peak-hour capacity, hindering the implementation of a wave-system structure. Barcelona had only two runways and they could not be used independently. Madrid was also equipped with only two independent runways, making it one of the most congested airports in Europe (Robusté and Clavera 1997).

Fourth, in the early 1990s there was only a limited competitive threat for Iberia. It did not face any significant competition on the Europe–Latin America market. Moreover, Iberia and its subsidiary Aviaco fully dominated the domestic market. Hence, competition as a driver for network change was still lacking at the beginning of the 1990s.

At first sight, there seemed to be a third international node (other than Madrid and Barcelona) in the Iberia network in the early 1990s: Santo Domingo (Dominican Republic). It was used as a fifth-freedom node for the Latin American network, connecting Spain and the rest of Europe through Madrid/Barcelona and Santo Domingo with Latin America (see Figure 6.13). A closer look reveals, however, that Santo Domingo was not a hub. It did not generate any indirect connections and no wave-system structure was operated there. Instead, Santo Domingo was used as an intermediate node for once-a-week flights to the Latin American capitals (see also Chapter 2). For example, Iberia flight 935 was operated on Thursdays as Madrid–Santo Domingo–Panama City, whereas flight 936 was operated on Saturdays as

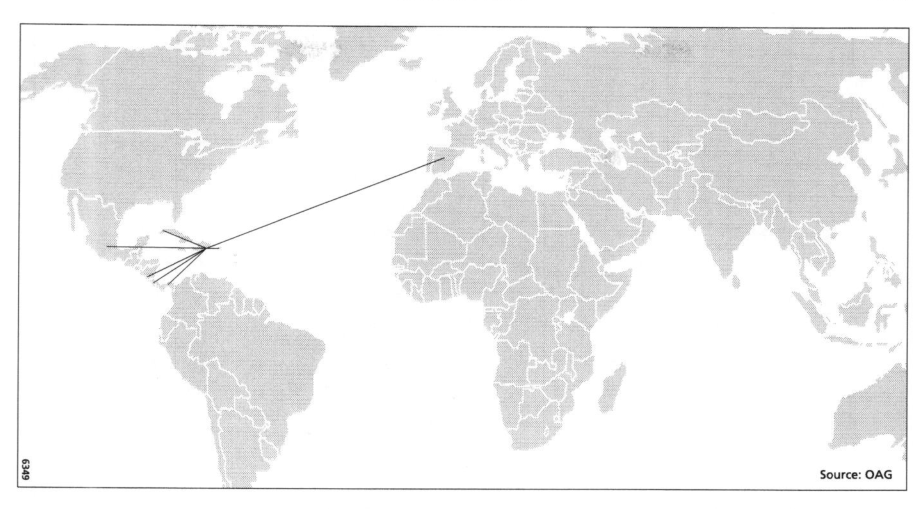

Figure 6.13 Iberia services through Santo Domingo, July 1990

Madrid–Santo Domingo–Guatemala. In conclusion, Iberia offered virtually no hub connections at Santo Domingo.

The operations through Santo Domingo cannot be compared with the hub operations Iberia started later on at Miami. Iberia developed Miami into a fifth-freedom hub for the Europe–Latin America market during the early 1990s. In fact, Iberia has been the only carrier to operate a hub on US territory. This exceptional position was created by the bilateral agreement between the US and Spain in 1991. Iberia was given the traffic rights to operate its Latin America–Europe flights through Miami.

From a network point of view, Miami was much more attractive for the carrier than Santo Domingo. Because of the large origin–destination market in Miami, the carrier could benefit from a much larger demand compared with its operations through Santo Domingo. In addition to the transfer traffic between Europe and Latin America, the local Europe–Miami market and the local Latin America–Miami market could be served (Figure 6.14).

In July 1992 Iberia started to use the Miami hub with a single late-afternoon wave. In July 1993 the operation was extended to two waves (morning and late afternoon), using four DC-9 aircraft based at Miami. The twice-a-day flight from Madrid to Miami connected at Miami with various flights to Latin America.

In 2003 the carrier still operated its Miami hub with four A319 aircraft based at Miami. However, in 2004 Iberia announced its intention to dehub Miami. As a result of September 11th, the security measures at Miami had been tightened and the connecting times between arriving and departing flights at Miami had doubled. From October 2004 the twice-a-day frequency between Madrid and Miami was reduced to once a day. Instead, Iberia began to fly daily to San José and three times per

Figure 6.14 Iberia routes to Latin America, July 1999

week to Panama City and Guatemala. In addition, passengers could connect to Latin American destinations via Iberia's Latin American code-share partner TACA.

1996–2003: Rationalization and hubbing

In 1996 the carrier reported a profit for the first time following a radical restructuring programme called the 'New Competitive Environment'. This programme was initiated after a major financial crisis in 1995 and the losses of the company in the previous six years. One reason for the deteriorating position of Iberia in 1995 involved the aggressive price competition of Air Europa and Spanair, which had entered the Spanish domestic market in 1994 (CAA 1998; Williams 2002). Until 1996 Iberia did not match the lower fares of the domestic competitors but relied on the attractiveness of its network. The strategy did not work well: Iberia quickly lost market share. On the Madrid–Barcelona route, for example, the carrier's share in seat capacity dropped from 98 per cent in 1994 to 69 per cent in 1995 (Williams 2001). Another reason was the intensified competition from other major EU airlines, which increasingly started to learn the rules of the hub-and-spoke game. As a result, they drew away connecting traffic from Madrid and Barcelona (Iberia 1996).

In reaction to its awkward financial position, Iberia sold its stake in Aerolineas Argentinas, VIASA from Venezuela was liquidated, and a number of Iberia's employees were laid off (Iberia 1997). Moreover, the carrier started to compete aggressively with Air Europa and Spanair by means of its low 'Estrella' fares on domestic routes. Another important step was the reorganization of the Iberia network.

First, a substantial wave-system structure was implemented at Madrid in 1996–1997. Consequently, Madrid became a hub in a strict sense. Madrid was not only

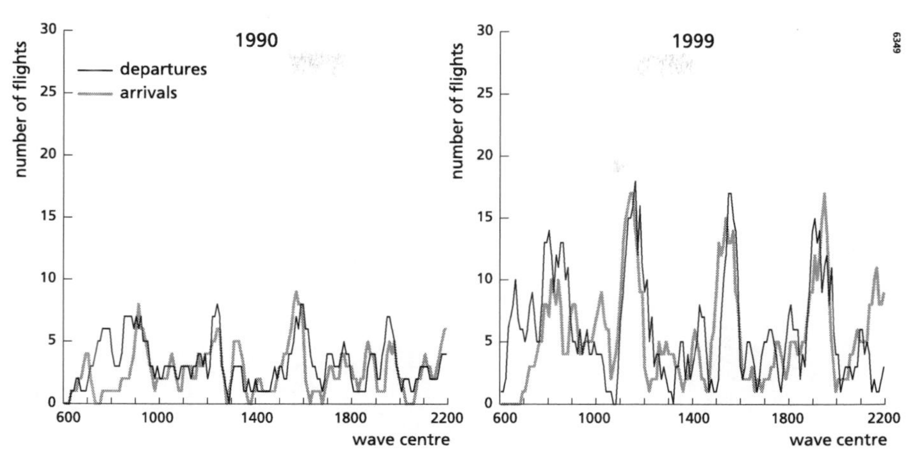

Source: OAG

Figure 6.15 Wave-system analysis of Iberia at Madrid

a spatial junction in the network of Iberia, but also became a significant temporal junction. The wave-system structure that was developed consisted of four waves: early morning, late morning, late afternoon and early evening (Figure 6.15). Nevertheless, the lack of slots at Madrid was a significant barrier to further development of the wave-system structure in subsequent years. The schedule structure could only be further optimized by 'reaching agreements with the third parties who operate existing slots' (Iberia 1997, 66). Therefore, no additional waves had been added by 2003, although the number of departures per wave had increased as well as the number of off-wave frequencies. It can be expected that the expansion of the Madrid–Barajas airport (two new runways and a new terminal by 2005) will offer a new opportunity for Iberia to optimize its schedule structure in order to improve indirect connectivity, since the new runway will add significantly to the peak-hour capacity.

In addition to that at Madrid, we also identified a wave-system structure at Barcelona in 1999 in our wave-system analysis of Chapter 4. Barcelona's wave-system structure consisted of two waves of domestic connections and connections between Spain and the rest of Europe in the morning and the afternoon. In 1990 the structure was not yet in place; it was developed following the major network restructuring in 1996/1997 (Figure 6.16).

However, the resulting wave-system structure was anything but ideal. Between 1997 and 2003 a first wave could be found between 9.00h and 10.00h. But this wave missed the opportunity of carrying local, high-yield business traffic. The same holds true for the second wave during the middle of the day. The business community prefers frequencies in the early morning and late afternoon. For a hub carrier, this would translate into a wave-system structure with waves at the 'edges of the day'. However, the wave-system structure of Iberia at Barcelona did not meet this criterion.

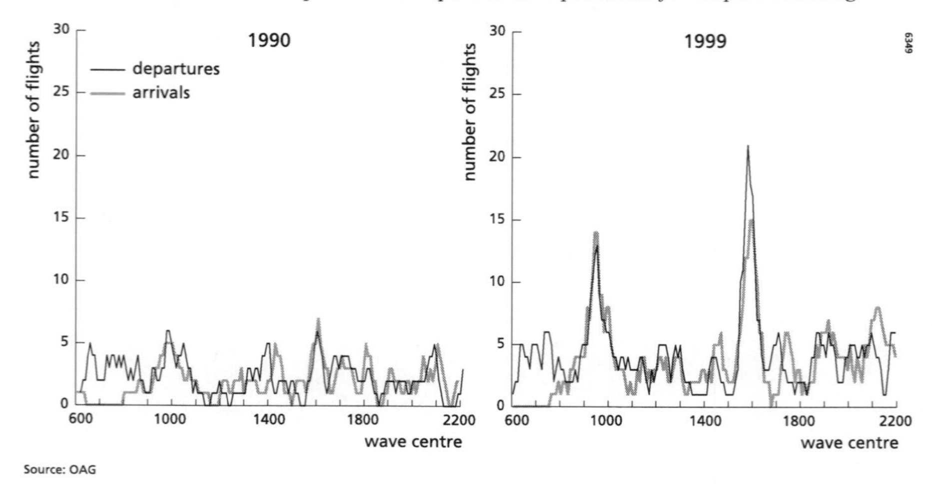

Source: OAG

Figure 6.16 Wave-system analysis of Iberia at Barcelona

Iberia is fully aware of the low quality of the structure at Barcelona. As a network manager of Iberia put it in 2003:

> We have a wave in the middle of the day at Barcelona that we have to live with. It doesn't make sense to have a wave in the middle of the day. You don't have a good product for the local market. Hubbing is good because you get connections and you get a multiplier effect for the markets you serve with your aircraft. But at the same time you have to offer a good product for the local market. The local market does not want a 10 o'clock flight. They want to leave before 9 o'clock in the morning and they want to return in the afternoon. If you can't provide that, you lose your local market. And if you lose market share in the local market, the economics of hubs don't work. If you can't hold your local traffic, your yields go down and you don't make a profit.

So why did Iberia choose to operate such a structure instead of developing a wave-system structure with much better timing of the waves? The reason for the bad timing lies in the coupling of the operations of the Madrid and Barcelona hubs, called 'double use'.

Historically, flights left from Madrid in the early morning (now Madrid's first wave) for Barcelona (now Barcelona's first wave) and continued under the same flight code to European destinations. For example, in July 1999 Iberia flight 6905 would leave Madrid at 8.20h in Madrid's first wave, arrive at Barcelona in Barcelona's first wave at 9.20h, and depart from Barcelona for the flight to Dublin at 10.00h. The aircraft would depart from European airports again to arrive at Barcelona during the middle of the day (Barcelona's second wave) and continue under the same flight code to arrive at Madrid in the evening (Madrid's fourth wave). The resulting wave-system at Barcelona was further supplemented by non-stop domestic and international flights to and from Barcelona.

This system created quite a large number of frequencies on the Madrid–Barcelona route, the largest European route in 2003 in terms of seat capacity. Iberia integrated the multi-stop flights into its Air Bridge (Puente Aereo) between Madrid and Barcelona, where flights were operated every 15 minutes in peak hours.

In essence, Iberia operated a dependent wave system at Barcelona from the second half of the 1990s on, because of the coupling of the operations with Madrid's wave-system structure. However, this system was far from optimal. The saturation of Barcelona-El Prat in terms of available runway slots restricted Iberia from further developing its wave-system structure at the airport. Barcelona's third runway, which became operational in 2005, will create the first opportunity for Iberia to implement additional waves and optimize the timing of the waves.

Second, the Aviaco network was integrated into the Iberia network from 1997 on. In 1997 most of the Aviaco flights were carried out under the Iberia flight code. Duplicated routes were largely removed and in 1998 Aviaco's operations were fully merged with those of Iberia. Third, non-profitable, thinner domestic routes were abandoned and taken over by Iberia's franchise partner Air Nostrum (Iberia 1997, 73).

Third, Iberia concentrated the growth of international services on Madrid and, to a lesser extent, on Barcelona. Madrid's share of the total number of Iberia flights from Spanish airports increased from 48% in 1990, to 51% in 1997, and to 57% in 1999. Barcelona's share decreased from 35% in 1999 to 32% in 1990, but the number of Iberia flights grew significantly during the same period.

Fourth, Iberia was seeking a way to resolve the competitive disadvantage of the decentralized geographical location of Madrid and Barcelona by taking advantage of the free-market regime with respect to the intra-EU market. One of the initiatives was the Hamburg hub, where Iberia attempted to serve the local Hamburg-to-Scandinavia market. In 1997 Iberia established a rudimentary mini-hub operation at Hamburg. Flights from Madrid and Barcelona arrived at 12.20h and flights to Oslo and Helsinki departed from Hamburg at 13.10h. However, the initiative was short-lived because local traffic did not materialize (Spaeth 2002).

The result of the network rationalization and the integration of Aviaco and the implementation of a wave-system structure at Madrid was increases in the frequencies of Iberia at Madrid and Barcelona under the Iberia flight code and subsequently a growth in the number of weighted indirect connections (Chapter 4). In 2003 Iberia's hub at Madrid was one of the largest in Europe, ranked just behind Heathrow, Paris Charles de Gaulle, Frankfurt and Amsterdam.

Conclusions

Iberia was an example of a somewhat inefficient European flag-carrier during the first half of the 1990s, with no serious hub-and-spoke operations. The carrier successfully made the transition to one of the most important hub-carriers in Europe. Although the advantages of the hub-and-spoke network had been recognized at an early stage, a major crisis within the airline was needed to trigger network reorganization. The resulting wave-system structure at Madrid significantly improved the airline's competitive position with regard to hub connections. The Barcelona hub was dependent on the Madrid operation as a result of the system of 'double use'. Both hubs suffered from the limited peak-hour capacity, however. The foreseen investments in a new runway and terminal capacity at both airports will substantially improve peak-hour capacity. This improvement will allow Iberia to develop further and optimize its hub-and-spoke system at Madrid and Barcelona.

Swiss International Airlines

Swiss came into existence after the bankruptcy of Swissair in October 2001 (Penney 2002). Investors decided that Swissair's daughter Crossair would have the best chance of becoming Switzerland's new national carrier. Crossair was renamed Swiss International Airlines. Swiss took over most of the medium- and long-haul aircraft of the bankrupt Swissair as well as its network. In essence, these moves amounted to the partial integration of the Crossair and Swiss networks.

Swissair and Crossair

In the 1990s Swissair operated its network out of its primary home base Zurich and secondary home base Geneva. Swissair had developed Zurich from a hub with a poorly developed wave-system structure of three waves at the beginning of the 1990s into a structure with six waves in 1999, according to our model and definition of a connection wave (see Chapter 4).

In 1999 Zurich served mainly the intra-EU, the Asia-Pacific, and North American hub markets. Swissair's hub in Zurich was the fifth EU hub in 1999 and the number of waves seems impressive. Nevertheless, since peak-hour capacity at Zurich has been very restricted compared with the other large EU hubs, the carrier has had to increase the number of waves in order to offer the desired city-pair combinations.

In 1999 Swissair served mainly EU destinations and a few intercontinental destinations (New York, Moscow, for example) from Geneva. However, Swissair decided to consolidate its intercontinental services at Zurich during the 1990s to obtain better hub connectivity. The result of this consolidation was a decrease in the Network Concentration index: large dual hub networks have higher Network Concentration indices than single hub networks. Hence, the consolidation of services at Zurich was accompanied by a decline in the Network Concentration index for its network.

Crossair had operated mainly from Basle and to a lesser extent Zurich, Geneva and Lugano. One the one hand Crossair fed Swissair's network through Zurich, while on the other hand Crossair developed its own regional hub at Basle with two small waves. The Eurocross connected nodes in Germany and Scandinavia with destinations in Switzerland and Southern Europe (Figure 6.17). Its network became

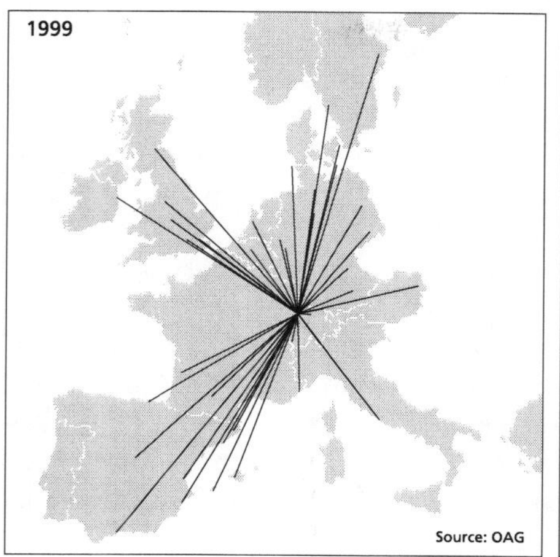

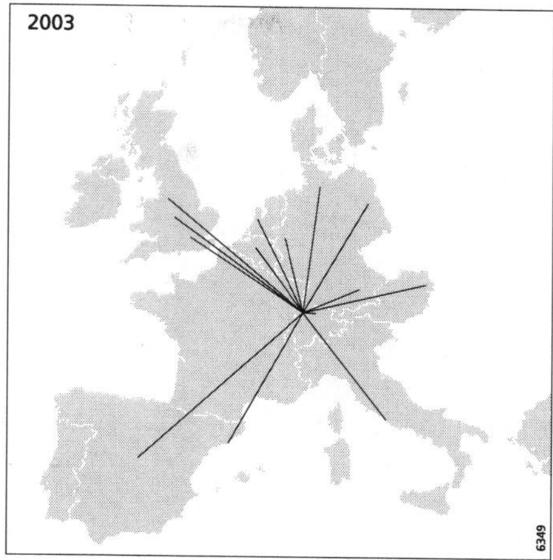

Figure 6.17 Scaling down Crossair's Basle hub

more concentrated between 1990 and 1999 owing to its more proliferative position compared with the other home bases and stations in the network.

Swiss

The new airline Swiss operated out of three home bases in 2003: the former Swissair nodes Zurich and Geneva and Crossair's regional hub at Basle. In contrast with the Brussels hub of the bankrupt carrier Sabena, Zurich did not see any decrease in terms of indirect connectivity. The number of indirect connections even increased slightly between 1999 and 2003. The difference between Brussels and Zurich was partly caused by the fact that Swiss successfully entered the Oneworld alliance, securing traffic from the Oneworld alliance hubs, whereas SN Brussels was still a stand-alone airline in 2003. However, the increase in indirect connectivity was only small compared with hubs such as Paris CDG, Amsterdam, Frankfurt, Madrid and Munich. The carrier moved from fifth to seventh position in terms of indirect connections in 2003. Madrid and Munich took over Zurich's fifth position.

Basle's role as a mini-hub decreased (Figure 6.17). The Eurocross did not prove to be profitable and Swiss decided to scale down the hub. Although Swiss still operated a very limited wave-system structure at the airport in 2003, the number of indirect connections decreased between 1999 and 2003. This decrease reemphasizes our earlier observations that regional hubs are generally not considered to be structurally profitable network strategies when a large origin–destination market is lacking; nearby hubs compete for transfer traffic and competition from low-cost airlines is increasing.

Braathens

Braathens was established in 1946 by the Norwegian ship-owner Ludwig Braathen (Penney 2002) and was named Braathens South American and Far East air transport (Braathens SAFE). Until 1954 this privately-owned airline operated scheduled international services. However, in 1954 its licence to operate these services was withdrawn and Braathens concentrated on the Norwegian domestic market instead.

Although not part of the EU, Norway adopted the packages of deregulation measures. The Third Package opened the international routes to Norway in 1993. The Norwegian government postponed the opening of the domestic market for domestic carriers until April 1994. Only in April 1994 did the domestic[6] Norwegian carriers obtain the right to develop their networks freely (Randoy and Pettersen Strandenes 1997). However, Wideroe's services to the more remote Norwegian airports were exempted from deregulation until 1997, when the Public Service Obligation was applied to many of these essential air services (Chapter 2).

In 1990 Braathens still operated a primarily domestic network focused on the southern part of Norway, with some international services to Copenhagen. Then, its network had only a moderately concentrated character in terms of the spatial distribution of seat capacity over the airports served. Oslo Fornebu was the primary node in the network, closely followed by Stavanger, Bergen and Trondheim, while the structure of its route network could be characterized as point-to-point/criss-cross. Originally Braathens was designated to serve routes only in the southern part of Norway. Its designation was later extended to routes along the west coast and routes connecting north and south (Williams 2002). The geography of the network still reflected the government regulation of the domestic market. Larger routes were served with Boeing 737 aircraft, thinner routes with Fokker F27 and F50 equipment.

Between 1990 and 1994 the Norwegian networks of the carriers Braathens, SAS and Wideroe's were still heavily regulated. Subsequently the temporal and spatial network development of Braathens remained quite stable. Until 1994/1995, the spatial distribution of seat capacity could be characterized as moderately concentrated.

Deregulation in 1994 offered new opportunities to the carrier. Frequencies on the existing network were increased. In addition, some new international routes to the UK (London and Newcastle) were initiated. However, in his analysis of the impact of deregulation on the Norwegian domestic market, Williams (2002) showed that deregulation was mainly beneficial for the tri-national flag carrier SAS.[7] SAS was much more successful than Braathens in attracting the high-yield business traffic. Braathens generated much lower yields and faced lower load factors. Another complicating factor for both SAS and Braathens was the atypical Norwegian aviation system: limited market size and many small routes (Morocco 2001).

6 The domestic Norwegian market was opened up for foreign carriers in 1997 when restrictions on cabotage were lifted.

7 Flag carrier of Norway, Sweden and Denmark.

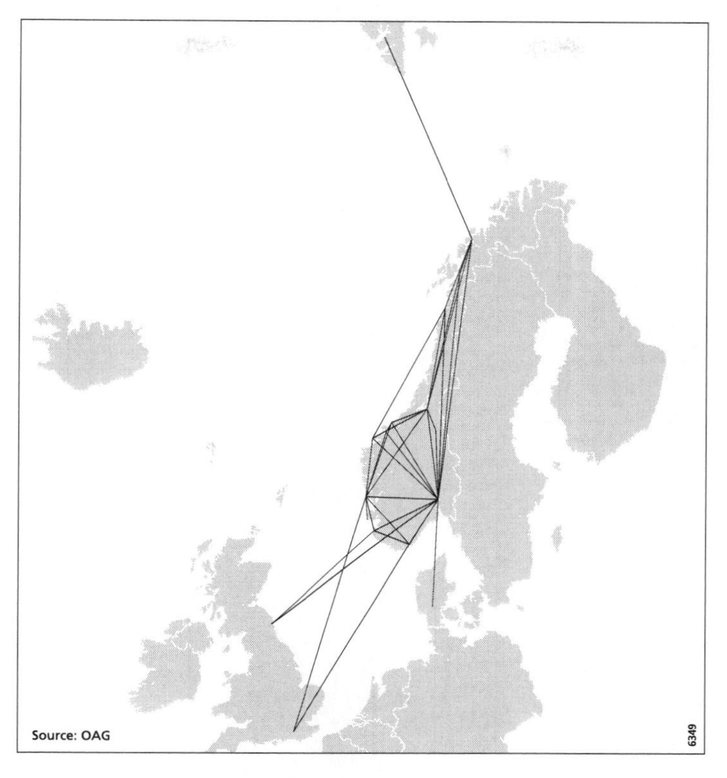

Figure 6.18 Network of Braathens, July 1994

To counter SAS's dominance and attract more traffic, Braathens joined KLM in August 1997. KLM acquired 30 per cent of Braathens. KLM's objective was to increase its feeder services to Amsterdam without having to make major investments in new aircraft (Dierikx 1999, 251). Moreover, Braathens had acquired Transwede in 1996 and Malmö Aviation in 1998 to support its strategy of entering the Swedish market.

As a result, the spatial distribution of seat capacity started to change. The Network Concentration index increased, indicating a fairly concentrated distribution of seat capacity. Oslo in particular and to a lesser extent Stavanger and Bergen saw their relative share in total capacity in the network grow, partly because of the connections to the KLM hub in Amsterdam. Hence, between 1996 and 1999 the morphology of the route network became more radial (Figure 6.19), including a new traffic node at Stockholm and a high density connection between Stavanger/Bergen and Amsterdam. However, Braathens did not operate a wave-system structure at any of its primary nodes (Oslo, Bergen, Stavanger, Stockholm), although a considerable number of indirect connections was generated at Oslo owing to its central position

Figure 6.19 Network of Braathens, 1999

in the network. However, the services to Amsterdam fitted into the wave-system structure of KLM.

Braathens' performance continued to be weak in spite of its cooperation with KLM. In 2001 it became clear that KLM was no longer interested in continuing

Figure 6.20 Network of Braathens, 2003

Note: As part of the SAS group.

the alliance (Williams 2002). Braathens itself argued that only KLM had 'benefited from the agreement through a dramatic increase in traffic to Amsterdam, [...] while *Braathens* had not seen corresponding gains' (Morocco 2001, 40). Moreover, cooperation with SAS was seen to be the only solution capable of guaranteeing the survival of Braathens in a market with only limited traffic demand.

Hence SAS announced in 2001 that it would buy the KLM share as well as the 38.8 per cent still held by the Braathens family. The services to Amsterdam were gradually decreased and finally abandoned (Morocco 2001; Penney 2002). Moreover, Braathens' network was further rationalized. The Swedish part of the network was transferred to SAS and other partners. SAS took over some markets with large volumes of business traffic, whereas Braathens concentrated on the thinner and lower-yield routes. The international network was extended with services from Oslo to leisure destinations in Southern Europe (Figure 6.20). In 2004 the carrier was fully integrated into the SAS group and was renamed SAS Braathens.

Meridiana

In 1964 the regional Italian carrier Meridiana, named Alisarda at that time, started operating scheduled air services from Olbia (Sardinia) to Rome (Finelli 2003). In 1990 the carrier operated a network concentrated around the airports of Rome Fiumicino, Milan Linate and the Sardinian cities of Olbia and Cagliari. The carrier's strategy was to concentrate on connecting the holiday destinations of Sardinia's Costa Smeralda and Sicily with the major Italian cities and a few cities outside Italy such as Paris and Frankfurt.

In 1991 the carrier changed its name to Meridiana and started to take advantage of the liberalized environment by adding new domestic and international nodes to its network. The carrier diversified from its leisure-oriented network to serving business destinations. Florence and Verona in particular became important nodes in the network. The introduction of the BAe146-200s to the airline's fleet in 1991 allowed Meridiana to operate services from Florence's very short runway, including international services to Paris CDG, Frankfurt and London Gatwick. Its fleet of DC-9s and MD-82 was not suitable for these services. An agreement with the Italian carrier Alpi Eagles in 2003 extended the Meridiana network with more point-to-point services to and from such airports as Venice and Palermo.

The gradual extension of the network with more central nodes resulted in a more equal spread of seat capacity over the population of nodes between 1990 and 2003. Meridiana's network gradually evolved from a very concentrated network into a moderately-concentrated/deconcentrated network, as Figure 6.21 shows. In 2003 the carrier mainly operated point-to-point services between Italian airports and some European destinations. In 2003 the route network morphology could be characterized as a criss-cross/non-radial network, although some airports such as Olbia, Rome and Cagliari are central nodes in the network; together they accounted for 39 per cent of total seat capacity. Florence was an important node in the network in terms of destinations, but less so in seat capacity, since it was only served by small-capacity aircraft (BAe-146).

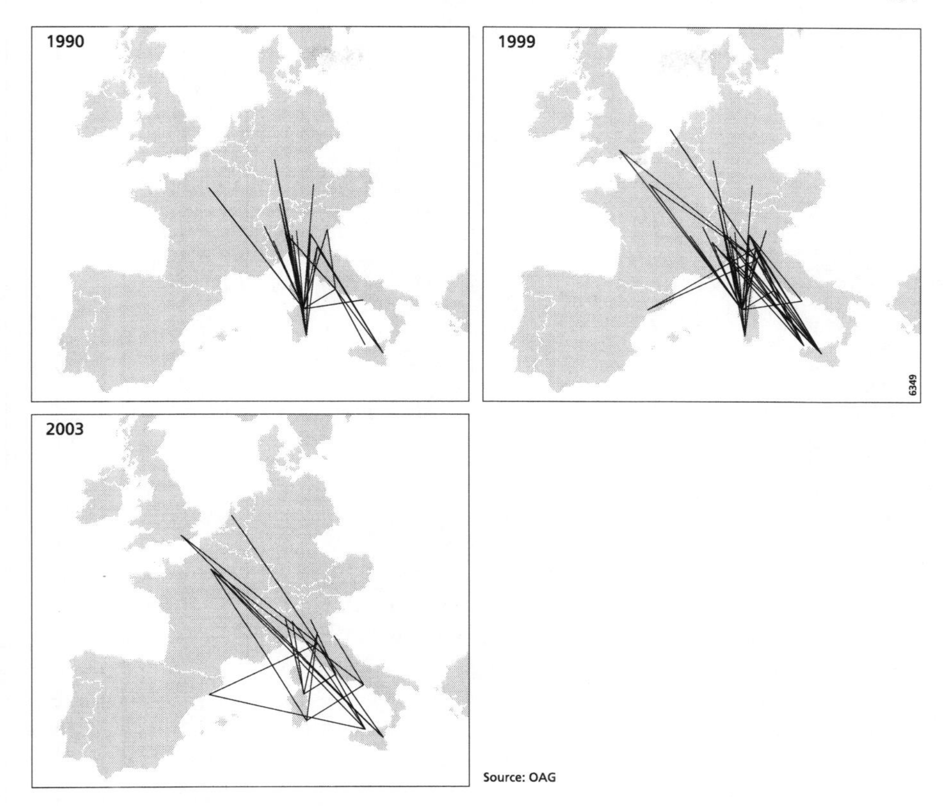

Figure 6.21 Route network of Meridiana

According to our WNX model, the airline generated some indirect connections via Rome FCO. Olbia was more important in terms of frequencies and seat capacity. However, its decentralized location compared with the destinations served resulted in a large routing factor and therefore virtually no indirect connectivity. At none of its stations did the airline operate a wave-system structure. The absence of such structures mirrored the carrier's network and pricing strategy in 2003: to serve point-to-point markets with low ticket prices.

In short, Meridiana's network is an example of a regional, deconcentrated network. The focus is on non-stop connections between Italian cities and some international destinations for both business and leisure traffic.

Régional Airlines

Régional Airlines (formerly known as Air Vendee) established a highly efficient hub at Clermont-Ferrand in 1994/1995. Régional Airlines was one of the few examples of airlines in Europe that reorganized their networks from a deconcentrated to a more

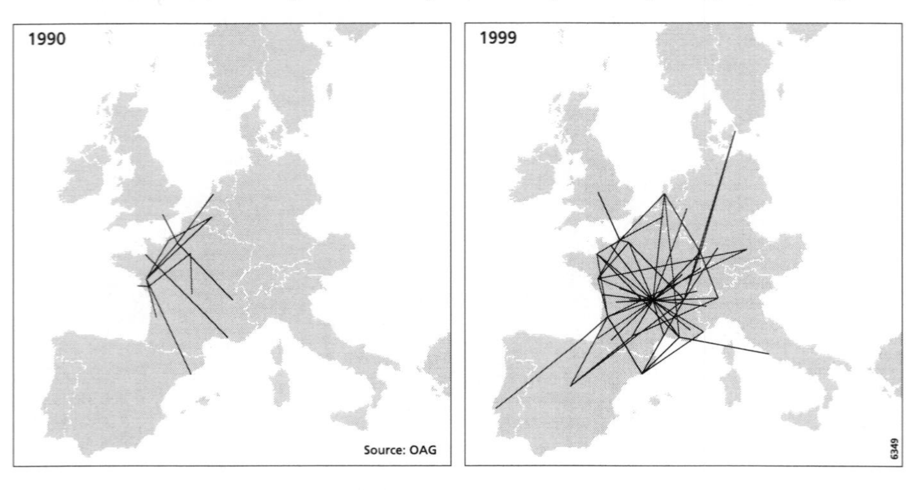

Figure 6.22 Route network of Régional Airlines

concentrated network as part of a hubbing strategy. The Network Concentration index of Régional increased from 0.40 in 1990 to 0.60 in 1999.

In 1999 the hub operation of Régional at Clermont-Ferrand consisted of an almost perfect wave-system structure of four daily waves (Figure 6.23). The Régional hub connects nodes in Western France with nodes in Eastern France, Italy, Germany, Switzerland and the Netherlands using regional jet and turboprop aircraft (Figure 6.22). In 2000, in the absence of any substantial origin–destination traffic, about 80–90 per cent of its traffic at Clermont-Ferrand was transfer traffic. Hence Clermont-Ferrand could be characterized as a wayport or desert hub (Chapter 2).

The airport of Clermont-Ferrand had been renovated to guarantee very short minimum connecting times. According to the OAG guide of 1999, the standard minimum connecting time was 20 minutes for domestic flights and one hour for international flights. The minimum connecting times for Régional Airlines flights were even lower (10 minutes). Short minimum connecting times are essential for a regional, mini-hub operation, as we saw in Chapter 2.

In 2000 Air France acquired Régional Airlines (l'Humanité 2000). However, the Clermont-Ferrand hub operation duplicated substantially the hub-operation of Air France at Lyon Satolas. Together with Flandre Air and Proteus, Régional Airlines was renamed Regional in 2001: an Air France subsidiary. Air France announced its intention to scale down the hub-operations at Clermont-Ferrand as of February 2004 (Régional 2004). Feeder frequencies to Paris CDG would be increased. Air France preferred Lyon to Clermont-Ferrand because of the much larger origin–destination market. However, according to the airline's website, in September 2004 Air France was still operating its hub at Clermont-Ferrand.

Interestingly, as a consequence of the dehubbing of Clermont-Ferrand, a number of small French communities would lose their air services altogether. These communities could only be served because of the economies of scope, density

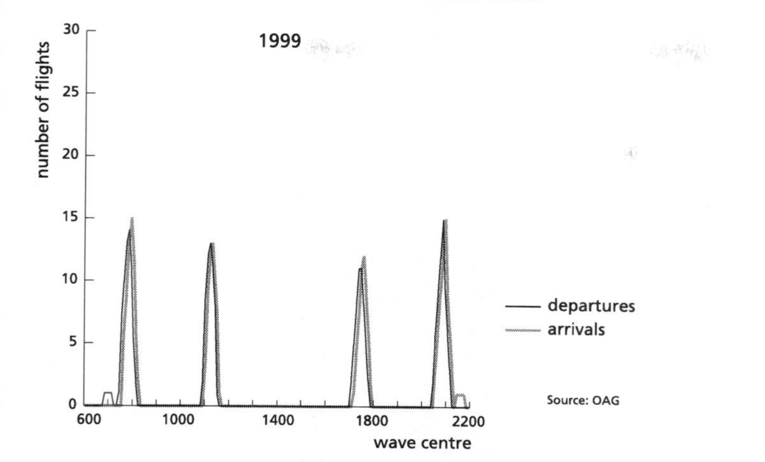

Figure 6.23 Wave-system of Régional Airlines at Clermont-Ferrand, 1999

and scale generated by the hubbing activities of Régional Airlines. This state of affairs underlines our earlier statements about the advantages of airline hub-and-spoke systems in terms of greater network coverage (Chapter 2). Small French communities without any services, or with only very limited provision, were invited by Régional and Air France to claim financial support through the Public Service Obligation (Régional 2004).

easyJet

The low-cost airline easyJet was founded in 1995 by the Greek shipping magnate Stelios Haji-Ioannou (Airliner World 2003). The carrier started operating from London Luton to avoid the congestion at Heathrow and Gatwick. The focus was on destinations in northern UK and southern Europe. From that moment on, the carrier was characterized by tremendous network growth: the number of airports served increased from 7 in 1996 to 43 in 2003.[8]

EasyJet expanded its network along central home bases in the UK and later on the European continent. The carrier mainly served medium/high-density markets. In contrast with a low-cost carrier such as Ryanair, easyJet serves primarily large airports, although in 2003 some thinner routes such as Venice–East Midlands and Inverness–London Gatwick were also served with one weekday return flight. On some of its routes, the focus on large airports resulted in heavy head-to-head competition with other carriers, such as the Amsterdam to Barcelona route (2003).

In 1996 easyJet's network could be characterized as a concentrated network and its route network morphology as radial, with London Luton as the central node. Between 1996 and 1999 the network was extended by means of new home bases

8 Including easyJet Switzerland.

Figure 6.24 Route network of easyJet

in the UK. In 1999 Luton was still the primary home base, flanked by Liverpool, Belfast and Glasgow as secondary home bases. The northern part of the UK, Amsterdam and southern Europe were served by Boeing 737-300s. At the end of the 1990s easyJet Switzerland was set up together with a new home base in Geneva. Bilateral constraints limited the possibility of serving the Geneva market as a UK-based carrier. Switzerland was not part of the Common European Aviation Market at that time (see Chapter 2). As a UK-based carrier, easyJet's services from Geneva to other EU countries would be seventh-freedom operations (see Annex 2). As a Swiss-based carrier, the airline could reap the benefits from the many liberal agreements drawn up between Switzerland and the EU countries and would circumvent any restrictions on seventh-freedom operations.

At the end of 2002 easyJet announced its takeover of Go, resulting in a new home base at London Stansted. London Gatwick, Edinburgh and Amsterdam became increasingly important. In 2001 easyJet started to convert Amsterdam into its new continental home base. In 2003 the carrier operated out of two primary home bases (Stansted and Luton) and about five secondary home bases (Belfast, Gatwick, Edinburgh, Liverpool, Amsterdam, Glasgow and Geneva).

The expansion of the number of home bases between 1996 and 2003 was mirrored by a decrease in the Network Concentration index. The carrier's network

Figure 6.25 Route network of Air Berlin

evolved from a concentrated network in 1999 to a moderately concentrated network in 2003. The airline did not operate a wave-system structure at any of its home bases. Nevertheless, several indirect connections were generated at Stansted and Luton in 2003. The high frequencies of services result in some viable connections, although serving these indirect markets is not a deliberate strategy of the carrier. Connecting flights cannot be booked as such through the airline's website.

Air Berlin

Air Berlin can be considered as a mixed low-cost and charter airline. However, the airline is anything but new to the air transport market. In 1979 the airline started its first services between Berlin and Palma de Mallorca (Airliner World 2003). Originally Air Berlin was a full charter airline. However, when deregulation removed the distinction between charter services and scheduled services in the intra-EU market, the airline took advantage of its new freedom and started to sell seat-only tickets to individual consumers through its website, in addition to its traditional holiday package product for tour operators. The airline first appeared in the OAG database in 1999.

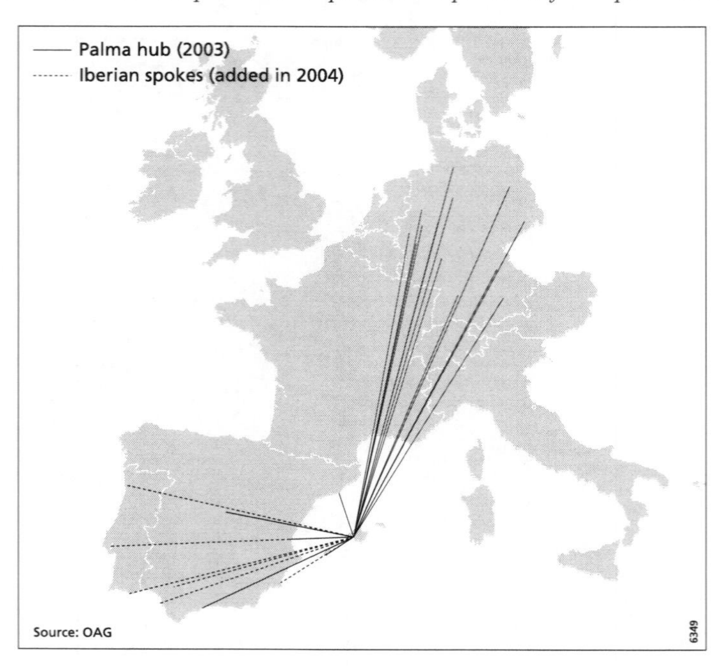

Figure 6.26 The Palma hub of Air Berlin

In 2003 Air Berlin's network included more than 50 destinations within the EU; they were served by Boeing 737-400 and 737-800 aircraft. The geography of its network was characterized by a strong north–south orientation, typical of the holiday charter airlines that connect the European 'sunbelt' with destinations in northern Europe (Figure 6.25). For such airlines, the level of tourist attraction is the main driver for the network structure.

In 2003 Palma de Mallorca (Germany's most popular holiday destination) was the most important southern destination in its network in terms of seat capacity, followed by Malaga, Alicante, Rome, Milan, Almeria and Faro. The most important destinations in the northern part of Europe included Berlin Tegel, Hamburg, Dortmund, Muenster, Paderborn, Dusseldorf and Hanover. The network of the carrier is characterized by many small German airports. To serve these 'marginal airports' is one of the carrier's explicit strategic objectives. The many central nodes in northern and southern Europe resulted in 1999 and 2003 in a low Network Concentration index reflecting the deconcentrated network pattern (see Chapter 3).

In 2002 the airline started to deviate from the north–south network pattern by introducing a low-cost City Shuttle service on routes between German airports and airports such as London Stansted, Zurich and Vienna. Interestingly, the City Shuttle service also included routes between its primary node Palma de Mallorca on the one hand and Madrid, Barcelona, Alicante and Ibiza on the other. The latter services were concentrated in an outgoing afternoon wave at around 15.00h so that

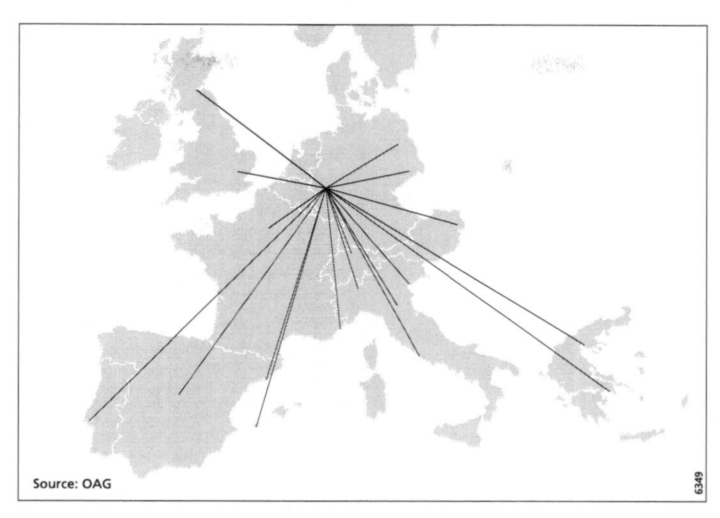

Figure 6.27 Route network of Germanwings, 2003

the incoming flights from Stuttgart, Hamburg, Dusseldorf, Munich, Berlin Tegel, Cologne, Paderborn and Muenster could connect to it. A second incoming wave from Spain arrives at around 20.00h with onward connections to German destinations.

In essence, Air Berlin was developing a low-cost hub operation that was built on top of a strong origin–destination market between Germany and Palma. Gradually, more hub connections were added to this origin–destination operation. In the summer of 2004 the Palma hub was further extended with connections to and from Faro, Lisbon, Porto, Seville, Jerez, Murcia and Valencia (Figure 6.26).

Germanwings

Germanwings is a low-cost carrier formed out of the German regional airline Eurowings in October 2002 (Airliner World 2003). Eurowings itself continued to operate as a regional airline partly under the Lufthansa flight code. In 2003 Germanwings operated out of a single home base at Cologne/Bonn airport (Figure 6.27). Not surprisingly, the network of Germanwings had a high Network Concentration index, indicating a concentrated, radial network structure.

The strategy of the carrier is to serve the major EU metropolitan areas from its Cologne/Bonn home base and, since 2004, from its secondary home base at Stuttgart. In 2003 the carrier served out of Cologne major destinations in southern Europe such as Madrid, Barcelona and Athens and major airports in the rest of Europe such as London Stansted, Paris CDG, Vienna, Berlin, Milan and Zurich. The focus is on routes with a large origin–destination demand. Owing to the fact that the home base Cologne is also centrally located in the network in a geographical sense, the airline generated some indirect connections through Cologne. Nevertheless, Germanwings

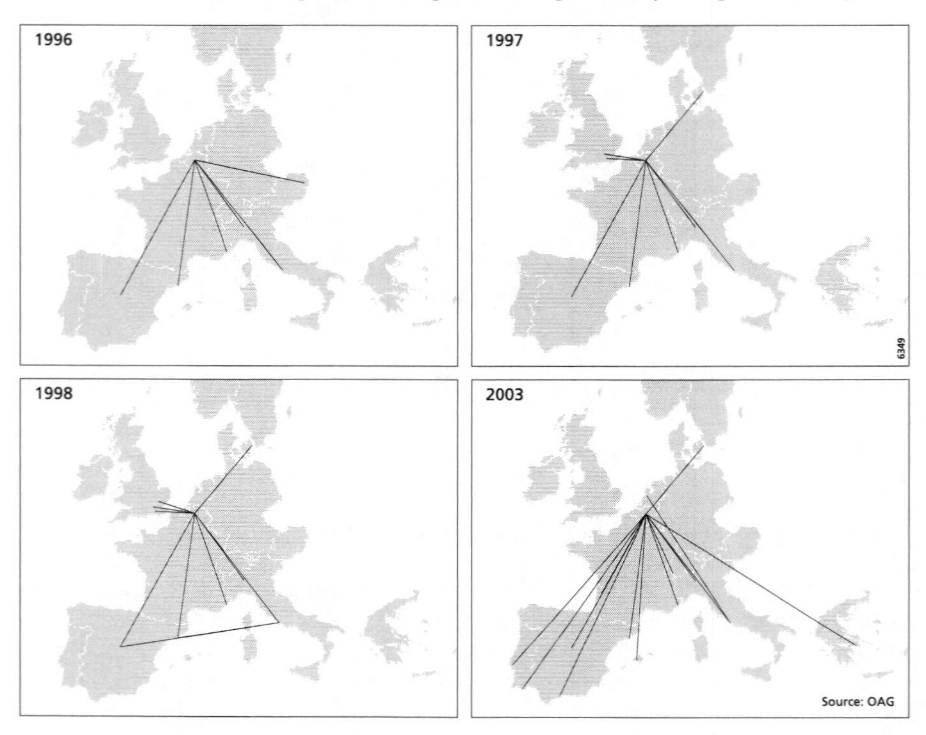

Figure 6.28 Route network of Virgin Express

did not operate a wave-system structure at the airport in 2003; neither were transfer connections offered through its website.

Virgin Express

Virgin Express began operations in 1996 as the first low-cost branch of Richard Branson's Virgin Group (Airliner World 2003). The carrier was formed out of the small Belgian charter and scheduled carrier Eurobelgian Airlines.

Virgin Express' network development between 1996 and 2003 was characterized by modest growth in terms of the number of destinations served. In 1996 the carrier started from the heritage of its predecessor Eurobelgian: a network centred at Brussels with a few routes to major destinations in Southern Europe. Not surprisingly, its network could be characterized as concentrated, according to the Network Concentration index.

The airline took advantage of the liberalized market and extended its Brussels network with Rome–Madrid and Rome–Barcelona links in 1997. Routes to London Heathrow, London Gatwick, Copenhagen and Nice were added in 1996–1997. In 1997 Virgin agreed to a block-space agreement with Sabena on routes to London,

Barcelona and Rome that had been dropped by the Belgian flag-carrier. Sabena bought about half the seats of the Virgin flights on these routes, with the requirement of in-flight catering and a two-class cabin. Moreover, transfers between the two carriers were possible and even encouraged (CAA 1998; Doganis 2001). Unlike many other low-cost airlines, Virgin mainly served the larger airports rather than the cheaper, secondary airports, partially because of its agreement with Sabena.

In this respect, Virgin was an unusual low-cost carrier, since virtually no low-cost airlines engaged in code-sharing agreements and interlining with major carriers. Neither did they engage in hubbing activities in the late 1990s or have a two-class cabin with in-flight service. Doganis (2001) argued that the lack of a clear focus with regard to its low-cost activities resulted in the heavy financial losses suffered in 1999. In 2000 Virgin began to drop routes from its network. Among other things, it withdrew the unprofitable services to Shannon of its Irish subsidiary Virgin Express Ireland as well as the routes between Madrid, Barcelona and Rome.

Sabena's bankruptcy in 2001 offered the carrier new opportunities. Some of Sabena's services to Southern Europe were taken over by Virgin Express, which even presented itself as the new Belgian flag carrier. In addition, a secondary base was opened in Amsterdam with services to Rome Fiumicino. The strategy of Virgin Express became more focused in 2004. According to Neil Burrows, Managing Director of Virgin Express, the emphasis was on low-cost operations to the major Mediterranean leisure destinations (Virgin Express 2004).

The increase in the number of destinations and services resulted in a small number of indirect connections through Brussels Zaventem. The number of connections is limited owing to the focus on Southern Europe. All indirect connections involve the Copenhagen service – the only service where hubbing would be attractive.

BMIBaby

BMIBaby operations were launched in March 2002 as a British Midland low-cost subsidiary. The launch of the carrier was mainly a reaction to the changing holiday preferences of consumers who increasingly prefer to book hotels and flights separately through the internet instead of buying all-inclusive holiday packages.

The airline began operating from East Midlands, its primary home base. Secondary home bases at Cardiff and Manchester were added to the network later that year. Cardiff was chosen because of its growing economy and origin–destination market as well as the absence of any operating restrictions at the airport.

In 2003 the carrier had a moderately-concentrated/concentrated network in terms of the spatial distribution of seat capacity. Each of these home bases was connected on the one hand to leisure destinations in Southern Europe (Barcelona, Palma de Mallorca, Nice, Malaga, for example) and destinations in continental Europe (Amsterdam, Brussels, Paris, Munich) and destinations in the UK and Ireland on the other hand (Edinburgh, Dublin, Glasgow, Cork, for example). About 50 per cent of the nodes served were smaller 5th tier airports (see also Chapter 3 and 6), which

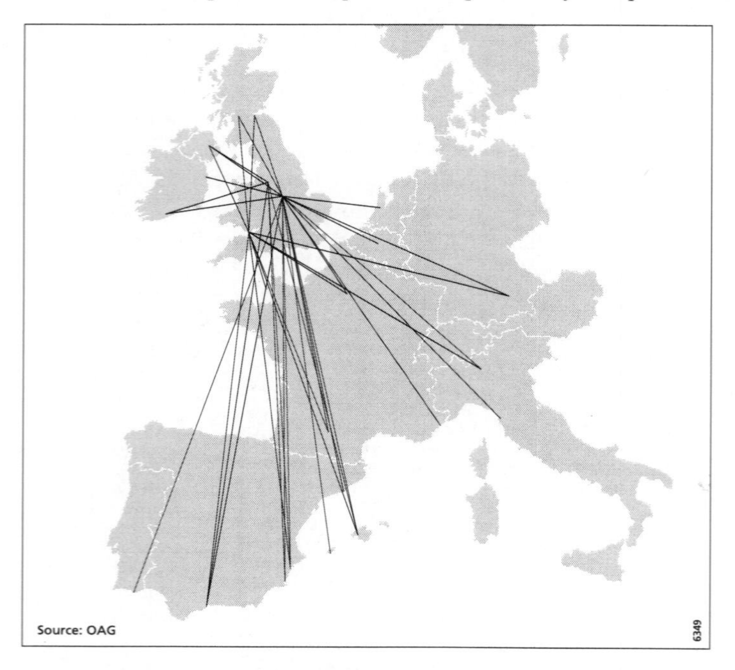

Figure 6.29 Route network of BMIBaby, 2003

means that the carrier was focused on somewhat smaller markets compared with the low-cost airlines such as Germanwings and Virgin Express.

BMI offered some indirect connections through its primary home base East Midlands in 2003. However, there was no wave-system structure at the airport. In addition, potentially viable transfer connections at East Midlands could not be booked through the airline's website.

Concluding comments

In this chapter a number of airlines were considered in more detail so as to understand better the network developments in deregulated markets. In particular, attention was paid to the network developments of KLM, British Airways and Iberia. It was shown that, for all three carriers, deregulation induced the building or intensification of hub-and-spoke systems. Deregulation offered the carriers the opportunity to optimize their intra-EU feeder network and increase the number of indirect connections offered via their hubs. The ideal hub-and-spoke operation is based on the following key drivers of hubs: a large, stable and high-yield origin–destination market, sufficient peak-hour capacity, and short connecting times to optimize the wave-system structure and a central location of the hub(s) in the geography of continental and intercontinental traffic flows. The development of their networks can be understood to a large extent within the context of these key drivers.

British Airways tried to resolve the lack of peak-hour capacity at its home base London Heathrow by developing a hub at Gatwick. This strategy failed, however, mainly because of the lack of peak-hour capacity at Gatwick itself and the consequences of a split home based operation (the duplication of European feeder services and the loss of intercontinental hub connections). British Airways retrenched to its core strength: the size of the origin–destination market of London. In 2003 the carrier was a point-to-point carrier rather than a hub-carrier in terms of its flight schedule structure. KLM's hub development was driven by the lack of a large origin–destination market to maintain a worldwide network. Hence the network strategy was focused on optimizing the connection complex at Amsterdam Airport Schiphol by making use of the strengths of its home base: the short minimum connection times of the airport, Schiphol's potential for growth in peak-hour capacity, and a central geographical location with respect to the continental and intercontinental passenger flows. In the beginning of the 1990s Iberia was an inefficient state-owned carrier without a serious hub-and-spoke network. Only after a major financial crisis in 1995 did the carrier reorganize its network. In developing a hub-and-spoke network, Iberia suffered first from a lack of peak-hour capacity at Madrid and Barcelona. Second, its hubs were less attractive than the hubs in North-western Europe because of the large detours for many connections. Instead, Iberia concentrated on developing its network based on two key strengths: its location with respect to the flows between Europe and Latin America and the flows between the Iberian Peninsula and the rest of the continent. In 2003 Iberia was the largest carrier for indirect intra-EU connections (between Spain and the rest of the EU countries) and the indirect connections between Europe and Latin America. The lack of peak-hour capacity at Madrid and Barcelona continued to be a major constraint for the development of efficient wave-system structures. Nevertheless, new runways and terminals were under construction at both airports in 2004. The added capacity will offer the carrier the opportunity to further strengthen its hub operations.[9]

9 In June 2006 Iberia announced a decrease in its hub-operations at Barcelona. The viability of the Barcelona hub had already been questioned by Dennis (2005).

Chapter 7

The Impact of Airline Network Configurations on the EU Airport Hierarchy

Introduction

Having paid attention to the dynamics in airline network configurations, we now turn from the airline level to another level of analysis: the airport. Our intention in this chapter is to provide an answer to the question, to what extent has the reconfiguration of European airline networks had an impact on the distribution of air-service supply in the EU airport hierarchy?

We begin this chapter by discussing some findings of previous research on airport connectivity and the airport hierarchy. Then we describe the methodology for the analysis reported in this chapter. The changing distribution of seat capacity in the European airport hierarchy is considered. In addition, we look at the connectivity of the smallest European airports in more detail.

Literature review of airport connectivity issues

Spatial concentration

The distribution of air traffic in the airport hierarchy has always been highly skewed towards the upper end of the airport hierarchy (that is, the largest airports), even before the deregulation of various air transport markets (see Reynolds-Feighan 2000, for example). However, several authors argue that the adoption of hub-and-spoke network structures by airlines in free-market regimes has resulted in a further concentration of connectivity and passenger flows at a few key airports in the hierarchy. Since airline hub-and-spoke networks require a concentration of traffic in space and time (Chapter 2), such network strategies may result in spatially-concentrated traffic patterns at the level of the aggregated aviation network.

In the case of US air passenger flows, the spatial concentration of airport traffic flows was addressed by McShan and Windle (1989), Goetz and Sutton (1997) and Reynolds-Feighan (2000) for the periods 1970–1984, 1978–1993, and 1969–1997 respectively. These studies concluded that the airports that were the home bases of hub-and-spoke carriers grew faster than non-hub airports, widening the gap between large and small airports. According to Reynolds-Feighan (2000, 561) the share of the top one hundred US airports accounted in 1993 for 96 per cent of total US domestic passenger enplanements against 92 per cent in 1969. As Goetz and Sutton (1997, 252) put it: 'these changes [spatial concentration, GB] are attributable in part to general population and economic trends, but they also reflect the importance of airline hubs and international gateways [...].'

Chou (1993a), on the other hand, did not find any enhanced spatial concentration of US domestic passenger flows in an analysis of nodal accessibility for the period 1970–1989. According to Chou, the increased airline hubbing operations at different hubs actually decreased the spatial concentration of air passenger flows. However, the study only considers 84 large/medium cities, primarily concentrated in the western part of the country.

In a study of the evolution of the European aviation network (1990–1998), Burghouwt and Hakfoort (2001) distinguish between extra-EU and intra-EU seat capacity. Using five clusters of airports, they concluded that a small number of very large airports increased their share in intercontinental seat capacity. However, intra-European seat capacity became spread over more airports during the same period.

Nyfer (2000), on the other hand, did not find any evidence of substantial concentration or deconcentration trends in the EU airport hierarchy. The share of the top 50 airports in the total number of annual passenger movements remained virtually stable between 1991 and 1998. However, unlike the study by Burghouwt and Hakfoort (2001), Nyfer (2000) did not distinguish between intra-European and extra-European traffic.

Peripheralization

In correspondence with the hypothesis of spatial concentration, it can be argued that airline hub-and-spoke operations and the freedom of route exit in deregulated markets have not been at all beneficial for airports at the lower end of the airport hierarchy: the regional or small community airports (Dempsey 1990). For the United States, GAO (1997), Goetz and Sutton (1997) and Reynolds-Feighan (1995; 2000) found empirical evidence for US airlines' frequent removal of unprofitable routes from their networks under a free domestic market regime. Direct flights between medium-sized and small airports were increasingly replaced by indirect flights via the hub (Graham 1995). As Reynolds-Feighan (1995, 467) states:

> For small communities with limited air services, the danger is that competition and network reorganisation by the airlines will focus on the major airports and cities leaving the smaller communities with much reduced services or with a loss of all air services.

As a result, many small community airports lost destinations, frequencies and a more convenient jet service (GAO 1997). Some airports even lost all their air services. 'Of the 514 nonhub communities receiving air service in 1978, 167 were terminated by 1995, while only 26 gained a new service' (Goetz and Szyliowicz 1997, 254).

GAO (1997, 2) found that 'a primary reason for these differences has been the greater degree of economic growth that has occurred [...].' Carriers were attracted by the relatively strong economic growth of the communities these airports serve. In addition to economic growth, capacity constraints at the major hubs may limit the ability of new entrants to link small airports with the larger ones.

For the European aviation network, Reynolds-Feighan (1995) concluded that, under a free-market regime, the smallest airports were the most vulnerable with respect to the changing airline network strategies in times of economic recession or airlines' financial problems. Based on a case study of the Irish and English commercial airports for a period of three years, she found that regional airports experienced a decline in the number of enplanements during the economic downturn at the beginning of the 1990s. Thompson (2002) found similar evidence for the French small-community airports. Similarly, Graham (1997a; 1998) argued that the possibilities of increasing services between European regional airports are limited, since many regional airlines are incorporated into the networks of major airlines. Hence, regional airlines concentrate increasingly on their hub-feeding role. Moreover, 'traffic volumes will increase largely within [the] existing [economic] geographical parameters' (Graham 1998, 102).

The findings of these studies were empirically supported by De Wit and colleagues (1999), who found that between 1984 and 1997 the routes between large and small European airports had grown faster than the routes between small airports in terms of total seat capacity and flight frequencies.

However, although the direct connectivity at small airports may decline in a free-market regime where hub-and-spoke airlines concentrate on a few key nodes on the network, the onward connectivity at small-sized airports may very well increase. Button (2002, 181–2) capped the discussion by stating:

> the network features of hub-and-spoke operations actually stimulate the provision of services to smaller communities. [...] The traffic volumes that could be anticipated on some of the routes in a direct service network would be so thin that services over these routes would not be commercially viable. [...] Even for smaller communities that could be viably served by direct service to each destination, the quality of that service in terms of frequency and convenience of service offered is almost inevitably lower.

In other words, small-community air passengers have a wide range of one-stop, onward destinations and frequencies once connected to one or several airline hub(s) (DoT 1990b).

In addition to the argument of onward connectivity from small airports, Dennis (2002) asserted that small European airports have significant growth opportunities. The introduction of more cost-efficient regional jets, regional hubbing, together with the growth of low-cost carriers using secondary airports are stimuli for air service to and from small airports.

Finally, both the Essential Air Service Programme in the United States and the Public Service Obligation in the EU have proven to be effective in maintaining a minimum service level to small airports, albeit to a different extent. The US government implemented the Essential Air Service Programme as part of the 1978 Airline Deregulation Act to guarantee continuous service to smaller communities by means of subvention to air carriers (Reynolds-Feighan 1999, 2000).

The Public Service Obligation is the European equivalent of the Essential Air Service Programme. To ensure the continuation of air services on non-commercially viable routes, the European Council of Ministers has enacted legislation permitting the provision of direct subsidies to airlines by the individual Member States. By 1997 161 PSO routes had been imposed by the Member States (Reynolds-Feighan 1999). As Williams (2002, 136) put it, 'it is at the discretion of each government to determine the level of service and the fares to be charged.' Since (unlike the US EAS system) the PSO system depends on the aviation policies of the individual Member States, the effectiveness of the PSO system in maintaining essential, but non-commercially viable routes to small European airports can be questioned (Reynolds-Feighan 1999; Williams and Pagliari 2004).

What this overview suggests is that it is not clear to what extent the observed network strategies of European airlines (as discussed in Chapters 3 and 4) have actually influenced the spatial distributions of air-service supply (in terms of seat capacity offered, or number of connections, for example) in the European airport population. Have the hub-and-spoke and radial network strategies induced the concentration of traffic on a few key airports in Europe? Neither has the existing body of literature provided an answer to the question to what extent small European airports benefit from airline hub-and-spoke strategies in terms of onward connectivity through hubs.

Methodology

The analysis reported in this chapter used two methodologies. For the analysis of the impact of airline network configurations on air-service supply in the EU airport population, we used the subgroup and source decomposition of the Gini index. We used the weighted indirect connectivity methodology for the analysis of small airport peripheralization. The methodologies had already been used in a simplified and slightly different format in the analyses reported in Chapters 3 and 4 respectively.

Subgroup decomposition of the Gini index

We used the Gini index to describe the capacity distributions in the European airport hierarchy. The same Gini index was introduced in Chapter 3 in the description of the determination of the level of spatial concentration in European airline networks. In the work reported in this chapter, however, we used the Gini index at a different level of analysis. The Gini measures the level of concentration of seat capacity in the overall airport hierarchy instead of the level of concentration in individual airline networks.

Apart from the different level of analysis, in the analysis described in this chapter the Gini methodology was extended. To assess the impact of airline network configurations on spatial concentration in the EU airport hierarchy, the source and subgroup decomposition of the Gini index was used. The subgroup decomposition has made it possible to determine the impact of various population subgroups on the overall concentration/inequality of seat capacity in the EU airport population. The source decomposition has enabled us to attribute the overall concentration of seat capacity to each individual airline network.

The methodology of the Gini decompositions by subgroup and source is commonplace in poverty research. The methodology has mainly been used to measure the impact of various income sources and population categories on the overall levels of income inequality (see Alayande 2003; Lerman and Yitzhaki 1985; Milanovic and Yitzhaki 2004; Yitzhaki 2002; Wodon and Yitzhaki 2001, for example). Reynolds-Feighan (2004) first introduced the Gini decomposition methodology into air transport research. She determined the contribution of US airline networks to overall traffic concentration in the US aviation network.

Decomposition by subgroup The most convenient way of decomposing the Gini index by subgroup and source starts by using a slightly different computation of the Gini coefficient (the covariance computation) from the method presented in Chapter 3. The Gini index can then be written as:[1]

$$G = \frac{2 * COV[y, F(y)]}{\mu} \tag{1}$$

We denote the total seat capacity per EU airport by y, the cumulative distribution function for the total per airport seat capacity by $F(y)$ (ranging between 0 and 1), and the mean total seat capacity per airport by μ. We refer the reader to Chapter 3 for an interpretation of Gini coefficients.[2]

We then break down the Gini coefficient into different categories of airport. This step allows us to know to what extent seat capacity concentration in the EU airport hierarchy is generated by seat capacity gaps within and between certain categories of airports. We distinguish five airport categories: 1st tier (1t), 2nd tier (2t), 3rd tier (3t), 4th tier (4t), and 5th tier airports (5t).

Yitzhaki (2002, 69) showed that the overall Gini index G_{yo} of seat capacity y is composed of:

$$G_{yo} = \sum_{i=1}^{i} P_i S_i G_{yi} + G^b \tag{2}$$

where G_{yi} denotes the Gini coefficient of seat capacity, y; i is the airport category ($i=1t;\ 2t;\ 3t;\ 4t;\ 5t$); and P_i is the share of the airport category in the total airport

1 We refer to Lerman and Yitzhaki (1985), Yitzhaki (2002) and Wodon and Yitzhaki (2001; 2004) for the derivation of the formulas presented here.

2 We have not used the NC index here since it does not lend itself to decomposition. Given the reasonable stability in the number of airports per airport category, we do not consider this to be a problem.

population. G^b denotes the between-category inequality. S_{yi} is the airport category's share in total seat capacity and can be written as:

$$S_{yi} = P_i \mu_{yi} / \mu_{yo} \tag{3}$$

where μ is the mean seat capacity per airport.

Finally, the share of each component w in the overall level of concentration of seat capacity in the EU airport population can be defined as:

$$w_i = \frac{P_i S_i G_{yi}}{G_{yo}}; \quad w^b = \frac{G^b}{G_{yo}} \tag{4}$$

and

$$\sum_{i=1}^{i} w_i + w^b = 1 \tag{5}$$

Airport groups

In order to analyze the contributions of various types of airports to the overall concentration of seat capacity in the EU airport population, we classified the European airports with regard to their function in the various airline networks. We have used the number of weighted indirect connections (Chapter 4) per airport (WNX) in 1999 to categorize the airports in the European airport hierarchy. We distinguish between 1st, 2nd, 3rd, 4th, and 5th tier airports.[3] The airports are listed in Figure 7.1. We acknowledge the fact that the boundaries of our categorization are arbitrary and could be disputed. Nevertheless, as we see in this chapter, the Gini index itself supports the categorization presented here.

- 1st tier airports: At the upper end of the airport hierarchy we find the 1st tier airports (Paris CDG, London Heathrow, Frankfurt, Amsterdam, Zurich). They are the primary home bases of carriers that operate on a global or continental scale. The home carrier may (Amsterdam, Frankfurt, Paris CDG, Zurich) or may not (London Heathrow) operate a wave-system structure at such an airport.
- 2nd tier airports are somewhat smaller airports in terms of the indirect connections generated compared with the 1st tier airports. These airports are the home bases of at least one home carrier that operates a specialized hinterland, a European, or directional hub/traffic node. Brussels, Copenhagen and Vienna are examples of 2nd tier airports. A wave-system structure may or may not be present here.

3 In the case of more than one airline offering indirect connections through a specific airport, the number of indirect connections of the various airlines that offer indirect connections has been totalled.

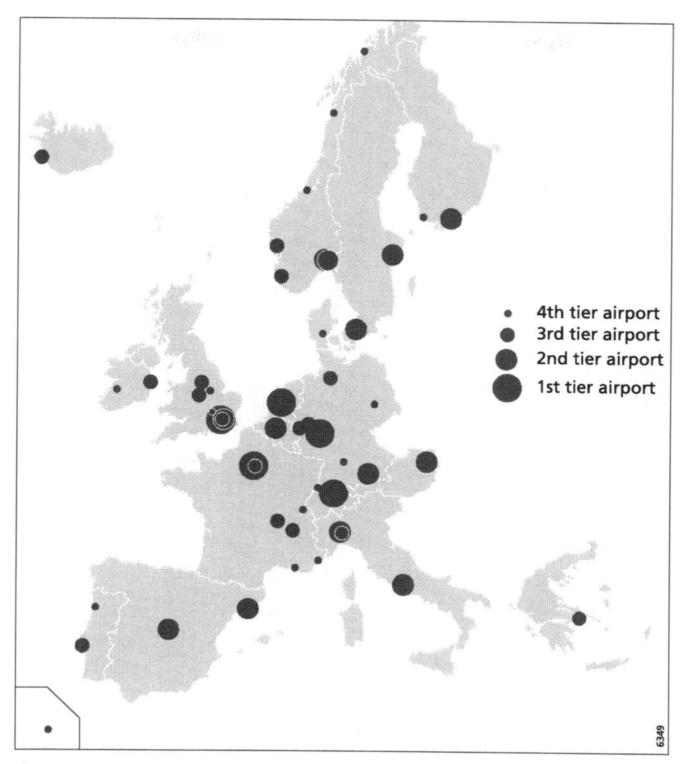

Figure 7.1 Airport classification

Note: *Only 1st–4th tier airports are shown.*

- 3rd tier airports: Most of the 3rd tier airports are the home base of at least one airline operating a European traffic node or hub. Apart from a few exceptions (Reykjavik, Clermont-Ferrand, Lyon) no wave-system structure can be found at these airports. The 3rd tier airports are used as secondary or tertiary nodes in networks of large airlines (Birmingham [BA], Lyon [Air France], for example) and as primary nodes in the networks of smaller airlines (Clermont-Ferrand in 1999, for example).
- 4th tier airports: at 4th tier airports, home based airlines offer only very few indirect connections. Most 4th tier airports are used as secondary or tertiary nodes in airline networks. No wave-system structure is present. Examples are Billund, Oporto and Shannon.
- 5th tier airports: the 5th tier airports are the smallest airports in the airport hierarchy and do not offer any significant amount of indirect connections. In other words, 5th tier airports do not have an intermediate function in the aviation network, but are the terminal destinations for virtually every air passenger (Fleming and Hayuth 1994). For a hub-and-spoke airline, such airports may function as spokes in the route network. The category of 5th

Table 7.1 Classification of European airports

WNX/ day	Category	Number of airports	Average seat capacity per airport per week (1999)	Average number of direct destinations per week (1999)	Average number of direct flights per week (1999)
>2500	1st tier airports	5	579528	193	3701
501–2500	2nd tier airports	13	241165	113	2116
61–500	3rd tier airports	16	119686	63	1049
10–60	4th tier airports	16	55638	35	604
<10	5th tier airports	520	5692	7	85

Source: *OAG*

tier airports covers a wide range of airports, ranging from Malaga to Bristol, Bordeaux and Groningen Airport.

Source decomposition of the Gini index

The source decomposition of the Gini index is presented here as a methodology to measure the impact of an individual airline network configuration on overall seat capacity concentration/inequality in the EU airport hierarchy. The decomposition methodology is based on the procedure described by Yitzhaki (2002). It was used because of its convenience for computation, although alternative procedures are available (Mussard et al. 2003). We refer the reader to Lerman and Yitzhaki (1985) and Yitzhaki (2002) for a derivation of the formulae used.

The Gini elasticity, η, is the marginal change in the overall Gini index G_y following a small proportional change in the seat capacity offered by airline x. The Gini elasticity can be defined as:

$$\eta_x = \frac{COV[x, F(y)]}{COV[y, F(y)]} * \frac{\mu_y}{\mu_x} = \frac{b_{xy}}{S_{xy}} \tag{6}$$

and

$$S_{xy} = \frac{\mu_y}{\mu_x} \tag{7}$$

b_{xy} is the Gini regression coefficient with x as the dependent and y as the independent variable (Yitzhaki 2002); b_{xy} varies between -1 and 1; b_{xy} will equal 1 (-1) when an airline's seat capacity is an increasing (decreasing) function of total seat capacity. When airline seat capacity is constant, b_{xy} will equal 0, implying that the source's share of the Gini is 0. S_{xy} is the average propensity of an airport in the overall airport population to be served by airline x.

Dividing b_{xy} by S_{xy} yields the Gini elasticity. If η_x>1 (<1), a marginal increase (decrease) of the network configuration of airline x increases (decreases) the overall

Gini index (that is, the concentration of seat capacity in the EU airport hierarchy). If η_x=1, the airline network configuration has no effect on the overall distribution of seat capacity at EU airports. The Gini elasticity depends on the Gini index of the individual airline network and the size and ranking of the airports served by this airline with respect to the overall airport population.

In order to estimate the absolute change in the overall initial Gini index following a 1 per cent change in the seat capacity of airline x, we need to compute ΔG (Wodon and Yitzhaki 2001). ΔG takes into account the market share of airline x in total seat capacity. This is important because, all other things being equal, a 1 per cent change in the airline seat capacity of a large airline is bound to have a larger impact on the overall Gini coefficient than a change for a small airline (Wodon and Yitzhaki 2001). ΔG can be defined as:

$$\Delta G = S_{xy} * G_y * (\eta - 1)/100 \tag{8}$$

It should be noted that ΔG assumes a small proportional change in the seat capacity of airline x. According to Wodon and Yitzhaki (2001, 100), a large change may alter the cumulative distribution and ranking of airport capacity, in which case the impact measured at the margin may no longer 'be a valid representation of the overall impact. Still, even in such a case, the impact at the margin would give a good idea of the direction of the distributional impact of the shift […]'.

In our source and subgroup decomposition analysis, we consider per year (1990–1999 and 2003) all the airports that had a scheduled service. Airlines and airports without a scheduled service in a certain year are left out of the analysis for that year.

Connectivity analysis

In addition to the Gini decomposition methodology, we have used the following indicators for the analysis of airport connectivity in relation to the small airport peripheralization:

- Number of direct and onward connections to capture the connectivity of a 5th tier airport (see Figure 7.2).
    - A direct connection is a non-stop connection between airport H and airport B. The measurement unit for direct connectivity is the individual direct flight.
    - An indirect is a connection between airport H and airport B via airport A. Again we have used the methodology of weighted indirect connectivity (Chapter 4). However, we have aggregated the weighted indirect connections to the level of the spoke airport instead of the airport where the transfer takes place
- The number of airports per category to capture the size of the airport population.

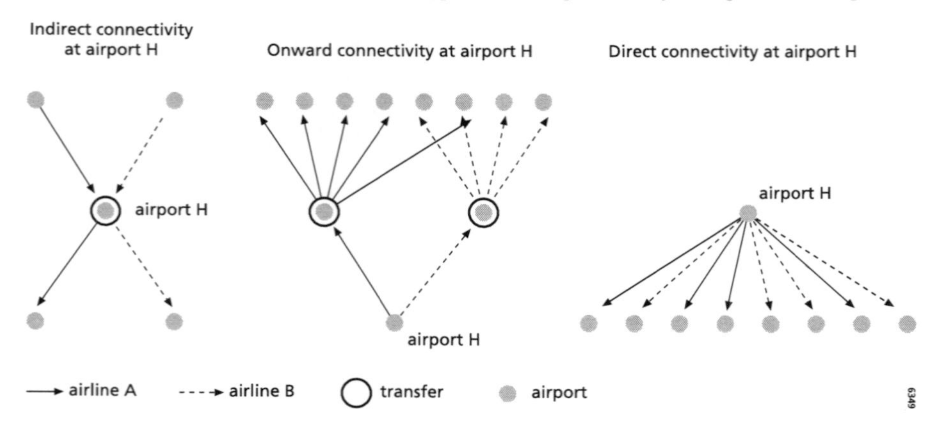

Figure 7.2 Direct, indirect and onward connectivity

The dataset consists of OAG data for the years 1990–1999. Since we need a complete time series for our analysis, the data for 2003 are left out of the analysis.

Spatial concentration in the EU airport hierarchy?

One of our intentions in this chapter is to present an answer to the question, to what extent have the changing airline hub-and-spoke strategies and alternative airline network strategies influenced the distribution of seat capacity in the European airport hierarchy. The hypothesis is that hub-and-spoke and radial network strategies of EU airlines stimulated spatial concentration in the airport hierarchy during the period of analysis.

We start this section with a description of the development of concentration of seat capacity in the European airport hierarchy and the contribution of various airport categories to this concentration pattern. We then turn to the effect of individual airline network strategies on the overall level of concentration by using the source decomposition of the Gini index.

Subgroup decomposition of the spatial distribution of seat capacity in the European airport hierarchy

The growth of seat capacity in Europe is not evenly distributed over the five airport categories. Table 7.2 makes it clear that with an average yearly growth rate of 6 per cent the 2nd tier airports were above the overall growth index during the period 1990–2003. The growth rate for the 1st tier and 4th tier airports was below the overall average. The growth rates between 1995 and 1996 coincide with the top of the economic cycle, whereas the very small or even negative rates between 1990

Table 7.2 Yearly growth rates (%), seat capacity

	90/91	91/92	92/93	93/94	94/95	95/96	96/97	97/98	98/99	1999–2003	average
1st tier	4.0	10.2	5.7	-0.4	0.3	11.9	6.4	8.0	7.3	1.5	5.5
2nd tier	-1.0	14.5	1.2	0.1	5.5	13.4	7.9	7.2	16.4	0.6	6.6
3rd tier	12.3	-1.3	5.5	11.0	5.9	15.3	-0.7	7.6	1.9	2.1	6.0
4th tier	0.0	2.7	3.1	3.9	3.0	20.3	4.0	5.3	11.9	1.6	5.6
5th tier	-0.6	7.0	3.5	4.5	7.2	10.9	9.4	5.1	11.9	6.3	6.5
All	2.7	7.8	3.8	3.1	4.4	13.2	6.0	6.8	10.1	2.6	6.0

Source: *OAG*

Note: *Total intra-EU and extra-EU seat capacity per airport category, 1990–2003. Estimated yearly growth based on the percentual growth of total seat capacity between 1999 and 2003.*

and 1991 were mainly the consequence of the economic downturn and the first Gulf War.

But the question arises: did the growth differences between airport categories result in a substantial shift in spatial concentration of airport capacity in the European airport hierarchy?

Intra-EU market Let us first consider the intra-EU market. The radial and hub-and-spoke strategies of EU airlines described in Chapters 3 and 4 do not seem to have resulted in a spatial concentration of intra-EU airport capacity on a small number of key airports. On the contrary, a small deconcentration of seat capacity took place during the period of analysis, as Table 7.3 indicates. More to the point, in 2003 the total seat capacity for intra-European destinations was more equally distributed over the European airports than in 1990. The share of the 2nd tier and to a lesser extent the 5th tier airports increased at the expense of the 1st tier airports.

However, these conclusions may very well have been influenced by the categorization of airports employed here. We therefore computed the Gini index of concentration for intra-EU seat capacity and broke the Gini index down by airport category. As we see below, the Gini subgroup decomposition offers a much more differentiated view of the distribution issue.

Table 7.3 Distribution (%) of intra-EU seat capacity

	1990	1993	1996	1999	2003
1st tier	21.1	21.6	18.3	17.8	15.5
2nd tier	24.7	24.6	24.5	26.5	25.0
3rd tier	17.3	17.6	20.0	17.6	17.2
4th tier	8.6	7.9	8.6	8.6	8.3
5th tier	28.3	28.3	28.5	29.5	34.0
All	100.0	100.0	100.0	100.0	100.0

Source: *OAG*

Table 7.4 Gini coefficients, intra-EU

	Within-group					Between group	Overall
	1st tier	2nd tier	3rd tier	4th tier	5th tier		
1990	0.2151	0.2539	0.3886	0.4445	0.6922	0.6473	0.8283
1993	0.2045	0.2478	0.3810	0.4746	0.6957	0.6451	0.8265
1996	0.1873	0.2495	0.4077	0.4273	0.6934	0.6387	0.8208
1999	0.1499	0.1781	0.3102	0.3806	0.7197	0.6306	0.8248
2003	0.1725	0.2370	0.3098	0.3941	0.7158	0.5838	0.8061

Source: *OAG*

Note: *Intra-European seat capacity only.*

The overall intra-EU Gini index decreased between 1990 and 2003 (Table 7.4). In other words, intra-EU seat capacity was increasingly deconcentrated, supporting the results presented above. The chosen categorization of airports (1st to 5th tier) does not violate the deconcentration conclusion.

The deconcentration pattern was the result of decreasing the within-group inequality of 1st–4th tier airports and a reduction of between-group inequality. These reductions were larger than the increase of the within-group inequality (Table 7.4) and the Gini share (Table 7.5) of the 5th tier airports.

Indeed, when we look at the growth of the individual airports from a geographical perspective for the period 1990–1999, we see that the growth of EU seat capacity was not constrained to a few very large airports in the hierarchy (Figure 7.3). The geographical pattern of seat capacity growth at airports largely followed the pattern of the airports that were important in the networks of airlines for generating indirect connections (1st to 4th tier airports) as well as a few 5th tier airports. The growth of a few 5th tier airports is captured by the increase of the within-group Gini index of the 5th tier airports.

During the period of analysis, the within-group inequality among 5th tier airports increased (Table 7.4) and its impact on the overall Gini index increased (Table 7.5). In specific terms, the seat capacity inequality among the 5th tier airports increased during the period of analysis. One reason for this outcome is the fact that only a

Table 7.5 Gini shares, intra-EU

	Within-group					Between group	Overall
	1st tier	2nd tier	3rd tier	4th tier	5th tier		
1990	0.0006	0.0020	0.0028	0.0016	0.2115	0.7815	1
1993	0.0006	0.0020	0.0029	0.0016	0.2122	0.7806	1
1996	0.0005	0.0020	0.0036	0.0016	0.2141	0.7781	1
1999	0.0004	0.0015	0.0023	0.0014	0.2300	0.7645	1
2003	0.0004	0.0019	0.0023	0.0014	0.2698	0.7242	1

Source: *OAG*

Note: *Share (wi) of different airport categories in the Gini coefficient of intra-EU seat capacity, 1990–2003.*

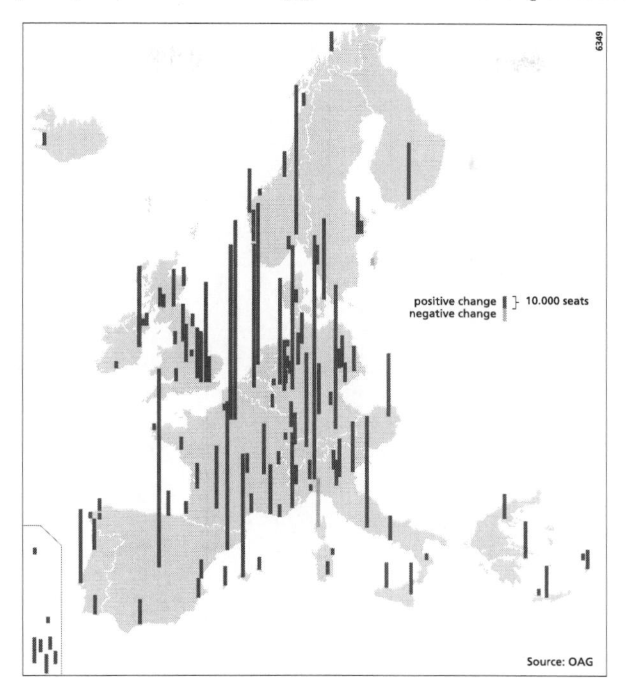

Figure 7.3 Growth intra-EU seat capacity, 1990–1999
Note: Absolute change per airport, 1990–1999.

small number of the 5th tier airports benefited from the reduction of between-group inequality in the overall airport hierarchy. In particular, the seat capacity growth at major leisure destinations (Palma de Mallorca, Heraklion, Malaga, Faro, Florence, Trapani, for example) and regional capitals (Edinburgh, Glasgow, Naples, Palermo, Bordeaux, Toulouse, Bilbao, Thessaloniki, for example) was responsible for the increase in capacity share of the 5th tier airports between 1990 and 2003.

One of the reasons for the growth of a selected number of 5th tier airports is likely to be found in the increase in low-cost services and former charter airlines increasingly selling seat-only tickets in the scheduled, low-cost market as well as an increase in competition between hub carriers for feeder traffic at these airports. The ten largest 5th tier airports in 1999[4] accounted for almost 30 per cent of total intra-EU seat capacity growth at 5th tier airports between 1990 and 1999. Almost 75 per cent of the growth in intra-European seat capacity at 5th tier airports took place at just 9.6 per cent (50) of the 5th tier airports. In other words, intra-EU seat capacity is increasingly deconcentrated, but in this deconcentration process airports of larger size are favoured over smaller airports.

4 Palma de Mallorca, Edinburgh, Glasgow, Toulouse, Venice, Hanover, Malaga, Catania, Las Palmas and Bologna.

Table 7.6 Distribution (%) of extra-EU seat capacity

	1990	1993	1996	1999	2003
1st tier	48.6	50.7	54.1	55.1	56.7
2nd tier	27.7	27.7	25.8	28.1	24.5
3rd tier	13.3	13.9	13.1	10.9	11.8
4th tier	4.7	4.9	4.0	3.3	3.4
5th tier	5.6	2.8	2.9	2.6	3.6

Source: *OAG*

Extra-EU market The picture is quite different for the extra-EU market (the market from EU airports to destinations outside the EU). The growth of seat capacity was to a large extent concentrated on the 1st tier airports (Table 7.6): London Heathrow, Paris CDG, Amsterdam and Zurich (Figure 7.4).

Again, these conclusions may well depend on the categorization used here. We therefore verified the results with the Gini subgroup decomposition. The computation of the (decomposed) Gini index supports our initial conclusions: extra-EU seat capacity was indeed less equally distributed in 2003 than in 1990. Inequality within every airport

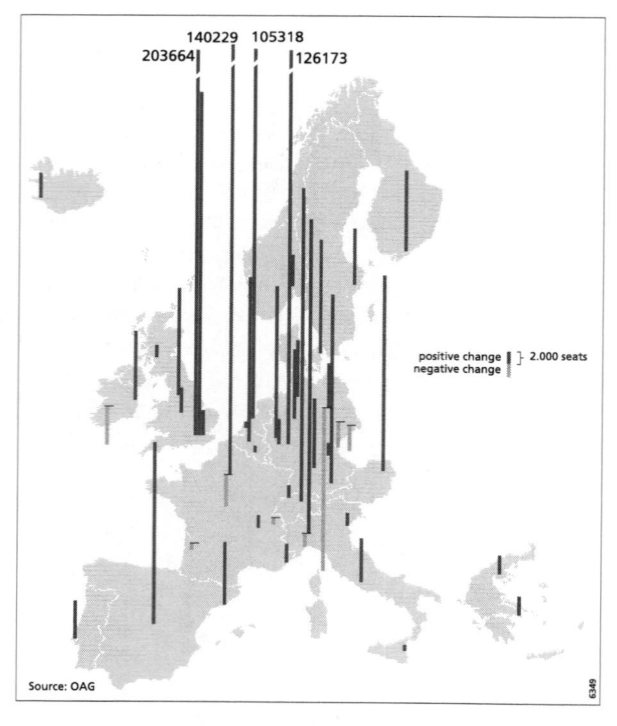

Figure 7.4 Growth extra-EU seat capacity, 1990–1999

Note: *Absolute change per airport, 1990–1999.*

Table 7.7 Gini coefficients, extra-EU

	Within-group					Between group	Overall
	1st tier	2nd tier	3rd tier	4th tier	5th tier		
1990	0.2597	0.4132	0.6206	0.5549	0.7747	0.7314	0.7955
1993	0.2370	0.3644	0.6494	0.5651	0.6659	0.7732	0.8206
1996	0.2440	0.3569	0.4947	0.5206	0.6594	0.7767	0.8191
1999	0.2333	0.3276	0.4727	0.4642	0.6572	0.7990	0.8360
2003	0.2520	0.3239	0.4081	0.5558	0.6370	0.8131	0.8499

Source: *OAG*

Note: *Extra-EU seat capacity only.*

tier decreased during the period of analysis (Table 7.7), as did the share of the within-group inequalities in the overall Gini coefficient (Table 7.8). Between-group inequality increased, however. Given the growth in market share of 1st tier airports, the increase in between-group inequality and Gini share (w_i) can be largely attributed to the above-average growth of the 1st tier airports *vis-à-vis* other airport tiers.

To conclude this discussion of the spatial distribution of seat capacity in the European airport hierarchy, we report that, at the intra-European level, no spatial concentration of seat capacity at a limited number of airports took place during the period of analysis. We even found a slight deconcentration pattern of intra-EU seat capacity. This dispersion was largely the consequence of a more equal distribution of seat capacity within the 1st–4th tier airport categories and the high growth levels at a small number of large 5th tier airports. Most small 5th tier airports did not really benefit from capacity growth. This difference resulted in a less equal capacity distribution among small, 5th tier airports. In contrast, extra-EU seat capacity was increasingly concentrated on a small number of large airports: the 1st and, to a lesser extent, 2nd tier airports.

So far, we have provided a description of the changes in the spatial concentration of seat capacity in the EU airport hierarchy. But how does this pattern relate to the (developments in the) individual airline network configurations? Let us now turn to the source decomposition of the Gini index to consider this question.

Table 7.8 Gini share, extra-EU

	Within-group					Between group	Overall
	1st tier	2nd tier	3rd tier	4th tier	5th tier		
1990	0.0102	0.0222	0.0159	0.0034	0.0289	0.9195	1
1993	0.0084	0.0169	0.0165	0.0039	0.0121	0.9422	1
1996	0.0091	0.0152	0.0116	0.0034	0.0125	0.9482	1
1999	0.0081	0.0139	0.0085	0.0021	0.0117	0.9557	1
2003	0.0077	0.0103	0.0062	0.0027	0.0164	0.9567	1

Source: *OAG*

Note: *Share (wi) of different airport categories in the Gini coefficient, 1990–2003 (extra-EU seat capacity).*

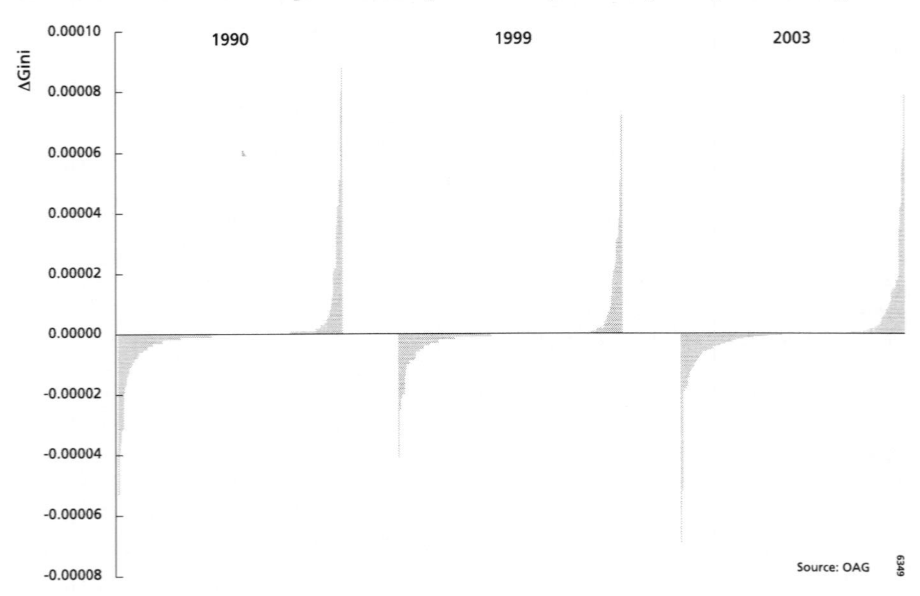

Figure 7.5 ΔG per airline, intra-EU

Note: *Absolute impact on the initial overall Gini coefficient of a 1 per cent increase in individual airline intra-EU seat capacity.*

Source decomposition of the spatial distribution of seat capacity in the European airport hierarchy: Intra-EU market

In this section we describe our decomposition of the Gini index by airline source. By so doing, we could determine the impact of individual airline network configurations on the overall distribution of seat capacity in the EU airport population. We first consider the distribution of intra-EU seat capacity. Then we turn to the extra-EU seat capacity distribution.

As we saw earlier, intra-EU seat capacity was more equally distributed over the EU airports in 2003 than in 1990. That is not to say, however, that every airline contributed to this deconcentration pattern to the same extent. The change in the Gini index is the consequence of the net effect of the various airline network strategies (Figure 7.5). Part of the airline network configurations increased the overall inequality of the intra-EU seat capacity distribution ($\Delta G<0$), whereas the other part decreased it. The decreasing impact was greater than the increasing impact. We return later to the impact of individual airlines.

Now let us contrast this deconcentration pattern with our findings in Chapter 3. There we concluded that most airline network configurations are highly concentrated in space. Indeed, Figure 7.6 shows that high levels of airline network concentration can have a substantial progressive marginal (η) or absolute (ΔG) impact on overall inequality in the intra-EU aviation network. But at the same time, high levels of

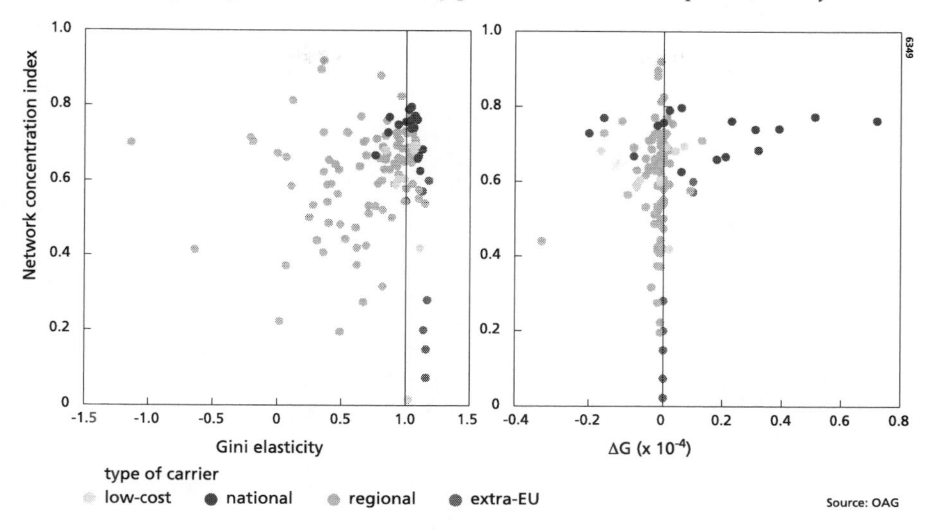

Figure 7.6 ΔG, Gini elasticity and NC values

Note: Intra-EU seat capacity only.

airline network concentration can have a regressive impact on overall inequality in the aviation network, whereas low levels of network concentration may have a progressive effect on the overall Gini. How can we understand this apparent contradiction?

As we shall see later on, much depends on the ranking of the airports served in each individual airline network and the airline's market share. Let us first consider the various airline categories in more detail.

National airlines The networks of national carriers such as Lufthansa, KLM, British Airways, Iberia, Swissair/Swiss, Air France, Austrian, Alitalia and Sabena/SN Brussels showed an overall inequality-increasing impact during the period of analysis (Table 7.9 and Figure 7.7). What this increase suggests is that these airline

Table 7.9 ΔG per airline category, intra-EU

	Low-cost	National	Regional	Extra-EU
1990	-0.000007	0.000330	-0.000390	0.000067
1993	-0.000003	0.000306	-0.000352	0.000048
1996	-0.000006	0.000266	-0.000272	0.000012
1999	-0.000027	0.000244	-0.000223	0.000006
2003	-0.000014	0.000307	-0.000297	0.000004

Source: OAG

Note: ΔG effect on the initial Gini of a 1 per cent change in intra-EU seat capacity of all airlines per category. The rows of this table add up to zero: a 1 per cent increase in seat capacity of all airlines in a particular year does not change the Gini index.

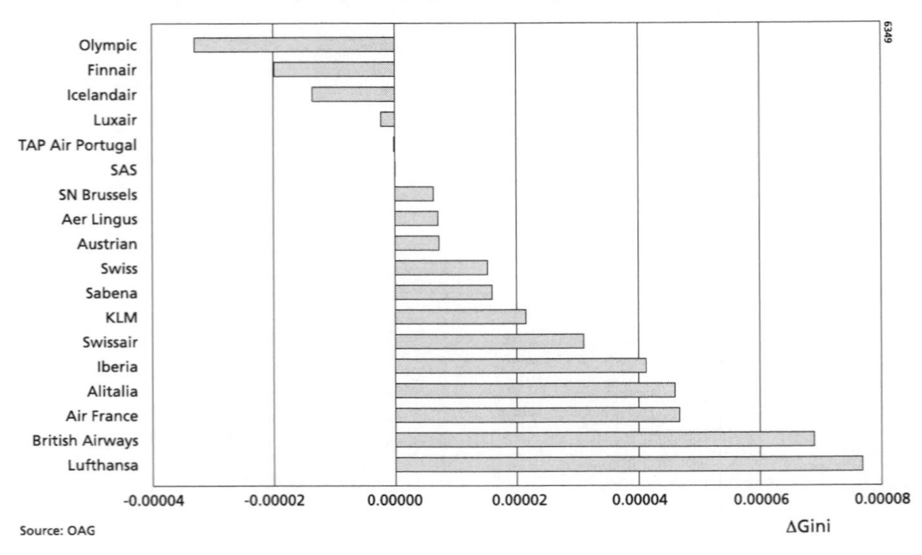

Figure 7.7 Average ΔG per national airline, 1990–1999 and 2003
Note: Intra-EU seat capacity only.

networks are concentrated around traffic nodes and hubs at the 1st to 3rd tier airports while mainly serving the 1st to 4th tier and larger 5th tier destinations.

Olympic Airways and Finnair on the other hand had spatially concentrated networks during the period of analysis, but showed an equalizing impact on the intra-EU airport hierarchy. Olympic, for example, has a network focused on Athens and a number of larger 5th tier airports (Rhodos/Thessaloniki/Corfu/Heraklion). Many very small destinations in the Greek archipelagos are served from these airports, while, compared with other national airlines, the number of 1st to 4th tier destinations is relatively small. This has resulted in a decreasing impact on overall inequality.

The signs of the national airline networks did not change during the period of analysis, indicating a structural impact on the distribution of capacity in the EU airport population.

Low-cost airlines Low-cost airlines had an inequality-reducing impact between 1990 and 2003 (Table 7.9). However, the individual low-cost carriers differ (Figure 7.8). The airlines having 1st to 3rd tier airports as their major traffic nodes and hubs had an inequality-increasing impact. Airlines with a network focused on serving 4th and 5th tier airports showed an inequality-decreasing impact on the overall Gini index. Ryanair, for example, operated traffic nodes at two 3rd tier airports in 1999 (Dublin and London Stansted); however, it served virtually no other 1st to 4th tier airports, resulting in an inequality-decreasing impact of the carrier on the overall Gini.

Hapag Lloyd had a moderately concentrated network in 1999 (NC=0.58) with its main bases at Hanover and Palma de Mallorca. The carrier was originally a charter airline, but it became also a scheduled airline after the full deregulation of the market

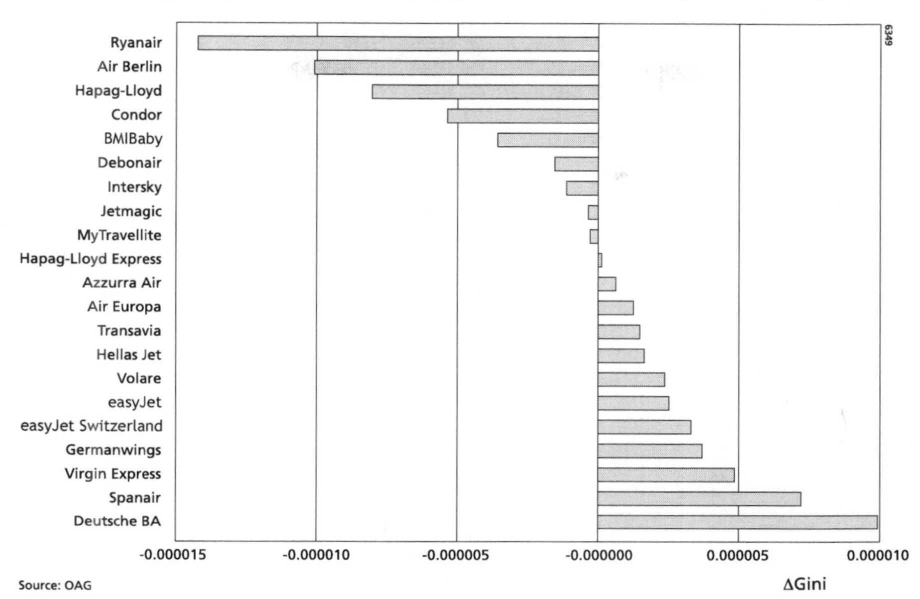

Figure 7.8 Average ΔG per low-cost airline, 1990–1999 and 2003
Note: *Average has been computed for operating years of each airline only.*

in 1997. The carrier connects smaller German airports (Hanover, Hamburg, Bremen and Nuremberg, for example) with leisure destinations in Southern Europe. Clearly such a network that connects the smaller airports in the network has a regressive impact on the inequality in the overall aviation network. The same holds true for Air Berlin (Chapter 6).

In contrast, a low-cost airline such as Virgin Express (Chapter 6), with its main traffic node at Brussels in 1999 and serving mainly the larger EU airports, stimulated – on average – the concentration of intra-EU seat capacity in the airport hierarchy. The network of Deutsche BA also concentrated on connecting larger airports, primarily within Germany, resulting in a concentrating impact on the EU airport hierarchy.

Regional airlines Regional airlines had a net decreasing impact on inequality with respect to the distribution of intra-EU seat capacity (Table 7.9). Some regional airlines fed the large airline hubs or operated independent traffic nodes at a 1st–3rd tier airport (British Midland, Air Europe, Viva Air, for example) while serving mostly 1st–4th tier and larger 5th tier destinations. Such airlines had an increasing impact on the overall Gini coefficient (Figure 7.9).

Most regional airlines however served in particularly small 5th tier airports. The best example is Wideroe's Flyveselkap, operating an extensive deconcentrated network along the coastline of Norway, and connecting many small airports in that region. Even a regional hub carrier such as Régional Airlines had a regressive impact in 1999 on the Gini index. Régional Airlines served mostly lower-ranked airports.

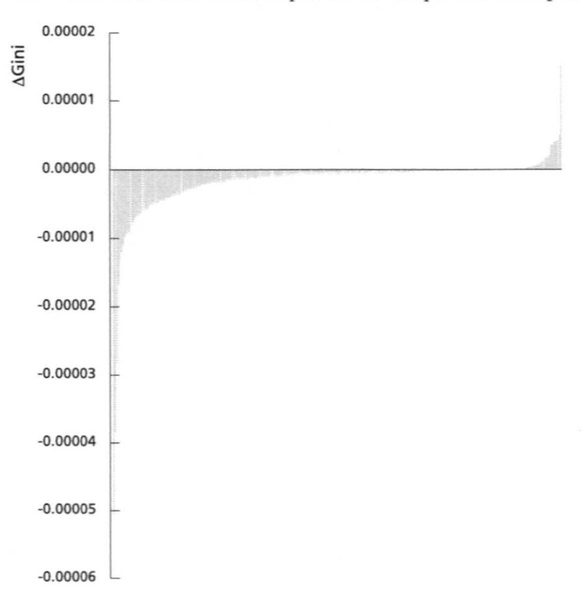

Figure 7.9 Average ΔG per regional airline, 1990–1999 and 2003
Note: Average has been computed for operating years of each airline only.

The individual absolute impact of most regional carriers was small compared with the national airlines and even the low-cost airlines. However, the large number of regional airlines in the airline population makes this group as a whole important in the understanding of the changes in concentration of seat capacity at EU airports.

Extra-EU airlines On average, the extra-EU airlines had a concentration-increasing impact (Table 7.9). This, of course, was the result of their fifth-freedom of traffic within Europe. They mainly offered connections between the 1st to 3rd tier airports (see also Chapter 3). However, as we saw earlier, the extra-EU airlines gradually retreated from the intra-EU market. During the first half of the 1990s carriers such as Pan Am, TWA, United and Delta still operated substantial intra-EU services. Their impact on the overall Gini index decreased significantly during the period of analysis and eventually became negligible in 2003 (Table 7.9).

Source decomposition of the spatial distribution of seat capacity in the European airport hierarchy: Extra-EU market

During the period of analysis, the Gini index of extra-EU seat capacity increased. Such an increase indicates a less equal distribution of extra-EU seat capacity over the EU airport population. How does this concentration pattern relate to the individual airline network configurations?

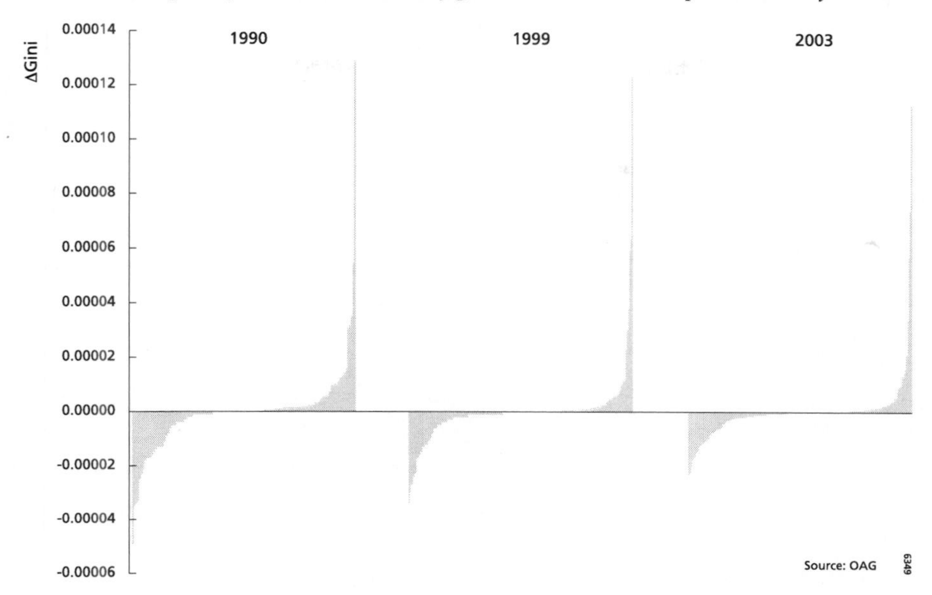

Figure 7.10 ΔG per airline, extra-EU

Note: *Absolute impact on the initial overall Gini coefficient of a 1 per cent increase in individual airline extra-EU seat capacity.*

The increasing inequality of extra-EU seat capacity is the net result of the impact of various airline network configurations on the overall concentration levels in the EU airport hierarchy (Figure 7.10).

Only the national airlines and extra-EU airlines played a significant part in the distribution of extra-EU seat capacity (Table 7.10). Their impact on the overall Gini increased between 1990 and 2003. National airlines had an inequality-increasing effect. Extra-EU airlines had an increasingly inequality-reducing impact on the capacity distribution.

Table 7.10 ΔG per airline category, extra-EU

	Low-cost	National	Regional	Extra-EU
1990	0.000000	-0.000028	-0.000042	0.000070
1993	0.000000	0.000111	-0.000028	-0.000083
1996	-0.000003	0.000154	-0.000042	-0.000109
1999	-0.000019	0.000155	-0.000022	-0.000114
2003	-0.000079	0.000192	-0.000015	-0.000097

Source: *OAG*

Note: *ΔG effect on the initial Gini of a 1 per cent change in extra-EU seat capacity of all airlines per category. The rows of this table add up to zero: a 1 per cent increase in seat capacity of all airlines in a particular year does not change the Gini index.*

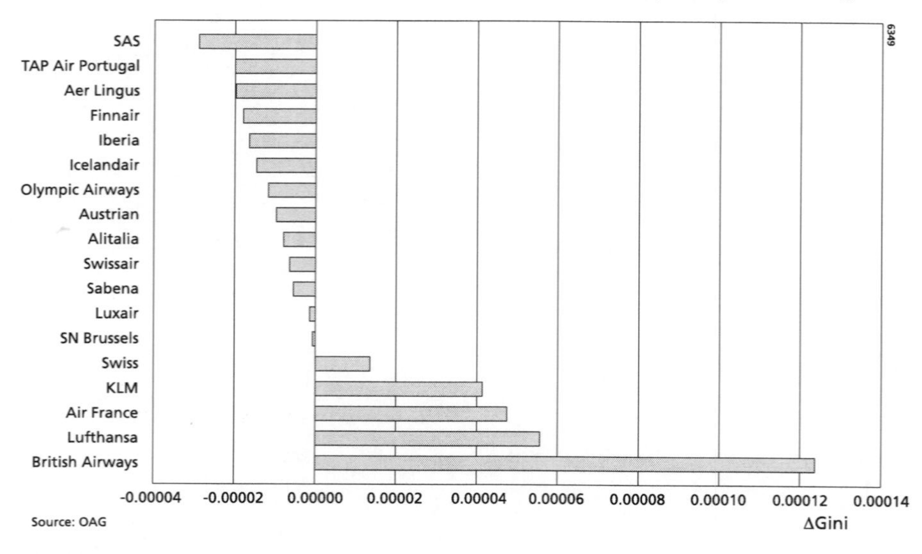

Figure 7.11 Average ΔG per national airline, extra-EU

Ongoing bilateral regulation of extra-EU services still determines to a large extent the number of airlines operating them. In most cases, these designated airlines are the national airlines of each country. Low-cost and regional airlines play virtually no part in the supply of extra-EU air services. Because of the dominance of the national and extra-EU carriers, we only discuss the impact of national and extra-EU airlines here.

National airlines National airlines had a net positive impact on the Gini coefficient following a one per cent change in their extra-EU seat capacity (Table 7.10). Figure 7.11 shows, however, that this progressive impact is dependent on five airline networks: British Airways, KLM, Lufthansa, Air France and Swiss/Swissair. These airlines had the largest market shares in extra-EU seat capacity during the period of analysis. Moreover, their extra-EU networks were concentrated on the five largest airports in the population: London Heathrow, Paris Charles de Gaulle, Frankfurt, Amsterdam and Zurich. Since the airport population for extra-EU airports is smaller, these five airports are above what is referred to as the poverty line: an increase in capacity of the five airports leads to an increase in inequality. As a consequence, the above-average growth of these airline networks stimulated further inequality in the extra-EU seat capacity distribution.

Extra-EU airlines Extra-EU airlines had a net decreasing-inequality effect during the period of analysis (Table 7.10). The impact of most extra-EU airlines is relatively small compared with the impact of the national carriers. Nevertheless, because of the large number of extra-EU airlines, this category is still important in the understanding of the development of the inequality levels.

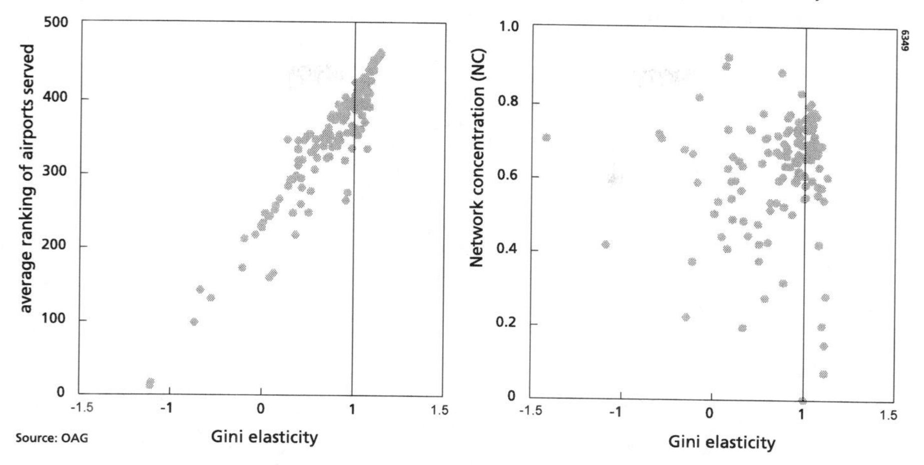

Figure 7.12 Gini elasticity, airport ranking and network concentration
Note: *Figure shows the Gini elasticity versus the average ranking of the airports served (left) and NC index (right) per airline in 1999 (intra-EU seat capacity) (1=lowest rank).*

During the period of analysis, the extra-EU airlines had an increasingly concentration-reducing impact on the EU airport hierarchy with respect to extra-EU seat capacity (Table 7.10), except for a very small positive impact in 1990. This means that extra-EU airlines increasingly served lower-ranked airports (other than the 1st tier). One of the reasons for this development might be the market growth during the 1990s (in particular with regard to the Europe–Asia market). The increase in demand justified more direct EU destinations. Moreover, the introduction of more efficient long-range aircraft types such as the Airbus A330/A340, Boeing 767ER and Boeing 777 enabled extra-EU airlines to serve more 2nd to 4th tier destinations directly. The 5th tier airports saw an increase in extra-EU capacity operated by extra-EU airlines, whereas the share of extra-EU capacity from 5th tier airports operated by national airlines decreased in the same period.

The spatial concentration hypothesis

On the basis of an extensive literature review, we expect airlines' adoption and intensification of hub-and-spoke and radial network configurations to increase concentration levels in the overall European airport hierarchy. However, we cannot accept this hypothesis. Intra-EU seat capacity showed a deconcentration pattern during the period of analysis.

We showed that various airlines have different marginal impacts on the overall distribution of seat capacity in the airport hierarchy. The differences can be explained by the rank of the airports the airlines serve (Figure 7.12): if the average rank of the airports served increases, so does the airline's Gini elasticity. For the actual absolute impact on the Gini coefficient, the market share of the airline is important. However,

Table 7.11 Gini elasticity and airline network concentration

		Gini elasticity (marginal impact on the Gini coefficient)	
		<1	>1
Airline network concentration	Small	Deconcentrated airline networks serving primarily lower-ranked airports (Wideroe's/ Ryanair, for example)	Deconcentrated airline networks primarily serving higher-ranked airports (most extra-EU carriers)
	Large	Concentrated airline networks, primarily serving lower-ranked airports (most regionals, for example, Braathens, Olympic Airways, Régional Airlines)	Concentrated airline networks (radial or hub-and-spoke) with higher-ranked traffic node(s)/hub(s) and serving primarily higher-ranked destinations (most national airlines)

the spatial configuration of the individual airline network (concentrated versus deconcentrated) has virtually no influence on the impact of the airline network on the overall Gini coefficient of the total European airport hierarchy. An airline can operate a deconcentrated, criss-cross network. If the carrier mainly serves higher ranked airports, it still has a progressive impact on the overall concentration level of seat-capacity.

Table 7.11 summarizes the different airline network configurations and their impact on the Gini index with respect to intra-EU traffic.

With respect to the distribution of intra-EU seat capacity, growth in most of the spatially-concentrated (radial/hub-and-spoke) network configurations of national airlines tends to increase overall concentration levels. The same effect holds true for the more deconcentrated extra-EU airline networks, since they serve primarily the largest airports in the airport population. However, their actual impact is negligible, because of their increasingly small market shares.

Low-cost, and in particular regional, airlines show a much more diverse pattern. Overall, low-cost carriers and regional airlines were responsible for the deconcentration of intra-EU seat capacity. Their inequality-decreasing effect was larger than the inequality-increasing effect of the national and extra-EU airlines. With the recent growth of low-cost airlines using smaller, secondary airports, a further reduction of the Gini index can be expected.

The extra-EU distribution followed an entirely different picture. Here, a concentration pattern could be observed. The four largest national airlines (British Airways, KLM, Lufthansa Air France) were largely responsible for the increase in inequality. The growth of extra-EU seat capacity took place at the four largest airports. Not surprisingly, the hubs of these airlines (London Heathrow, Amsterdam, Frankfurt, Paris Charles de Gaulle) were also the main European gateways of the global airline alliances (Oneworld at London Heathrow, Wings at Amsterdam, Star at Frankfurt and SkyTeam at Paris Charles de Gaulle). Other national airlines such as Iberia and SAS showed an inequality-decreasing impact. The impact of extra-EU airlines on the concentration level was increasingly negative in direction between 1990 and 2003. We offered a number of possible reasons for this development.

In conclusion, we cannot accept the spatial concentration hypothesis. The spatial concentration of airline networks does not automatically result in more concentration in the EU airport hierarchy. The impact of each individual airline network is not only related to the spatial configuration of its network; much more important is the overall ranking of the airports being served and the airline's market share. The eventual distributional shifts in the airport hierarchy are the net result of the various airline network strategies.

Finally, we turn to the second part of this chapter: the peripheralization of small EU airports.

The peripheralization of small airports?

In the previous section we concluded that the larger 5th tier airports benefited most from the growth of seat capacity. In this section, we look at them in more detail. How did direct and onward connectivity to 5th tier airports develop during the period of analysis?

First, we present our analysis of the number of 5th tier airports with scheduled air service and the spatial distribution of air-service terminations. As we saw in the literature review of this chapter, small airports are most vulnerable for air-service terminations under a free market regime and some may even lose air service altogether. Second, we consider the growth of direct versus onward connectivity. As discussed above, some studies on US small community airports concluded that smaller-sized airports may face a decrease in direct connectivity, but that, as a consequence of airline hub-and-spoke strategies, such a decrease may very well be compensated by an increase in onward connections via (with a transfer at) a hub. In other words, direct connectivity to airports with hub operations may be more important than direct connectivity per se.

Let us first consider the 5th tier airports that lost air service altogether during the period of analysis. We have considered the period 1990–1999, because we needed a complete period for the analyses to be carried out.

Loss of scheduled air service

The number of 5th tier airports with scheduled service was not stable during the period of analysis, but varied from year to year according to our OAG database. Figure 7.13 provides an overview of the dynamics in their number. During the 1990–1999 period, 184 airports lost intra-EU scheduled air service altogether from one year to the next. There were 181 airports that gained new air service without having had a scheduled air service in the previous year. Many airports in the 5th tier airport hierarchy were 'sleeping' or 'traffic light' airports: in some years they did have scheduled air service, but in others they did not.

The net gains and losses seem to correlate with the economic growth cycle. The number of airports that lost air service was much larger during the economic decline

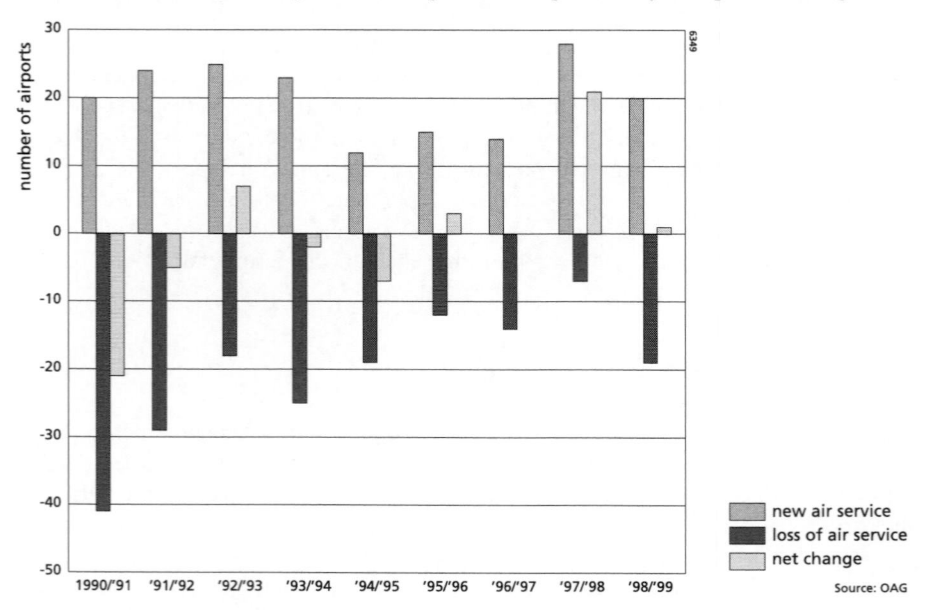

Figure 7.13 5th tier-airport connectivity dynamics

Note: *Figure shows the air-service terminations, new air service and net gain of air service in the 5th tier airport category, 1990–1999, intra-EU air service only.*

of 1990–1992 than during the second half of the 1990s. The airports that lost air service were mostly airports with a capacity of less than 4000 seats/week in any of the years under consideration. Most of these airports are located in the more remote regions of Europe: Scandinavia, Iceland, northern Portugal and the northern part of the UK. However, some airports in the core area of Europe (France, Germany) also fell out of the population of scheduled airports.

The results presented here correspond with earlier studies of small community airports in the UK, Ireland and USA (Goetz and Sutton 1997; Reynolds-Feighan 1995, for example). Small airports are most vulnerable with respect to airline network rationalization, especially in periods of (regional) economic downturns.

Direct and onward connectivity

Obviously, not every airport facing a decrease of air-service loses its scheduled network completely. Let us consider the changes in the direct connectivity versus onward connectivity at 5th tier airports that did not lose scheduled air service completely. Are decreases in 5th tier airport connectivity compensated by a growth of onward connectivity through the major EU airports? One might expect such a development because of the adoption and intensification of hub-and-spoke and radial network configurations by EU airlines.

Table 7.12 5th tier-airport connectivity

		Direct connectivity			
		No change	**Increase**	**Decrease**	**All airports**
Onward connectivity	No onward connectivity in 1990 and 1999	3.1	12.6	16.4	32.0
	No change	0.0	0.7	0.7	1.4
	Increase	4.0	39.1	11.6	54.7
	Decrease	2.1	4.3	5.5	11.8
	All airports	9.2	56.6	34.1	100.0

Source: *OAG*

Note: *Percentage (%) of the number of 5th tier airports and changes in daily direct and weighted onward connectivity (n=422). 5th tier airports with intra-EU scheduled air service in 1990 or 1999.*

Table 7.12 reveals that 34 per cent of the 5th tier airports that had scheduled service in both 1990 and 1999 faced a decrease in direct connectivity. The majority of these airports did not have onward connections in 1990 or 1999 (16.4 per cent). These airports remained outside the connecting complexes of airline networks that generate transfer opportunities at the hubs and traffic nodes. This figure should be treated with caution, since in our analysis we did not take the regional alliance partners or inter-line connections into account. These regional carriers may be particularly important for the small-sized airports in generating onward connections.

About 34 per cent (11.6 per cent of all airports or 49 airports) of the airports with a decrease in direct connections faced an increase in the amount of onward connectivity through the various airline hubs and traffic nodes. Such an increase may be the consequence of a growth in the number of hubs/traffic nodes to which the 5th tier airport is connected. It may also be the consequence of an increase in frequencies to the same hub/traffic node that meet minimum and maximum connecting times and routing factors (see also Chapter 4). This figure would actually have been much higher if alliance connections had been included in the analysis. In this respect, it can be concluded that losses of direct connectivity are frequently compensated by gains in onward connectivity.

The growth of direct connections still seems to be highly associated with the growth of onward connections. Direct connectivity increased at almost 57 per cent of the 5th tier airports. At 39 per cent of these airports onward connectivity increased also. The apparent relationship is likely to be the consequence of the increased hubbing activities of the major carriers, which increasingly compete for transfer passengers at the spoke airports (Frenken et al. 2004). In addition, the growth of frequencies as such generates more onward frequencies, regardless of any hub strategies of the hub carriers.

However, a small percentage of the 5th tier airports can be considered as 'pockets of pain'. These airports faced either a decrease/an equal number of onward connections and at the same time a decrease/equal direct connectivity or they did not have any onward connections at all. Just as for the airports with scheduled air service terminations, the 'pockets of pain' are concentrated in certain areas. In specific terms, these areas can be found in the northern part of Norway, Sweden, Iceland, the Shetlands, the Orkney Islands, Scotland, northern Portugal and the Frisian Islands. Again some caution is needed here since we have not included transfer connections between alliance partners or interline connections in the WNX-model used.

Conclusions and discussion

In the previous chapters we described our analysis of the changing network configurations of EU airlines. We concluded that most EU airlines adopted or intensified hub-and-spoke networks and concentrated their networks in space. In this chapter we have assessed the consequences of these changing network strategies for the European airport hierarchy and its spatial distribution.

We concluded that the growth of EU seat capacity was unevenly distributed in space between 1990 and 2003. Moreover, major differences can be found between the different markets. Intra-EU seat capacity spread over more airports. The 1st tier airports lost intra-EU market share at the expense of 2nd, 4th, and 5th tier airports. Moreover, a small number of larger 5th tier airports were responsible for the growth of the seat capacity share of 5th tier airports. These airports included some major leisure destinations in Southern Europe and regional capitals. Interestingly, no concentration pattern as seen in the development of the US airport hierarchy could be found.

The decomposition analysis of the Gini index showed that the low-cost airlines, regional airlines and a few national carriers were responsible for this deconcentration trend. Most national carrier and extra-EU carriers had a progressive impact on the overall concentration level.

However, the European airport hierarchy concentrated on a smaller number of airports with regard to extra-EU seat capacity. Its growth took place at the 1st and, to a lesser extent, the 2nd tier airports. The 1st tier and some of the 2nd tier airports play a part as the primary continental connection complexes for global alliance networks. Not surprisingly, KLM, British Airways, Air France and Lufthansa were largely responsible for the increase of concentration levels with respect to extra-EU traffic. The main hubs of these carriers are the primary European gateways for the global alliances.

When looking at the 5th tier airports alone, we note that a substantial number of them lost air service altogether during the period of analysis. Many of these airports are 'sleeping' temporarily; the availability of scheduled air service varies from year to year. Most probably, this state of affairs depends on the (regional) economic circumstances and individual airline network strategies.

A substantial part (34 per cent) of the airports that lost air service partially (but not completely) was compensated by an increase in the number of one-stop onward connections through other airline hubs and traffic nodes. Since we did not include onward connections between alliance partners, this figure can be assumed to be too conservative and slightly higher in reality. Nevertheless, it is clear that a decrease in direct connectivity is frequently compensated by a larger indirect connectivity.

Chapter 8

Airport Planning in a Free-Market Regime

A free-market regime is likely to speed up airline network change; deregulation removes the regulatory impediments to rapid modifications of airline networks (de Neufville and Odoni 2003). As we saw in the preceding chapters, European airline networks in a free-market regime are dynamic structures in both space and time that show discontinuous changes.

Since airport connectivity is the aggregate product of overall airline network behaviour, the connectivity and traffic volumes at the airport level may also become much more dynamic and turbulent. In other words, an important effect of airline network strategies in free market regimes is that overall airport traffic, together with the composition of the traffic, may become more volatile (De Neufville and Barber 1991). Following De Neufville and Barber (1991), we refer to volatility as the average year-to-year variation in (the composition of) airport traffic compared with the overall trend of traffic. De Neufville and Barber showed in their paper entitled *Deregulation induced volatility of airport traffic* that volatility levels at US airports increased dramatically after US deregulation in 1978. Free route entry and exit, hub building and de-hubbing, the low-cost effect at secondary airports, airline bankruptcies and network optimization of merged airline networks are all important sources of high volatility levels.

Given the volatility of airport traffic demand in free-market regimes, future airport traffic volumes and traffic composition may be increasingly difficult to predict. Apart from the fact that forecasting suffers from many well-documented limitations (De Wulf 1991; Flyvbjerg et al. 2003, Hogarth and Makridakis 1981; Mintzberg 1994, for example), volatility as a result of deregulation further reduces the reliability of detailed traffic forecasts, particularly for the distant future.

The free-market regime and the related airline network behaviour make the context in which airport planners operate increasingly problematic. In essence, volatility of (the composition of) airport traffic means greater uncertainty and risk for airports. Volatility and the associated uncertainty with respect to future traffic volumes have implications for the planning of airport capacity. Airport revenues become much more uncertain as the instability of airport traffic grows. Because traffic forecasting is central to airport master planning, the risks associated with investments in facilities increase.

The question we ask in this chapter is how airport planners can deal with the tension between the long-range planning of airport capacity and the rapid changes in airline network behaviour. In this chapter we argue that a paradigm shift towards a more flexible, dynamic approach to airport planning is needed to deal with the free-market regime in the EU air transport industry.

We begin by examining the notions of strategic planning. Then we discuss the traditional approach to strategic airport planning and its pitfalls. Lastly, we shift our attention to an alternative model of strategic airport planning: Flexible Strategic Planning (FSP). FSP deals explicitly with volatility, uncertainty and risk.

Strategic planning

In order to discuss the role of volatility and uncertainty in strategic airport planning, we first have to define what we mean by strategic planning. However, strategic planning is not an easy concept to define. The academic literature offers a myriad of definitions. Following the work of Kreukels (1980), we define strategic planning here as the most systematic form of action that intends to match long-term goals with short- and mid-term objectives, primarily driven by goal-oriented rationality. In this context, goal-oriented rational decision-making can be defined as the 'acquisition of all the information necessary, comparing the information on different options, and then selecting the option which will enable him to achieve his goals and interests' (Parsons 1995, 272).

Strategic planning styles

The history of strategic planning has brought forward numerous approaches, styles and models. It is not our intention to give an overview of these approaches. Numerous publications are available on this subject. In the context of this study, we discuss briefly the characteristics of three strategic planning styles: long-range planning, strategic planning and strategic management, based on the work of Harrison and Taylor (Crol 1999; Genus 1995; Wilson 1998, for example). It should be noted that we use the term strategic planning here as a planning style, in contrast with the former section, where strategic planning was used as a general concept of action.[1]

Long-range planning After the Second World War, Western countries experienced a relatively high degree of stability and economic growth. Economies were primarily supply driven. Keeping costs down and productivity high entailed mass production and economies of scale. The 1950s saw the rise of long-range planning. Such planning was typically based on extrapolations of historical trends. The annual

1 This overview is based on the evolution of strategic planning as a corporate activity. Planning within public organizations such as spatial planning agencies shows a quite different development (see Kreukels 1978, for example). In general terms, it can be said that corporate planning developed from operational, short-term planning into strategic planning from the 1950s onwards. Spatial planning however developed from a long-range type of planning to a strategic type of planning that combined long-term visions with short-term goals and resources.

budgeting process was expanded to produce long-range forecasts. A single long-range sales forecast would be the main input for the operating plans and budgeting. The continuing economic growth made such extrapolations possible and fostered the opinion that organizations could determine, or at least forecast, their environment.

Strategic planning The popularity of long-range planning faded away, since few planners had foreseen the oil crisis of 1973/74 and the recessions of the early 1980s. The world economy became transformed from being supply driven into demand driven. The answer to the changing circumstances and growing uncertainty was the development of a number of analytical tools and concepts to facilitate understanding of the nature of the macro-environment. Tools were developed for strategic planning to identify and assess the opportunities and threats in the macro-environment of organizations in relation to the strengths and weaknesses of an organization. Strategic planning combines the assessment of the external and internal environment (Kreukels 1978). Scenario building became an important aspect of the planning exercise. Quantitative forecasting techniques were further developed.

Initially, strategic planning was primarily a top-down process (Crol 1999). It was the task of corporate managers and strategic planners who relied on 'hard data' (reports, numbers). But the research of Mintzberg (1994), for example, showed that relying on hard data alone could easily result in strategic failure. Hard data often omits important non-quantitative factors, is limited in scope, arrives too late, or is too aggregated for effective use. Operational management did have access to soft data, but it was detached from the strategy-making itself. Strategic management tried to resolve this 'fallacy of detachment'.

Strategic management Globalization, deregulation, the ICT revolution, demographic shifts and growing social and environmental responsibility resulted in rapidly-shifting economic patterns from the 1980s on. The long-range and strategic planning approaches were not suitable for a changing environment. The reliance of long-range and strategic planners on forecasting techniques became inappropriate for the constantly changing conditions.

The dynamic macro-environment required the input of managers in the strategy-making process since managers have easy and real-time access to 'soft' information. Organizations searched for better possibilities to 'sense' external change and deal with uncertainty. Strategic management places part of the responsibility of strategy-making in the hands of operating managers rather than corporate managers. The top-down approach was combined with a bottom-up approach.

Kreukels (1978) addressed the characteristics of the strategic management style very well, although he labelled it strategic planning:

- existing strategy and plans are the starting point for the planning process
- the external environment and the internal environment are both assessed
- objectives and resources are interactively developed

- objectives of the plan and strategy are not given *a priori*, but are gradually developed in a top-down, bottom-up, inside-out and outside-in process of communication and analysis.

Flexible strategic planning Flexible strategic management (Genus 1995), flexible strategic planning (Dempsey et al. 1997) or dynamic strategic planning (de Neufville 2000) was embraced in the 1990s as a result of ever-increasing uncertainties. We use the concept of Flexible Strategic Planning in this book. Flexible Strategic Planning explicitly addresses uncertainty in strategy formation and planning. The Flexible Strategic Planning style is the core of our framework for the analysis of airport planning in free-market regimes.

First, we turn to the pitfalls of long-range and strategic planning using insights from the rational planning model.

The rational planning model

The normative model of planning that traditionally underlies long-range planning and strategic planning styles can be described as the rational planning model (Dempsey et al. 1997; Goetz and Szyliowicz 1997; Ruefli and Sarrazin 1981).[2]

The rational strategic planning process involves a linear, step-by-step, planned search for optimal solutions. The rational model of strategic planning is built on the congruence or fit between internal and external organizational factors (Mintzberg 1994, 36) and organizational goals and resources (Kreukels 1978). The process of rational planning is depicted in Figure 8.1.

According to Ruefli and Sarrazin (1981), the elements that characterize the rational model are:

- strategic decision-making is centralized in top (corporate) management
- the environment can be dominated, influenced or at least forecast
- there is an assumption of strict rationality on the part of decision-maker
- there are specified long-range strategic goals
- complete information is available concerning the constraints and other relationships affecting strategic decision-making. The decision-makers have all the resources required for understanding and analyzing the strategic issues (Genus 1995)
- goals, objectives and values are shared between the decision-makers.

The rational planning model has received severe criticism:

- The informational requirements of the rational planning model are unrealistic (Goetz and Szyliowicz 1997). Simon (Parsons 1995) developed the concept

2 Also referred to as the classical normative approach (Ruefli and Sarrazin 1981), linear model (Genus 1995), core design school model or SWOT model (Mintzberg 1994).

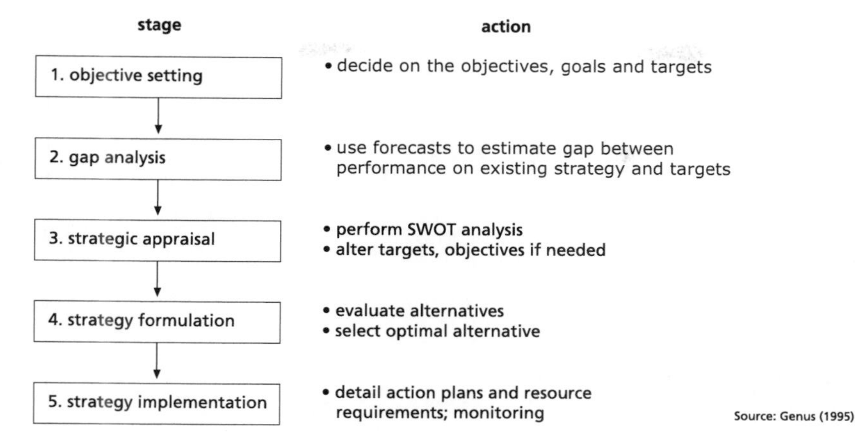

Figure 8.1 The rational model of strategic planning

of 'bounded rationality'. Human rationality is limited. Human beings have only limited information and decision-making capabilities. Moreover, they cannot have access to all the necessary data (Rycroft and Szyliowicz 1980).

- The rationality assumption can be questioned. According to Lindblom (Lindblom 1990; Parsons 1995; Rycroft and Szyliowicz 1980), decision-making exhibits 'muddling-through' characteristics: change is incremental rather than quantum; it involves mutual adjustment and negotiation; it proceeds through a succession of incremental changes; and it involves trial and error. In other words, in Lindblom's incremental approach decision-making evolves through small steps rather than the rational evaluation of all alternatives. Moreover, political (power) relations can easily distort the quest for optimal solutions. Economic rationality is not the same as political rationality (Bryson 1995).
- The rational planning model implicitly ignores uncertainty (Ruefli and Sarrazin 1981) in the political, economic and technological context. As a result, too much emphasis is placed on forecasting (Goetz and Szyliowicz 1997). Reliance on forecasting has been discredited empirically and theoretically (Hogarth and Makridakis 1981; Sanders 1998).
- The rational model can lead to conservative decision-making in the short term. Because of the assumption that the environment can be controlled or influenced, decision-making is directed to those areas where actions are most effective: low-risk areas (Ruefli and Sarrazin 1981).
- Decision-makers seldom share goals, values and objectives. Frequently a multiplicity of them exists within a single organization (Genus 1995). Strategy, goals and objectives may not be clearly articulated at the start, but may be sought for during the planning process.
- Strategy formation needs input from all layers of an organization to be successful. Strategy cannot be developed by corporate management alone

(Mintzberg 1994; Simpson 1998). Corporate management is usually too detached from operations to develop strategy successfully by itself. Moreover, detachment may result in resistance in the rest of the organization with respect to adopting the strategy (Genus 1995).

In this section we have discussed the concept of strategic planning as well as various strategic planning styles. The long-range and strategic planning styles are based on the rational model of decision-making. However, the rational model has a number of serious pitfalls. In the context of airport planning in a free-market regime, the fact that rational planning ignores or underestimates uncertainty is particularly important.

Traditional airport master planning

Traditionally, airport master planning showed a strong resemblance to the model of rational planning. What are the characteristics of traditional airport master planning?

Introduction

In the early days of aviation (before the Second World War) airport planning in Europe was a somewhat *ad hoc* activity (Caves and Gosling 1999). Airport planning was mainly driven by airline preferences, military objectives and architectural expression (Gordon 2004). After the completion of Ford Airport near Detroit in 1927 by the Ford Motor company (Mom et al. 1999, 21), US approaches to airport planning started to gain momentum in Europe. Ford Airport, with its concrete runways, taxiways and aprons became a role model for a number of European airports such as Amsterdam Schiphol, Helsinki and Stockholm.

As air travel grew and aircraft size increased, basic industry standards in airport design were required to achieve safer air travel. The standardization of facilities, ground equipment and procedures was needed.

One of the first guidelines for airport planning was the ICAO set of standards of 1947. The ICAO (International Civil Aviation Organization) was created in 1947 as a United Nations specialized agency following the Chicago Convention of 1944 (Zacher and Sutton 1996). The ICAO was designed to help develop an orderly and safe international air transport market. The ICAO adopted the safety annexes of the Chicago Convention in 1951. Annex 14 describes the standards and recommendations for the design of airports (ICAO 2000; Kazda and Caves 2000); the prescription has been regularly amended since its inception. In contrast with the Standards, the Recommendations of the ICAO are not binding on its Member States but, according to Zacher and Sutton (1996), states are conscientious in seeking to implement them. The reasons are obvious: major aviation accidents usually involve the death of the passengers and the ensuing publicity may result in a reluctance to travel by air. In addition, the ICAO has published other annexes and manuals that

Box 8.1 Key stages of the master planning process

1. Preplanning phase

- Work programme
    - Organization
    - Project scoping
    - Consultant contracts
    - Application for project funding

2. Analysis

- Inventory of existing conditions and issues
- Air traffic demand forecast
- Airport facility requirement analysis
- If not possible at existing site: site selection for new airport
- Inventorying of potential and existing constraints to investments in airport capacity (including environmental constraints)
- Development of several master plan alternatives for comparative analysis
- Selection of the most acceptable and appropriate master plan

3. Airport Master plan

A set of drawings and plan report, including:

- Policy/coordinative plan
    - Aims and objectives
    - Implementation schedules
- Physical plan
    - Airport layout plan
    - Land use plan
    - Terminal plan
    - Landside access plan
- Environmental plan
    - Environmental impact
    - Project development of the impact area
- Financial plan
- Technical annexes

4. Master plan implementation

5. Master plan updates

- Revision and review at least every two years
- Thorough evaluation and modification at least every five years

complement Annex 14 on many different issues, ranging from airport design and airport service to environmental protection and birds striking information systems. The Airport Master Planning Manual (Doc 9184) is the most important document with respect to strategic airport planning.

Some countries have their own sets of standards and recommendations. The US Federal Aviation Administration Advisory Circulars 139 and 150 are the most important non-ICAO planning documents. Although the ICAO and FAA documents differ in detail (de Neufville and Odoni 2003), they are the next most commonly used sources for airport planners (Kazda and Caves 2000). Both the ICAO and FAA documents provide airport planners throughout the world with general guidelines about airport master planning. The master planning based on the FAA master plan Advisory Circular 150 is referred to here as traditional airport master planning.

The airport master plan

What is an airport master plan? The Airport Master Planning Manual (ICAO 1987, 1–2) defines an airport master plan as 'the planner's conception of the ultimate development of a specific airport'. According to the FAA (1985, 2) an airport master plan is 'the planner's concept of the long-term development of an airport'. More recently, Kazda and Caves (2000) defined the airport master plan as 'a guide as to how the airport development should be provided to meet the foreseen demand while maximizing and preserving the ultimate capacity of the site'. Additionally, they stress that it is important to consider not only the airport site itself, but also the land and communities in the airport region. Dempsey (2000, 224) defines the airport master plan as 'a comprehensive conception of the long-term development of an existing airport, or the creation of a new airport and land adjacent thereto'.

The goal of a master plan is 'to provide guidelines for future airport development which will satisfy aviation demand in a financially feasible manner, while at the same time resolving the aviation, environmental and socioeconomic issues existing in the community' (FAA 1985, 2).

A typical master planning process has a number of stages (de Neufville and Odoni 2003; Dempsey 2000; FAA 1985; Kazda and Caves 2000; Lane et al. 2001); they are outlined in Box 8.1. Each stage ends with a 'gate' at which the project solution is considered by the stakeholders and approval is given to proceed to the next stage (Lane et al. 2001). Hence the traditional master planning process is a strictly linear and staged process.

In this chapter we refer to a traditional master planning process (Box 8.1) as a process that is based on the FAA guidelines. The master planning process based on the ICAO guidelines (ICAO 1987) is slightly different, but in essence it contains the same elements as the FAA model. The main elements can be found in airport master plans throughout the world. Table 8.1 shows three master plan examples. Although they differ slightly in structure, the typical master planning format can be clearly recognized in each of them.

Traditional airport master planning and the rational model

The traditional master planning style shows a remarkable resemblance to the rational model of strategic planning. Various authors have pointed out the parallels between the traditional master planning/FAA model and the rational model (see Dempsey et al. 1997; Dempsey 2000; Goetz and Szyliowicz 1997; Freathy and O'Connell 1999; De Neufville and Odoni 2003, for example). As we saw earlier, the rational planning

Table 8.1 Summarized tables of content of three airport master plans

Future Spatial Planning Vision 2020, Amsterdam Airport Schiphol (2004)	Sydney Airport, Preliminary Draft Master Plan (2003)	Chicago O'Hare International Airport Master Plan (2003)
1. Introduction: Mandates, mission, values, constraints, goals 2. Strategic issues 3. Air transport developments 4. Traffic forecasts 5. Runways and taxiways 6. Passenger facilities 7. Cargo facilities 8. Maintenance facilities 9. Landside access 10. Land use outside airport boundary (Airport City) 11. Environmental impact 12. Implementation plan and capital implementation costs 13. Plan currency	1. Introduction: Vision, purpose, assumptions, objectives 2. Background: Sydney's airports 3. Regulatory framework 4. Economic, social and strategic significance 5. Regional development 6. Aviation activity forecasts 7. Airfield-indicative development concept 8. Terminal and passenger systems-development concept 9. Freight-development concept 10. Aviation support facilities-development concept 11. Landside access-development concept 12. Commercial development-development concept 13. Land use zoning plan 14. Airspace protection 15. Utilities 16. Sydney airport environment management 17. Community values 18. Implementation and review	1. Introduction and background 2. Inventory a. Airport setting b. Historical background c. Airspace and air traffic control facilities d. Terminal facilities e. Support/ancillary facilities f. Ground access g. On-airport passenger movements h. Other facilities i. Airport environs and land-use 3. Aviation activity forecasts 4. Demand/capacity analysis and facility requirements a. Airfield demand/capacity and facility requirements b. Passenger terminal area facility requirements c. Support/ancillary facility requirements d. Ground access facility requirements 5. Alternatives a. Airfield alternatives analysis b. Terminal facilities alternatives analysis c. Support/ancillary facilities alternatives analysis d. Ground access facilities alternatives analysis e. On-airport passenger movements 6. Preferred development plan a. Airfield plan b. Terminal plan c. Ground access d. On-airport passenger movements e. Other facilities f. Land acquisition g. Additional capabilities 7. Implementation plan a. Phasing plan b. Implementation schedule c. Capital development program costs d. Financial feasibility 8. Airport layout plan

Source: Chicago O'Hare International Airport (2003), Schiphol Group (2003c), Sydney Airport Corporation Limited (2003)

model has received severe criticism. Given the characteristics of the rational model and current market uncertainties, the traditional airport master planning has a number of serious drawbacks.

There is no best plan The informational and analytical requirements of the traditional master planning model are unrealistic. The rational model involves a 'step-by-step planned search for optimal solutions to definable problems' (Genus 1995, 11). The rational model of strategic planning is built on the congruence or fit between internal and external organizational factors (Mintzberg 1994, 36) and aims to maximize utility. Uncertainties are thought to be resolved by data analysis or are implicitly ignored (Ruefli and Sarrazin 1981). Analysis provides synthesis (Mintzberg 1994).

In the same way, traditional master planning is a strictly linear, step-by-step process that seeks to match facilities at the airport with projected aviation demand by means of a rational choice for the optimal alternative.

However, these informational and analytical requirements are unrealistic, as we discussed earlier. Market conditions change quickly (volatility), future demand is uncertain, decision-making and planning are not fully rational ('bounded rationality') activities, the planning process exhibits certain 'muddling through' characteristics, and data may be incomplete or unreliable. Hence airport planning is a 'satisficing' exercise rather than an optimizing one. There is no such thing as a single 'best' and final plan (de Neufville 2000). An additional problem of a final, blue-print style master plan is that it may create resistance in the organization to a commitment to change when it is needed. Given the uncertainties and risks, the building of a commitment to deal with change is required.

The future is uncertain and cannot be known Much emphasis is placed on air-traffic forecasting in the traditional master planning model. Airport capacity requirements are based on single point demand forecasts. In other words, they are based on expectations about a specific future. 'Estimates of the timing of certain threshold events are the basis for effective planning. In airport planning, these events correspond to levels of aviation demand which exceed existing or planned capacities at the airport' (FAA 1985, 21).

The performance of air-traffic demand forecasting has been poor (de Neufville and Odoni 2003; Dempsey et al. 1997), is likely to get poorer in volatile, deregulated markets (de Neufville and Barber 1991), and can be criticized in many respects (de Neufville 1991a). One of the major criticisms is that the forecast is invariably wrong as a result of the highly volatile market environment. The future cannot be known, let alone mastered.

Traditional airport master planning does acknowledge the existence of market uncertainties, which may have serious effects on the reliability of forecasting (de Neufville 1991a). However, the prevailing argument is that the anticipated air traffic will occur in any case, given general economic growth and the scarcity of airport capacity. Traditional airport master planning is supply-driven rather than demand-driven. As a result of this 'build it and hope they'll come' (Meyer 1993) or 'concrete will fly' vision, the postponement of investments is the only flexibility that is thought to be needed in airport master planning. It is the case, however, that demand may grow much faster than predicted, may not grow at all, or may occur in an entirely different composition with different airport facility requirements (de Neufville 1991a).

The FAA recognized that the single point forecasts may be wrong owing to market uncertainties. These may lead to significant 'forecast error costs' (FAA 1985). In the report 'Forecasting Aviation Activity by Airport', the FAA (2001) suggests – in three paragraphs – a way to deal with uncertainty and forecast errors. An alternative to the single point forecasts is the use of scenario forecasts with a 'most likely', 'highly likely' and 'low likelihood' forecast. But even then, single future assumptions are generally being made on airfares, fuel prices and load factors. Moreover, in many cases the alternative scenarios are 'window dressing': although alternative forecasts are presented in the master plan, the baseline/'most likely' forecast is used to determine the airport facility requirements. Finally, the FAA does not call for flexibility in the master plans to deal with the potential range of possible future outcomes other than an appropriate timing of the investments. Traditional airport master planning is inflexible. The ICAO guidelines (ICAO 1987) are less traditional in this respect. The ICAO calls for the development of different traffic scenarios as well as sensitivity analyses of the parameters used in the traffic forecasts.

In short, traditional airport master planning is based on a single expectation about a specific future. And since that expectation is nearly always incorrect, so is the master plan that is based on it. In essence, traditional airport master planning is reactive (reacting to unanticipated change) or at best adaptive: master planning offers a 'once-and-for-all' solution for expected change.

Airport planning is not a top-down, inside-out process The rational planning model assumes the existence of a powerful, unitary actor (Goetz and Szyliowicz 1997). Decision-making power is centralized in top-management, and top-management works with specifiable long-range goals. Only in a few circumstances, such as the centralized, authoritarian bureaucracy (the 'machine organization'), do these assumptions hold (Bryson 1995, 11; Mintzberg 1994). In other organizations the powerful, unitary actor that can influence or know its environment is rarely present.

First, airport planning takes place in a context with a multiplicity of external stakeholders, most notably the airlines, regional authorities and the local community. These stakeholders can have considerable negotiating power (Dempsey et al. 1997; Ruefli and Sarrazin 1981) and quite different agendas, values and goals. The participation of these actors during the process (and not just at the start) may be necessary for successful planning (Dempsey et al. 1997; Kreukels 1978). Hence the planning process should not only be inside-out, but also outside-in.

Second, Mintzberg (1994) and Simpson (1998) showed that bottom-up processes are essential for successful planning and strategy formation. Airport line managers have access to 'soft' information: they are the first to detect new market developments, opportunities and threats, whereas corporate management can easily become disconnected from reality while relying on 'hard' data.

Finally, airport management may have vague or non-specified strategies, goals and objectives at the beginning and during the planning process (Genus 1995). Strategies are created not only by the master planning process (Mintzberg 1994), but also in an ongoing top-down and bottom-up process of the research, intelligence, brainstorming and creativity of individuals. Commitment building to such goals and objectives may be needed in various layers of the organization for effective strategy formation.

The failure of the traditional airport planning model was most convincingly demonstrated in the study by Dempsey and colleagues of Denver International Airport and smaller case studies by Dempsey (2000). Another (non-air) transport example is the research by Flyvbjerg and colleagues (Bruzelius et al. 2002; Flyvbjerg et al. 2003) of the Channel Tunnel, the Great Belt rail and road link between Denmark and continental Europe, and the Øresund link between Sweden and Denmark. General (empirical) studies of the failure of the rational planning model in uncertain environments include the work of Rycroft and Szyliowicz (1980) and Mintzberg (1994).

In short, the traditional airport master planning model can be characterized as a rational model of strategic planning. The traditional model shares with the rational model several serious drawbacks and inaccurate assumptions that make it far from ideal for airport planning in an uncertain market environment. Various studies have indicated the failure of the traditional (airport) planning model and the rational model in general terms.

A threefold dilemma for airport master planning

The characteristics of the model of traditional airport master planning, volatility of airport traffic volumes and the associated uncertainty with respect to future traffic volumes and composition result in a threefold dilemma for airport master planning.

Volatility and airport traffic forecasts

If the volatility of airport traffic demand increases, the ability to forecast for airport planning may become weaker (de Neufville and Barber 1991). Various studies have addressed the growing gap between (airport) traffic forecasts and actual traffic developments. Errors in forecasts are normal owing to the well-described problems, including poor data (DeWulf 1991; Flyvbjerg et al. 2003; Hogarth and Makridakis 1981), major weaknesses in econometric forecasting models, inaccurate assumptions (de Neufville 1991a, 1992), biased forecasting consultants (Flyvbjerg et al. 2003) and the inability to forecast discontinuities (DeWulf 1991; Mintzberg 1994; Prud'homme 2004, for example). In general, the discrepancies between forecasts in airport master plans and actual traffic volumes increase as the horizon of the forecast becomes more distant. Maldonado (in: de Neufville 1992; de Neufville and Odoni 2003, 78) found average errors of 23 per cent, 41 per cent and 78 per cent respectively for five, ten and fifteen year airport traffic volume forecasts.

However, in a free-market regime the reliability of traffic forecasts is even further reduced (de Neufville 1991a; de Neufville and Barber 1991; de Neufville and Odoni 2003; Dempsey et al. 1997; Graham 1999). The free-market regime broadens the unconstrained field of action for airlines to configure their network. As discussed earlier, airlines can and do make sudden changes in their network configuration. Not surprisingly, De Neufville (1991a, 8) reported that 'no single forecast can be trusted as "right"'. In their book about mega-project planning Flyvbjerg and colleagues (2003, 31) advised decision-makers to 'take with a grain of salt any traffic forecast that does not explicitly take into account the risk of being very wrong'. Finally, Dempsey (2000, 211) stated that 'forecasting is more an art than a science, and as an art form, more impressionism or surrealism than realism.'

Volatility, uncertainty and risk

If future airport traffic volumes do indeed become more difficult to forecast, what will be the risks associated with an approach to airport planning that does not take full account of the uncertainties with respect to future traffic volumes?[3]

In general, the projects included in the airport master plans will be based on shakier assumptions and will therefore become more risky (de Neufville and Barber 1991). In specific terms, airports that do not fully acknowledge the volatility and uncertainty of airport traffic are more likely to face some serious risks:

- Capacity shortages. Capacity shortages can result in short-term congestion costs for an airport (Doganis 1992). Unexpected demand can result in inconvenience for passengers as well as a rush to construct (Karlsson 2003, 3). This rush increases the chance of planning errors, premium construction costs and negative media coverage. Moreover, capacity shortages can imply missed growth opportunities. Capacity shortages are often associated with low-cost carriers starting a new service at a small airport, and with airlines building new hubs or airports in dense metropolitan areas with little expansion opportunities. Examples include Baltimore-Washington International Airport (Southwest), London Heathrow (British Airways) and Frankfurt (Lufthansa).
- Overcapacity. Investments that are made too soon create overcapacity. Because airports require by nature large indivisible investments such as runways, the risk that decisions will lead to serious overcapacity increases (Porter 1980, 328–39). Overcapacity involves higher short- and medium-term unit costs (Doganis 1992). This higher cost comes not only from higher depreciation and other capital costs, but also from higher operating costs (heating, lighting,

3 It is important to note that there are many more uncertainties and risks associated with investments in airport infrastructure, such as technological risks, legal and regulatory risks, interest rate risks (Clarke and Varma 1999). Given the scope of this study, we have concentrated on the uncertainties and risks associated with airline network behaviour, airport traffic demand and the composition of airport traffic demand.

maintenance, labour, and so forth). Overcapacity is often related to newly-constructed airports, major expansions of airport infrastructures or the failure of a home-based carrier.

- Losses. Developments on too grand a scale (compared with demand) can lead to heavy financial losses if the higher unit costs are not compensated by larger revenues. Moreover, the development of underused facilities may result in the loss of resources (land, finances) which could have been used for other, more profitable investments.
- Competitive loss. Since hub airports compete for transfer traffic and to a certain extent for origin–destination markets in a multi-airport region, investments in infrastructure may result in revenues that are lower than expected, because competitors also invest and take their share of the (transfer) market.
- Mismatch between the investment of infrastructure facilities and services versus the actual development of traffic composition and airline-user requirements. Such a mismatch may result in unnecessarily high unit costs per passenger, considerable reconstruction costs of airport facilities, loss of passenger/airline demand or missed revenues. For example, intercontinental traffic results in higher unit costs per passenger since more space is required for customs, immigration and health (Doganis 1992). At the same time, intercontinental traffic generates more revenues through the higher revenues from shopping and higher aeronautical charges. Building an intercontinental terminal while, unexpectedly, continental traffic grows at the expense of intercontinental traffic may result in much higher unit costs and revenues that are lower than those forecast (de Neufville and Odoni 2003).
- Lack of public support. Large airport investments which do not meet expectations in terms of revenues, traffic volumes and costs can easily weaken public support, in particular when the investments are financed by the public sector and environmental problems are at stake. According to Flyvbjerg and colleagues (2003, 4): 'The success of these projects is so important [...] that [...] even governments can collapse when they fail.'

All EU commercial airports are subject to the uncertainties and risks of the free-market regime. However, not every airport or every new investment in airport infrastructure will face these risks to the same extent (Karlsson 2003). The importance of dealing with these risks in various airport investment projects depends on both the probability of certain events that drive the future development of (segments) of airport traffic as well as the impact of these events on airport operations.

In practice, some airports – those for which the probabilities are extremely difficult to determine – face particularly high levels of uncertainty and risk. These vulnerable airports include newly-constructed airports, existing commercial airports with low levels of airline activity and closed military bases which are being converted to commercial airports. Such airports have little advance knowledge of the characteristics of future demand or when demand will materialize.

A threefold dilemma for airport master planning

The growing uncertainties and risks in the context of airport planning bring us to a threefold dilemma for airport master planning.

- Traditional airport planning is based on (detailed) estimates of future traffic demand to determine facility requirements. The style of traditional airport master planning was developed in the regime of *quid-pro-quo* bilateralism. However, traffic demand may be increasingly difficult to forecast and may frequently show discontinuous changes in the current free-market regimes.
- Such an uncertain market environment demands flexibility in planning. However, the traditional airport master planning process is inflexible. As a result, it is not capable of dealing with the reality of uncertainty.
- Airport master planning as a formal procedure is nevertheless essential for the successful development of an airport:
    - The airport infrastructure is the platform for creating the future growth of the airport (Smit 2003). The quality and quantity of the infrastructure is its most important strategic asset. Investments in the airport need to be coordinated to benefit from growth opportunities. The greater the resources needed for investments in airport infrastructure, the more carefully must these resources be controlled in advance (Mintzberg 1994). These resources can be financial, but also environmental (air quality, a safe and liveable environment, and so forth) and spatial (land).
    - Airports are characterized by activities with tightly-coupled operations. Many airport operations are highly structured and depend on each other (in aircraft handling, passenger and baggage handling, for example) for safety, economic and environmental reasons. Planning is needed to guarantee the coupling of the operations.
    - Airport master plans function as communication and control devices, both internally and externally. Internally, master plans can help create an awareness of and commitment to the strategy followed by the airport. Moreover, the vocabulary may enhance communication between different departments of the airport. Good communication is particularly important at larger airports with thousands of employees.
    - Externally, there may also be a need for master planning. Airport investments may be funded with public money. Furthermore, airports have large impacts on the surrounding community, both negative (noise, air quality, safety) and positive (economic effects). Airport master plans can be used to evaluate airport development from a public perspective or may even be used by governments to control airport development.

How can this threefold dilemma be solved? A more flexible and pro-active planning style is required. Let us therefore turn to the planning style of Flexible Strategic Planning.

Flexible Strategic Planning

Introduction

Airport planning needs flexibility to deal with the volatile market environment and associated uncertainty of future traffic demand and composition. De Neufville (de Neufville 1991b; de Neufville and Barber 1991; de Neufville and Odoni 2003), Dempsey et al. (1997) and Freathy and O'Connell (1999) put forward a flexible and dynamic approach to strategic planning that deals explicitly with uncertainty and risk in (airport) planning. Richard de Neufville of the Massachusetts Institute of Technology can certainly be considered to be one of the leading advocates of flexibility tailored to airport planning and design. We call such a planning style Flexible Strategic Planning (FSP). Flexible Strategic Planning identifies, re-anticipates and provokes changes in the environment.

The Flexible Strategic Planning style emerged in corporate planning during the 1990s as a branch of strategic management. Although its theoretical roots can be traced back to the late 1950s and the 1960s, it started to gain momentum in the 1980s. Because of the changing economy, planners paid increasing attention to uncertainty in strategic planning (see Michael 1979; Weber 1984; Ruefli and Sarrazin 1981; Amara 1979, for example).

In our view, FSP can be seen as an 'alternative paradigm of rational analysis' as Rosenhead described it (in Parsons 1995, 426–7) (see Table 8.2). The alternative paradigm *accepts* that present society and its future cannot be known (Gunsteren and Ruyven 1993). That paradigm takes the uncertainty and complexity in the real world as a starting point and adapts the rational model to these real-world circumstances.

This alternative paradigm can also be found in other disciplines under different names, such as dynamic strategic planning and robust planning in systems analysis and operations research (de Neufville 2000, 2001; Landeghem and Vanmaele 2002; Neely and de Neufville 2001; Paraskevopoulos et al. 1991; Parsons 1995), market place planning in aviation system planning (Caves and Gosling 1999) and flexible strategic management in management studies (Genus 1995).

Table 8.2 The alternative paradigm of rational analysis

Rational model	Alternative paradigm of the rational model
Optimizing	Non-optimizing. 'Satisficing'
Overwhelming data demands	Reduced data demands. Hard and soft data
Assumption of a single decision-maker with abstract objectives from which concrete actions can be deduced for implementation though a hierarchical chain of command	Facilitates planning from the bottom up
People are treated as passive objects	People are seen as active subjects
Implicitly ignores or attempts to abolish uncertainty	Accepts and deals with uncertainty

Source: Adapted from Parsons (1995, 426)

In this section, we elaborate the framework of Flexible Strategic Planning. Given the limited scope of this research we have concentrated on the aspect of uncertainty in airport planning. The alternative paradigm of the rational model has a much broader scope than the way in which uncertainty is dealt with. Future research may wish to deal with these other aspects. First, we ask, 'what is flexibility?' We then ask, 'what are the characteristics of Flexible Strategic Planning?'

Flexibility

What do we mean by flexibility? Flexibility is not a concept that is easy to define and so many definitions and dimensions of flexibility exist. In everyday language, flexibility is the ability to bend, or the ability to adapt. Genus (1995) and Goetz and Szyliowicz (1997) offer a list of concepts that are closely associated with the notion of flexibility:

- adaptability: the ability to make a singular and permanent adjustment to a new environment;
- re-adaptability: the ability to make continuous adjustments to a new environment;
- corrigibility and reversibility: errors associated with strategic decisions that can be remedied or completely undone to allow a new course of action;
- strategic renewal: organizations continuously improve their strategy to changing conditions;
- hedging: protecting or insuring against risk;
- robustness: the degree to which facilities are able to function efficiently in a new environment;
- resiliency: the ability of an organization to continue to function after unexpected events.

Although useful in giving a first impression of flexibility, the above list still does not give us a precise definition. Godet and Roubelat (1996), from the school of the French futurist philosopher Gaston Berger, and Russell Ackoff (1974, 22–31) offer a useful perspective for the definition of flexibility and relate it to different airport planning styles. Four different attitudes or 'postures' (Ackoff 1974, 27) of humans and organizations to deal with future change can be distinguished:

- Passive/inactive: do nothing. Inactivist planning reflects satisfaction with the way things are going. It only reacts to serious threats by means of crisis-management.
- Reactive: react to unanticipated change. Reactivists prefer the previous state to the one in which they are situated. Reactive planning seeks to undo changes that come across the organization. It is a remedial type of planning: 'muddling-through'. Judgement, common sense and intuition based on experience are more important in decision-making than analysis and experimentation.

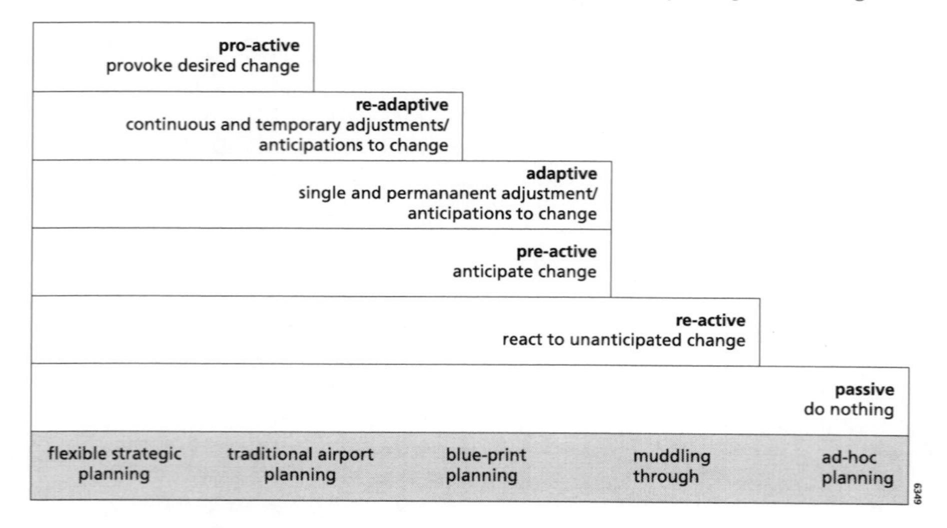

Figure 8.2 Attitudes to change

- Pre-active: anticipate change. Pre-activists try to predict and prepare *for* the future. Pre-active planning and decision-making is based on logic, science and experimentation rather than experience, common sense and intuition.
  According to Genus (1995) anticipation and adjustment can be:
  - adaptive: single and permanent anticipation and adjustment to change
  - re-adaptive: continuous anticipation and adjustment to change (flexibility).
- Pro-active/interactive: provoke desired change. Pro-activists do not plan for the future, but rather they plan the future. Pro-active planning seeks self-development, self-realization and self-control. Pro-activists consider experimentation as the best way of learning and pursuing desired goals.

We define flexibility here as the 'ability to make continuous adjustments in constantly changing conditions' (Dempsey et al. 1997, 475). In other words, flexibility is the same as re-adaptability. To be able to adjust to changing conditions, airport planning has to continuously anticipate and adjust to change.

The other concepts related to flexibility we listed earlier (corrigibility, reversibility, strategic renewal, hedging, robustness, resiliency) can only be categorized as flexible concepts when they are used in a re-adaptable fashion. We return to the characteristics of flexibility in the next section.

Based on the positioning of flexibility *vis-à-vis* other ways of reacting to future change, we can position FSP *vis-à-vis* other airport planning styles in a cumulative way (Figure 8.2). By cumulative we mean that FSP is not an entirely different approach to airport planning. FSP still remains to a considerable extent a rational model, but adds elements of flexibility and pro-activity to traditional airport planning styles. This notion about the cumulative and compatible character of FSP is not unique.

FSP can be considered to be part of the 'alternative paradigm of rational analysis'. This alternative paradigm does not discard the rational model completely, but rather it adapts the rational model to real world circumstances (Parsons 1995). De Neufville and Odoni (2003, 91) addressed the same issue with regard to airport planning: 'it [dynamic strategic planning] is entirely compatible with and builds on traditional airport master planning and with strategic planning in management.' Dempsey and colleagues come to the same conclusion: 'we do not advocate that the analytic (rational) approach be completely abandoned; rather it must be improved and made more realistic in terms of how planning actually occurs.'

Traditional airport master planning can be described as an adaptive and reactive planning style. On the one hand it implicitly ignores uncertainty and reacts to unforeseen and unanticipated new market environments (re-activity). On the other hand traditional master planning offers one solution for one specific expectation of the future based on the most-likely forecasting of traffic demand (adaptivity).

At the other end of the cumulative hierarchy we find Flexible Strategic Planning. FSP still carries some of the characteristics of traditional airport master planning. Some airport facilities that are characterized by internal and external forces with low uncertainty levels can be very well planned in a more traditional, rational way. Here, point-specific forecasts are reliable and traditional planning processes sufficient, although future outcomes will never be 100 per cent predictable (Courtney 2001). However, FSP adds two new dimensions to airport planning: pro-activity and flexibility. In the next section we give an account of the characteristics of pro-activity and flexibility.

Finally, it is important to keep in mind that flexibility can be ex ante or ex post (Genus 1995). Ex ante flexibility refers to actions taken now which allow the organization to be flexible in the future. Ex ante flexibility has to do with anticipation. Reserving land at an airport for future use is an example of ex ante flexibility. Ex post flexibility refers to actions that are adjustments to change now, which are possible because of decisions taken in the past. Deciding to develop a low-cost concourse on 'banked' land after experiencing an unexpected growth of low-cost traffic is an example of ex post flexibility. In that same facility, one could build in ex ante flexibility by creating the option to expand it in the future. Let us now turn to the characteristics of Flexible Strategic Planning.

The characteristics of Flexible Strategic Planning

Introduction

What are the additional elements of a flexible strategic approach in airport planning compared with traditional airport master planning? On the basis of an extensive survey of literature on planning theory, systems analysis, management studies and business economics a number of characteristics of flexibility and pro-activity in planning can be distinguished.

These characteristics are:

- real options
- multi-future robustness and backcasting
- contingency planning
- scanning and experimenting
- proactivity
- diversification
- flexible organizations.

Real options

One of the most important elements of FSP is the creation of real options. Whereas traditional airport master planning makes a single, once-and-for-all commitment to an expected future, FSP makes a much more flexible commitment to deal with an uncertain and risky future (Courtney 2001). FSP minimizes irreversible commitments and opts for the possibility of delaying, postponing, changing, staging or abandoning investments in airport infrastructure. Such flexible commitments are known as real options.

An option is 'the right, but not the obligation to take action some time in the future, usually for a predetermined price and a given period' (de Neufville 2001, 7). Options are rooted in financial analysis. Here, options can be either call options (buying into a good situation) or put options (insurance to get out of a bad situation). Call options increase in value with favourable movements in the underlying asset price. Put options pay dividends when the asset drops in value. Hence, call options maintain access to higher payoffs whereas put options protect against downside losses.

A real option is in fact a financial option translated into planning and design. A real option is an option that is related to the physical part of a certain design (de Neufville 2001). The payoff of the real option is the value of the investment. In contrast with traditional airport master planning, FSP is not passive or reactive to risk, but deals with it pro-actively; by creating real options, uncertainty can be dealt with and even exploited (de Neufville 2001). We can distinguish a number of real options in relation to airport master planning (Day 2003; de Neufville 2001; Goetz and Szyliowicz 1997; Nutt 1988):

Call-like options:

- Growth options: the option to invest in airport infrastructure such as investing in a new runway or cargo facility. This option can be used to temporize investments (de Neufville 2001, 16): this is the possibility to postpone or accelerate proposed investments. An airport can wait to invest until the market is more favourable and the investment is more valuable. For example, many EU airports postponed investments after September 11th to await more favourable circumstances. Another reason to wait is that time reduces uncertainty, so it may make sense to postpone an investment until more information is available and lower levels of uncertainty arrive (Courtney 2001). A special growth option is land banking, or land reservation: an airport acquires off-airport land for possible future growth.

- Another type of call-like option is the option to expand: the option has been exercised, but it is still possible to accelerate or broaden the investment in an airport facility.

Put-like options:

- Insurance: an option to divest in the airport infrastructure, that is, to scale or close down airport facilities. The option to divest is also known as insurance or reversibility.
- Option to delay: the option has been exercised, but there is still a possibility to delay or contract the investments in an airport facility. Amsterdam Airport Schiphol used the option of the delay for its fourth module of its new Terminal West. Although construction had already started, the project was temporarily halted after September 11th.
- A special type of option is the flexible design (de Neufville 2001; Greden and Glicksman 2004; Nutt 1988; Sanchez and Collins 2001). Such an option can be call-like, but also put-like. Greden and Glicksman (2004) distinguish two types of flexible design: the macro-level flexible design and operational flexibility.

  Macro-level flexible design is also known as modularity. An airport facility is modular if its architecture allows for the most desirable variation in its components (Sanchez and Collins 2001). These components may be functional components (physical features) or activity components (non-physical features such as service routines). In a modular design, the interfaces between the components are designed to allow for some variation in the components.

  When an airport facility is modular, the airport may or may not decide to upgrade, replace or remove certain components of its facilities. Examples include the option to add tube gates to a simple passenger terminal building in order to create a more convenient connection between an aircraft and the terminal building. Another example is the use of non-load-bearing walls, which make it easy to expand terminal infrastructure (Karlsson 2003). In essence, modularity loosens the tightly-coupled operations of the airport system and so allows easier mutations of that system.

  Operational flexibility refers to airport facilities that can handle different levels and types of traffic flows/functions without major mutations in the components of the facility. Operational flexibility is also known as the option of switch use (Real Options Group 2004).
- Modularity may also facilitate incrementalism. This is the option to invest in airport infrastructure in very small steps for the optimal match of traffic

demand and infrastructure supply. Such an option is of course closely related to growth options and options to expand.
- Many options with respect to the planning of airport facilities are referred to as compound or nested options. The airport development project is constituted of many, even an infinite number of different coexisting real options that build on each other. Most strategic investments in airport capacity are compound options: not only is a new terminal a valuable terminal by itself, it is also a condition for subsequent investment opportunities (additional piers, commercial development, for example).

Real options have to be analyzed carefully. In many cases, the creation of real options costs a considerable amount of money and there is no guarantee that they will generate good returns. Appropriate valuation of the options is therefore an indispensable part of their creation. Traditional net present value methods are less suitable for volatile markets since they do not fully incorporate uncertainty or the value of flexibility (Leslie and Michaels 1997).

Two important methods for the analysis of risky projects are of primary importance in the FSP model: decision analysis and real option analysis. These have well-described advantages over conventional methods for the valuation of projects such as net present value analysis (Day 2003; de Neufville 2001; Neely and de Neufville 2001; Smit 2003). The conventional methods do not incorporate uncertainty sufficiently well, or the possibility of expanding, delaying, abandoning or changing an investment (Day 2003; Leslie and Michaels 1997). Here, we only discuss briefly some of the general characteristics of real option and decision analysis. Numerous textbooks and articles are now available on this subject.

Decision analysis – in relation to operational research – 'is an organized way to analyze the complex combinations of possibilities and probabilities of occurrence' (de Neufville and Odoni 2003). Decision analysis intends to yield logical, systematic choices given a set of (1) development alternatives, (2) potential outcomes, (3) the probabilities of potential outcomes, and (4) the objectives and risk attitude of the organization (Bresina et al. 2002; Courtney 2001; Parsons 1995). Simple decision analysis is frequently visualized by using decision tree structures (de Neufville and Odoni 2003).

Real option analysis on the other hand consists of a set of procedures for calculating the value of a real option compared with its costs, given the volatility of the underlying asset of the option (Courtney 2001; Day 2003; de Neufville 2001; Karlsson 2003). Real option techniques provide a dynamic framework for analyzing strategic capital investments by enabling investments to be treated as opportunities rather than now-or-never type investment decisions. In essence, real option analysis considers the value of flexibility or, in other words, of keeping options open.[4]

4 Real option analysis is rooted in the financial option valuation model developed by Myron Scholes and Fischer Black (Black and Scholes 1973). The model was later adapted by

Since real option analysis is complex and requires a vast amount of data, which may not always be available, more qualitative procedures ('real options thinking') have been proposed (Courtney 2001; de Neufville 2001; Leslie and Michaels 1997; Real Options Group 2004). In short, real options thinking does away with the one-time decisions for multi-year investments and the minimization of uncertainty. Instead, real-options thinking stresses the fact that options allow for changing course as market conditions change and more information becomes available. Owing to the nature of a real option (maintaining access to high payoffs while constraining downside losses), real-options thinking seeks gains from uncertainty rather than reducing uncertainty.

Multi-future robustness and backcasting

Real options make it possible to postpone, change, accelerate, expand or abandon investments in airport infrastructure according to market conditions. Real options are an alternative to 'big bet' investments and blue-print/deterministic plans. A 'big bet' investment can be dangerous in volatile markets because it is single-future robust. 'Big bet' investments deal with only one expected future, or can only deal with alternative futures at very high costs.

Real options allow the planning process to be phased in relation to air-traffic demand. Real options make it possible to create a multi-future robust plan. Multi-future robustness refers to an airport master plan as a guideline that would best cope with the widest range of probable scenarios (Caves and Gosling 1999). Or in other words, a multi-future robustness approach yields plans 'that remain valid for a longer time period' (Landeghem and Vanmaele 2002, 773), even in volatile markets.

Hence, the flexible strategic master planning process is quite different from the traditional airport master planning process. Let us consider this process.

Multi-future robustness starts with planning backwards from a long-term or ultimate critical future state toward clearly-defined commitments in the short term (Ruefli and Sarrazin 1981). Such a planning process is also called backcasting or normative forecasting. Note that the traditional airport master planning plans forward from the present conditions using detailed traffic demand forecasts (see also Figure 8.4).

The long-term or ultimate critical future state is a set of broad, long-term strategic goals driven analytically and creatively by:

- the general expectations about the development of the market. These expectations consist of the traffic demand in different scenarios as well as the major components of traffic demand. This is not a detailed, single point-specific forecast as in traditional airport master planning, since the forecast is invariably wrong. The expected long-term traffic growth under different

---

Robert Merton. Scholes and Merton won the Nobel Prize for their work on options in 1997 (Leslie and Michaels 1997).

scenarios is used as a guideline for development and as a tool to facilitate the understanding of the level of risk (DeWulf and van der Schaaf 1998; Heracleous 1998). Tools such as scenario planning (DeWulf and van der Schaaf 1998; Doorn and Vught 1978), Delphi techniques (Doorn and Vught 1978), brainstorming and mind-mapping (Parsons 1995) may be used. Expected long-term traffic demand can be tied to a particular year or period (the planning horizon) or can depend on the maximum, ultimate development of the airport

- the associated opportunities and threats, given:
  - the vision, mission, strengths, weaknesses, objectives, resources and mandate of the airport
  - the agendas of important stakeholders (airlines, air traffic control, the community, and so forth)
  - the airport's appetite for risk (risk averse or risk seeking)
  - the creativity of the people involved in the planning process.

The resulting long-term or ultimate strategic goals can be translated into planning activity levels or PALs (Houston Airport System 2004). Planning activity levels correspond to a certain traffic demand and components of the demand in different scenarios (peak-hour demand, for example). The PALs can be used to determine the airport facility requirements (runway capacity, the capacity of passenger buildings, and so forth) in different scenarios following well-described procedures (Ashford et al. 1997; FAA 1983; Odoni and de Neufville 1992; Wells and Young 2004, for example).

Sensitivity analysis is needed to test the many assumptions used in determining the facility requirements, such as the assumptions on aircraft mix, load factor, acceptable level of delay and required level-of-service (LOS),[5] and so on.

The airport facility requirements are then worked out for several different alternative developments for the airport. Such a development alternative is in fact a portfolio of real options in a context of changing market conditions (Smit 2003). Since the number of alternatives is infinite, designers and planners normally base their search strategy on heuristics. These are ways of reducing a search in order to economize on time and resources. They normally lead to a 'satisficing' rather than an optimizing alternative (Frenken 2001). A first qualitative screening results in a short-list of development alternatives.

Decision analysis, real option analysis, multi-criteria analysis, game theory and other evaluation techniques can then be used to test the performance of each short-listed alternative under different scenarios (de Neufville 2000; Smit 2003, for example). The best long-term alternative is that which performs best over the range of future scenarios, but may very well not be the optimal alternative in any single

5 With regard to passenger terminal buildings, for example, the level-of-service refers to the amount of space available per passenger. IATA defines six level-of-service standards ranging from A (excellent) to F (unacceptable).

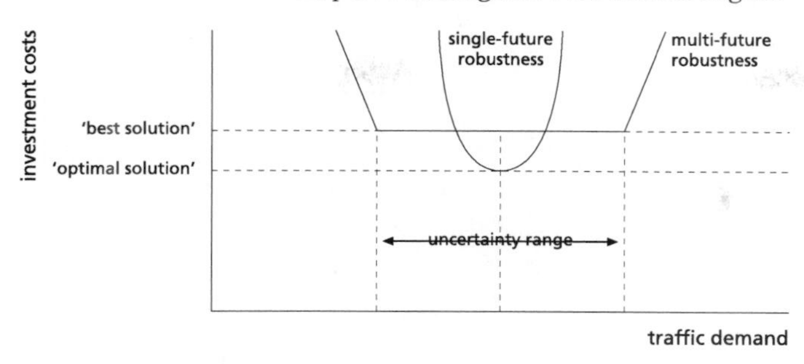

Figure 8.3 Multi-future versus single-future robustness

traffic demand scenario. In other words, the best long-term alternative is robust for a wide range of probable scenarios (Landeghem and Vanmaele 2002). The Dutch airport consultancy firm NACO, for example, uses a multi-criteria methodology to evaluate long-term alternatives. Weighted criteria include the financial implications of each alternative, the level of flexibility of each alternative, environmental impact, and so forth.

In essence, FSP searches for the alternative with the highest 'common factor' in a set of alternatives. Figure 8.3 shows that a multi-future robust alternative may not be the optimal alternative in any single scenario of traffic demand and traffic composition. However, it performs best over a range of probable scenarios in contrast with single-future robust alternative.

However, the long-term alternative that is eventually preferred may differ from the best, robust alternative. Airport planning normally takes place in a context of many stakeholders with different agendas. The negotiation process between those stakeholders will be important in the choice of a preferred alternative. In contrast with traditional airport master planning, FSP acknowledges that there is no unitary, powerful actor who can dictate the planning process. The preferred alternative is likely not to be the best solution, but the most 'satisficing' solution (Simon 1957) for the stakeholders involved. The shareholder value may differ from the societal value (Smit 2003). We refer to the work of Altschuler and Luberhoff (2003), Flyvbjerg and colleagues (2003) and Dempsey, Goetz and Szyliowicz (Dempsey et al. 1997) for a discussion on the role of politics in the planning and development of large infrastructure projects.

Next, the long-term, preferred alternative is decomposed into a number of phases or trajectories (McLoughlin 1979, 231). A trajectory charts the course of action for acquiring and exercising real options.

The master planning process then focuses on the first phase of the preferred alternative (Nutt 1988). A more detailed airport development plan or site plan is worked out for this first phase. In so doing, the first phase development keeps open the widest possible range of probable futures, since the long-term preferred alternative is multi-future robust (Figure 8.4). Hence, FSP draws a clear distinction between the broad, long-term master plan and the more detailed, medium-term development plans.

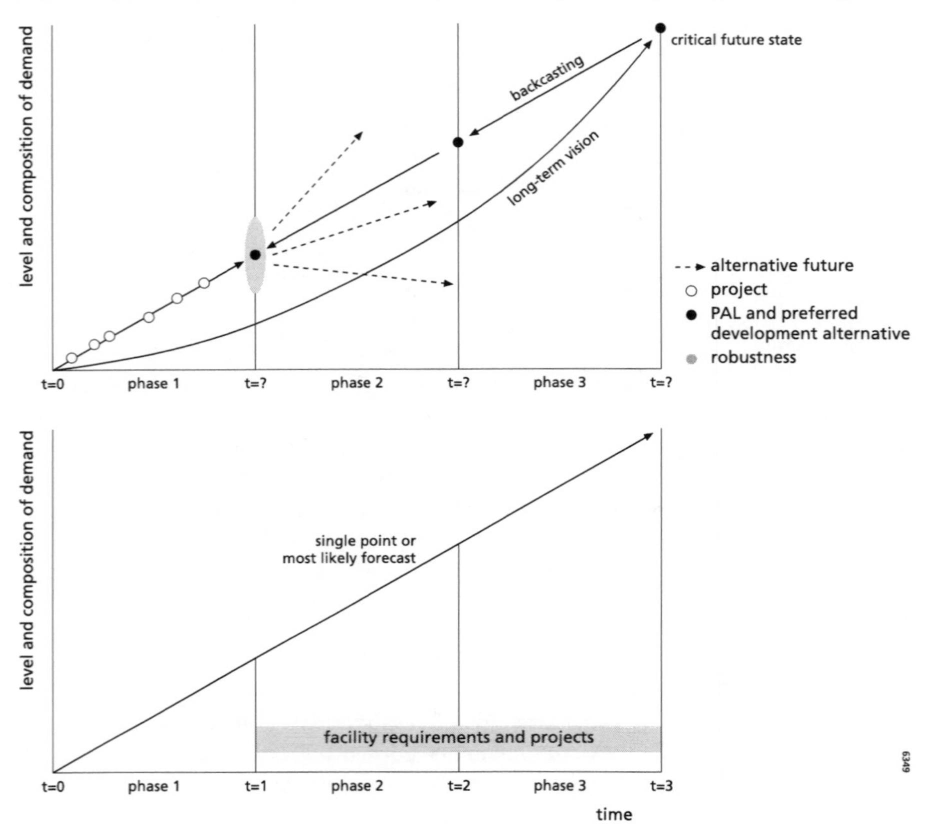

Figure 8.4 Backcasting versus forecasting

Commitments are only made to first phase developments, and not to developments in later phases. Since FSP considers the master plan as a portfolio of real options, proposed developments for later phases can be changed as conditions change and new information becomes available. Other trajectories are still possible (Figure 8.4). In general, it will be necessary to work out the next phase and update the master plan at the end of each phase. But, even during a phase, there may be a need to alter the objectives and planned developments if market conditions change.

Consequently, the phases and specific investments in a specific phase are not tied to a specific year (as in traditional master planning), but are tied to traffic demand and the composition of demand. FSP is demand driven. Commitments are made just-in-time: no earlier than necessary and as late as possible. FSP replaces the 'build-it-and-they'll-come' principle of traditional master planning with the 'build-it-as-if-it-is-likely-they'll-come' approach. In short, the master plan creates an indeterminate airport architecture (Nutt 1988) by incorporating flexibility through real options and a phased process.

The detailed first-phase development plan has to be assessed on its level of robustness under more detailed, traffic demand scenarios. The timing and sequencing of individual projects can be assessed by using the real-option analysis or decision-analysis techniques (Courtney 2001; Day 2003; de Neufville 2001).

Contingent road maps can also help airports decide on the sequencing and timing of investments. A contingent road map specifies the actions to be taken when important contingencies (scenarios) arise (Courtney 2001). The road map identifies the important key value drivers for each contingency and the associated triggers or thresholds that indicate when new projects have to be started. Such thresholds or triggers depend on the planning activity levels of the proposed developments the growth rate of the key value drivers, the maximum acceptable level of delay, and the lead time[6] of the proposed project. The triggers and thresholds help establish the just-in-time delivery of the projects (Lepardo and Lane 2002). Contingent road maps need to be updated continuously with new market information to be realistic and effective. The whole process must be continuously monitored and regularly updated so as to take into account the changing market conditions.

In short, by backcasting and creating multi-future robustness, FSP combines long-term strategic direction with short-term, more detailed objectives and commitments that allow the course of action to be changed in later phases, or even during phases, when conditions change. Hence flexible airport planning can be considered to be hybrid planning. FSP includes a fairly formalized programme for the first phase of airport development. For later phases, the airport master plan is nothing more than a state-of-the-art vision: the plan involves the documentation of a strategic-thinking exercise that serves as an input for the first phase plan, but is unlikely to be realized.

Contingency planning

Contingency planning can be useful in certain specific circumstances. Contingency planning develops alternative plans for alternative scenarios (Michael 1979; Mintzberg 1994). The organization is then prepared for whatever scenario may materialize. In real-option terms, contingency planning creates two or more coordinated portfolios of real options at the same time. In practice, scenario planning is only possible and practical when there is a limited number of scenarios covering the whole or a clearly defined range of possible futures. Otherwise, the contingencies that arise may not be the contingencies for which the planning is directed (Bresina et al. 2002; Mintzberg 1994).

The second problem associated with contingency planning concerns commitment and costs. It is difficult to create commitment in an organization for the planning for different scenarios knowing that most of these scenarios and associated contingency plans will never materialize (Mintzberg 1994). Moreover, the development of various detailed, fully worked out plans requires considerable resources in the organization in terms of personnel and costs. Nevertheless, if there is a discrete, well defined

6 The time required for a development to move from conception to completion.

alternative scenario with a high probability and high risk, the development of a contingency plan may be an option to consider.

Scanning and experimenting

As we saw earlier, flexibility means re-adaptability: the ability to make continuous adjustments to a continuously changing environment. Hence, FSP is not a single, once-a-year planning exercise, but a continuous endeavour. The quickly changing environment has therefore to be scanned continuously for new opportunities, threats and the associated risks. Such a continuous effort needs a well-developed 'radar network' to collect, communicate and synthesize market information (Clarke and Varma 1999; Courtney 2001; Davies and Petrie 2002; Porter 1980).

The information gathering is both focused and peripheral (Sanders 1998). For one thing, it has to be focused on the variables that really matter for the success of the strategy (Courtney 2001). Focus is also necessary because not everything can be scanned fully and rationally. These focus variables are the key value drivers; they are the main inputs for the different analytical tools used in a process such as decision and real option analysis, together with the general assessment of the environment. As De Neufville (2001, 15) puts it: 'it is necessary to commit to ongoing processes of information gathering to ensure that real options can be exploited at the correct time.'

On the other hand, information gathering that is only focused on the current key value drivers can miss early indicators of the key value drivers of tomorrow. A broader scanning process that seeks peripheral developments is needed. Sanders (1998, 74) calls such early indicators 'perking information': 'the changes that are already taking shape just below the surface, and which can only be seen with peripheral vision or well-developed foresight skills'. This perking information is the input for the identification of new market opportunities and threats, the design of new scenarios, investments in real options and the critical assessment of current strategies. Creativity and soft analysis play an important role in the gathering of perking information.

FSP complements the 'radar network' with learning options. Courtney (2001, 70–71) states that these 'provide a preferential position to invest in the future'. They include, for example, continuous experimentation in products, services and business systems. Learning options provide an airport with the latest information on specific opportunities and threats, potential new solutions and solutions without potential through the small-scale testing of certain development alternatives (Ackoff 1974; Lepardo and Lane 2002).

Proactivity

Proactivity means the provocation of desired change. In other words, proactive actions are designed to increase the probability of certain events (Courtney 2001, 39). Examples of pro-active planning activities include:

- influencing competitors' conduct. With regard to airport planning, this influencing has to do with strategic investments to pre-empt competition. An airport may invest strategically to pre-empt competitors (Smit 2003) and 'catch' a disproportionate share in, for example, transfer traffic demand
- locking up key resources in the industry to hinder the moves of competitors in the same market
- introducing a new product or service that redefines competition (Courtney 2001)
- restructuring the industry by means of mergers, acquisitions, alliances, and joint-ventures
- creating an industry standard
- replicating existing business systems in new markets
- influencing regulatory changes to their organization's own benefit.

Diversification

By diversifying investments, airports can spread risks. In contrast with the real options approach, diversification is reactive to uncertainty and risk since it seeks to minimize both. Such diversification can first of all consist of investing in a collection of independent strategic investments that have uncorrelated, or only weakly correlated, uncertainties and risks. Airports that develop significant air and landside commercial activities as well as real estate ('airport cities'), which depends less on the traffic demand compared with aeronautical revenues, is an example of such an approach. Second, a slightly different form of diversification is hedging: choosing investments with offsetting payoff structures; if one investment performs 'badly', the other goes 'well' (Courtney 2001). The dual strategy of Denver International Airport is an example of a hedging strategy. The airport has the strategic goal to be a home base for a major hubbing carrier (United) and to be a home base of a major low-cost airline (Frontier). Many low-cost airlines have proven to be successful and have grown during the recent economic recession, whereas the hub carriers have had to downsize and face significant financial problems. Moreover, the current terminal and concourse capacity restrictions at the airport guarantee that any slots that are eventually given up by United are taken up quickly by expanding Frontier.

Flexible organizations

One of the most important elements of a flexible organization is a 'think risk culture' (Clarke and Varma 1999, 418). The problem with flexibility in strategic planning is that organizations show a resistance to change (DeWulf and van der Schaaf 1998; Mintzberg 1994). First, management frequently has an overconfidence in the chosen strategy (DeWulf and van der Schaaf 1998). Moreover, members of the organization are reluctant to accept change since it may bring organizational restructuring, change of position, and so forth.

Hence, Davies and Petrie (2002) argued that risk and uncertainty have to be an intrinsic part of the way an organization works. Flexible organizations have 'learned to love change' (Wall 2004, 217). Risks and the risk vision (such as the maximum acceptable level of risk for the organization) have to be communicated throughout the organization and made explicit whenever possible.

Another important issue is the top-down, bottom-up, inside-out and outside-in character of the planning process. The traditional airport planning process is generally a top-down process steered by corporate management and planners. Flexible planning stresses the need for input from different parts and levels of the organization during the planning process. First of all, this is needed to build commitment to the strategic plan. Second, the knowledge and insight from planners and corporate management on the different aspects of the airport planning process are limited. Continuous input from line management is therefore needed.

The integration of different stakeholders in the planning process is also important. Stakeholders such as airlines, air traffic control, government authorities and local communities have to be informed and involved in the planning process at an early stage. On the one hand stakeholders can provide valuable information on the opportunities and threats in the market and the level of risk and uncertainty associated with the proposed airport developments (de Neufville 2000). On the other hand the involvement of the stakeholders in the planning process can help create external commitment to the master plan and enhance flexibility (Dempsey et al. 1997).

Limits to flexibility

The FSP planning approach seems to be the panacea for strategic airport planning in a volatile market environment. There are, however, several limitations to the approach.

- There is still little empirical evidence of the effectiveness of the FSP approach in airport planning (Freathy and O'Connell 1999). De Neufville (1991b) assessed the potential benefits of the flexible approach for Sydney. The planning for Sydney anticipated future needs by securing a site for a second airport well ahead of future needs. The result is that Sydney can add capacity when it is needed. Karlsson (2003) demonstrated the benefits and limitations of a flexible approach for Pease International Tradeport (United States). Caves and Gosling (1999) demonstrated the problems and benefits associated with the dual-track strategy for the airport development of Minneapolis/St. Paul.

  More empirical research on the effectiveness of FSP at various airports is needed to obtain an accurate insight into the applicability of the FSP framework in different contexts.
- Flexibility can be built into airport master planning, but usually only by accepting increased costs or lower returns in the short term (Clarke and Varma

1999; Greden and Glicksman 2004). Not every real option is attractive from a cost-benefit viewpoint. On the other hand, it most be recognized that the value of an option increases if uncertainty increases and can lead to significant cost savings and benefits in the long run (Lepardo and Lane 2002). The flexible planning process itself is a more demanding exercise than the traditional approach to airport planning from an organizational perspective. There is a need for the constant assessment of the existing plans and scanning and experimenting with the environment.

- Some airports do not have a master plan. Small European airports in particular may have insufficient resources to start a master planning process. However, even without a master plan, airports can benefit from certain characteristics of FSP.
- The choice for flexibility is frequently a 'wicked problem'. A 'wicked problem' exists when there are competing requirements between stakeholders or within the same organization (Lepardo and Lane 2002). Since airport development usually takes place in dense urban areas, the competition between stakeholders for such resources as land is intense. An airport that opts for off-airport land for potential future growth guarantees its own flexibility, but inhibits the surrounding community from using the land (and frequently the surrounding area, because of noise issues). Flexibility for the airport can result in inflexibility for other stakeholders or for other activities at the airport.
- Political power: FSP acknowledges that (political) negotiation between stakeholders is part of the planning process and its outcomes. However, narrow political interests can overly influence decision-making and limit flexibility (Caves and Gosling 1999, 252).
- Analysis paralysis: investing too much time in analysis with the purpose of reducing uncertainty can result in the loss of growth opportunities, competitive loss, or a master plan that is overtaken by reality.

Conclusions

In this chapter we have argued that strategic airport planning faces a threefold dilemma. First, traditional airport master planning is based on detailed airport traffic forecasts. The volatility of airport traffic and the associated uncertainty with respect to future traffic volumes is likely to increase in a free-market regime. Hence, traffic forecasts are likely to become less reliable. Second, uncertainty requires flexibility in airport planning. However, traditional airport master planning is not able to cope with such uncertain and risky market conditions. Its characteristics as a rational model of decision-making make traditional airport master planning passive, reactive or at best adaptive to uncertainty and risk. Various studies have shown the failure of the traditional (airport) planning model. Airports that are not able to deal with uncertainty in a flexible way face significant risks in terms of overbuilding, under-building, mismatches between demand and supply, higher unit costs, losses and

Table 8.3 Characteristics of Flexible Strategic Planning

Traditional airport master planning	Flexible strategic planning
Passive, reactive, adaptive	Re-adaptive, pro-active
Once-and-for-all anticipation/adjustment to change	Continuous anticipation/adjustments to change
Supply driven	Demand driven
Forecasts as predictions of the future	Backcasting. Scenarios as guidelines of what might happen in the future
Single-future robustness of plan and projects	Multi-future robustness of plan and projects
Long-term and short-term commitments	Short-term commitments, long-term strategic thinking
Preferred analytical tools: forecasting and net present value analysis	Preferred tools: scenario planning, decision analysis and real option analysis, contingent road maps, scanning, experimenting
Preferred alternative is optimal solution for a specific future	Preferred alternative is best alternative across a range of probable future scenarios
Risk implicitly ignored or risk aversion	Think risk culture. Risk as an opportunity
Top-down/inside-out	Top-down/bottom-up, inside-out/outside-in

negative media attention. Third, strategic airport planning is nevertheless essential for the successful development of an airport.

In our view a paradigm shift towards a flexible, dynamic approach to strategic airport planning is needed to deal with the free-market regime in the EU air transport industry, given the risks associated with investments in airport infrastructure. We call this approach the model of Flexible Strategic Planning or FSP. However, little is yet known of the extent to which EU airports apply FSP.

In this chapter we have put forward a number of essential characteristics of FSP, based on an extensive literature review. FSP is re-adaptive (flexible) and proactive towards risk and uncertainty and builds on the traditional model of airport planning. Table 8.3 lists the most important differences between traditional airport master planning and FSP. The most important elements are the creation of real options, multi-future robustness and backcasting, contingency planning, diversification and flexible organizations. In addition, we discussed a number of limitations to the real-world application of FSP.

In the chapter that follows, we shift our focus to a detailed analysis of the planning process at Amsterdam Airport Schiphol from the perspective of FSP.

Chapter 9

Flexible Strategic Planning: The Case of Amsterdam Airport Schiphol

To what extent can the airport planning process for Amsterdam Airport Schiphol be characterized as a flexible planning style? What, in practice, are the limitations for such a planning style? In this chapter we report our assessment of the master planning process for Amsterdam Airport Schiphol (Schiphol, hereafter). We have made our assessment by using the theoretical framework of Flexible Strategic Planning (Chapter 8).

Our analysis is based on an extensive review of planning documents and studies, participation in and observation of various meetings of the Airport Development Department of the Schiphol Group in 2004 and interviews with various stakeholders outside the Schiphol Group.[1] A list of respondents can be found in Annex 4.[2]

In this chapter we follow a funnel format. We start by introducing the airport in its national planning context. Gradually we proceed through the analysis of the master planning process of Schiphol in more detail. Lastly we end up with an analysis of a specific airport plan against the background of the model of Flexible Strategic Planning.

We show that Schiphol's approach to airport planning clearly exhibits a number of characteristics of Flexible Strategic Planning. At the same time, some important elements of traditional airport master planning and limitations to flexibility are identified.

Context of the planning process

Concentration of traffic growth

In 1999 the Dutch Government decided, after a lengthy consultation process about the locational options for future growth of air transport in the Netherlands, to concentrate further growth of air transport on the Amsterdam Airport Schiphol location in the Strategic Policy Decree regarding the National Airport (Ministerie van Verkeer and Waterstaat/Directoraat-Generaal Rijksluchtvaartdienst 1999; Strategische Beleidskeuze Toekomst Luchtvaart 1999). The option to move the

---

1 All quotes from Dutch respondents were translated in English by the author.

2 Because of confidentiality and the sensitivity of some of the information used for this chapter, not all sources and references are cited in the text.

airport to a new, offshore location in the North Sea was considered to be a realizable, but not a viable alternative for the medium/long term, given the major uncertainties in terms of future traffic demand (Ministerie van Verkeer and Waterstaat 2003).

The initial growth limits of 44 million passengers and 3.3 million tons of freight were lifted. However, the airport would have to meet the environmental and spatial restrictions laid down in the Airport Planning Decree and the Civil Aviation Act. Growth had to be accommodated by limited modifications of the runway configuration as well as technological enhancements of airport capacity (air traffic management, for example).

Abandoning the (ultra) long-term growth option

For the long term (2020–2025), the North Sea airport was still considered an option. In 2000 the Dutch Government set up Flyland: a research programme that would further study the offshore alternative.

Flyland was eventually dismantled in 2003. The Netherlands Ministry of Transport, Public Works and Water Management argued that an offshore airport was not likely to be needed before 2020 (as was previously envisioned), but might well be in 2040. The recent developments in the air transport sector (decline in economic growth, 11th September, SARS) had changed the prospective for traffic demand growth at Schiphol. Hence Schiphol airport ought to be able to handle traffic growth until 2040. In addition, it is likely that the closing-down of Flyland was the result of extensive cuts in expenditures in the Ministries that financed Flyland.[3]

From a real-option perspective (Chapter 8), the decision to discontinue Flyland, or an alternative trajectory to facilitate long-term growth, deserves attention. Airport traffic may become more volatile in free-market regimes. The differences between forecast and realized traffic volumes can reach levels of up to 78 per cent in 15 years (de Neufville 1992). The prospect that the currently envisioned ultimate future capacity of Schiphol (85–90 million passengers) will certainly *not* be reached by 2020 is as valid as the prospect that it certainly will be reached by 2020.

On the one hand, the important sets of forecast documents for Boeing and Airbus both predict that air traffic demand growth in Europe will recover from its current crisis in the next few years (Airbus 2002, for example). Schiphol's traffic demand has already caught up, principally because of the growth of low-cost airlines and transfer passengers (Schiphol Group 2004f). On the other hand, the future strategic position of Schiphol in the Air France–KLM network remains unclear, oil prices reached all-time highs in 2004, and the international political arena continued to be unstable, resulting without doubt in more uncertainty about future traffic volumes.

In real-option terms (Chapter 8), the Dutch government no longer considers the offshore alternative to be a growth option (the right, but not the obligation to realize a

3 Netherlands Ministry of Transport, Public Works and Water Management; Netherlands Ministry of Economic Affairs; Netherlands Ministry of Spatial Planning, Housing and the Environment.

Box 9.1 Amsterdam Airport Schiphol

The modern history of Schiphol started in 1967, when the airport took on its current shape. In 1967 a completely renewed airport was opened on the western side of the old airport to facilitate future traffic growth. The layout of the new airport was characterized by a one-terminal concept with finger piers, a tangential runway system of four runways (to deal with the frequent and heavy crosswinds in the Netherlands) and many opportunities for further growth.

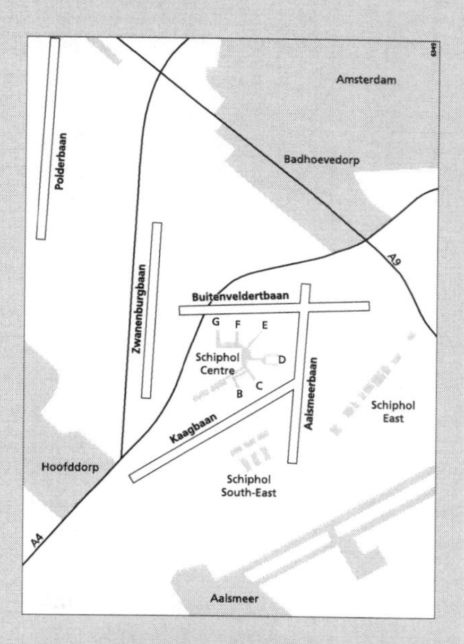

Figure 9.1 Layout, Amsterdam Airport Schiphol

The current airport layout still consists of a centralized passenger terminal area with a tangential system of five runways: three parallel runways and two crosswind runways. The Southern and Southeastern parts of the airport are dedicated to cargo handling, while the maintenance facilities are concentrated on Schiphol-east. On the landside of the airport we find a commercial development axis that runs from the central terminal area to the Southwestern part of the airport. In 2003 the airport area covered 2878 hectares.

Since 1958 Amsterdam Airport Schiphol has been a limited liability company: NV Luchthaven Schiphol. The name was changed to Schiphol Group in 1999, although the legal name is still NV Luchthaven Schiphol. The Schiphol Group covers not only Amsterdam Airport Schiphol, but also a few regional airports (Rotterdam Airport, Eindhoven Airport and Lelystad), international participations (Brisbane and New York JFK, for example) and a Real Estate division (SRE).

Box 9.1 Continued

The Schiphol Group is legally a private entity, but at the same time it is publicly owned. The national government holds 75.8 per cent of the shares, the Municipality of Amsterdam 21.8 per cent, and the Municipality of Rotterdam 2.4 per cent. Since the end of the 1990s there have been various political debates about the privatization of the Schiphol Group (CPB 2000, for example). In 2004 the Dutch Cabinet announced that the national government would put at least some of its shares on the stock market. In 2006 partial privatization was still under discussion.

In 2003 the airport handled more than 40 million passengers against 16.5 million in 1990. Particularly since the 1990s, Schiphol has grown at a tremendous rate in terms of passenger numbers, frequently showing double-digit growth rates. Passenger movements increased from 159,000 in 1980 to 202,000 in 1990 to 393,000 in 2003. The airport handled about 1.3 million tonnes of freight in 2003 against 300,000 tonnes in 1980 and 600,000 tons in 1990.

long-term growth alternative). The focus on just the Schiphol location would only be a short/medium-term fix for the accommodation of traffic demand in the Netherlands.

We do not intend to argue for the revival of the offshore option. Various studies have indicated that investing in a brand new offshore airport would not be the best choice from a flexible planning perspective (de Neufville 1995, for example). An offshore airport requires very large and irreversible initial investments. These are unlikely to be economically viable 'under any standard commercial accounting practice' (de Neufville 1995, 23).

From the perspective of national consumer welfare, however, abandoning *any* long-term growth option completely calls into question the flexibility of the planning process at the national level, especially because of the extremely long lead times associated with the development of new runway infrastructure, let alone the development of a completely new (offshore) airport.

Initiating a new planning process

The government commissioned the Dutch civil aviation sector to formulate and evaluate different growth alternatives for the Schiphol location: the *Business Case Redesign*. The different alternatives were to be analyzed in a cost-benefit analysis carried out by the Netherlands Bureau for Economic Policy Analysis. If considered feasible, an Environmental Impact Analysis was to be carried out to evaluate the environmental impact of the alternatives. Finally, the government would decide about the possibilities for the future development through the Airport Planning Decree[4] and Airport Traffic Decree.[5] Among other things, the Airport Planning Decree specifies the spatial layout of take-off and landings strips and terminals and defines the areas

4 'Luchthavenindelingsbesluit'.

5 'Luchthavenverkeersbesluit'.

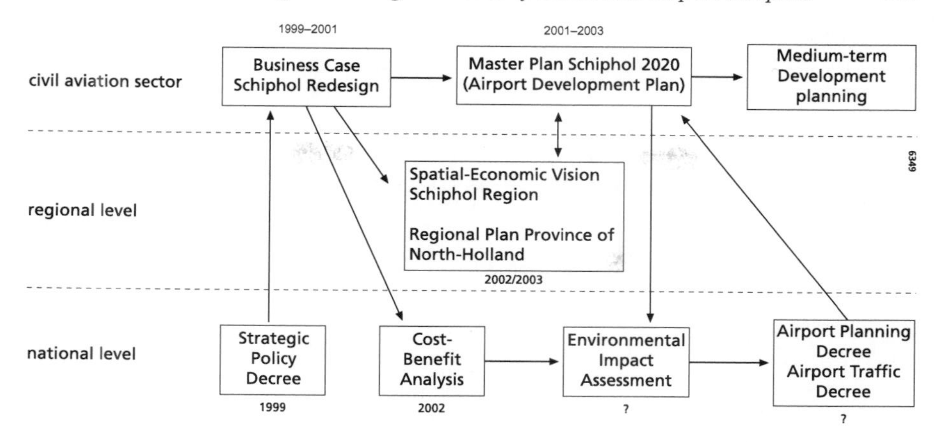

Figure 9.2 The planning process for Schiphol

around the airport where there is a need for a complete ban, or at least restrictions on land uses for noise and safety reasons. Local government authorities have to adapt their Municipal Zoning Plans according to the Airport Planning Decree. This Decree sets the environmental and safety standards at the national level. The Airport Traffic Decree lays down the rules for airport use and stipulates limits for noise levels, air pollution and risk to public safety.

In 2002 the government adopted the Airport Planning Decree and Airport Traffic Decree for Schiphol's current runway configuration (five runways). Further modifications of the runway system will need a new Airport Planning Decree and Airport Traffic Decree. In fact, these Decrees define the mandate of the Schiphol Group with regard to the master planning of its capacity.

Conclusions

The decision of the Dutch government to concentrate the future growth of air transport on Amsterdam Airport Schiphol initiated a new master planning process within the Schiphol Group (Figure 9.2). Nevertheless, the final decision-making concerning the redesign of the runway system still rests at the national level. As a result of more conservative long-term growth expectations, the long-term growth option of an offshore island in the North Sea was abandoned. We argued in Chapter 8 that abandoning any long-term growth option (not necessarily the North Sea option) contrasts with the model of Flexible Strategic Planning, which emphasizes the creation of real options instead of deterministic plans. Given the uncertainties with respect to future airport traffic demand, the prospect that the currently envisioned ultimate future capacity of Schiphol will certainly not be reached by 2020 is as true as the prospect that it certainly will be reached by 2020. Hence, the choice of Amsterdam Airport Schiphol as the preferred alternative for both the medium and very long term can be characterized as a type of deterministic, traditional

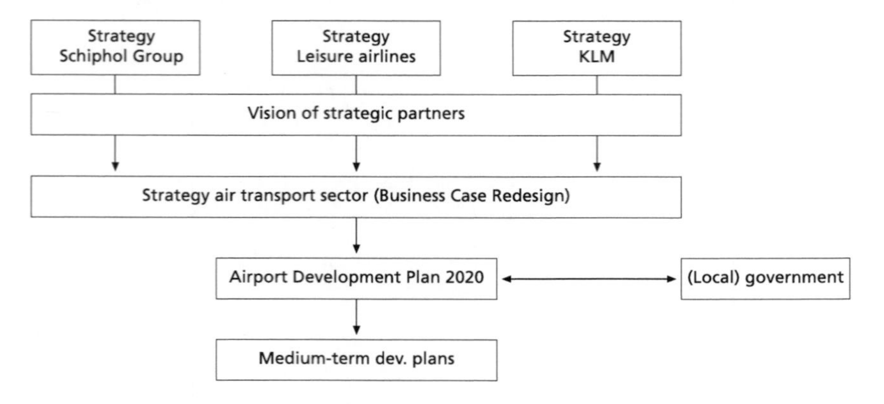

Figure 9.3 Structure of the master planning process at Schiphol

airport planning, which insufficiently addresses the uncertainties and risks in airport planning in free-market regimes.

Stakeholders in the master planning process

Overall structure of the master planning process

The decision to concentrate growth on the Schiphol location in both the short and long term gave rise to a new master planning process for Schiphol. The planning process is outlined in Figure 9.3. The master plan is called the *Airport Development Plan 2020* (ADP) or *Ruimtelijke Toekomstvisie Schiphol 2020*. As Figure 9.3 shows, the ADP is part of a much broader planning process. This process also includes the strategic vision of the air transport sector (the *Business Case Schiphol Redesign*) and medium-term development plans, which can be geographical, but also sectoral in scope.

The overall structure of the master planning process outlined here cannot be well understood without a brief introduction to the most important stakeholders in the master planning process: the Airport Development Department of the Schiphol Group, NACO, the MT Schiphol Group, the airlines and the local, regional and national government authorities.

The Schiphol Group

The master planning of Amsterdam Airport Schiphol takes place within the context of various organizational units of the Schiphol Group. A number of them have a significant impact on the process and content of master planning (Figure 9.4). We restrict our discussion here to the most important features in the context of our research: the Airport Development Department and the Management Team Schiphol Group.

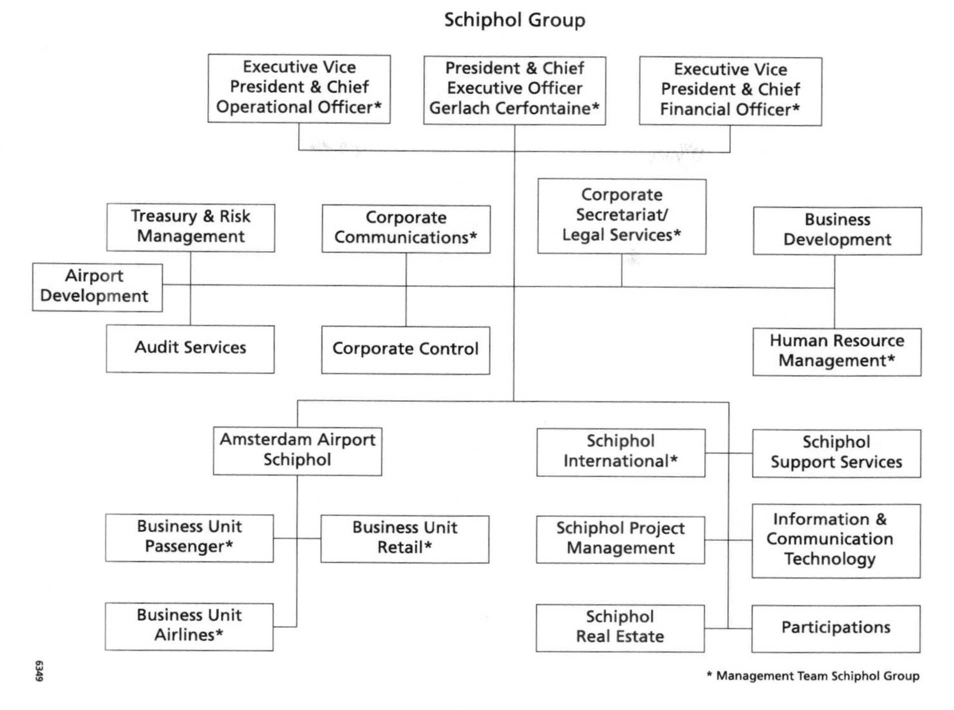

Figure 9.4 Organization of the Schiphol Group, January 2004

Airport Development Within the Schiphol Group, the Airport Planning (AD) Department is responsible for the long-term and medium-term strategic planning of Amsterdam Airport Schiphol, or in other words, the master planning and medium-term development planning. The planning 'philosophy' of the Airport Development Department could be characterized as the SWOT model of strategic planning (Porter 1980, for example). According to a planner of AD, the master planning of AD is based on the future perspectives about the trends that affect airport traffic demand. In this context, AD has the objective of matching the airport's resources with the external business environment while taking into account the uncertainties and risks of today's market environment. Master planning is about making strategic reservations for future growth and keeping options open. Moreover, airport master planning is not a once-and-for-all exercise, but a continuous, iterative process to anticipate continuous, new developments. The master plan is clearly no blueprint. The following quotation of an AD planner illustrates this:

> [...], you should not put the opening of the Northwest terminal in your diary for 31 March 2015. The master plan deals with the land we need for future development.

Flexibility is one of the main objectives of the master planning of Airport Development. The following quotation about the definition of a master plan by an AD employee illustrates this conclusion:

> [A master plan] is the long-term direction to develop the airport. You make a nice scale-model of the airport […]. That is what attracts people. But you can't know how the market will evolve. You have to live with that. The master plan is really a contingency plan: you look for the highest common factor. […]. For me, the master plan is one big reservations plan. […], for me it's the creation of land reservations that can deal with an uncertain future.

Furthermore, master planning has to be functional and should be aimed at value creation for the stakeholders (Schiphol Group 2003b). Compared with some other airports in the world, master planning at Schiphol is less focused on the realization of 'airports as temples' with high-standing architecture. As one of the AD planners put it:

> With regard to the elaboration [of the master plan] we are quite Calvinistic: we prefer functionality in airport planning, without forgetting completely about the value of architecture and design. This is quite a difference from Aéroports de Paris, for example […] with its famous architects, […] we look more at cost control and functionality.

Specifically, the following tasks of the Airport Planning Department are important with respect to this chapter:

- contribution to company-wide strategic thinking and analysis
- long-term and medium-term airport planning
- contribution to specific projects
- organization of the master planning process. The AD coordinates the master planning process both internally and externally. Consequently, among other things, during the *ADP 2020* planning process, Airport Development ensured the input from and communication to the different Business Units and departments of the Schiphol Group. Furthermore, AD communicated regularly with the air transport sector and the local government authorities about the *ADP 2020*.

Management Team Schiphol Group The Airport Development department has no strategic decision-making power, however. Decision-making rests with the Management Team Schiphol Group. This Group consists of the chief executive, chief financial and chief operational officers, the director of Schiphol International, the director of Communications, the director of Legal Services, the director of Human Resources, the directors of the four Business Units and, if required, the directors of other departments (see Figure 9.4).

KLM Group

KLM and partners (Northwest and regional partners) accounted for 60 per cent of total passenger numbers in 2003. Hence KLM is the main user of the airport's infrastructure. KLM's main requirement for Schiphol is optimal accommodation of its hub-operation. For the KLM group, the hub-operation translates into 'user requirements' of sufficient peak-hour capacity, a dedicated terminal area, short taxi times from apron to runway, an efficient and reliable baggage handling system, the reliability of the runway system and good landside accessibility (KLM 2002). We listed these factors as essential key drivers for an airline hub-operation in Chapter 2.

The KLM Group has been involved in the ADP planning process from the start. Together with Netherlands Air Traffic Control (LVNL) and Schiphol, KLM provided the strategic input for the *Airport Development Plan 2020* through the *Business Case Schiphol Redesign.* During the planning process, the Airport Development Department also communicated frequently with the KLM Group.

The involvement of KLM in the planning process from the start has brought about a major improvement in the airport's master planning process. This improvement was partly the result of a change in national aviation policy, putting much more responsibility on the stakeholders in the air transport industry itself. As one KLM executive put it:

> In the past, there was always some KLM involvement in major issues. But now, the planning process has a well-defined structure that starts with the airlines [...] and their user requirements. The user, in fact, defines what it wants.

Hence, there had been a substantial input from the largest user of the airport into the airport planning process, as we see later on.

Local, regional and national government

The relationship between an airport and its local community is crucial for the airport's future (Caves and Gosling 1999, 101). On the one hand, while it may well bring substantial economic and social benefits to its region and even to an entire country, an airport will also cause substantial negative external effects in terms of noise, odour, safety, congestion and building restrictions within noise contours. On the other hand, an airport needs its region for a strong origin–destination market, local and regional accessibility, a suitable workforce and reservations of land for future growth. The national government, the Province of North-Holland, the Municipality of Haarlemmermeer and the Municipality of Amsterdam are some of the most important stakeholders in this respect.

The National Government decides about any substantial reconfiguration of the airport's infrastructure through the Airport Planning Decree[6] (Ministerie van Verkeer and Waterstaat/Directoraat-Generaal Rijksluchtvaartdienst 1999). This

6 'Luchthavenindelingsbesluit'.

Decree defines the airport area and 'the areas within which there is a ban on housing construction and where existing housing will no longer be used for that purpose' (Ministerie van Verkeer and Waterstaat/Directoraat-Generaal Rijksluchtvaartdienst 1999, 12; Staatsblad van het Koninkrijk der Nederlanden 2002, 5). The building plans of the local authorities will have to be assessed in the light of the Airport Planning Decree.

Whereas the Airport Planning Decree deals with the spatial layout of the airport and the airport region, the Air Traffic Decree[7] sets environmental and safety standards at the national level (Staatsblad van het Koninkrijk der Nederlanden 2002). It defines the limits for the use of runways, flight paths and traffic regulations (Ministerie van Verkeer and Waterstaat/Directoraat-Generaal Rijksluchtvaartdienst 1999). Any reconfiguration of Schiphol's runway system requires an Airport Planning Decree and an Airport Traffic Decree. These Decrees have to be backed by an Environmental Impact Assessment,[8] which has to be initiated by the Dutch civil aviation sector.[9] History shows that the Environmental Impact Assessment appeals against the Airport Planning Decree, and final decision-making by the government take at least five years, and frequently much more.

Through the Regional Plan, the Province of North-Holland can facilitate or limit the future growth of the airport. In particular, new runway infrastructure requires building restrictions at the regional level because of noise nuisance and safety issues. The Regional Plan can enforce these building restrictions since the Zoning Plans of the Municipalities have to fit into the Regional Plan.

Schiphol is located within the boundaries of the Municipality of Haarlemmermeer. Formally, developments at the airport have to meet the Municipal Zoning Plan. In practice, the Zoning Plan is very general in scope with respect to developments on the airside of the airport. In addition, the zoning plan has to be adapted according to the Airport Planning Decree at the national level.

NACO

NACO (Netherlands Airport Consultants) is an airport engineering and consultancy firm based in The Hague. It has been involved in numerous airport planning and development projects throughout the world. NACO was partly responsible for the design of the central passenger terminal building for the new Schiphol airport of 1967 (Bouwens and Dierikx 1996, 207). NACO has been highly involved in the planning and design of the airport's infrastructure ever since.

Because of the tasks of the Airport Development Department of the Schiphol Group, NACO is not responsible for the entire master planning process for Schiphol, in contrast with its role in many other airport planning and development projects.

7 'Luchthavenverkeersbesluit'.

8 'Milieu-effect Rapportage'.

9 A Strategic Partnership of the most important stakeholders of the civil aviation sector.

Instead, the Schiphol Group frequently asks NACO to work out certain smaller aspects of the master planning process in a more *ad hoc* manner.

The Business Case Redesign

Background

In the Strategic Policy Decree of 1999 on the future of air transport in the Netherlands, the national government chose to concentrate the further growth of Schiphol airport at its present location. It should be possible for growth to meet strict environmental standards. Such growth should be facilitated by means of (limited) adjustments to the runway system and technological measures to increase airport capacity (Air Traffic Control solutions, slot coordination).

As a consequence of the Strategic Policy Decree[10] and on the request of the Minister of Transport, Public Works and Water Management, the Dutch civil aviation sector initiated a study on the future development alternatives for the airport in 1999. A strategic partnership of the Schiphol Group, KLM, Martinair, Transavia and LVNL (air traffic control) carried out the ensuing *Business Case Redesign.* Its objective was to 'create spatial opportunities and capacity for sustainable growth of the Schiphol location in the long run (after 2010)' (Nederlandse Luchtvaartsector 2001a, 6) within the context of the Strategic Policy Decree. The *Business Case Redesign* was completed in 2001. It is important to note that it was a civil aviation sector study. Hence it considered the business-economic value of the growth alternatives for the air transport sector, but not for other stakeholders or other interests (local and regional governments, for example).

The *Business Case Redesign* was later used as the input for the master plan of Schiphol, the *Airport Development Plan 2020*. A clear advantage of the relationship between the *Business Case Redesign* and the Airport Development Plan was the early involvement of the airlines in the master planning process. In our view, this approach eliminated the 'build it and they'll come' approach, which is characteristic of the traditional airport master planning style (Chapter 8). Instead, the master planning process was demand driven from the very beginning (Schiphol Group 2001a, 3). A demand-driven approach is one of the requirements of Flexible Strategic Planning. Schiphol was informed about the requirements of its major users. Moreover, the approach ensured more commitment to the Airport Development Plan from the airlines. Let us consider the main elements of the *Business Case Redesign.*

Capacity requirements

The cornerstone of the *Business Case Redesign* was the traffic demand forecast for 2020, the peak-hour requirements given KLM's strategy and the subsequent growth

---

10 Ministerie van Verkeer and Waterstaat (2000).

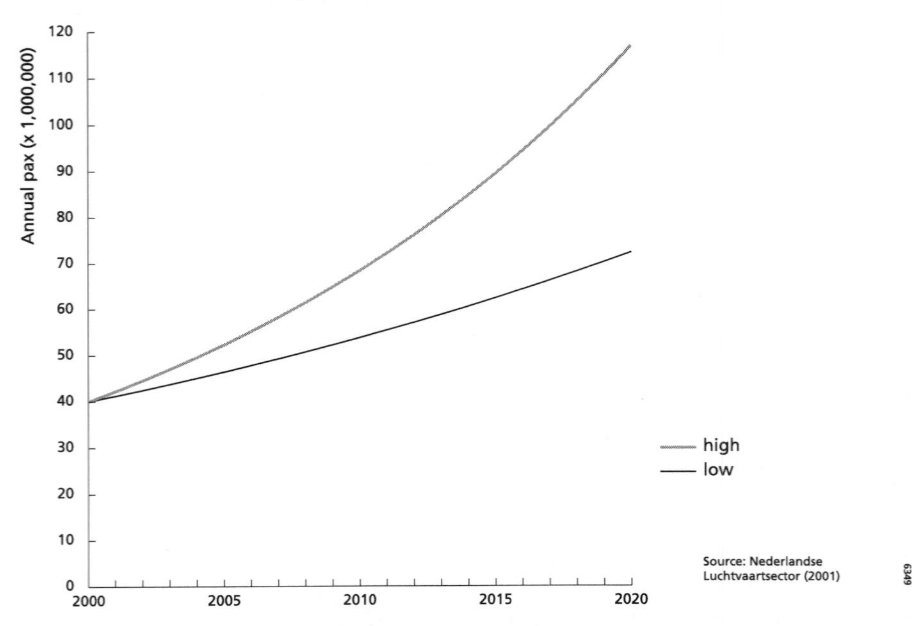

Figure 9.5 Passenger traffic demand forecast, Business Case Redesign

potential for Schiphol. Based on simple linear trend projections of 3 per cent and 5.5 per cent growth per year, high and low (unrestricted) demand forecasts for passenger traffic were generated respectively. Forecasts were also generated for the freight market, various traffic segments of the passenger market (origin–destination versus transfer traffic, KLM group versus other carriers), and the number of aircraft movements.

For example, the *Business Case Redesign* forecast 72–116 million passengers for the year 2020 (Figure 9.5) and 620,000–1 million aircraft movements, with the assumption of 113 passengers per aircraft movement on average. The percentage of transfer passengers was projected to increase from 40 per cent in 2001 to 50 per cent in 2010 and was assumed to remain stable after 2010 owing to the saturation of the transfer market.[11]

The forecasts were based on the assumption that KLM would intensify its hub-operation. Specifically, it was expected that KLM would add new waves to its existing wave-system in the future in order to offer more competitive frequencies per day and more connections per wave (KLM 2002). Other (non-hub) scenarios for the KLM operation at Schiphol, such as those developed during the TNLI and ONL process, were not considered (Scenario Werkgroep ONL 2001).

11 If traffic flows are not large enough for a direct connection between two cities, the hub-and-spoke network is an optimal solution. With the ongoing growth of traffic demand in Europe, more city-pairs will have sufficient demand for a direct connection. Hence, transfer traffic at the EU hubs is not expected to grow indefinitely.

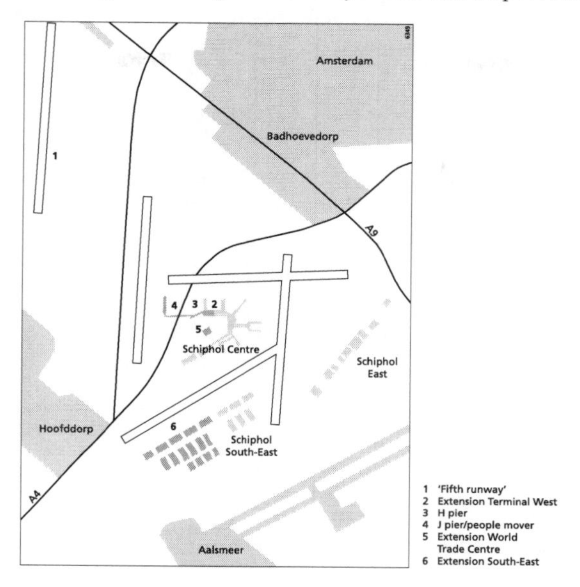

Figure 9.6 Extensions Site Plan 2010

The existing *Site Plan 2010* (based on the previous Schiphol Master Plan, the *Master Plan 2015*) allowed for a maximum growth of 600,000 aircraft movements, 60 million annual passenger movements and a maximum peak-hour demand of 120 aircraft movements (Nederlandse Luchtvaartsector 2001a). This growth would be accommodated by building a fifth runway,[12] extending Terminal West,[13] by constructing a J-pier and H-pier, and the optimization of the five-runway system[14] (Figure 9.6).

However, the system of five runways would not be able to accommodate the capacity requirements in terms of the peak-hour capacity associated with the traffic forecasts of the *Business Case Redesign*. Hence, at the end of the planning horizon (2020), it was considered likely that there would be a capacity gap in the range of 10 to 60 million passengers per annum. Additional runway and terminal capacity was considered essential for further growth.

There was another problem. The *Business Case Redesign* estimated that the maximum peak-hour capacity of 120 movements per hour would be available for 90 per cent of the time during the year in the system of five runways. Unfavourable weather circumstances would reduce peak-hour capacity to 80 movements per hour during 10 per cent of the time.[15] Such capacity reductions would cause significant delays and

12 Completed in 2003.

13 Completed in 2004.

14 Technical-operational measures, adapted use of runways, distribution of flights during the day (CPB and NLR 1998).

15 Strong southwest winds of more than 25 knots.

cancellations. It is obvious that such delays would result in considerable costs for the carriers and would reduce the attractiveness of Schiphol as a transfer airport.

Hence the *Business Case Redesign* evaluated different growth alternatives given Schiphol's weather conditions, capacity requirements and national policy context (most notably the Strategic Policy Decree of 1999) in the high and low forecasts. Criteria for the evaluation included the increase in peak-hour capacity, the reliability of the runway system (in terms of weather conditions) and value creation for Schiphol and KLM (net present value). On behalf of the civil aviation sector, a well-reputed consultant carried out a study on the net present value of different runway configurations for the civil aviation sector.

The consultant considered four options that would meet the requirements set down in the Strategic Policy Decree of 1999 (standstill in terms of environmental effects and only a limited redesign of the runway system).[16] Figure 9.7 illustrates the following options:

- 5P (reference situation): a configuration of five runways, with a fifth runway parallel to the North–South runways (present situation). The 5P configuration would allow the airport to grow to 60 million and eventually 67 million passengers a year and a peak-hour capacity of 120 aircraft movements per hour.
- 6PK: a six-runway configuration, with a sixth runway parallel to the existing Southwest–Northeast runway ('Kaagbaan'). This configuration would offer a limited increment in peak-hour capacity (growth to 140 movements per hour) and a growth to 78 million passengers a year.
- 6P: a six-runway configuration, with a sixth runway parallel to the existing North–South runways. The 6P alternative would offer the airport the opportunity to grow to 160 movements per hour and 78 million passengers a year.
- 7PK: a seven-runway system, with a sixth runway parallel to the existing North–South runways and a seventh runway parallel to the existing Southwest–Northeast runway ('Kaagbaan'). The 7PK alternative is in fact the combination of 6PK and 6P. The alternative would allow the airport to grow to 160 aircraft movements per hour and 90 million annual passenger movements.

The runway systems 6P and 7PK would create most value for the stakeholders compared with the 5P system, since 6P and 7PK would simply add most peak-hour capacity. The 6PK system would not do so, because it only offers a minor increase in peak-hour capacity. The 6PK runway configuration does not allow for the independent and parallel use of two runways for take-off and two for landing under normal weather conditions. The 7PK system would be more expensive, however,

16 Earlier studies had shown that other runway configurations than those shown here would either increase the airport region's exposure to aircraft noise, would not deliver the desired increases in peak-hour capacity, or would be too costly.

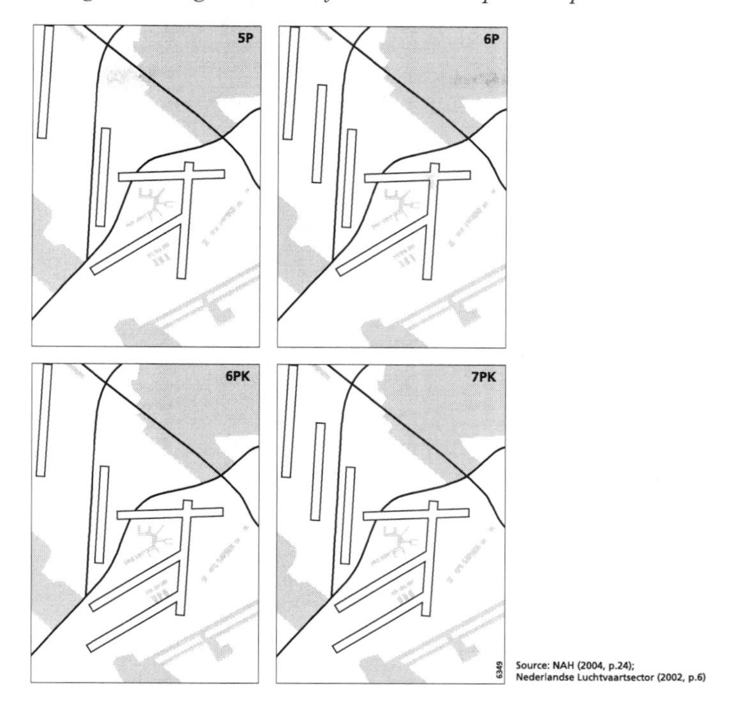

Figure 9.7 Runway configuration alternatives

because of the substantial deconstruction costs of facilities in the southeastern part of the airport. The study concluded that the 6P runway configuration would be the most attractive from a peak-hour capacity-enhancing perspective.

Nevertheless, in bad weather conditions (heavy crosswinds) the peak-hour capacity would very probably be heavily reduced since there would not be sufficient crosswind runway capacity available. The *Business Case Redesign* concluded that more research on this topic was needed.

The consultant A.T. Kearney (2001) later quantified and reconfirmed this preliminary conclusion of the *Business Case Redesign* on the capacity reductions in the 6P system. The A.T. Kearney study concluded that the 6P runway system would lead to a situation where 40 per cent of the flights would be delayed or cancelled for 10 per cent of the year as a result of heavy crosswinds (Nederlandse Luchtvaartsector 2002). The study showed that the 6P runway system would lead to insufficient reliability of the required peak-hour capacity.

The 6PK, 6P and 7PK runway configurations require additional terminal, apron and other facilities. The *Business Case Redesign* estimated that the maximum capacity of the central terminal area would be reached with 600,000 annual aircraft movements and 60 million passengers per year. A secondary terminal area would eventually be needed in the north-western area of the airport. This would mean abandoning the one-terminal concept of the airport.

The *Business Case Redesign* of 2001 concluded by requesting land reservations for the 6P alternative and the 7PK runway system. The *Business Case Redesign* was sent to the Minister of Transport, Public Works and Water Management. The Minister commissioned an evaluation of the various alternatives in preparation for national decision-making about the future of Schiphol airport (Ministerie van Verkeer and Waterstaat 2000). The Minister initiated a cost-benefit analysis, carried out by the Netherlands Bureau for Economic Policy Analysis (CPB) (CPB 2002). The CPB made positive recommendations about creating growth options for a sixth and seventh runway.

Dealing with uncertainty

A noteworthy aspect of the *Business Case Redesign* is the fact that it explicitly acknowledges and deals with the uncertainty associated with the forecasts and the proposed alternatives:

> The sector wants to stress that a number of variables associated with the market and technology are uncertain. Further analysis [...] will not be capable of reducing this uncertainty substantially (Nederlandse Luchtvaartsector 2001a, 2).

The most important elements of flexibility brought forward by the *Business Case Redesign* are the creation of growth options, sensitivity analyses with respect to the parameters used in the evaluation process, and a demand-driven planning process.

First, the *Business Case Redesign* called for 'land reservations' in the Regional Plan of the Province of North-Holland to facilitate additional runways and terminal capacity (Nederlandse Luchtvaartsector 2001a, 2002). We can consider such land reservations growth options in order to deal flexibly with market uncertainty: the possibility, but not the obligation, to develop new runway and terminal capacity, according to market circumstances.

Second, the capacity requirements and valuations presented in the *Business Case Redesign* were not definitive. In other words, they are based on certain assumptions about the future traffic mix, the mix of traffic during the day, and so forth. These future parameters cannot be known and might differ substantially from today's assumptions. For the *Business Case Redesign*, a reputed consultant carried out a sensitivity analysis for several 'what if' scenarios. 'What if' scenarios varied, for instance, on the percentage of transfer traffic, size of aircraft and maximum capacity per runway. In addition, the consultant provided the civil aviation sector with a computer-based tool to carry out additional sensitivity and scenario analyses.

Third, a strategic partnership of the airport, airlines and air traffic control carried out the *Business Case Redesign*. As discussed earlier, this approach ensured more commitment and input from the most relevant stakeholders. The result was a demand-driven approach, as that put forward by the model of Flexible Strategic Planning.

However, there was also a drawback associated with the demand-driven approach. The *Business Case Redesign* turned out to be heavily rooted in the objectives of the hub carrier KLM. The *Business Case Redesign* is essentially a hub-oriented study. Low-cost airlines such as easyJet (in July 2003 the third largest carrier at the airport in terms of seat capacity) were not included in the study team for the traffic scenarios. Both traffic scenarios were based on the assumption of a growing and dominant hub carrier. Alternative scenarios were not considered.

In other words, there was a bias towards the demands of the main user (KLM). This is hardly a surprise given the dominant position of KLM at the airport, its participation in the *Business Case Redesign* and the current strategy of the Schiphol Group: to be a 'mainport' or major hub for the European continent (see Schiphol Group 2000, for example).

Although the potential for low-cost operations was recognized later on in the planning process for the Schiphol Group, the 'hub' orientation of the *Business Case Redesign* would challenge the assumptions on which the master planning process was based. We discuss this issue later in this chapter where we consider the *GHJ-plan*.

Final recommendations of the Business Case Redesign

The Dutch civil aviation sector published its final report on Schiphol's Redesign in 2002 (Nederlandse Luchtvaartsector 2002). The report stated that connectivity and sustainability were the cornerstones for the future growth of Schiphol. Connectivity means destinations, frequencies and indirect connections. Hence connectivity requires peak-hour capacity. Sustainability entails the reliability of the peak-hour capacity in all weather circumstances. Sustainability requires additional east–west runway capacity (the 6PK alternative) before any investment in additional north–south runway capacity (the 6P alternative). Enhancing peak-hour capacity by means of an additional north–south runway would only be possible if an additional east–west runway was in place to deal with the expected reductions in peak-hour capacity. This conclusion is clearly in contrast with the initial preference of the *Business Case Redesign* for the 6P alternative (Nederlandse Luchtvaartsector 2001b). In fact, the study prefers the 6PK alternative with the possibility of developing 6PK into 7PK.

The final report again called for land reservations for a sixth and seventh runway and for building restrictions for the associated noise impact areas in the Regional Plan of the Province of North-Holland. The request of the civil aviation sector was backed by the cost-benefit analysis of the CPB Netherlands Bureau of Economic Policy Analysis (CPB 2002). The civil aviation sector finally announced that it would start an environmental impact assessment at short notice.

Conclusions regarding the Business Case Redesign from the perspective of FSP

In short, the *Business Case Redesign* marked the start of a new master planning process for Schiphol. Important to note is that it was not the airport or a consultant that was responsible for the forecasting, definition of capacity requirements and initial evaluation of planning alternatives. Instead, a temporary coalition of airlines, air traffic control and Schiphol airport initiated the *Business Case Schiphol Redesign* that incorporated the forecasting and defined the basic capacity requirements. Hence the master planning process was demand-driven from the outset. From the perspective of Flexible Strategic Planning, the demand-driven approach needs to be favoured, since it is better suited to allow the airport to anticipate and adjust to market demand.

Moreover, the study acknowledged the existence of market uncertainty and set out various ways indicating how to deal with it. These included an explicit request for a growth option for possible future growth. Such an option would give the air transport sector the possibility, but not the obligation to continue to grow at Schiphol. In Chapter 8 we emphasized the need for growth options as a central element to a more flexible approach to airport planning. Nevertheless, the *Business Case Redesign* was heavily centred on the hub operation of KLM. The quickly changing market circumstances were to challenge the orientation towards the hub carrier at a later stage.

Airport Development Plan 2020

Plan preparation

In 2001 the Airport Development Department of the Schiphol Group started its internal master planning process for the development of the airport for the period 2003–2020. The starting point for the process was the *Business Case Redesign*. The civil aviation sector had forecast significant growth that would probably result in a capacity gap of 10–60 million passengers in 2020. The internal master planning process should result in an airport master plan with a long-term planning horizon of 2020 to cope with this capacity gap: the *Airport Development Plan 2020* (ADP) (Schiphol Group/Afdeling Airport Development 2003a, 2003b). The Airport Development Department was responsible for the master planning process and the writing of the master plan itself on behalf of the Schiphol Management Team.

The objectives of the ADP planning process were to:

- outline the potential for the physical, spatial and functional development of Schiphol in the case of a growth to 85 million passengers and 3 million tons of freight in 2020 and the associated development trajectory. With regard to passenger movements, this development would equate to a scenario of 4.5 per cent annual growth of passenger movements
- indicate which land reservations would be required on and off the airport site
- provide a framework for the medium-term airport site planning (*development plans*).

Flexibility requirements

In the plan preparation phase the Airport Development Department set out a number of requirements for the planning process which are noteworthy from the perspective of flexible planning (Schiphol Group 2001a).

First, the Airport Development Department considered the communication with the civil aviation sector and, to a lesser extent, the (local) government to be important. On the one hand, communication was necessary to ensure the most relevant input from the most relevant stakeholders for the plan for it to be demand driven. At the same time, communication was considered essential to build up the commitment of other stakeholders to the ADP. According to Flyvbjerg and colleagues (2003, 88), a lack of stakeholder involvement tends to create 'a situation where those groups who worry about the project and are left without information and influence are inclined to act destructively [...]'. In other words, the planning process should be an outside-in and inside-out process of communication. We identified interactivity as a condition for flexible planning in Chapter 8.

As indicated in an interview with a local government representative, the local government authority has only been involved formally in a limited way during the ADP process. This limited involvement bears the risk of generating the limited commitment of the local authorities. Although the airlines would be regularly involved, they would not however play the same role as they did during the *Business Case Redesign*. The airlines were considered as customers during the ADP planning process to safeguard the independent strategy formation and decision-making of the airport itself.

Second, the master planning process would start immediately (2001), although the final report of the civil aviation sector with respect to the Redesign Schiphol was not yet available. Waiting for this report would have led to unnecessary delays in the planning process in a market that was changing rapidly. In terms of the flexible planning approach, ADP tried to avoid analysis paralysis (Skinner 2001).

In addition, the simultaneous development of the Redesign Business Plan and the *ADP 2020* would offer the opportunity to develop goals and resources in a continuous interactive search process. In our opinion, this search process is certainly much more valuable than a traditional, linear approach to planning, where goals are set at the very start. In Chapter 8 we argued that goals are rarely given and clearly defined at the very start of the planning process, one of the assumptions of the rational process in which the traditional airport master planning model is rooted. Flexible Strategic Planning develops objectives and means in a continuous process of communication and interaction with the most relevant stakeholders. As we shall see, the objectives of the ADP have indeed changed during the planning process because of new information becoming available through the *Business Case Redesign*.

Third, the phasing and the development trajectories of the *ADP 2020* should be sufficiently robust to withstand the 'fallback scenarios': scenarios with less traffic than the base forecast of 4.5 per cent, or different types of traffic. In other words, the ADP should be multi-future robust for alternative scenarios. Hence Airport Development announced a scenario/risk analysis in a later phase.

Fourth, the Airport Development Plan would have to be worked out in terms of detailed medium-term development for the period 2003–2007. The site plans have to be updated every year in order to reassess changing market circumstances.

From the perspective of flexible planning, the airport master planning process is characterized by what is variously referred to as backcasting, backfolding or backrolling: the master planning works backwards from the long-term critical state defined in the Redesign Business Plan and the Airport Development Plan to the medium-term development plans and business plans. We identified backcasting as an essential characteristic of flexible planning in Chapter 8: a decision in the medium term can only be optimal in the long term if all subsequent decisions are optimal or, in other words, if the ultimate critical future state is multi-future robust. The risk and scenario analysis would help to formulate a multi-future robust and flexible airport master plan.

Finally, the Airport Development Plan has to be actively managed:

> The Airport Development Plan has to be managed actively. If it is not managed properly, the divergence between the medium-term development plan and ADP will become too large for the latter to lead the medium-development plan (Schiphol Group 2001a).

In other words, we observe a double re-adaptation process to respond to changing market circumstances. The first re-adaptation process concerns the yearly updates of the medium-term development plans. The second concerns the management of the ADP itself:

> Experience tells that such a plan [*ADP 2020*] has to be updated at least every five years or even earlier, whenever structural developments require (Schiphol Group/Afdeling Airport Development 2003a, 42).

It can be concluded that the ADP process stressed the need for flexibility from the start. The ADP process explicitly recognized the volatility and uncertainty of airport traffic demand and composition and Airport Development designed a planning process to deal explicitly with this uncertainty. The result is a phased process of continuous interaction between the more general, long-term master plan and the more detailed, medium-term development plans.

Strategic premises

In contrast with many other master planning processes, the forecasting and definition of runway alternatives was not carried out by the Airport Development Department of the Schiphol Group, but by the civil aviation sector (the *Business Case Redesign*). Hence the ADP planning process started by mapping its strategic premises given the *Business Case Redesign* and Schiphol Group's own mission, vision and goals (Schiphol Group 2001a). In our view, the latter were quite important given the fact that the *Business Case Redesign* was carried out in partnership with the airlines and air traffic control. The recommendations of the *Business Case Redesign* were focused almost exclusively on the operations of the home carrier KLM.

The most important strategic premises of the *ADP 2020* are:

- Schiphol has the objective of being one of the four major hubs in Europe by optimally accommodating one of the three major worldwide alliances.

- Since the origin–destination market is not large enough to maintain an extensive and frequent network, a hub carrier that generates sufficient transfer demand is needed to maintain such a network.
- Although accommodating the hub carrier is still a prime objective, the ADP aims to create the option of accommodating simultaneously other markets, such as other alliances and low-cost airlines. This strategic objective clearly differs from the objectives put forward by the *Business Case Redesign*, which concentrated only on the hub carrier KLM.
- The development of Schiphol as an Airport City: according to the Schiphol Group, Schiphol is more than just an air transportation node. It is also a multi-modal transport and urban node with the opportunity to generate revenues. About 50 per cent of the revenue generated by the Schiphol Group is nowadays non-aeronautical.
- The *ADP 2020* is based on a 'most likely scenario' of growth towards 85 million passengers in 2020 ('2x Schiphol' scenario). This scenario corresponds to 4.5 per cent growth in annual passenger movements. Of these 85 million passengers, about 55 million are projected to be carried by KLM and partners and 40 million by other carriers. Moreover, in this scenario, total traffic consists of 37 million transfer and 48 million origin–destination passengers. This most likely scenario is derived from the scenarios developed for the *Business Case Redesign*.

Scenario and risk analysis

In 2001 a parallel study project on the uncertainties and risks surrounding the *Airport Development Plan 2020* was initiated: the *Long-term Scenario Study* (Schiphol Group 2001b). In our view, this study was important, since the *Business Case Redesign* scenarios were biased towards the assumption of growing hub operations by the KLM group. The *Business Case Redesign* did not consider explicitly such scenarios as a declining KLM hub operation, or very high growth rates of the low-cost airlines and so forth. Such scenarios might have significant implications for the *ADP 2020*. Neither was it clear whether the '2x Schiphol' was indeed the most-likely expectation.

Hence the aim of the Scenario Study was to analyze the probability of the 'most likely scenario' of the *Business Case Redesign*. In addition, the Scenario Study had the objective of providing the input for the 'robustness' testing of the *Airport Development Plan 2020* if the future were to develop differently from the most-likely forecast. Figure 9.8 places the Scenario Study in the context of Schiphol's master planning process.

Flexibility and multi-future robustness From the viewpoint of a flexible planning approach, the Scenario Study is noteworthy. In essence, it tries to guarantee the multi-future robustness of the Airport Development Plan. The Scenario Study aims to bring forward the other probable scenarios with a high impact that ought to be

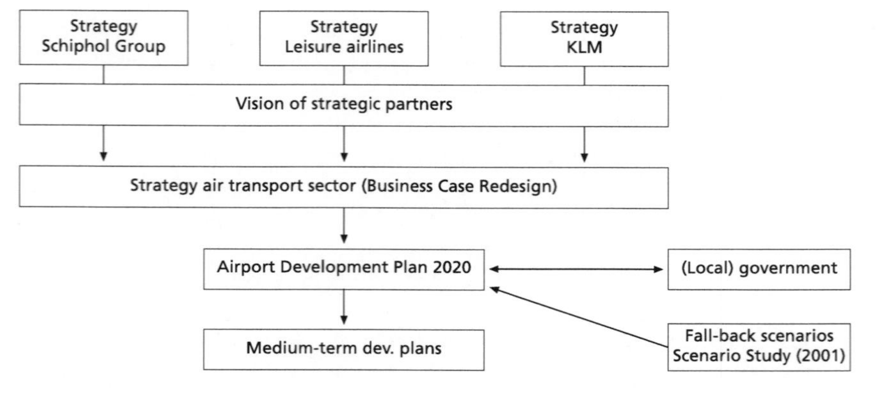

Figure 9.8 Scenario study in a broader planning context

taken into account in the *ADP 2020*. Only then can a master plan be formulated that is multi-future robust, is based on the highest 'common factor' for different scenarios, and is valid for a longer period.

In addition, the study considers flexibility as a broader concept than just the phasing of investments. In Chapter 8 we stated that traditional airport master planning considers the temporization of investments as one of the most important elements of flexibility needed in airport master planning in order to deal with the risks of overbuilding and under-building. However, Flexible Strategic Planning acknowledges that the composition of traffic may develop differently from what was initially envisioned, resulting in different capacity requirements.

The Scenario Study makes the same acknowledgement: the study tries to isolate those scenarios that are not just part of the phasing problem and could be resolved by accelerating or postponing investments (the option to accelerate or postpone investments). The Scenario Study searches for those scenarios that have an impact on the spatial layout of the airport or business concept, and hence on the content of the ADP.

As the Scenario Study puts it (Schiphol Group 2001b, 3):

> [...] the ADP should be sufficiently robust to deal with changing conditions flexibly. In this context, we do not just mean that investments can be accelerated or delayed. [...] The task force has searched for those 'what if' scenarios with a large impact on the spatial layout of the airport or business concepts.

In relation to the option of acceleration or delay, the Scenario Study mentions that the planning horizon has limited value. Traffic demand is much more important in relation to exercising growth options. This statement is in line with the characteristics of Flexible Strategic Planning. Flexible plans do not have a rigid planning horizon, but are based on triggers, planning thresholds or, in the words of the Schiphol Group, stepping-stones. In specific terms, it is not certain moments in time that trigger investments; it is certain volumes of traffic demand and the composition of these volumes that trigger new developments of airport infrastructure.

Identifying relevant what-if scenarios How did the Scenario Study isolate the most relevant 'what-if' scenarios, those which might have a large impact on the *ADP 2020*, are probable, and cannot be dealt with by simply postponing or accelerating investments (phasing)? The Scenario Study distinguished five major drivers for the development of the airport as an air traffic node: (1) economic growth, (2) network development of carriers, (3) environmental policy and regulations, (4) general air traffic and freight demand, and (5) aircraft technology.

The study describes different scenarios for each of the major drivers. With respect to our framework of Flexible Strategic Planning (Chapter 8), it is important to discuss two scenarios in relation to network development that might have a significant impact on the *ADP 2020*. The Scenario Study elaborated and assessed many more scenarios. Here we present just two that are highly relevant in the light of the following sections:

- Alternative alliances: the *Business Case Redesign* implicitly assumed that KLM would find an equal European partner to extend the Wings alliance (including Northwest Airlines, Kenya Airways). Wings would be the smallest of the four global alliances (Wings, SkyTeam, Oneworld, Star). In this scenario, Amsterdam would be the main hub with a large scope of intercontinental destinations. The Scenario Study concluded that four other scenarios were conceivable and would have quite a large impact on the Airport Development Plan (Table 9.1).
- Low-cost airlines: the *Business Case Redesign* did not explicitly consider the low-cost market in the forecasting models and the evaluation of the development alternatives. The Scenario Study distinguished between two scenarios with regard to low-cost network development. On the one hand, the Scenario Study formulated a scenario of stagnating low-cost growth. This scenario was not considered very realistic given the current growth of the low-cost segment and experiences in the United States. On the other hand, a scenario of radical low-cost growth was considered more realistic given the experiences with the radical growth of the low-cost market in the United States. Radical low-cost growth would have a very large impact on the master planning of Schiphol. It was recognized that the *Business Case Redesign* did not explicitly consider the growth of low-cost airlines.

  Low-cost airlines would demand dedicated, simpler and more efficient facilities with shorter aircraft turn-around times. If the airport were to decide to accommodate the low-cost market, specific facilities would be needed:

  > […] because the low-cost segment puts pressure on turn-around times and subsequently the controllability of the boarding/de-boarding process, the ADP can

Table 9.1 Alternative alliance scenarios in the Scenario Study

Scenario	Impact
KLM does not find a partner, Wings does not become a global airline alliance	• Loss of market share. • Amsterdam remains a primary hub for Wings, but on a smaller scale than in 2001.
KLM joins Star Alliance	• Networks of KLM and Lufthansa partly overlap. • Amsterdam becomes the secondary hub in the alliance, with Frankfurt as the primary hub. Intercontinental destinations may be under pressure.
KLM joins SkyTeam	• Paris Charles de Gaulle remains the primary hub of the SkyTeam alliance. Paris still has significant growth options. • Route networks of KLM and Air France partly overlap. • Amsterdam becomes the secondary hub. Intercontinental destinations may be under pressure.
KLM joins Oneworld	• London remains a primary hub as the home base of Oneworld's major partner British Airways. • The overlap between the KLM and British Airways network is quite small. Moreover, London airports are very congested. • As a result, Schiphol remains a primary hub and keeps its intercontinental destinations.

Source: *Adapted from Schiphol Group (2001b, 13)*

be expected to have to put forward specific, dedicated facilities to accommodate the growth of this market (if it is required) (Schiphol Group 2001b).

The Scenario Study identified these alternative scenarios very well. First, the Wings alliance has not become the fourth global alliance. KLM joined the SkyTeam alliance in 2004, following the Air France–KLM merger in 2003. Second, low-cost carriers were indeed becoming increasingly important at the airport. In July 2003 easyJet was the third carrier at the airport in terms of seat capacity.

It would not be possible to deal with these scenarios by simply accelerating or postponing investments. Hence the Scenario Study might deliver a useful input for testing the multi-future robustness of the *ADP 2020*. Nevertheless, the *Business Case Redesign*'s 'most likely' scenario and the need for land reservations brought forward by the *Business Case Redesign* (7PK and terminal Northwest) were still considered realistic. The Scenario Study concluded that the Redesign 'most likely' scenario could be used for the development of the ADP.

In our opinion, there were three problems associated with the Scenario Study. First, it could not assess the detailed implications for the master plan, because the *Airport Development Plan 2020* was still in a development stage.

Second, and perhaps more significant, the Scenario Study did not offer any combinations of different 'what-if' scenarios. The scenarios considered every key driver separately. However, it was this combination of a radical low-cost growth scenario and the SkyTeam scenario that was to undermine the strategic premises of the Airport Development Plan.

Finally, according to sources within the Airport Development Department, the impact of the Scenario Study on the *ADP 2020* was limited. The study ought to be followed up by a monitoring system of key drivers and thresholds that would trigger new investments or delay/change/abandon planned investments. Such a system might be comparable to the contingent road maps (Chapter 8), which guide the development of the airport in different scenarios. The system was never further elaborated and implemented. Instead, corporate strategy again turned its attention to '2x Schiphol' (85 million passengers in 2020), as initially laid down in the *ADP 2020*. Faludi (1973) helps to explain this observation: organizations in a turbulent environment tend to become involved in *a priori* decision-making. The complexity of the forces, or a lack of understanding of those forces, may result in organizations committing themselves prematurely to a strategy or plan to reduce complexity and the perceived uncertainty.

In summary, the Scenario Study was the reaction of the Schiphol Group to the uncertainties and risks associated with investments in airport capacity. The aim of the study was to formulate probable alternative scenarios, to assess the value of the most-likely scenario, and to 'test' the *ADP 2020* on it robustness for alternative futures. From a flexible planning perspective, we have to appreciate the Scenario Study efforts. The exercise bears witness to the recognition of risk and uncertainty as an inescapable reality in airport planning and helps to reassess these uncertainties and risks. Moreover, the study successfully identified two alternative scenarios that later became reality. The impact of the Scenario Study on the Airport Development Plan was limited, however. Low-cost airlines did not find favour at Schiphol for a long time as we shall see. Moreover, no follow-up of the Scenario Study was ever undertaken.

Alternatives

After the strategic premises had been formulated and the forecasting work done, the next step was to formulate various master plan alternatives. Why was the preferred alternative eventually chosen? What were the criteria for this choice?

The final *ADP 2020* master plan does not give us any information about the evaluation of the different development alternatives. Obviously, such an evaluation of alternatives must have taken place. According to a NACO representative, NACO together with the architects of Benthem Crouwel designed about 17 alternatives for the ADP. We could not trace the exact decision-making process in relation to these development alternatives. It is likely, however, that the evaluation of long-listed alternatives followed the regular procedure. As a planner from the Airport Development Department stated:

> We always design different development alternatives. We then compare these alternatives using multi-criteria analyses. This process leads to certain preferred alternatives, which we subject to risk analyses in different scenarios.

Three important alternatives included the development of (1) a new terminal area between the Zwanenburgbaan and the Polderbaan, (2) a new terminal area in the North-western area ('Noordwest') of the airport and (3) the extension of the existing terminal area in the KLM cargo area. The first development alternative had already been included in the Masterplan 2015, published in 1997. The last was an entirely new development alternative. Schiphol concluded that the first development option would make a seventh runway between the Zwanenburgbaan and Polderbaan impossible, although it was not clear whether such a runway would ever be needed. The alternative 'Northwest' would still allow for such a runway development, should a serious capacity gap arise. An extension of the terminal complex to the KLM cargo area would still allow for a seventh runway, but it would carry the heavy disinvestments costs of the deconstruction of the KLM cargo buildings.

In our opinion, three factors determined the number and type of alternatives: the prior decision-making process, the results of the Scenario Study and the strategy of the Schiphol Group. First, the prior decision-making processes at the national level and the recommendations of the civil aviation sector in the *Business Case Redesign* limited the scope of the evaluation of alternatives. In other words, the evaluation of development alternatives for the Schiphol-location took place within the framework of earlier decision-making.

In 1999 the Dutch government decided to concentrate further growth on the Schiphol location, but kept the option open to move to an offshore island in the long run. The government abandoned the latter option in 2003. Then, the Dutch civil aviation sector evaluated the different alternative runway configurations. On the basis of the conclusions of the A.T. Kearney study, the *Business Case Redesign* finally concluded that the 6PK and eventually a 7PK runway system would be best able to accommodate and realize future growth from cost, environmental, peak-capacity and reliability perspectives. The *Business Case Redesign* also stressed the need for additional, decentralized terminal capacity since the central terminal area would not be able to cope with the final traffic growth. Since the runway capacity largely leads for the other facilities at the airport such as terminals and aircraft-stands, the evaluation of alternatives for the *ADP 2020* took place within a pre-defined context. This reinforces our declaration in Chapter 8 that the choice of a certain alternative is not a fully rational process, but is also path-dependent on decisions made earlier.

Second, the strategy of the Schiphol Group changed from being an airline hub to a more diverse strategy early in 2000. In the Master Plan of 1989, the major objective of Schiphol was the mainport strategy: 'the mainport strategy means that there has to be sufficient capacity at the airport to accommodate passenger and freight demand' (N.V. Luchthaven Schiphol 1989, 13). In the master plan of 1997, the objective was not only the mainport strategy, but also the 'development of the airport as a(n) (inter)national and regional traffic node' and 'the development of the airport and region into a multifunctional centre of facilities, services and firms (Amsterdam Airport Schiphol 1997)'. Schiphol labelled this more diverse strategy the AirportCity strategy. Finally, the Airport Development Plan of 2003 confirmed that the AirportCity strategy was still the core strategy, but added that the airport also wanted to facilitate low-cost carriers and other alliances. Let us consider this in more detail.

With regard to other alliances, the (informal) policy in 2001–2003 was to cluster other alliances. The underlying idea was that clustering might eventually contribute to the hubbing operations of a non-KLM alliance at the airport. This clustering would reduce the dependency on KLM, enhance competition, reduce prices and increase traffic demand. However, the Scenario Study concluded that such a secondary hub operation was not a very likely scenario: Schiphol would not have enough runway capacity to facilitate two full hub operations side by side. Moreover, the nationality clauses in bilateral air-service agreements made it virtually impossible for foreign airlines to start a hub operation at Schiphol (Chapter 2). Nevertheless, the idea concerning the potential for other alliances had its effect on the *ADP 2020*, as we see below.

With regard to the low-cost carriers, the *ADP 2020* planned to facilitate not only the KLM hub operation, but also other alliances and origin–destination airlines (including charter and low-cost airlines). The Scenario Study identified the potential for low-cost carrier growth. Low-cost carriers might help the airport to reduce its dependency on KLM. The business model of these carriers differs from that of a full-service carrier such as KLM (see Chapter 2). Accommodating low-cost airlines would require specialized, dedicated facilities. Including low-cost carriers in the airport's strategic market portfolio was all but evident. According to one Schiphol planner:

> The tremendous growth of low-cost carriers has long been neglected. The general opinion was: they are difficult, we don't want them, they're just joyriders, it's a wild trade. Low-cost air transport has no place in a high-quality airport.

According to another Schiphol planner:

> There has been a development in the conception of low-cost airlines, running from 'we don't want them' to 'toleration' to 'keeping the option open' and, in the future, to 'stimulation'.

In short, the evaluation of alternatives exhibits the characteristics of a funnelling process: decisions made earlier (including the *Business Case Redesign*) largely defined the action space of Airport Development and Benthem Crouwel-NACO in designing the alternatives. In essence, this procedure is normal for human beings and organizations in overcoming the limitations of the decision-maker to deal with highly complex decision-making processes. Funnelling, or sequential decision-making, allows a problem to be broken down into 'a sequence of similar problems which could be resolved one after the other, none of which exceeded the information-handling capacity of the decision-maker' (Faludi 1973, 111).

The problem with the funnelling approach, however, is that there is a risk of abandoning certain alternatives prematurely. Airport planning takes many years. Circumstances may change during the planning process; more attractive alternatives may have been abandoned at an earlier stage. The combination of the funnelling process, the role of KLM in this process and market volatility would challenge the strategic premises of the *ADP 2020*.

The Airport Development Plan 2020

In 2003 the first draft of the *Airport Development Plan 2020* was finalized. In July 2004 the plan still awaited the approval of the Board of Directors of the airport. Consequently, at that time the document was therefore still an internal, confidential document. Let us briefly consider some elements of the *ADP 2020* that are interesting from the perspective of Flexible Strategic Planning and are important in relation to the analysis in the final section of this chapter.

The objective of the *ADP 2020* was 'to provide a guideline of how the airport might develop in the long run as an AirportCity, taking into account environmental and safety issues, as well as the impact on land-use in the airport region'. In practice, this guideline calls for the accommodation of the recently-formed KLM–Air France Group, other alliances, low-cost airlines, other airlines and the further extension of Schiphol as an AirportCity.

The *ADP 2020* acknowledged the increasingly dynamic character of the airline industry (Schiphol Group/Afdeling Airport Development 2003a) and its potential impact on the future development of facilities at the airport. The ADP acknowledged the need for flexibility, mainly through remarks made about the guideline character of the ADP and the creation of real options.

The *ADP 2020* stressed that it is only a guideline. It indicates which land reservations are needed on and off the airport site to accommodate traffic growth, given current insights, forecasts and conditions. However, the ADP is not a blueprint, a deterministic plan. The Dutch title of the ADP is *Ruimtelijke Toekomstvisie*, which can be translated as a *Spatial Perspective on the Future*. This title further underlines the guideline character of the plan and its intention not to be deterministic. Unlike the *ADP 2020*, the former plans of 1989 and 1997 were called master plans.

The ADP has to be updated at least every five years, or when changing circumstances so require:

> Planning is a continuous process. Frequently, new developments and insights are integrated into policy. Given the dynamics in the air transport industry and the airport, there have to be sufficient opportunities for such integration. Hence, the ADP is not a blueprint for the future that cannot be changed. This vision is more a guideline for policy and development thinking, given the current insights, forecasts, and conditions [...] Investments and trajectories are based on traffic forecasts. If the insights regarding the development of traffic forecasts change, the planning can be changed (Schiphol Group/Afdeling Airport Development 2003a, 41–2).

This definition of airport master planning is in line with the earlier discussion about the planning culture within Airport Development, which considers the airport master planning as a continuous process of making strategic land reservations and keeping options open. Using the framework of Flexible Strategic Planning (Chapter 8), the

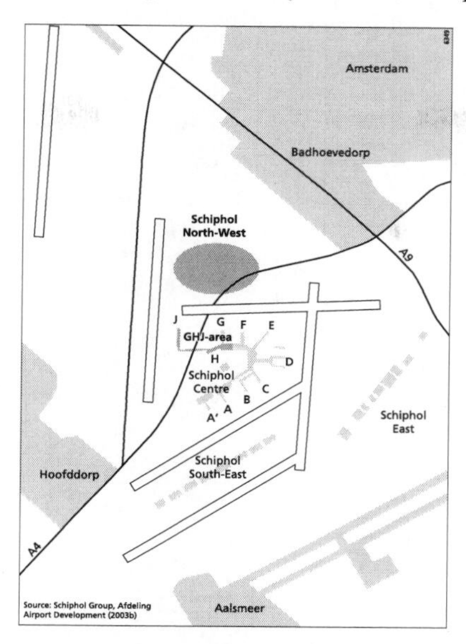

Figure 9.9 Possible spatial layout of Schiphol in 2020

Airport Development Department therefore considers master planning a process of creating real options of continuously anticipating changes in the environment.

The *ADP 2020* creates an endless number of real options. We do not intend to summarize the *ADP 2020* here. However, for a good understanding of the next two sections, we highlight two groups of real options in the *ADP 2020*: the extension of the runway system and the terminal, pier and gate facilities. Figure 9.9 gives an overview of some important real options in the plan.

A sixth runway (crosswind) The *ADP 2020* planning process started with the assumption that the 6P alternative would be the most suitable alternative, although the civil aviation sector had not yet brought forward a preferred alternative regarding the future growth of the airport (Schiphol Group 2001a). If the civil aviation sector were to make new information available, the ADP would incorporate it and adapt the plan if necessary. Indeed, during the planning process the *ADP 2020* included new information that would have a significant impact on the initial plan.

First, the results of the A.T. Kearney Study led to changes in the ADP. As we saw earlier, this study concluded that a sixth parallel runway would result in a significant fallback in capacity during 10 per cent of the year because of heavy crosswinds. Such a reduction in capacity would result in delays, cancellations and extra costs for the airlines and the airport. Hence the ADP study eventually preferred the 6PK alternative (with possible expansion to 7PK if required); for the sake of peak-hour reliability, an additional crosswind runway would be required before any commitment to an additional north–south runway could be made.

Second, the 6PK alternative was initially rejected because it would not deliver the desired increase in peak-hour capacity for the airport. In 2001 the maximum peak-hour capacity of the 6PK runway system would be 140 movements per hour, decreasing to 120 in the case of heavy crosswinds. However, the assumptions made concerning the maximum peak-hour capacity per runway turned out to be too conservative. Technological improvements and more aggressive air traffic control stimulated the peak-hour capacity per runway and subsequently increased the maximum number of movements per hour.

Hence the ADP planning process started with the assumption that a sixth parallel runway was needed. However, on the basis of new information, a sixth crosswind runway was eventually preferred. The *ADP 2020* still called for land banking with regard to a seventh parallel runway, although the runway was not thought to be needed within the planning horizon.

Terminal, pier and gate facilities The runway facilities lead for most of the other investments in airport capacity. The growth in peak-hour traffic demand that a sixth runway would accommodate would need additional terminal facilities, piers, aircraft stands, and so forth. The ADP envisioned the location of the KLM–Air France and Sky Team alliance partners being primarily in the central terminal area. This location was to ensure short minimum connecting times, one of the key drivers for a hub-operation (Chapter 2). However, the possibilities for an additional terminal, pier and gate infrastructure were limited since the central terminal area had nearly reached its maximum layout. Growth opportunities for the hub carrier were created with the option for an additional A-pier and A'-pier (Figure 9.9). Furthermore, the ADP created the option to free-up capacity in the central terminal area by relocating non-hub carriers to a new, decentralized terminal area.

The *ADP 2020* envisioned the non-hub carriers at different locations at the airport. First, the non-hub carriers could be located in the central terminal area during the non-peak periods (off-wave) of the hub system. Second, origin–destination airlines (alliances, low-cost, charter) would move to a decentralized, full-service J-pier on the other side of the motorway A4 (Figures 9.9). A People Mover System would connect the pier with the central terminal area. The J-pier was supposed to be the next extension of the terminal area. An H-pier might be built to solve temporary capacity problems, but it would only deliver a very limited growth in gate facilities.

Finally, the ADP planned the origin–destination airlines in a decentralized area on the Northwestern side of the airport, 'Noordwest'. The Noordwest area was expected to be needed in 2020, based on the most-likely scenario.

Conclusions

The *ADP 2020* planning process started in 2001. The strategic premises of the ADP were based on the results of the *Business Case Redesign* together with the strategy of the Schiphol Group itself. From the start, the Airport Development Department of the Schiphol Group recognized the need for flexibility in the master plan and the planning process. Not surprisingly, the ADP planning process exhibits some important characteristics of the model of Flexible Strategic Planning as discussed in Chapter 8. Some of the important flexible planning characteristics are the oscillation between the long-term Airport Development Plan and the medium-term development plans, the guideline character of the *ADP 2020*, the creation of real options and the extensive scenario and risk analysis.

We have however also identified the bias towards the hub carrier in the *Business Case Redesign* and the importance of this study for the *ADP 2020* as a potential limitation to the flexibility of the planning process. In addition, some interesting initiatives towards a contingent planning model as a follow up of the Scenario Study were abandoned.

We now turn to the volatility of the airport transport market. We show below how market dynamics can undermine the strategic premises of a master plan and challenge the master planning process.

Changing tides

The current deregulated air transport market is likely to become increasingly volatile. The future of airport traffic is becoming increasingly uncertain. Airline network behaviour is becoming more dynamic in both the short and the long term, with major effects on the connectivity and traffic demand of individual airports. Schiphol has been no exception in this respect. Consequently, a quickly changing market context invalidated some of the assumptions underlying the Airport Development Plan. Let us consider this changing context and the consequences for the planning process with regard to the GHJ-area. This consists of the G-pier, H-apron and J-apron at the airport (Figure 9.9).

The past

The *Airport Development Plan 2020* was based on the strategic premise of a highly dominant and successful hub carrier (KLM group), as was argued earlier. The related forecasts showed high growth rates of annual passenger volumes and peak-hour capacity demand (Schiphol Group 2004e). Not surprisingly, the *Business Case Redesign* and *ADP 2020* concentrated on an optimization of the hubbing process at the airport, just like the earlier Master Plans 2003 and 2015. This optimization was referred to as the 'mainport strategy'. In addition, the aim was to cluster other alliances and create the option for other alliances to start limited hub operations at the airport. The *ADP 2020* envisioned more peak-hour capacity of the runway system to facilitate KLM's hubbing strategy. Furthermore, the KLM group would be clustered in the central terminal area. Other alliances would have their own terminal area: the J-pier. This would be a full-service pier, connected with the central terminal area by a People Mover System. Low-cost carriers would be tolerated as far as capacity would permit.

An H-pier was an option should a small increment in the number of gates be needed (Figure 9.9). But the H-pier, the predecessors of which can be found in the master plans of 1989 and 1997, was not thought to be a very efficient solution. Since the H-pier could only be used on one side, its unit costs per passenger would be relatively high compared with a pier that can be used on both sides. In the long term there would be the option to accommodate other alliances and low-cost carriers in a decentralized terminal area: Schiphol Noordwest (Figure 9.9).

The present

The airport context started to change rapidly in 2001. Because of September 11th, the economic recession, SARS and soaring oil prices, the growth of traffic slowed down and even became negative for Schiphol in 2003 (compared with 2002). As a result, the new traffic demand forecasts were much more conservative than those originally used for the *Business Case Redesign* and the *ADP 2020* (Schiphol Group 2004e).

Moreover, the low-cost airlines showed themselves to be 'recession-proof'. Whereas most full-service carriers experienced declining growth figures and yields, low-cost carriers enjoyed high growth rates during the period 2000–2004. According to a Schiphol planner:

> The importance of low-cost carriers was not considered to be very great, until misfortune struck: the first Gulf War, SARS and September 11th. The major carriers faced serious problems, but the low-cost carriers did not. In fact, the low-cost carriers were a buffer in this period.

Because of the growth of the low-cost carriers, the marketing department of the airport forecast a shortage of 13 aircraft stands in 2013. The low-cost airlines (in particular easyJet) had frequently asked the airport for dedicated facilities. On the other hand, there were still major uncertainties about the long-term stability of low-cost growth. Analysts expect a shake-out in the low-cost market following its recent and enormous growth, a development that could be observed in the United States some years ago (Gelten 2004).

Lastly, Air France took over KLM in September 2003. Suddenly Schiphol was no longer the only hub available to KLM. Paris Charles de Gaulle, an airport with options to expand its peak-hour capacity significantly, became a second growth option for the KLM–Air France hub operations. The Dutch government reached an agreement with the newly-formed airline on 42 'key destinations' that would be operated from Schiphol during the next five years under 'normal economic circumstances' (Ministerie van Verkeer and Waterstaat 2003). In the long term, however, network reorganizations are likely to be expected. Paris Charles de Gaulle may have better chances of becoming the primary hub airport for SkyTeam because it has better key drivers for a hub operation (Chapter 2) than Amsterdam: a larger origin–destination market, better landside accessibility and more growth options. Hence the Air France–KLM merger created uncertainty for the future role of Schiphol in the network of its most important carrier.

In summary, traffic forecasts became much more conservative because of the changing market circumstances. The need for more peak-hour capacity was only moderate, but low-cost airlines were knocking at the gate. These new developments undermined the strategic premises of the original *ADP 2020* and created a strategic mismatch between the envisioned projects in the *ADP 2020* and market developments (Schiphol Group/Afdeling Airport Development 2004d). This mismatch could not simply be resolved by the phasing of investments, but only by changing the plans for the spatial layout of the airport. Ironically, the Scenario Study of 2001 had already addressed the potential impacts of the changes in the market environment in 2002–2004.

The risks of a strategic mismatch

What did the strategic mismatch comprise? The original *ADP 2020* envisioned a first increment in gate facilities by investing in a decentralized, full-service J-pier. An automated people mover system would connect this pier to the central terminal area. In the long term, a terminal and aircraft stand capacity were planned in the Schiphol Noordwest area. However, serious risks would accompany this first step towards the J-pier:

- The risks of overcapacity: investing in a full-service J-pier when facing low-growth levels might result in a shift of non-KLM carriers and low-cost airlines to the J-pier, leaving some of the gates at the B and G-pier underused.
- The risks of a mismatch between user requirements and the supply of facilities: low-cost airlines proved to be an opportunity for the airport to diversify aeronautical revenues and become less dependent on a potentially footloose hub carrier. However, the user requirements of low-cost airlines differ from those of the full-service airlines for which the J-pier had been planned. Low-cost airlines require short turn-around times, the clustering of operations, self-service check-in with baggage drop-off points, very simple passenger handling (no tube gates, no buses) and low-cost facilities (cheaper building materials, no tapis roulants, and so forth). A full-service J-pier with a people mover would certainly not satisfy these criteria.
- The risk of higher unit costs per passenger: the J-pier would be a very costly option. The investments in a people mover system to make the pier accessible for passengers would be considerable. Moreover, such an investment is very difficult to reverse. Investing in a big-bet, irreversible facility is not wise from a flexibility point of view. A J-pier would be a single solution for a single expected future (clustering alliances). Lower than expected growth rates might be a burden on the finances of the airport for a long time.
- Not investing in new aircraft stand capacity and simply delaying the J-pier was not an option either: the airport would face a limited shortage in aircraft stands and would miss the opportunity to accommodate low-cost growth and diversify revenues.

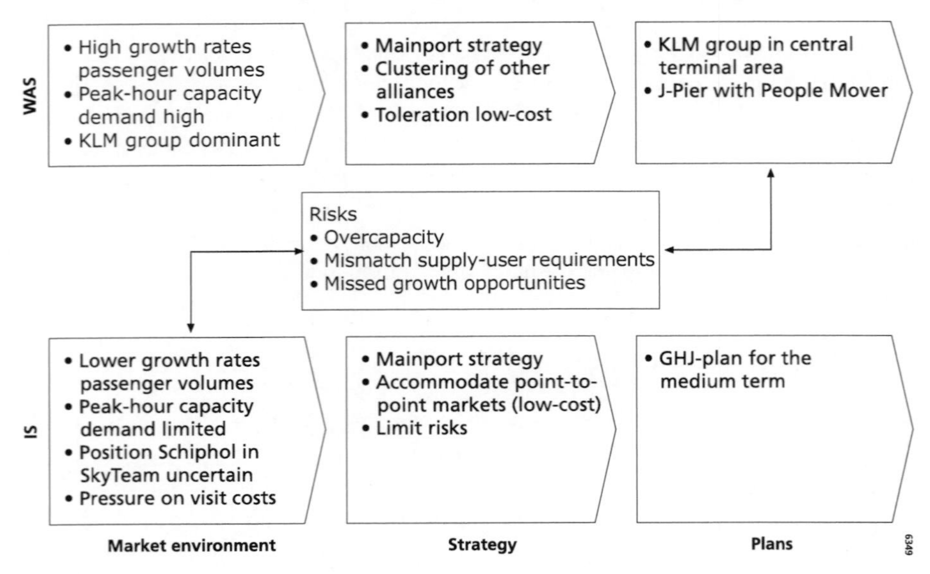

Figure 9.10 Changing tides, changing policies, changing plans

In conclusion, the J-pier with a people mover was no longer considered the best growth option in the uncertain and risky market environment. The strategy of the airport changed. The mainport strategy (accommodating the hub carrier) was still the most important strategy, but the accommodation of point-to-point airlines (low-cost carriers) – while minimizing risky investments – also became important. Airport Development translated the new strategy into a new medium-term plan – the *GHJ-plan* – that would be more suitable for the new circumstances (Figure 9.10).

Let us consider the planning process and content of the *GHJ-plan*, then review the plan and planning process from the perspective of flexible strategic planning.

The GHJ-plan

In the previous section we showed that the changing market environment gave rise to the opinion within Airport Development and the Schiphol Group in general that investing in the J-pier was no longer the best solution. At the same time, the airport wanted to take advantage of the opportunity to accommodate low-cost growth and resolve limited capacity problems in the medium term without taking major risks.

In June 2003 the Chief Operational Officer commissioned the Airport Development Department to resolve the strategic issue at stake: the *GHJ-plan*. This plan is in fact part of a much broader revision of the Airport Development Plan owing to structural changes in the market environment (Schiphol Group 2004c). Here we focus on the *GHJ-plan* alone.

The planning process within the Airport Development Department to resolve the issue consists of a number of steps:

- formulation of the objectives
- evaluation of the long-listed alternatives
- evaluation of the short-listed alternatives
- plan design
- decision-making.

Let us briefly consider these steps. It is important to note that the steps discussed here are not necessarily sequential. The development of the GHJ-plan has been a continuous search and communication process with a continuous oscillation between analysis, formulation of objectives and formulation of the plan.

Formulation of objectives

The initial objectives of the plan were:

- to resolve capacity problems in the short and medium term
- to accommodate low-cost airlines by means of a tailor-made product
- but to do so without doing any damage to the hub-operation of KLM
- to minimize risks of investments in an uncertain market
- to reduce visit costs for the airlines to which the new product will be offered.

With respect to the accommodation of the low-cost airlines, no dedicated facilities for low-cost airlines were present at the airport at that time. Low-cost airlines were tolerated at the airport as long as they fitted into the 'normal' operation. Dedicated facilities would require the airport to take into account the specific user requirements of low-cost airlines and, by so doing, to reduce the costs for airlines to visit the airport. Specifically, this would mean dedicated facilities where low-cost airlines could be clustered, a facility with short turn-around times, self-service check-in and baggage drop-off points, boarding without buses or tube gates, boarding and de-boarding at two aircraft doors, lower levels of service, cheaper materials and limited frills (Schiphol Group 2004d).

From a flexible planning perspective, we can say that the *GHJ-plan* was demand driven: the *GHJ-plan* was not only a reaction to the changing market circumstances, although the *GHJ-plan* was demand-driven, it might also be considered a solution that followed a previously established market trend. The *GHJ-plan* is not a proactive development, which intends to provoke a well-defined future, but is rather a reaction to market developments.

With respect to the minimization of risks, Airport Development would have to formulate a plan that would be sufficiently flexible to deal with the uncertainties and risks of the free-market regime.

Table 9.2 Evaluation of long-listed alternatives

Alternative	Valuation
Low-cost to J-pier with People Mover System (original plan)	• High-cost option • Irreversible investment • Risk of overcapacity • No product differentiation
Lelystad airport (Province of Flevoland)	• Risks of unlimited low-cost growth and 'cannibalization' of KLM hub-operation • Large investments needed to convert Lelystad into a commercial airport • Would not be ready when needed
Low-cost to 'Noordwest' area	• Large investments needed (accessibility, baggage handling, for example) • Would not be ready when needed
Low-cost to Schiphol-East ('Oost')/ Southeast ('Zuidoost')	• Runway-crossings: decrease in peak-hour capacity
A-pier	• Risk of interference with KLM operation and its growth opportunities
Dedicated low-cost facility in GHJ-area	• Meets aircraft stand requirements until 2007–2010 • Limited investment • Phasing possible

Source: *Schiphol Group (2004d)*

Long-listed alternatives

The evaluation of alternatives followed a sequential decision-making procedure. First, there was a valuation of the long-listed alternatives based on general criteria. Second, the short-listed alternatives were subjected to more detailed financial analysis and robustness analysis. Table 9.2 gives an overview of the long-list of alternatives and the final valuation of each of the alternatives (Schiphol Group 2004d). Figure 9.11 illustrates the search areas on the airport site. The Airport Development Department concluded that a solution to the strategic issues was to be found in the GHJ-area of the airport. This area best met the airport's objectives in terms of risk minimization; it would solve capacity problems in the short-term; and, because of the limited scope, it would not be a threat to, or interfere with, the KLM hub operation.

Short-listed alternatives

The Airport Development Department subsequently developed several detailed alternatives for the GHJ-area. These included:

1. A low-cost H-pier with peak and buffer aircraft stands in the J-area, but without an extensive bus service to the J-apron. The J-apron would only be used for peak demand and buffering of aircraft (see Figure 9.12).
2. A low-cost H-pier with a J-apron. Additionally, there would be a dedicated J-apron for Transavia/Basiq Air with extensive bus operation to the J-apron.

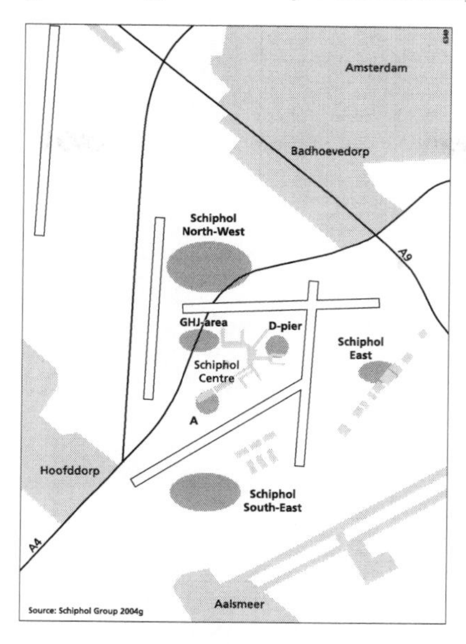

Figure 9.11 Search areas for dedicated low-cost facilities

3. A low-cost J-terminal with a bus or walking bridge connection over the A4 motorway to the central terminal area.

The short-listed alternatives were evaluated according to three criteria: (1) user requirements; (2) investment costs and operational expenses; (3) multi-future robustness. The financial consequences were analyzed by using a net present value methodology.

With regard to the user requirements, alternative A would be a facility tailored to the preferences of the low-cost airlines. However, there would be no possibility of accommodating Transavia/Basiq Air in a dedicated facility. On the other hand, it would be the least costly alternative and it would be robust for various future scenarios.

B would be the best alternative from the viewpoint of user requirements: a dedicated product for both Transavia/Basiq Air and other low-cost airlines, such as easyJet. However, this would be the most expensive alternative owing to the large bus operation. Moreover, the alternative bears the risk of overcapacity in the central terminal area: Transavia/Basiq Air uses gates in the central terminal area outside the peaks (off-wave) of SkyTeam. Moving Basiq to a J-apron might result in lower occupancy rates of the gates in the central terminal area.

Alternative C meets the user requirements of the low-cost carriers, and it would be easier to expand, but it is also quite an expensive solution. Moreover, it bears the risk of creating overcapacity in the central terminal area. In addition, alternatives B and C would have a negative impact on the commercial revenues of the airport. Passengers tend to leave the terminal earlier when they depart from a decentralized

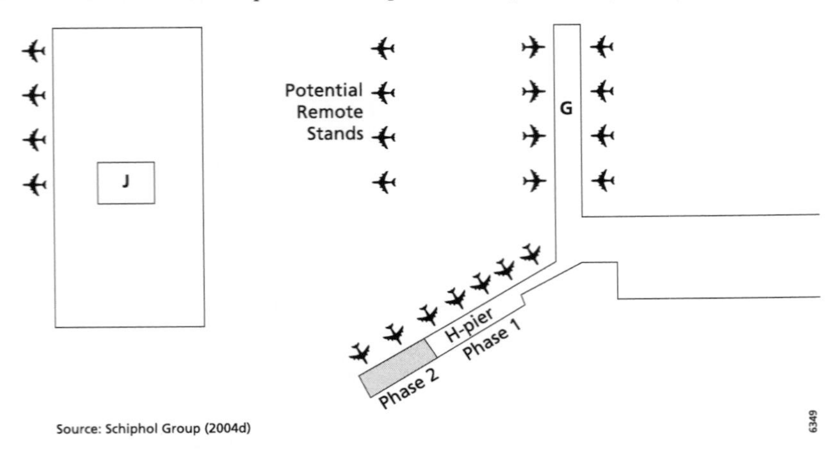

Figure 9.12 Alternative A

pier or terminal area. Hence they spend less time and money in the shops and restaurants of the central terminal area.

From a financial point of view, alternative A turned out to be the most attractive solution. It was not the most desirable solution from the user requirement viewpoint, but other solutions would be much more costly.

Recapturing the framework of Flexible Strategic Planning, the quantitative evaluation of short-listed alternatives followed a commonplace, traditional net present value (NPV) methodology (see Chapter 8). Uncertainty and flexibility were not taken into account in the NPV analysis. Robustness analysis of uncertainties and risks was only carried out for a previously chosen alternative, based on the NPV methodology. Such an approach may lead to a premature commitment to a particular alternative. Some deferred alternatives might be more valuable if uncertainty and risk had been taken explicitly into account by means of decision analysis, real option analysis or scenario analysis.

Robustness analysis

Airport Development subjected the preferred alternative A to an extensive robustness analysis. This took place by means of 'what-if' thinking. Various scenarios that could possibly affect the preferred plan (alternative A) were analyzed according to the potential implications they might have. Table 9.3 summarizes the results of the robustness analysis, based on the author's insight and information. The Airport Development Department thus concluded that the low-cost H-pier was the best alternative given the objectives of the plan, current market conditions and the results of the financial and robustness analyses.

From a flexibility point of view, the robustness analysis deserves appreciation, since the uncertainty was explicitly taken into account. Nevertheless, as we stated in Chapter 8, such robustness-thinking is still quite subjective. In this respect, there are

Table 9.3 Robustness of the GHJ-plan (alternative A)

	Higher than expected growth of SkyTeam hub operation and low cost	**Decrease SkyTeam hub operation, growth low-cost**	**Stagnation/decrease hub operation and low-cost**	**Growth Sky Team, decrease/stagnation low-cost growth**
Short-term	• Expansion of H pier (11 gates), peak capacity in J-area • Build A pier for hub operation	• Minimum investments to convert full-service gates to low-cost gates in central terminal area (G-pier for example) • Analysis of the possibilities of extending H-pier to 11 and 25 gates	• Stop all investments • H-pier is a no-lose option: low-cost option=low-risk option	• Delay H-pier • Do not extend H-pier any further • Upgrade H-pier to full-service pier • Demolish H-pier and build full-service pier
Long-term	• Demolition of H-pier, low-cost to Schiphol Noordwest • Upgrading H-pier to full-service pier, low-cost to Noordwest/ other airport	–	–	–

better methods of valuing flexibility and uncertainty, such as decision-analysis and real option analysis. Moreover, the preferred alternative was not compared with other alternatives. In the planning process, the financial analysis ruled out the other short-listed alternatives before the robustness analysis of the preferred alternative started.

Finally, in April 2004 the Management Team Schiphol Group decided to adopt the *GHJ-plan* (alternative A). The development trajectory of the GHJ-area was a phased trajectory. In the first stage, additional aircraft stands would be built on the J-apron to compensate for the loss of disconnected aircraft stands on the H-apron. In addition, the first phase of the H-pier would be realized (five gates) with peak aircraft stands on the J-apron. According to market conditions, in a second phase the H-apron could be extended to seven gates and an additional four aircraft stands at the G-pier. Further extensions of the H-area to 11 and 25 gates would be studied (Schiphol Group 2004d).

The Airport Development Department received the commission in 2003. The formulation of the plan took about three weeks. Commitment building in the various Business Units and the Management Team and subsequent revisions of the plan took about 10 months, according to one Schiphol planner. The first phase of the H-pier was completed in October 2005.

To conclude, none of the short-listed alternatives turned out to be an optimal solution for every criterion. However, the low-cost H-pier with J-buffer/peak-area was considered to be the most attractive alternative given current market conditions and future expectations. First, the plan proved to be robust for various future scenarios. Second, the plan was financially the most attractive and met most airline user requirements. Third, the development trajectory of the GHJ-area was phased to meet demand on a just-in-time basis.

Conclusions: the GHJ-plan from the perspective of flexible planning

What can we say about the H-pier alternative from the perspective of flexible planning? Is the *GHJ-plan* an example of a state-of the-art flexible plan, or does it still exhibit most of the characteristics of what we call traditional airport master planning? The GHJ planning process and final plan exhibit a number of important characteristics of flexible planning.

First, the *GHJ-plan* is demand driven. With the *GHJ-plan*, the Airport Planning Department anticipated new market developments and adjusted to them, most notably the changing position of Schiphol as a hub in the network of its home carrier KLM and the growth of the low-cost market. The *GHJ-plan* captured a 'window of opportunity'.

Second, the *GHJ-plan* is a multi-future robust plan. A 'what-if' analysis was performed to test the viability of the *GHJ-plan* in the most probable scenarios. Long-term implications of short-term actions were identified in a range of futures. The *GHJ-plan* is not the optimal alternative for any single scenario, but performs best over a range of probable scenarios.

Third, the GHJ-planning process shows clearly the value of an airport planning process that oscillates between the medium and long term. The very existence of medium-term plans such as the *GHJ-plan* allows the airport to reassess changing circumstances. The Airport Development Plan can again be updated on the basis of these new market circumstances and new medium-term plans. We identified the continuous updating of the long-term master plans and medium-term development plans as a major prerequisite of a flexible planning style in Chapter 8.

Fourth, the *GHJ-plan* acknowledged the uncertainties and the risks of the current air transport market from the start. Using the terminology of Chapter 8, we conclude that the Airport Development Department has a think risk culture. It all but considers the planning as deterministic and the future as controllable.

Fifth, the *GHJ-plan* contains real options:

- The plan is phased and modular. The modular H-pier can be built in phases. It will be investigated whether the H-pier can be further extended to 11 and 25 gates. The J-apron might eventually be upgraded to an apron with a full bus operation, a pier or small terminal if market circumstances require so.
- The H-pier is reversible: the H-pier is a low-cost investment. Because of its simple layout and the use of cheaper materials, the pier can be broken down if the land is required for other uses in the future.
- Both the H-pier and J-apron can be delayed, accelerated or expanded according to market circumstances.

As an AD planner stated:

> If we built a J-pier with an ATS[17] and tube gates [...], we would have a pier in its maximum, most expensive and least reversible form. Now imagine European traffic transforming into a low-cost operation. We would do better to start with open aircraft stands in the J-area (with buses from the terminal), probably with a small (low-cost) satellite at a later stage (with buses to the terminal), then a low-cost/charter terminal and finally, we could choose to convert the facility into a fully-fledged pier (with or without ATS).

Finally, the *GHJ-plan* contributes to a diversification strategy: the *GHJ-plan* facilitates the growth of low-cost airlines. Hence, the growth of low-cost revenues at the airport somewhat reduces the dependency on the dominant home-carrier.

We conclude that the *GHJ-plan* exhibits some important characteristics of the planning style of Flexible Strategic Planning, which we discussed in Chapter 8. However, we put forward some remarks also from the perspective of traditional airport master planning.

Conclusions: The GHJ-plan from the perspective of traditional airport master planning

First, the low-cost growth could have been anticipated much earlier. In this chapter we discussed the Scenario Study. This Study identified the scenario of high low-cost growth with its specific user requirements, the KLM–Air France merger and the delayed growth of air traffic demand. Unfortunately, the Scenario Study failed to combine these into one scenario. Moreover, the impact of the Scenario Study on the actual Airport Development Plan was slight. The possibility of low-cost growth in combination with dedicated facilities was not translated into the Airport Development Plan. One the one hand, the full-service J-pier did not meet the different user requirement of low-cost airlines. On the other, the Noordwest area would have been delivered much too late.

Second, there was no follow-up of the Scenario Study in terms of contingent road map planning. With such a system, the Airport Development Department might have discovered and anticipated the low-cost growth and uncertainty regarding the hub carrier much earlier.

Third, the identification and appreciation of the low-cost market as a growth opportunity and the translation into planning took a long time. Various respondents used the metaphor of the oil tanker to describe the process of strategic change within the Schiphol Group. What was the reason for the long lead times of the project? The potential for low-cost had been identified much earlier, but the translation into strategy took a very long time.

One reason is that the strategy of the Schiphol Group was to create a high quality airport. Low-cost airlines certainly did not fit into this picture, but a J-pier with an automated people mover would. Another reason is that organizations in general

17 Automatic Transport System.

show a resistance to change. Facilitating the low-cost market would mean extra work, a need for knowledge and, potentially, organizational changes. Moreover, one should not forget that the Airport Development Planning process had already started in 2001. Incorporating the low-cost growth with its specific user requirements would probably mean that the ADP planning process would have to be further delayed. According to a Schiphol planner:

> The *ADP 2020* was being overtaken by new developments. We had two choices: indicate the potential impact of these developments in a footnote of the plan, or start all over again. The H-pier is an example of the first choice. You have to finish your plan. It does not make sense to start over and over again.

According to the airport planning consultant NACO, too long lead-times of the master planning process are among the major problems in the highly turbulent market environment: by the time the master plan is finished, the world has changed too much for the master plan to be viable. As one director of a regional airport put it:

> You need a master plan to communicate your ideas to others or go to the Stock Exchange. But a master plan is too rigid for the air transport market of today. […] Besides, we are a small organization with limited resources to formulate a master plan as Schiphol does. It is more important for us to make a profitable business.

Fourth, the strategic premises of the *ADP 2020* were biased. KLM played an important part in the *Business Case Redesign*, which preceded the Airport Development Plan. KLM in fact defined what it wanted. The part KLM played is no surprise given its large market share and its history at the airport. As a result, the Airport Development Plan was heavily oriented towards the hub carrier. A more pluralistic process in the current, highly volatile market environments would seem to have been a better procedure for a Strategic Partnership than that of the *Business Case Redesign*.

Fifth, traditional evaluation tools were used to evaluate the *GHJ-plan*. The NPV methodology as applied in the project evaluation did not capture the value of flexibility in the plan, nor did it take into account the level of uncertainty. As we saw earlier, there are better alternatives capable of taking uncertainty and flexibility into account.

A sixth reason is that organizations tend to search for stability in times of environmental turbulence. A contingent road map system based on 'what if' scenarios and triggers apparently did not fit in the search for stability. In contrast, it was considered to complicate the context further.

Finally, Flexible Strategic Planning is pro-active: Flexible Strategic Planning provokes desired change. The GHJ-pier does not provoke a desired change, but follows market developments that could no longer be ignored. Pro-active planning might have stimulated low-cost growth at the airport from the start by functioning as a kind of breeding ground for low-cost airlines:

The low-cost market had been asking for additional facilities at Schiphol for some time. Yet Schiphol tried to keep them away as long as possible: we were a high-quality airport and we did not want the hub operation of KLM to be damaged.

Conclusions

The long-term planning of Schiphol's infrastructure is taking place in an uncertain market environment. In this chapter we analyzed the master planning process for Schiphol's *Airport Development Plan 2020*. In so doing, we have shown how airport planners deal with an increasingly uncertain, volatile and risky market environment.

What does this flexibility in the long and medium-term planning of Schiphol's infrastructure consist of? Although our results provide only a snapshot of the planning process, we can nevertheless put forward a number of important elements of Flexible Strategic Planning. At the same time, for every element of flexibility there is another side of the coin.

Backcasting

First, Flexible Strategic Planning is characterized by a continuous oscillation between the long term (the master plan) and the medium term (the development plan): the general level and the more detailed level. The master plan or Airport Development Plan is only a broad guideline for the future development of the airport. It is nothing more than a strictly coordinated portfolio of real options. It is a coordinated portfolio because an airport consists of a set of tightly coupled operations. Changes in one part of the airport may interfere with operations in other parts of the airport or the possibility of developing these operations in the future. Hence a master plan has to be highly coordinated. The master plan is a portfolio of real options because it does not prescribe a certain development. It only indicates the most-likely and robust way of developing the airport, but is not an obligation to do so.

The master plan is worked out in more detailed, medium-term development plans. In terms of the framework of Flexible Strategic Planning, the master plan is folded back or is backcast. This process helps to create robustness in the planning process internally (coordination between the development of different airport facilities) and externally (with respect to probable future scenarios: multi-future robustness). Moreover, backcasting creates a phased development process of the airport, which is able to anticipate and adjust to new developments.

In the medium-term development plans, new market developments can be incorporated and, if necessary, the master plan can be updated if the medium-term plan deviates too much from the master plan. The advantage of such a development plan was clearly demonstrated in the *GHJ-plan*, which is a medium-term development plan tailored to the recent low-cost market growth. However, this plan was not the result of the original *ADP 2020*. Because of the guideline-character of the ADP, new developments such as low-cost could still be incorporated.

However, there are also downsides. The *ADP 2020* process took about two years: four years if we include the *Business Case Redesign*. During this period market circumstances changed significantly: KLM merged with Air France, low-cost airlines grew significantly, the economy plunged into economic recession, oil prices rose and security became much more important.

As a result, the *ADP 2020* was no longer leading for all the medium-term developments at the airport. In other words, there was a certain amount of analysis paralysis (Chapter 8) in the master planning process. Various respondents indicated that the association of the lead times of the master plan with the strategic discussions and analyses was particularly to blame. According to NACO, today's master planning should ideally cover a period of 9 months to a year. In the case of Schiphol, the formulation of the master plan took much longer.

Another problem associated with the creation of real options is the fact that flexibility tends to be a 'wicked problem'. Schiphol would like to create the option to extend its runway system by two additional runways. However, this flexibility for the Schiphol Group is inflexibility for the municipalities in the Schiphol region. There are building bans and restrictions on noise and safety impact on areas around the airport. Moreover, the land needed for runway development could be used for other purposes. Flexibility for an airport may create inflexibility for other relevant stakeholders, in particular when the airport is located in a dense metropolitan area. The Province of North-Holland gave Schiphol the real option for new runway development. However, the option will expire in 2006 when Schiphol ought to have decided about its future expansion strategy.

Finally, the reconfiguration of the runway system of Schiphol or changes in the airport boundary can only take place by means of an Airport Planning Decree and Airport Traffic Decree from the national government. Hence, creating and exercising the most important growth option for an airport – runway development or runway relocation – is dependent on national political decision-making. To a certain extent, the outcome and duration of such political decision-making are uncertain. The start of the decision-making process for Schiphol's fifth runway (fully operational in 2003), for example, could be traced back to 1968 (Bouwens and Dierikx 1996, 269). According to our model of Flexible Strategic Planning, a flexible approach creates not only the option to undertake a certain action, but also the option to time that action as optimally as possible according to market developments. Only then will airport planning be fully demand driven. However, political decision-making interferes with the flexibility in the timing of airport investments and is, therefore, a major limitation to flexibility in airport planning.

Demand driven

Airport planning at Schiphol is demand driven: we found various examples of the demand-driven nature of airport planning at Schiphol.

First, planning horizons are not the most important anchors for planning. Planning horizons imply a 'build and they'll come approach': one of the characteristics of the traditional airport master planning style. Most of the plans still have a planning horizon in the plan title (the *ADP 2020*, for example), but these horizons are merely symbolic. New developments are triggered by certain key drivers (for example, peak-hour demand, demand for aircraft stands) rather than a certain year. By using the options to delay or accelerate and the option of modularity, airport facilities can be delivered according to demand in an incremental way. The GHJ-area, for example, is a phased project that permits development according to market circumstances. There are limits, however, to such a flexible development of facilities. There are significant costs associated with flexibility. Hence, the costs of flexibility have to be valued against the benefits. Alternatives to traditional net present value analysis, such as decision analysis and real option analysis, can be used to measure the value of flexibility in airport planning under uncertain market conditions.

Second, the most important stakeholders in the planning of airport capacity, the airlines, took part in the planning process from the start through the Strategic Partnership of the *Business Case Redesign*. As a result, Schiphol could clearly identify the user requirements of its main user KLM and formulate a plan to which the airlines were committed. It is not clear, however, to what extent this interactivity with the airlines was a deliberate strategy of the Airport Planning Department. The Strategic Partnership for the *Business Case Redesign* seems to have been formed on behalf of the Minister of Transport, Public Works and Water Management in 1999.

We have, however, also observed the downside of this relationship between KLM and Schiphol in the early stage of the planning process. The results of the *Business Case Redesign* and the *ADP 2020* were heavily oriented towards the hub carrier. The strategic premises were to be undermined by new market developments later in the planning process. Until now we have defined volatility as the variation in airport traffic. However, the importance of various stakeholders seems also to have become more volatile. The important airlines of today may not be the important airlines of tomorrow. A volatile planning context therefore requires a pluralistic approach. This approach identifies not only the most important stakeholders of today, but also the most probable stakeholders of tomorrow.

In addition, there seems to be a tension between demand-driven planning and pro-active planning. We concluded that the *GHJ-plan* was a plan that eventually followed the low-cost market, but certainly did not anticipate the low-cost market as a new opportunity at an early stage. Pro-activeness requires peripheral thinking: new solutions for existing developments or solutions for trends of tomorrow. Such an approach implies taking risks. In a highly uncertain environment, organizations tend to reduce risks as much as possible. As a result, the airport could very well miss viable opportunities.

Diversification

In this chapter we distinguished various diversification strategies of the Schiphol Group to reduce its dependency on the hub carrier KLM. One of these strategies is the investment in 'airport city' development in order to increase non-aeronautical revenues, such as revenues from real estate development. The GHJ-area plan is another example of diversification. With the dedicated facilities in the GHJ-area, the airport aims to diversify its aeronautical revenues.

Multi-future robustness

The Airport Planning Department aims to formulate a multi-future robust plan. Hence robustness thinking is an important element in the Schiphol planning process. We described robustness thinking in the case of the *GHJ-plan*. The preferred plan was tested against a range of probable future scenarios.

Another robustness analysis was the Scenario Study, which identified very accurately the alternative scenarios that the airport is facing today: an alternative alliance scenario for KLM (KLM–Air France) and a scenario of high low-cost growth. Yet the master planning process did not fully incorporate the results of Scenario Study. Attitudes within the organization with respect to low-cost carriers and the fact that organizations tend to reduce complexity in turbulent times restricted the possibilities for the Airport Development Department to anticipate alternative scenarios. Strategic change thus requires a flexible organization that is prepared to review constantly its own strategies in the light of new market developments.

To meet the multi-future robustness requirement of Flexible Strategic Planning, various authors (see Chapter 8) have argued that new investment valuation tools such as decision-analysis and real-option analysis are needed to supplement the more traditional net present value method, since these alternative methods incorporate uncertainty better and are able to value flexibility. In the case of Schiphol, only the traditional net present value methodology was used for the projects concerned. Although such alternative methods are more complicated and demanding of data than traditional valuation tools, a study of experiences with alternative valuation methods in, for example, the valuation of investments in the oil industry or Research and Development, might be highly beneficial for airport planners.

In conclusion, various elements of Flexible Strategic Planning were identified in Schiphol's airport planning process, which has to be appreciated in the light of an uncertain market environment. We also identified some areas where the characteristics of traditional airport planning practices could be found. Most notably, this concerns the evaluation of investments in airport infrastructure, the duration of the master planning process, the flexibility of the organization and the interaction with the most relevant stake-holder KLM. Moreover, we concluded that while Flexible Strategic Planning may help airport planners deal with uncertainty and risk, it is not a universal remedy for dealing with uncertainty and risk in the free-market regime. Almost every element of flexibility has another side of the coin. Many of the downsides of flexibility are related to the complex organizational, political, business and spatial contexts in which airport planning takes place.

Chapter 10

Conclusions

This book has dealt with the development of the European aviation network and its impact on airport planning. The starting point of the study was the notion that deregulation of air transport markets may have severe implications for the way airlines configure their networks in space and time. The adoption of spatially and temporally concentrated hub-and-spoke networks is certainly one of the most striking impacts of deregulation as is the rise of low-cost, no-frills carrier networks. In turn, changing airline network behaviour has consequences for airport connectivity as well as the way airports are planned and developed. How have airline networks in Europe developed after deregulation and what are the consequences for airport planning?

The era of bilateralism gave birth to the rise of the European flag carrier, operating radial networks centred on the national home base(s). Most of these carriers focused on their national origin–destination markets, while a few carriers managed to develop their home bases as sixth-freedom hubs. With the transition to an intra-EU free-market regime and the growth of air traffic demand came the development of wave-structured airline hubs in many of the EU countries.

From a spatial perspective, however, the route networks of the flag carriers remained remarkably stable. Ongoing bilateral regulation of air services to extra-EU destinations continued to pin them down to the airports of their home country. In addition, radical reorganization of large scale airline networks is costly and risky. Part of the costs to enter a new market is sunk: marketing activities, for instance, are irreversible commitments. Furthermore, airport capacity, which is suitable for substantial hub operations, is scarce in Europe. Moreover, the current allocation mechanism of slots through grandfather rights is a barrier to entry at congested airports. Finally, the network economies of hubbing favour the addition of connections to existing hubs rather than the development of new hubs that serve the same market.

Regional and low-cost airline networks were less stable than national airline networks. They frequently showed discontinuous changes. Some regional carriers established niche hubs, while others concentrated on traffic feed to the major carriers. The second half of the 1990s saw the rise of the low-cost carrier, dedicated to serving point-to-point markets only. Some of the low-cost airlines served primarily the smaller, non-hub airports; others concentrated on the major airports in Europe.

The rise of the low-cost carriers and the growth of regional operations contributed to a deconcentration of intra-EU traffic. However, only part of the smaller airports reaped the benefits from this concentration trend, leaving most of the other small airports with below average growth levels or even decreases in direct air service.

Mainly the upper end of the small airport hierarchy as well as low-cost carrier destinations experienced the new growth opportunities of the deregulated market. Nevertheless, many of the small airports saw increases in the number of onward connections via the major hubs. Hub-and-spoke operations stimulated the number of onward connections since hub-carriers compete for transfer passengers at the smaller spoke airports.

Extra-EU traffic started to consolidate into the larger hub airports, primarily as a consequence of the global airline alliances, which tend to choose one or two intercontinental hubs on every continent. The main hubs of Air France, British Airways, KLM and Lufthansa became the connection complexes for the global airline alliances (SkyTeam, Oneworld, Wings and Star), attracting a disproportionate share of intercontinental traffic flows. The future network strategies of these alliances will be of crucial importance to the future of the main European gateways.

The freedoms of the deregulated market make the future of many EU airports much more uncertain and risky. While in the bilateral regime airports could more or less wait for their share of traffic to materialize, today airports will have to work hard to retain existing traffic and win new traffic. There is no guarantee that projected traffic will materialize. The forecast is always wrong and so is the airport master plan based on it. This means an increased risk of capacity mismatches and destruction of economic value. Further deregulation of intercontinental markets, the expected shake-out under low-cost airlines, and the responsibility taken on by the EU for the extra-EU air-service relationships are likely to further increase volatility and uncertainty. Major shifts in EU airline networks still have to occur. The failures of Sabena and Swissair, the merger between Air France and KLM and the radical low-cost network growth in recent years might be the first indications of these shifts.

In a market environment where investments in airport capacity become riskier, airports are also faced with a commercialization trend in the airport industry itself. Airport managers must increasingly safeguard the economic performance of their airport (Barret 2000; Starkie 2002). This means economically sustainable investment programmes and the ability to self-fund these. Successful airports will be those with the ability to invest just-in-time in the right facilities in a way that contributes to good economic performance (Werson and Burghouwt 2006, 28).

However, the uncertainty and risk in airport planning are not necessarily negative features that need to be avoided at all costs. Volatility, uncertainty and risk can be exploited with the right approach to airport planning. An approach that sees an airport plan as a coordinated portfolio of real options does not have to be reactive to risk. Options limit downside losses but maintain upside gains. However, a paradigm shift towards a more flexible and dynamic planning process is needed to manage and exploit risk. Uncertainty and risk are conventionally avoided and reduced as much as possible. Nevertheless, a flexible approach to airport planning can exploit the growing uncertainties and risks that are rooted in the dynamic airline network behaviour of the free-market regime.

Annex 1

Definitions of the Hub-and-Spoke Network

Study	Definition
Berry et al. (1996, 1)	'[In hub and spoke networks], passengers change planes at a hub airport on the way to their eventual destination.'
Bootsma (1997)	'The network is designed as such, that routes are deliberately concentrated at a limited number of connection facilities, called hubs. [...] In order to maximize these connection possibilities, the hub carrier usually schedules its flights in a limited number of time-windows.'
Button (1998, 20)	'In hub-and-spoke operations, [...] carriers generally use one or more large airports [...]. Flights are arranged in banks which allow passengers continuing on to be consolidated on outbound flights to further destinations.'
Button (2002, 177)	'Airline networks that entail consolidating of traffic from a diverse range of origins and are destined to a diverse range of final destinations at large, hub airports.'
Dempsey and Gesell (1997, 200)	'Consolidation of operations around hubs by airlines.'
Dennis (1998, 2)	[Airline HS networks aim] 'to carry connecting passengers with both origin and destination outside their home country.'
Goetz and Sutton (1997, 243)	'Major connection complexes for airlines'.
Kanafani and Ghobrial (1985, 15)	'Hubbing occurs when airlines concentrate thier flights at a few airports which they use as collection-distribution centres for their passengers. [...] Connecting traffic is characterized by a banked schedule [...].'
O'Kelly (1998, 171)	'Hubs [...] are special nodes that are part of a network, located in such a way as to facilitate connectivity between interacting places.'
Oum et al. (1995, 837)	'Hub-and-spoke networks concentrate most of an airline's operations at one, or a very few, hub cities. Virtually all other cities in the network are served by non-stop flights from these hubs.'
Pels (2000, 13)	'In a HS-network, the hub airport is the only airport with a direct connection to all other airports. All passengers traveling between two "spoke airports" (an indirect market) are chanelled through the hub airport. The market between a hub and spoke is a spoke market.'
Shaw (1993, 47)	'In a hub-and-spoke network, hubs serve as central locations which collect and distribute passengers between a set of nodes connected to hubs.'
Reynolds-Feighan (2001, 265)	'The hub-and-spoke network requires a concentration of traffic in both space and time.'
Shy (1997, 216)	'[...] airline firms decrease the relative number of nonstop direct flights and reroute passengers via a third city which we will call the hub.'
Wojahn (2001)	'A hub-and-spoke network concentrates traffic in both space and time.'

Annex 2

Freedoms of the Air

Freedoms of the air

1st freedom: the right to overfly one country *en route* to another
2nd freedom: the right to make a technical stop in another country
3rd freedom: the right to carry traffic from the home country of the airline to another country
4th freedom: the right to carry traffic to the home country from another country
5th freedom: the right to carry traffic between two foreign countries by an airline of a third country, which carriage is linked with third- and fourth-freedom rights of the airline
6th freedom: the right to carry traffic between two foreign countries via the home country of the airline
7th freedom: the right to carry traffic between two foreign countries by an airline of a third country, which carriage is not linked with third- or fourth-freedom rights of the airline
8th freedom: the right to carry traffic between two points in a foreign country on a route with origin/destination in the home country of the airline
9th freedom: the right to carry traffic between two points in a foreign country, which is unrelated to the home country of the airline

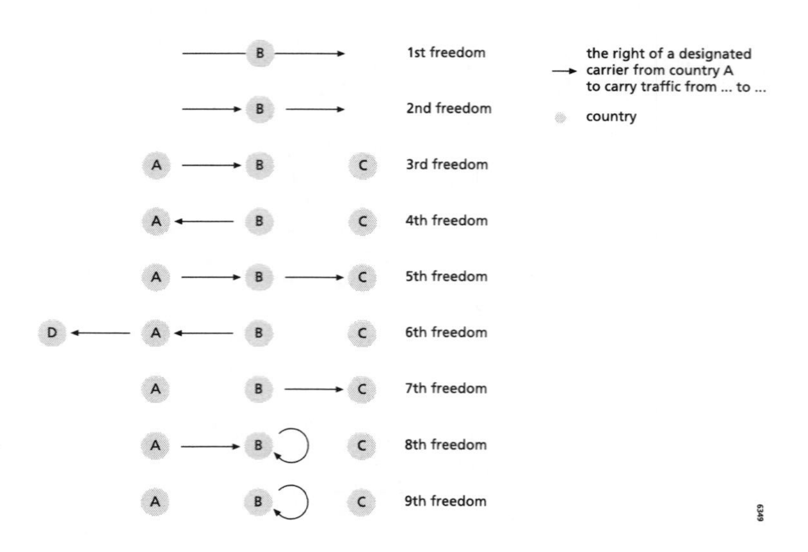

Annex 3

Airline Classification

Airline name	Airline code	Classification
Aer Lingus	EI	National
Air France	AF	National
Alitalia	AZ	National
Austrian Airlines	OS	National
British Airways	BA	National
Finnair	AY	National
Iberia	IB	National
Icelandair	FI	National
KLM-Royal Dutch Airlines	KL	National
Lufthansa German Airlines	LH	National
Luxair	LG	National
Olympic Airways	OA	National
Sabena	SN	National
SAS Scandinavian Airlines	SK	National
Swissair	SR	National
Tap Air Portugal	TP	National
Sn Brussels Airlines	SN	National (2003 only)
Swiss	LX	National (2003 only)
Deutsche BA	DI	Low-cost (2003 only)
Air Europa	UX	Low-cost
Condor Flugdienst	DE	Low-cost
Debonair Airways	2G	Low-cost
easyJet (Switzerland)	U2 (DS)	Low-cost
Hapag Lloyd Fluggesselschaft	HF	Low-cost
Ryanair	FR	Low-cost
Spanair	JK	Low-cost
Transavia Airlines	HV	Low-cost
Virgin Express	TV/BQ	Low-cost
Air Botnia	KF	Low-cost (2003 only)
BMIBaby	WW	Low-cost
Condor Flugdienst	DE	Low-cost
Germanwings	4U	Low-cost
Hapag-Lloyd Express	X3	Low-cost
Hellas Jet	T4	Low-cost
Intersky	3L	Low-cost
Jetmagic	GX	Low-cost
Mytravellite	VZ	Low-cost
Volare Airlines	VA	Low-cost
Other EU airlines	–	Regional
Other non-EU airlines	–	Extra-EU

Annex 4

List of Respondents and Informants

Aad Kieboom, Schiphol Group
Albert Doe, Gemeentelijk Havenbedrijf Rotterdam
Alex van Elk, Airport Niederrhein/Düsseldorf Weeze
Andrew Sentance, British Airways
Bert Uitterhoeve, Municipality of Haarlemmermeer
Dan Melfi, Denver International Airport
Delbert Brown, Director, Detroit City Airport
Desirée Breedveld, Rotterdam Airport
Mr Mohrmann, Amsterdam Institute of Technology
Mr Tindemans, Maastricht Aachen Airport
Dick Jansen, KLM
Elzeline de Jong, Municipality of Amsterdam
Eric P. Amel, Delta Air Lines
Frederick Busch, Denver International Airport
Hans van den Ancker, NACO
Hans Vonk, Province of North-Holland
Herman Neukermans, BIAC
Huib Heukelom, NACO
Jacco Hakfoort, Ministry of Economic Affairs
Jan Christian Schraven, Lufthansa
Jan Klaver, Ministry of Spatial Planning, Housing and the Environment
Jan Petit, Ministry of Foreign Affairs
Joop Krul, Schiphol Group
Joop Mulder, Schiphol Group
Joost Wagemakers, Airport Development, Schiphol Group
José Bolorinos Crémades, Iberia
Just Kerckhoff, KLM
Kimm Casella, Forest City Stapleton, Denver
Liesbeth Noorman, Schiphol Group
Lina G. James, Hartsfield Atlanta International Airport
Marc Dierikx, Instituut voor Nederlandse Geschiedenis
Mariska Kooi, Schiphol Group
Mark C. Gurney, Northwest Airlines
Mark Lammertink, Municipality of Haarlemmermeer
Martin Bijl, Schiphol Group
Maurice Klaver, Municipality of Haarlemmermeer

Maurits Schaafsma, Schiphol Group
Meiltje de Groot, Schiphol Group
Michael D. Floyd, Hartsfield Atlanta International Airport
Michiel Weijs, Municipality of Amsterdam
Olaf van Reeden, Schiphol Group
Paul Beck, NACO
Paul de Swart, SADC
Pieter Bootsma, KLM
Reinout Heering, NACO
Richard Boyle, British Airways
Sytze Rienstra, Ministry of Transport, Public Works and Water Management
Tom Huissen, Province of North-Holland
Vicky Braunagel, Denver International Airport
Wim Kranenburg, Schiphol Group
Xander den Uyl, Province of North-Holland

Annex 5

Classification of World Regions

World region code	World region name	Area
EU	EU	EU countries (until 2003) and Iceland, Norway, Switzerland Excluding overseas territories of EU countries, but including Canaries, Madeira and Azores
EUR	Other Europe	Albania, Belarus, Bosnia Herzegovina, Bulgaria, Croatia, Cyprus, Czech Republic, Estonia, Faroe Islands, Hungary, Latvia, Lithuania, Malta, Moldovo, Poland, Republic of Macedonia, Romania, Slovakia, Slovenia, Turkey, Ukraine, West Russia (West of Ural), Yugoslavia
NAM	North America	United States, Canada, Greenland
LAM	Latin America	Rest of the American continent, including the Caribbean
MEA	Middle East	Bahrain, Iran, Iraq, Israel, Jordan, Kuwait, Lebanon, Oman, Qatar, Palestine, Saudi Arabia, Syrian Arab Republic, United Arab Emirates, Yemen
AFR	Africa	Algeria, Angola, Benin, Botswana, Burkina Faso, Burundi, Cameroon, Cape Verde, Central Africa Republic, Chad, Comoros, Congo, Cote d'Ivoire, Djibouti, Egypt, Equatorial Guinea, Eritrea, Ethiopia, Gabon, Gambia, Ghana, Guinea-Bissau, Guinea, Kenya, Liberia, Libyan Arab Jamahiriyia, Madagascar, Malawi, Mali, Mauritania, Mauritius, Morocco, Mozambique, Namibia, Niger, Nigeria, Reunion, Rwanda, Sao Tome and Principe, Senegal, Seychelles, Sierra Leone, Somalia, South Africa, St Helena, Sudan, Tanzania, Togo, Tunisia, Uganda, Zaire, Zambia
APA	Australasia/Pacific	Australia, New Zealand, Pacific Islands (excluding US territories) and all other countries in Asia, except those countries belonging to EU, EUR, NAM, LAM, APA, MEA or AFR

Annex 6

Summary of the EU Packages of Deregulation Measures

	First Package From 1 January 1988	Second Package From 1 November 1990	Third Package From 1 January 1993
Fares	• Automatic approval discount fares within 'zones of reasonableness' • Double approval for other fares	• Extension 'zones of reasonableness' discount fares • Double disapproval for fully flexible fares • Double approval for other fares	Provisions for the Member States or Commission to intervene in case of a sustained downward development of fares or excessive basic fares
Designation	Multiple designation by a state allowed if: • 250,000 pas/year (1st year) • 200,000 pas/year (2nd year) • 180,000 pas/year (3rd year)	Multiple designation allowed if: • 140,000 pas/year (from January 1991) • 100,000 pas/year (from January 1992)	Not applicable
Capacity	Capacity shares between states: • 45/55 per cent (from January 1988) • 40/60 per cent (from October 1988)	• Capacity shares of a State up to 60 per cent • Capacity can be increased by 7.5 per cent points per year	Unrestricted
Route access	• 3rd/4th freedom to hub routes • 5th freedom allowed up to 30 per cent of capacity • Combination of points allowed	• 3rd/4th freedom between all airports • 5th freedom allowed up 50% of capacity • PSO for regional routes • 3rd/4th freedom can be matched by an airline from the other state	• Full access to international and domestic routes within the EU (exemptions for Greek Islands and Azores) • Cabotage unrestricted from April 1997 • Restricted cabotage for up to 50 per cent until April 1997 • Reformed PSO
Licensing of carriers	Not provided for	Not provided for	EU ownership and control

Source: *Button et al. (1998)*

References

Ackoff, R.L. (1974), *Redesigning the future* (New York: John Wiley & Sons).

Airbus (2002), *Global market forecast* (Blagnac Cedex: Airbus S.A.S).

'Airliner World' (2003), 'No frills', *Airliner World* October 2003, 39–79.

Airneth (2006), 'A note on the network performance of Dubai and Emirates', Presentation prepared for the Airneth-seminar 'The impact of the expansion of Dubai and Emirates on international airline competition', 7 April 2006, Amsterdam <http://www.airneth.com/documents/PresentationBurghouwt.pdf>, accessed 10 July 2006.

Airwise (2000), 'Heavy loss of traffic at KLIA due to airlines withdrawing services', *Airwise* (published online July 30 2001) <http://www.airwise.com>.

Airwise (2004), 'European Union transport ministers have rejected a US offer for a landmark aviation agreement', *Airwise* (published online June 11 2004) <http://www.airwise.com>.

Alayande, B. (2003), 'Decomposition of inequality reconsidered: some evidence from Nigeria', UNU-WIDER Conference on Inequality, Poverty and Human Wellbeing, 29–31 May 2003, Helsinki.

Allen, P.M., Alamdari, F., Cordey-Hayes, M. and Black, I. (1997), *Hub and spoke developments in Europe and their impact on uncertainties in future passenger demand at Schiphol Airport* (Bedford: Cranfield University).

Allison, P.D. (1978), 'Measures of inequality', *American Sociological Review* 43:6, 865-80.

Altshuler, A.A. and Luberhoff, D.E. (2003), *Megaprojects: the changing politics of urban public investments* (Washington: The Brookings Institution).

Amara, R. (1979), 'Strategic planning in a changing corporate environment', *Long Range Planning* 12:1, 2–12.

Amsterdam Airport Schiphol (1997), *Masterplan Schiphol 2015*, 22-8-1997 (in Dutch).

Arens, K.-J. (2004), *Europese luchthavens. Onderzoek naar een toegenomen volatiliteit*, Masters Thesis (Utrecht: Utrecht University) (in Dutch).

Arthur, W.B. (1989), 'Competing technologies: an overview', in G. Dosi (ed.), *Technical Change and Economic Theory* (London/New York: Pinter).

Ashford, N., Stanton, H.P.M. and Moore, C.A. (1997), *Airport operations* (Boston: McGraw-Hill).

A.T. Kearney (2001), *Operationele betrouwbaarheid 6P. Eindrapportage projectdirectie*, unpublished document (in Dutch).

Baarda, D.B., de Goede. M.P.M. and Teunissen, J. (2001), *Kwalitatief onderzoek. Basisboek* (Groningen/Houten: Stenfert Kroese) (in Dutch).

Back (2002), 'Hub de-peaking: AA at DFW, UA at ORD and CO at IAH, Back Aviation Solutions' (published online November 2002) <http://www.backaviation.com>.

Bailey, E.E. and Friedländer, A.F. (1982), 'Market structure and multiproduct industries', *Journal of economic literature* 20:3, 1024–48.

Balfour, J. (2002), 'EC aviation scene (No. 1: 2002)', *Air & Space Law* 18:4/5, 249–65.

Balfour, J. (2003), 'EC aviation scene (No. 2: 2003)', *Air & Space Law* 27:2, 106–25.

Bania, N., Bauer, P.W. and Zlatoper, T.J. (1998), 'U.S. air passenger service: a taxonomy of route networks, hub locations and competition', *Transportation Research E* 34:1, 53–74.

Barabasi, A.-L. (1999), 'Emergence of scaling in random networks', *Science* October 15.

Barabasi, A.-L., Réka, A. and Jeong, H. (2000), 'Scale-free characteristics of random networks: the topology of the world-wide web', *Physica* 281:1–4, 69–77.

Barrett, S.D. (2000), 'Airport competition in the deregulated European aviation market', *Journal of Air Transport Management* 6:1, 13–27.

Barrett, S.D. (2004), 'How do the demands for airport services differ between full-service carriers and low-cost airlines?', *Journal of Air Transport Management* 10:1, 33–49.

BCG (2004), *Airports – dawn of a new era* (Munich: The Boston Consulting Group).

Berechman, J. and de Wit, J.G. (1996), 'An analysis of the effects of European aviation deregulation on an airline's network structure and choice of a primary West European hub airport', *Journal of Transport Economics and Policy* September, 251–70.

Berry, S., Carnall, M. and Spiller, P.T. (1996), *Airline hubs: costs, markups and the implications of customer heterogeneity* (Cambridge: National Bureau of Economic Research).

Bissessur, A. and Alamdari, F. (1998), 'Factors affecting the operational success of strategic airline alliances', *Transportation* 25:4, 331–55.

Black, F. and Scholes, M. (1973), 'The pricing of options and corporate liabilities', *Journal of Political Economy* 81:3, 637–54.

Bootsma, P.D. (1997), *Airline flight schedule development: analysis and design tools for European hinterland hubs*, PhD Thesis (Utrecht: University of Twente).

Borenstein, S. (1989), 'Hubs and high fares: dominance and market power in the U.S. airline industry', *RAND Journal of Economics* 20:3, 344–65.

Borenstein, S. (1992), 'The evolution of U.S. Airline Competition', *Journal of Economic Perspectives* 6:2, 45–73.

Boschma, R.A., Frenken, K. and Lambooy, J.G. (2002), *Evolutionaire economie. Een inleiding* (Bussum: Coutinho) (in Dutch).

Bouwens, A.M.C.M. and Dierikx, M.L.J. (1996), *Building castles of the air: Schiphol Amsterdam and the development of airport infrastructure in Europe, 1916–1996* (Den Haag: Sdu Uitgevers).

Boyle, R. (2002), 'Presentation with slides. FSAS Part I' <http://www.ba.com>.

Braeutigam, R.R. (1999), 'Learning about transport costs', in J.A. Gómez-Íbáñez, W.B. Tye and C. Winston (eds), *Essays in transportation economics and policy. A handbook in honor of John R. Meyer* (Washington, DC: Brookings Institution Press).

Bresina, J., Dearden, R., Meuleau, N., Ramakrishan, S., Smith, D. and Washington, R. (2002), *Planning under continuous time and resource uncertainty: a challenge for AI* (Moffet Field, CA: NASA Ames Research Center).

British Airways (2003a), 'Key events' <http://www.ba.com>.

British Airways (2003b), 'British Airways Fact Book 2003' <http://www.ba.com>.

Brueckner, J.K. and Spiller, P.T. (1994), 'Economies of traffic density in the deregulated airline industry', *Journal of Law and Economics* 37, 379–415.

Bruzelius, N., Flyvbjerg, B. and Rothengatter, W. (2002), 'Big decisions, big risks: improving accountability in mega projects', *Transport Policy* 9:2, 143–54.

Bryson, J.M. (1995), *Strategic planning for public and nonprofit organizations: a guide to strengthening and sustaining organizational achievement* (San Fransisco, CA: Jossey-Bass Publishers).

Burghouwt, G. (2002), 'De onweerstaanbare opkomst van de airport city', *Geografie* September 2001 (in Dutch).

Burghouwt, G. and Ennen, E. (2002), 'De luchthaven als stedelijke ruimte', *Stedenbouw & Ruimtelijke Ordening* 83:1, 43-5 (in Dutch).

Burghouwt, G. and Hakfoort, J.R. (2001), 'The European aviation network, 1990–1998', *Journal of Air Transport Management* 7:5, 311–18.

Burghouwt, G. and Hakfoort, J.R. (2002), 'The geography of deregulation in the European aviation market', *TESG* 93:1, 100–106.

Burghouwt, G. and de Wit, J.G. (2005), 'Temporal configurations of airline networks in Europe', *Journal of Air Transport Management* 11:3, 185–98.

Burghouwt, G. and de Wit, J.G. (2005b), 'Strategies of multi-hub airlines and the implications for national aviation policies', Airneth report 1, workshop multi-hub development, 28 October 2005, The Hague (available online 24 November 2005) <http://www.airneth.nl/serve_file.php?dType=dDocument&id=89>, accessed 15 July 2006.

Burghouwt, G., Hakfoort, J.R. and Ritsema-Van Eck, J.R. (2003), 'The spatial configuration of airline networks in Europe', *Journal of Air Transport Management* 9:5, 309–23.

Button, K. (1999), 'The usefulness of current international air transport statistics', *Journal of Transportation and Statistics* May, 71–91.

Button, K. (2002), 'Debunking some common myths about airport hubs', *Journal of Air Transport Management* 8:3, 177–88.

Button, K. and Taylor, S. (2000), 'International air transportation and economic development', *Journal of Air Transport Management* 6:4, 209–22.

Button, K., Haynes, K. and Stough, R. (1998), *Flying into the future: air transport policy in the European Union* (Cheltenham: Edward Elgar Publishing).

CAA (1995), *The single European aviation market: progress so far* (London: Civil Aviation Authority/Westward Digital Ltd).

CAA (1998), *The single European aviation market: the first five years* (London: Civil Aviation Authority/Westward Digital Ltd).

Caves, R.E. and Gosling, G.D. (1999), *Strategic Airport Planning* (Amsterdam: Pergamon).

Caves, R.E., Christensen, L.R. and Tretheway, M.W. (1984), 'Economies of density versus economies of scale: why trunk and local service airline costs differ', *The RAND Journal of Economics* 15: 4, 471–89.

Caves, R.E. (1997), 'European airline networks and their implications for airport planning' *Transport Reviews* 17:2, 121–44.

CEC (1999), *Mededingingsrecht in de Europese Gemeenschappen. Volume IIA. Controle op steunmaatregelen van de staten* (Brussel, Luxemburg: Europese Commissie. Directoraat-Generaal Concurrentie) (in Dutch).

Chan, Y. and Ponder, R.J. (1979), 'The small package air freight industry in the United States: a review of the Federal Express Experience', *Transportation Research A* 13:4, 221–9.

Chang, Y.-H. and Williams, G. (2002), 'European major airlines' strategic reactions to the Third Package', *Transport Policy* 9, 129–42.

Chen, F.C.-Y. and Chen, C. (2003), 'The effects of strategic alliances and risk pooling on the load factors of international airline operations', *Transportation Research E* 39:1, 19–34.

Chicago O'Hare International Airport (2003), *O'Hare International Airport Master Plan* <http://egov.cityofchicago.org>.

Chou, Y.-H. (1993a), 'Airline deregulation and nodal accessibility', *Journal of Transport Geography* 1:1, 36–46.

Chou, Y.-H. (1993b), 'A method for measuring the spatial concentration of airline travel demand', *Transportation Research B* 27:4, 267–73.

Clarke, C.J. and Varma, S. (1999), 'Strategic risk management: the new competitive edge', *Long Range Planning* 32:4, 414–24.

Comité des Sages (1994), *Expanding Horizons: civil Aviation in Europe, an action programme for the future.* A report by the Comité des Sages for air transport to the European Commission (Brussels: European Commission).

Courtney, H. (2001), *20/20 foresight: crafting strategies in an uncertain world* (Boston: Harvard Business School Press).

CPB (2000), *Schiphol: een normaal bedrijf?* (Den Haag: Centraal Planbureau) (in Dutch).

CPB (2002), *KKBA Schiphol* (Den Haag: Centraal Planbureau) (in Dutch).

CPB and NLR (1998), *Geluidsproblematiek rond Schiphol*, 18 June 1998. <http://www.minvenw.nl> (in Dutch).

Creaton, S. (2004), *Ryanair: how a small Irish airline conquered Europe* (London: Aurum).

Crol, J.B. (1999), 'Het belang van strategisch denken in het bedrijfsleven', *Beleid en Maatschappij* 26:3, 163–9 (in Dutch).

Dagtoglou, P.D. (1994), *Air transport and the European Union: essays and comments* (Deventer: Kluwer).

Daudel, S. and Vialle, G. (1994), *Yield management: applications to air transport and other service industries* (Paris: Institut du Transport Aérien).

Davies, R.S. and Petrie, A. (2002), 'The road to effective risk management', *PN network* 54, 19–22.

Day, A. (2003), *Mastering risk modelling* (London: Prentice Hall).

Delta (2004), 'Delta through the decades' <http://www.delta.com>.

Dempsey, P.S. (1990), *Flying blind: the failure of airline deregulation* (Washington, DC: Economic Policy Institute).

Dempsey, P.S. (2000), *Airport planning and development handbook: a global survey* (New York: McGraw-Hill).

Dempsey, P.S. and Gesell, L.E. (1997), *Airline management: strategies for the 21st century* (Chandler, AZ: Coast Aire).

Dempsey, P.S., Goetz, A.R. and Szyliowicz, J.S. (1997), *Denver International Airport: lessons learned* (New York: McGraw-Hill).

de Neufville, R. (1991a), 'Understanding and using forecasts', foreword to *Passenger forecasts for Logan International Airport* (Boston, MA: Massport).

de Neufville, R. (1991b), 'Strategic planning for airport capacity: an appreciation of Australia's process for Sydney', *Australian Planner* 29:3, 174–80.

de Neufville, R. (1992), *Assessment of the 'Flight Plan' forecasts for Seattle Tacoma and regional airports together with reflections on the proper basis for airport planning*, Report for the Air Transportation Commission State of Washington (Cambridge, MA: Massachusetts Institute of Technology).

de Neufville, R. (1995), *Amsterdam multi-airport system: policy guidelines*, Final Report for Amsterdam Airport Schiphol (Cambridge: Massachusetts Institute of Technology).

de Neufville, R. (2000), 'Dynamic strategic planning for technology policy', *International Journal of Technology Management*, prepublication draft.

de Neufville, R. (2001), 'Real options: dealing with uncertainty in systems planning and design', 5th International Conference on 'Technology Policy and Innovation', Technical University of Delft, Delft, the Netherlands.

de Neufville, R. and Barber, J. (1991), 'Deregulation induced volatility of airport traffic', *Transportation Planning and Technology* 16, 117–28.

de Neufville, R. and Odoni, A.R. (2003), *Airport systems: planning, design and management* (New York: McGraw-Hill).

Dennis, N.P. (1994a), 'Scheduling strategies for airline hub operations', *Journal of Air Transport Management* 1:2, 131–44.

Dennis, N.P. (1994b), 'Airline hub operations in Europe', *Journal of Transport Geography* 2:4, 219–33.

Dennis, N.P. (1998), 'Competition between hub airports in Europe and a methodology for forecasting connecting traffic', 8th World Conference on Transport Research, 12–17 July 1998, Antwerp.

Dennis, N.P. (2001a), 'Developments of hubbing at European airports', *Air & Space Europe* 3:1/2, 51–5.

Dennis, N.P. (2001b), *Regional air services in Europe*, European Transport Conference, 10-12 September 2001, Cambridge.

Dennis, N.P. (2002), *Opportunities and problems in developing regional air services from European regional airports*, 6th Annual Air Transport Research Society Conference, 14–16 July 2002, Seattle, WA.

Dennis, N.P. (2005), 'Industry consolidation and future airline network structures in Europe', *Journal of Air Transport Management* 11:3, 175–83.

De Senarclens, P. (2001), 'Regime theory and the study of international organizations', *International Social Science Journal* 45:4, 453–62.

de Wit, J.G. (1995a), 'An urge to merge?' *Journal of Air Transport Management* 2:4, 173–80.

de Wit, J.G. (1995b), 'Concurrentie en concentratie in de Europese luchtvaart', *Tijdschrift voor Vervoerswetenschap* 95:4, 357–69 (in Dutch).

de Wit, J.G. (2004), 'Changing business models in the air transport supply chain: two traditional business models', in H. Meersman, P. Roosens, E. v.d. Voorde and F. Witlox (eds), *Optimising strategies in the air transport business: survival of the fittest?* (Antwerp-Apeldoorn: Garant).

de Wit, J.G. and van Gent, H. (1996), *Economie en transport* (Utrecht: Lemma B.V) (in Dutch).

de Wit, J.G., Uittenbogaart, P. and Wei-Yun, T. (1999), 'Hubbing and hub-bypassing: network developments in a deregulated European airport system', ATRG Conference, June 1999, Hong Kong.

DeWulf, G. (1991), *Limits to forecasting. Towards a theory of forecast errors*, PhD Thesis (Utrecht: Rijksuniversiteit van Utrecht).

DeWulf, G. and van der Schaaf, P. (1998), 'Portfolio management in the midst of uncertainties: how scenario planning can be useful', *Journal of Corporate Real Estate* 1:1, 19–28.

Dierikx, M.L.J. (1999), *Blauw in de lucht. Koninklijke Luchtvaartmaatschappij 1919–1999* (Den Haag: Sdu Uitgevers) (in Dutch).

Dierikx, M.L.J. and Lyth, P.J. (1994), 'The development of the European scheduled air transport network, 1920–1970: and explanatory model', European networks, 19th–20th centuries. New approaches to the formation of a transnational transport and communications system. 11th International Economic History Congress, Milan.

Doganis, R. (1991), *Flying off course: the economics of international airlines* (London: Routledge).

Doganis, R. (1992), *The Airport Business* (London, Routledge).

Doganis, R. (2001), *The airline business in the 21st century* (London and New York: Routledge).

Doorn, J. van and van Vught, F. (1978), *Forecasting. Methoden en technieken voor toekomstonderzoek* (Assen: Van Gorcum) (in Dutch).

DoT (1990a), *Secretary's task force on competition in the U.S. domestic airline industry*, U.S. Department of Transportation, Office of the Secretary of Transportation.

DoT (1990b), *Secretary's taks force on competition in the U.S. airline industry: industry and route structure.* Executive summary, U.S. Department of Transportation, Office of the Secretary of Transportation.

Dresner, M.E. and Windle, R.J. (1995), 'Alliances and code-sharing in the international airline industry', *Built Environment* 22:3, 201–11.

Eddington, R. (2002), 'FSAS Introduction' <http://www.ba.com>.

Etzioni, A. (1967), 'Mixed scanning: a 'third' approach to decision-making', *Public Administration Review* 27, 385–92.

EURAFOR (2000), *Airline alliances, European Civil Aviation Conference*, unpublished document.

FAA (1983), *Airport capacity and delay*, AC 150/5060-7, Federal Aviation Administration.

FAA (1985), *Airport master plans*, AC 150/5070-6A, Federal Aviation Administration. APP-400.

FAA (2001), *Forecasting aviation activity by airport*, Federal Aviation Administration.

Faludi, A. (1973), *Planning theory* (Oxford: Pergamon Press).

Finelli, M. (2003), 'Revolucionaria Meridiana', *Airliner World* October 2003, 26–9.

Fleming, D.K. and Hayuth, Y. (1994), 'Spatial chracteristics of transportation hubs: centrality and intermediacy', *Journal of Transport Geography* 4:1, 3–18.

Flyvbjerg, B., Bruzelius, N. and Rothengatter, W. (2003), *Megaprojects and risk: the anatomy of ambition* (Cambridge: Cambridge University Press).

Franke, M. (2004), 'Competition between network carriers and low-cost carriers: retreat, battle or breakthrough to a new level of efficiency?', *Journal of Air Transport Management* 10:1, 15–21.

Freathy, F. and O'Connell, F. (1999), 'Planning for profit: the commercialisation of European airports', *Long Range Planning* 32:6, 587–97.

Frenken, K. (2001), *Understanding product innovation using complex systems theory*, PhD Thesis (Amsterdam: University of Amsterdam).

Frenken, K., van Terwisga, S., Verburg, T. and Burghouwt, G. (2004), 'Airline competition at European airports', *Journal of Economic and Social Geography (TESG)* 95:2, 238–42.

GAO (1997), *Airline deregulation: addressing the air service problems of some communities*, General Accounting Office <http://www.gao.gov>.

Gelten, I. (2004), *Turbulence in the US airline industry: 'The low cost revolution'*, Masters Thesis (Utrecht: Utrecht University).

Genus, A. (1995), *Flexible strategic management* (London: Chapman & Hall).

George, K.D., Joll, C. and Lynk, E.L. (1992), *Industrial organization: competition, growth and structural change* (London: Routledge).

Ghobrial, A. (1983), *Analysis of the air network structure: the hubbing phenomenon* (Berkeley, CA: University of California).

Gillen, D. and Morrison, W. (2003), 'Bundling, integration and the delivered price of air travel: are low cost carriers full service competitors', *Journal of Air Transport Management* 9:1, 15–23.

Godet, M. and Roubelat, F. (1996), 'Creating the future: the use and misuse of scenarios', *Long Range Planning* 29:2, 164–71.

Goetz, A.R. (2002), 'Deregulation, competition and antitrust implications in the US airline industry', *Journal of Transport Geography* 10:1, 1–19.

Goetz, A.R. and Sutton, C.J. (1997), 'The geography of deregulation in the U.S. airline industry', *Journal of the Association of American Geographers* 87:2, 238–63.

Goetz, A.R. and Szyliowicz, J.S. (1997), 'Revisiting transportation planning and decision making theory: the case of Denver International Airport', *Transportation Research A* 31:4, 263–80.

Goh, J. (1997), *European air transport law and competition* (Chichester: John Wiley & Sons).

Gordon, A. (2004), *Naked airport: a cultural history of the world's most revolutionary architecture* (New York: Metropolitan books).

Graham, B. (1995), *Geography and air transport* (Chichester: John Wiley & Sons).

Graham, B. (1997a), 'Air transport liberalization in the European Union: an assessment', *Regional Studies* 31:8, 807–22.

Graham, B. (1997b), 'Regional airline services in the liberalized European Union single aviation market', *Journal of Air Transport Management* 3:4, 227–38.

Graham, B. (1998), 'Liberalization, regional economic development and the geography of demand for air transport in the European Union', *Journal of Transport Geography* 6:2, 87–104.

Graham, B. (1999), 'Airport-specific traffic forecasts: a critical perspective', *Journal of Transport Geography* 7:4, 285–9.

Greden, L. and Glicksman, L. (2004), 'Option valuation of architectural flexibility: a case study of the option to convert to office space', Real options 8th Annual Conference, 17-19 June 2004, Montreal.

Gudmundsson, S.V. and Rhoades, D.L. (2001), 'Airline alliance survival analysis: typology, strategy and duration', *Transport Policy* 8:3, 209–18.

Güller Güller architecture urbanism (2001), *From airport to airport city* (Barcelona: Litogama).

Gunsteren, H. van and van Ruyven, E. (1993), 'De ongekende samenleving (DOS), een verkenning', *Beleid en Maatschappij* 1993:3, 114–25 (in Dutch).

Gutiérrez Puebla, J. (1987), 'Spatial structures of network flows: a graph theoretical approach', *Transportation Research A* 21:6, 489–502.

Hakfoort, J.R. and Schaafsma, M. (2000), 'Planning Airport City Schiphol. Een heroriëntatie op de toekomst van de luchthaven', in L. Boelens (ed.) *Nederland Netwerkenland; een inventarisatie van de nieuwe condities van planologie en stedenbouw* (Rotterdam: NAi Uitgevers).

Hanlon, J.P. (1984), 'Sixth freedom operations in international air transport' *Tourism management* 5:3, 177–91.

Hanlon, J.P. (1996), *Global airlines: competition in a transnational industry* (Oxford: Butterworth-Heinemann).

Heracleous, L. (1998), 'Strategic thinking or strategic planning?' *Long Range Planning* 31:3, 481–7.

Hogarth, R.M. and Makridakis, S. (1981), 'Forecasting and planning: an evaluation', *Management Science* 27:2, 115–38.

Houston Airport System (2004), *William P. Hobby Airport Master Plan. Houston Airport System.*

IATA (2000), *Global airport connectivity monitor*, IATA/Hague Consulting Group.

Iberia (1996), *Annual report 1996* <http://www.iberia.com>.

Iberia (1997), *Management report 1997* <http://www.iberia.com>.

ICAO (1987), *Airport planning manual, part i, master planning*, Doc.9184-AN/902 (Montreal: ICAO).

ICAO (2000), *International standards and recommended practices: annexes to the Convention on International Civil Aviation* (Chicago: ICAO).

'Integrale Beleidsvisie. Hoeveel ruimte geeft Nederland aan luchtvaart? Integrale beleidsvisie over de toekomst van luchtvaart in Nederland' (1997) (in Dutch).

Investopedia (2004), 'Volatility: what does it mean?', Equade Internet Ltd. <http://www.investopedia.com/terms/v/volatility.asp>.

Irwin, M.D. and Kasarda, J.D. (1991), 'Air passenger linkages and employment growth in U.S. metropolitan areas', *American Sociological Review* 56:4, 524–37.

Ivy, R.J. (1993), 'Variations in hub service in the US domestic air transportation network', *Journal of Transport Geography*, 1:4, 211–8.

Ivy, R.J., Fik, T.J. and Malecki, E.J. (1995), 'Changes in air service connectivity and employment', *Environment and Planning A* 27:2, 165–79.

Jagersma, P.K. (2003), *KLM. Waarheen vliegt gij?* (Holland Business Publications) (in Dutch).

James, C. (2003), 'Increasing the firm's strategic IQ: dynamic versus static strategic planning', *Graziadio Business Report* 6:2, <http://gbr.pepperdine.edu/032/>.

James, G.A., Cliff, A.D. and Haggett, P. (1970), 'Some discrete distributions for graphs with applications to regional transport networks', *Geografiska Annaler* 52B:1.

Janssen-Jansen, L. (2004). *Regio's uitgedaagd. 'Growth Management' ter inspiratie voor nieuwe paden van pro-actieve ruimtelijke planning*, PhD Thesis (Utrecht: Utrecht University) (in Dutch).

Kanafani, A. and Ghobrial, A.A. (1985), 'Airline hubbing: some implications for airport economics', *Transportation Research A* 19:1, 15–27.

Karlsson, J. (2003), *Dynamic strategic planning in practice: Pease International Airport*, Aviation Management and Research Conference, Montréal.

Kazda, A. and Caves, R.E. (2000), *Airport design and operation* (Amsterdam: Pergamon).

Keaton, M.H. (1993), 'Are there economies of traffic density in the less-than-truckload motor carrier industry? An operations planning analysis', *Transportation Research A* 27:5, 343–58.

Kinnock, N. (1998), *Speech to the Association of European Airlines Presidents' Assembly* (Berlin: European Commission).

Klapwijk, P. (1996), *Global economic networks: how deregulation leads to a new economic landscape*, PhD Thesis (Amsterdam: University of Amsterdam).

KLM (2002), *Belang van de verdere groei van de Schiphol-hub*, op basis van de resultaten van een drietal studies uitgevoerd door AAE, o.a. uitgevoerd in opdracht van de Stichting Connekt, 9 April 2002, unpublished document (in Dutch).

Krasner, S.D. (1991), 'Global communications and national power: life of the Pareto frontier', *World Politics* 43:3, 336–66.

Kreukels, A.J.M. (1978), 'Toepassing van strategische planning in de ruimtelijke planning', *Planning; methodiek en toepassing* 1978:6, 21–31 (in Dutch).

Kreukels, A.J.M. (1980), *Planning en planningsproces* (VUGA) (in Dutch).

Kuby, M.J. and Gray, R.G. (1993), 'The hub network design problem with stopovers and feeders: the case of Federal Express', *Transportation Research A* 27:1, 1–12.

Landeghem, H. van and Vanmaele, H. (2002), 'Robust planning: a new paradigm for demand chain planning', *Journal of Operations Management* 20:6, 769–83.

Lane, R., Lepardo, V. and Woodman, G. (2001), 'How to deal with dynamic complexity on large, long projects', Paper presented at the ASCE's – IATA Conference, Orlando, Florida.

Langley, A., Mintzberg, H., Pitcher, P., Posada, E. and Saint-Macary, J. (1995), 'Opening up decision making: the view from the black stool', *Organization Science* 6:3, 260–79.

Lambooy, J.G. (1995), *Regionale economische dynamiek* (Bussum: Coutinho) (in Dutch).

Lepardo, V. and Lane, R. (2002), 'Wicked problems, righteous solutions: back to the future on large complex projects', *PB network* 2002:54, 4–11.

Lerman, R.I. and Yitzhaki, S. (1985), 'Income inequality effects by income source: a new approach and applications to the United States', *The Review of Economics and Statistics* 67:1, 151–6.

Leslie, K.J. and Michaels, M.P. (1997), 'The real power of real options', *The McKinsey Quarterly* 1997:3, 5–23.

l'Humanité (2000), 'Air France prend le contrôle de régional airlines', *Journal l'Humanité* 20 janvier (in French).

Lijesen, M.G. (2003), 'Customer valuation of flight characteristics: a stated preference approach', ATRS Conference, Toulouse.

Lijesen, M.G. (2004), *Home carrier advantages in the airline industry*, PhD Thesis (Amsterdam: Free University of Amsterdam).

Lijesen, M.G., Rietveld, P. and Nijkamp, P. (2000), 'Do European carriers dominate their hubs?', 4th ATRG Conference, 2–4 July, Amsterdam.

Lindblom, C.E. (1990), *Inquiry and change: the troubled attempt to understand and shape society* (New Haven: Yale University Press).

McLoughlin, J.B. (1979), *Urban and regional planning: a systems approach* (London: Faber and Faber).

McShan, W.S. and Windle, R.J. (1989), 'The implications of hub-and-spoke routing for airline costs and competitiveness', *Logistics and transportation review* 25:3, 209–30.

Mendes de Leon, P. (2002), *Before and after the tenth anniversary of the Open Skies Agreement Netherlands–US of 1992* (Leiden: Internationaal Instituut voor Lucht- en Ruimterecht van de Universiteit Leiden).

Mendes de Leon, P. (2003), *Van Open Skies naar open markten: het dilemma in de internationale luchtvaart* (Leiden: Internationaal Instituut voor Lucht- en Ruimterecht van de Universiteit Leiden) (in Dutch).

Meyer, M. (1993), 'Build it and hope they'll come: is Denver's new international airport a visionary coup or a monument to the excesses of the '80s?', *Newsweek* June 7, 1993.

Michael, S.R. (1979), 'Guidelines for contingency approach to planning', *Long Range Planning* 12:6, 62–8.

Milanovic, B. and Yitzhaki, S. (2004), *Decomposing world income distribution* (Washington/Jerusalem).

Miles, M.B. and Huberman, A.M. (1994), *Qualitative data analysis: an expanded sourcebook* (Thousand Oaks, CA, London, New Delhi: Sage Publications).

Ministerie van Verkeer & Waterstaat (1999), *Investeringskosten ONL. Kostenraming van een eiland in de Noordzee en een redesign van Schiphol* RLD 127 (in Dutch).

Ministerie van Verkeer & Waterstaat (2000), *Definitief kabinetsvoornemen Toekomst van de Nationale Luchthaven*, Brief aan de voorzitter van de Tweede Kamer der Staten Generaal (in Dutch).

Ministerie van Verkeer & Waterstaat (2003), *Brief aan de voorzitter van de Tweede Kamer der Staten-generaal*, 2 oktober 2003, (in Dutch).

Ministerie van Verkeer & Waterstaat (2003), *'Onderzoeksprogramma Flyland'*, Brief aan de voorzitter van de Tweede Kamer der Staten-Generaal <http://www.minvenw.nl> (in Dutch).

Ministerie van Verkeer & Waterstaat (2004), *Voorgeschiedenis Project Mainport Schiphol* <http://www.mainportschiphol.nl> (in Dutch).

Ministerie van Verkeer & Waterstaat/Directoraat-Generaal Rijksluchtvaartdienst (1999), *The future of the national airport*, 17 December 1999 (in Dutch).

Ministerie van VROM (2004), *Nota Ruimte* (Den Haag: Ministerie van VROM) (in Dutch).

Mintzberg, H. (1994), *The rise and fall of strategic planning* (New York: The Free Press).

Mom, G., Dierikx, M.L.J., van den Boogaard, A. and Werff, C. (1999), *Schiphol. Haven, station, knooppunt sinds 1916* (Zutphen: Walburg Pers/Stichting Historie der Techniek) (in Dutch).

Morocco, J.D. (2001), 'Major shake-up of the Scandinavian air travel market', *Aviation Week & Space Technology* 154:2, 40–2.

Morrish, S.C. and Hamilton, R.T. (2002), 'Airline alliances: who benefits?', *Journal of Air Transport Management* 8:6, 401–7.

Morrison, S.A. and Winston, C. (1995), *The evolution of the airline industry* (Washington: The Brookings Institution).

Moselle, B., Reitzes, J., Robyn, D. and Horn, J. (2002), *The impact of an EU–US open aviation area*, Prepared for the European Commission. Directorate-General Energy and Transport (London, Washington, DC: Brattle Group).

Mussard, S., Seyte, F. and Terraza, M. (2003), 'Decomposition of Gini and the generalized entropy inequality measures', *Economics Bulletin* 4:7, 1–6.

NAH (2000), *Ruimtelijk-economische visie Schipholregio*, Ambtelijk advies aan de voor Schiphol verantwoordelijke bestuurders Provincie Noord-Holland, Gemeente Amsterdam, Gemeente Haarlemmermeer (in Dutch).

Nayar, B.R. (1995), 'Regimes, power and international aviation', *International Organization* 49:1, 139–70.

Nederlandse Luchtvaartsector (2001a), *Voorlopige resultaten Businesscase Schiphol Redesign*, 1 januari 2001 (in Dutch).

Nederlandse Luchtvaartsector (2001b), *Brief aan de Minister van Verkeer en Waterstaat*, Schiphol, 3 mei 2001 (in Dutch).

Nederlandse Luchtvaartsector (2002), *Ruimte voor luchtvaart. Redesign: de mogelijkheden op Schiphol nader onderzocht*, Management samenvatting 2002, juni 2002 (in Dutch).

Neely, J.E. and de Neufville, R. (2001), 'Hybrid real options valuation of risky product development projects', *International Journal of Technology, Policy and Management* (prepublication draft).

Nijkamp, P. (1996), *Liberalisation of air transport in Europe: the survival of the fittest?* (Amsterdam: Vrije Universiteit van Amsterdam).

Nutt, B. (1988), 'The strategic design of buildings', *Long Range Planning* 21:4, 130–40.

N.V. Luchthaven Schiphol (1989), *Beleidsvoornemen Masterplan Schiphol 2003* (in Dutch).

Nyfer (2000), *Hub, of spokestad? Ruimtelijk-economische effecten van luchthavens* (Breukelen: Nyfer) (in Dutch).

O'Connor, K. (1997), 'The international air linkages of Australian cities 1985–1996', Department of Geography and Environmental Science, Monash University.

O'Connor, K. (2003), 'Global air travel: toward concentration or dispersal?', *Journal of Transport Geography* 11:2, 83–92.

Odoni, A.R. and de Neufville, R. (1992), 'Passenger terminal design', *Transportation Research A* 26:1, 27–35.

O'Kelly, M.E. (1998), 'A geographer's analysis of hub-and-spoke networks', *Journal of Transport Geography* 6:3, 171–86.

O'Kelly, M.E. and Bryan, D.L. (1998), 'Hub location with flow economies of scale', *Transportation Research B* 32:8, 605–16.

O'Kelly, M.E. and Miller, H.J. (1994), 'The hub network design problem', *Journal of Transport Geography* 2:1, 31–40.

Oum, T.H., Park, J.-H. and Zhang, A. (2000), *Globalization and strategic alliances: the case of the airline industry* (Amsterdam: Pergamon).

Oum, T.H., Taylor, A.J. and Zhang, A. (1993), 'Strategic airline policy in the globalizing airline networks', *Transportation Journal* 32:3, 14–30.

Oum, T.H., Yu, C. and Zhang, A. (2001), 'Global airline alliances: international regulatory issues', *Journal of Air Transport Management* 7:1, 57–62.

Oum, T.H., Zhang, A. and Zhang, Y. (1995), 'Airline network rivalry', *Journal of Economics* 18:4a, 836–57.

Paraskevopoulos, D., Karakitsos, E. and Rustem, B. (1991), 'Robust capacity planning under uncertainty', *Management Science* 37:7, 787–99.

Park, J.-H., Park, N.K. and Zhang, A. (2003), 'The impact of international alliances on rival firm value: a study of the British Airways/USAir Alliance', *Transportation Research E* 39:1, 1–18.

Parsons, W. (1995), *Public policy: an introduction to the theory and practice of policy analysis* (Cheltenham: Edward Elgar).

Pels, E. (2000), *Airport economics and policy: efficiency, competition, and interaction with airlines*, PhD Thesis (Amsterdam: Vrije Universiteit van Amsterdam).

Pels, E. (2001), 'A note on airline alliances', *Journal of Air Transport Management* 7:1, 3–7.

Penney, C. (2002), 'Braathens: Norway's airline', *Airliner World* February 2002, 22–6.

Penney, C. (2002), 'Swiss simplicity', *Airliner World* June 2002, 56–8.

Petzinger, J.R. (1995), *Hard landing: the epic contest for power and profits that plunged the airlines into chaos* (New York: Random House).

Porter, M.E. (1980), *Competitive strategy: techniques for analyzing industries and competitors* (New York: The Free Press).

Project Mainport & Milieu Schiphol (1995), *Planologische Kernbeslissing Schiphol en Omgeving*, Tweede Kamer der Staten-Generaal (in Dutch).

Provincie Noord-Holland (2003), *Streekplan Noord-Holland-Zuid*, Vastgesteld door Provinciale Staten van Holland op 17 februari 2003, Samenvatting (in Dutch).

Prud'homme, R. (2004), 'Infrastructure and development', Paper prepared for the ABCDE (Annual Bank Conference on Development Economics), 3–5 May, Washington, DC.

Randoy, T. and Pettersen Strandenes, S. (1997), 'The effect of public ownership and deregulation in the Scandinavian airline industry', *Journal of Air Transport Management* 3:4, 211–15.

Real Options Group (2004), 'Concepts in real options: an overview' <http://www.rogroup.com>.

Régional (2004), 'Clermont-Ferrand: a new orientation', 2004 <http://www.regional.fr>.

Reynolds-Feighan, A. (1995), 'European and American approaches to air transport liberalisation: some implications for small communities', *Transportation Research A* 29:6, 467–83.

Reynolds-Feighan, A. (1998), 'The impact of U.S. airline deregulation on airport traffic patterns', *Geographical Analysis* 30:3, 234–53.

Reynolds-Feighan, A. (1999), 'Subsidiation policies in the provision of air services to small communities: European and US approaches', Forum on Air Transport Provision in Europe's Remote Regions, Nairn, UK.

Reynolds-Feighan, A. (2000), 'The US airport hierarchy and implications for small communities', *Urban Studies* 37:3, 557–77.

Reynolds-Feighan, A. (2001), 'Traffic distribution in low-cost and full-service carrier networks in the US air transport market', *Journal of Air Transport Management* 7:5, 265–75.

Reynolds-Feighan, A. (2004), 'Application of Gini decompositions to analysis of transportation networks', ERSA 2004 Conference, 25-29 Augustus 2004, Porto.

Rhoades, D.L. and Lush, H. (1997), 'A typology of strategic alliances in the airline industry: propositions for stability and duration', *Journal of Air Transport Management* 3:3, 109–14.

Robson, C. (2002), *Real world research: a resource for social scientists and practitioner-researchers* (Malden: Blackwell Publishers).

Robusté, F. and Clavera, J. (1997), *Impacto economico del aeropuerto de Barcelona*, (Madrid: Editorial Civitas/Aena) (in Spanish).

Rosenau, J.N. (1992), 'Governance, order, and change in world politics', in J.N. Rosenau and E.-O. Czempiel (eds), *Governance without government: order and change in world politics* (Cambridge: Cambridge University Press).

RPB (2005), *Atlas of airports in Northwest Europe*, Netherlands Institute for Spatial Research <www.rpb.nl>, accessed 10 July 2006.

Ruefli, T. and Sarrazin, J. (1981), 'Strategic control of corporate development under ambiguous circumstances', *Management Science* 27:10, 1158–70.

Ruijter, P. de and Janssen, N. (1996), '(Real) options thinking and scenarios' <http://www.deruijter.net>.

Rycroft, R.W. and Szyliowicz, J.S. (1980), 'The technological dimension of decision-making: the case of the Aswan High Dam', *World Politics* 33:1, 36–61.

Sanchez, R. and Collins, R.P. (2001), 'Competing and learning in modular markets', *Long Range Planning* 34:6, 645–67.

Sanders, T.I. (1998), *Strategic thinking and the new science: planning in the midst of chaos, complexity and change* (New York: The Free Press).

Scenario Werkgroep ONL (2001), *Lange termijn scenerio's voor Schiphol* <www.flyland.nl> (in Dutch).

Schaafsma, M. (2001), 'Planning Schiphol Airport City', in B. Scholl and E.-A. Budau (eds), *Flughafen- und Raumentwicklung* (Karlsruhe: Institut für Städtebau und Landesplanung, Universität Karlsruhe).

Schiphol Group (2000), *Creating airport cities* (brochure).

Schiphol Group (2001a), *Definitief plan van aanpak. Airport Development Plan 2003-2020*, 16 juli 2001 versie 7 (in Dutch).

Schiphol Group (2001b), *Inventarisatie lange termijn scenario's* (in Dutch).

Schiphol Group/Afdeling Airport Development (2003a), *Ruimtelijke toekomstvisie Schiphol 2020*, Versie 29 oktober 2003 (in Dutch).

Schiphol Group/Afdeling Airport Development (2003b), *Ruimtelijke Toekomstvisie 2020*, Concept. Versie 24 november 2003 (in Dutch).

Schiphol Group (2003c), *Ruimtelijke Toekomstvisie Schiphol 2020*, Concept. Afdeling Airport Development (in Dutch).

Schiphol Group (2003d), *Jaarverslag Schiphol Group* <http://www.schiphol.nl> (in Dutch).

Schiphol Group/Afdeling Airport Development (2004a), *Plan van Aanpak. Studie Toekomstige Bedrijfsvoering Passagiers afhandeling Terminal Complex Schiphol Centrum*, Concept (in Dutch).

Schiphol Group/Afdeling Airport Development (2004b), *Passagiersvervoer via Schiphol in eerste halfjaar met 8% gestegen*, Press release (in Dutch).

Schiphol Group/Afdeling Airport Development (2004c), *Herijking 1e planfase RTV*, (in Dutch).

Schiphol Group/Afdeling Airport Development (2004d), *AAS MLT ontwikkelings-strategie passagiers -en vliegtuigafhandeling*, Presentatie Hoofdlijnen- Concept, Versie 19 januari 2004, (in Dutch).

Schiphol Group/Afdeling Airport Development (2004e), *AAS MLT ontwikkelingsplan passagiers- en vliegtuigafhandeling onderdeel GHJ-gebied*, Besluitvormingsdocument MT-SG 2 maart 2004 (in Dutch).

Schiphol Group/Afdeling Airport Development (2004f), *Statistical Annual Review 2003* <www.schipholgroup.nl>.

Schipper, Y. (1999), *Market structure and environmental costs in aviation: a welfare analysis of European air transport reform*, PhD Thesis (Amsterdam: Free University of Amsterdam).

Schipper, Y. and Rietveld, P. (1997), 'Economic and environmental effects of airline deregulation', in C. Capineri and P. Rietveld (eds), *Networks in transport and communications* (Aldershot: Ashgate).

Sen, A. (1976), 'Poverty: an ordinal approach to measurement', *Econometrica* 44:2, 219–31.

Shaw, S.-L. (1993), 'Hub structures of major US passenger airlines', *Journal of Transport Geography* 1:1, 47–58.

Shaw, S.-L. and Ivy, R. J. (1994), 'Airline mergers and their effects on network structure', *Journal of Transport Geography* 2:4, 234–46.

Shy, O. (1997), *The economics of network industries* (Cambridge: Cambridge University Press).

Simon, H. (1957), *Models of Man* (New York: Wiley).

Simpson, D. G. (1998), 'Why most strategic planning is a waste of time and what you can do about it', *Long Range Planning* 31:3, 476–80.

Skinner, D. C. (2001), *Introduction to decision analysis: a practitioner's guide to improving decision quality* (Gainesville, FL: Probabilistic Publishing).

Smit, H. (2003), 'Infrastructure investment as a real options game: the case of European airport expansion', *Financial Management Journal* 2003: Winter, 5–35.

Spaeth, A. (2002), 'Iberia in good shape', *Flug Revue*, August.

Staatsblad van het Koninkrijk der Nederlanden (2002), 'Besluit van 26 november 2002 tot vaststelling van een luchthavenverkeerbesluit voor de luchthaven Schiphol (Luchthavenverkeerbesluit Schiphol)', Jaargang 2002 (in Dutch).

Starkie, D. (2002), 'Airport regulation and competition', *Journal of Air Transport Management* 8:1, 63–76.

Stout, H. (2001), 'Capaciteitsmanagement van luchthaven Schiphol', in E.F. Ten Heuvelhof, K. Koolstra and H. Stout (eds), *Capaciteitsmanagement: beslissen over capaciteit van infrastructuren* (Utrecht: Lemma) (in Dutch).

Stratagem Amsterdam (1997), *Concurrentie analyse van Europese luchthavens*, Deel onderzoek netwerkontwikkelingen (Amsterdam: Stratagem Strategic Research BV) (in Dutch).

Strategische beleidskeuze Toekomst Luchtvaart (1998), *Waar ligt de toekomst van luchtvaart in Nederland?* <http://www.mainportschiphol.nl> (in Dutch).

Strategische beleidskeuze Toekomst Luchtvaart (1999), *Toekomst van de nationale luchthaven* (in Dutch).

Sydney Airport Corporation Limited (2003), *Sydney Airport Preliminary Draft Master Plan.*

Thompson, I.B. (2002), 'Air transport liberalisation and the development of third level airports in France', *Journal of Transport Geography* 10:4, 273–85.

Timberlake, M., Smith, D.A. and Shin, K.H. (2000), 'The relative centrality of cities based upon air passenger travel', GaWC Study Group and Network.

Tinkler, K.J. (1977), 'An introduction to graph theoretical methods in geography', *Modern Geography*, 14, 3–55.

Tinkler, K.J. (1979), 'Graph theory', *Progress in Human Geography*.

Toh, R.S. (1998), 'Towards an international open skies regime: advances, impediments, and impacts', *Journal of Air Transportation World Wide* 3:1, 61–70.

Toh, R.S. and Higgins, R.G. (1985), 'The impact of hub and spoke network centralization and route monopoly on domestic airline profitability', *Transportation Journal* 1985: Summer, 16–27.

Tretheway, M.W. (2004), 'Distortions of airline revenues: why the network airline business model is broken', *Journal of Air Transport Management* 10:1, 3–14.

Veldhuis, J. (1997), 'The competitive position of airline networks', *Journal of Air Transport Management* 3:4, 181–8.

Veldhuis, J. and E. Kroes (2002), 'Dynamics in relative network performance of the main European hub airports', European Transport Conference, 9–11 September, Cambridge.

Verbeek, B. (2001), 'De sturende overheid in het perspectief van internationalisering en europeanisering', in J.R. Hakfoort and R. Torenvlied (eds), *De staat buitenspel. Overheidssturing en nieuwe instituties* (Meppel: Boom) (in Dutch).

Verdaas, C. and Arts, G. (1999), 'Strategisch beleid: een diffuus begrip', *Beleid en Maatschappij* 26:3, 153–62 (in Dutch).

Virgin Express (2004), 'Virgin Express gives priority to flights to the South of Europe', Press Release, 27th April 2004.

Volten, P.M.E., Harryvan, A.G. and Harst, J. v.d. (1999), 'Inleiding', in. P.M.E. Volten, A.G. Harryvan and J. v.d. Harst (eds), *Internationale betrekkingen. Samenwerking en regimevorming in de internationale betrekkingen* (Assen: Van Gorcum) (in Dutch).

Wall, S. (2004), *On the fly: executing strategy in a changing world* (Hoboken: John Wiley & Sons).

Wassenbergh, H. (1996), 'The "Sixth" freedom revisited', unpublished document.

Wassenbergh, H. (2003a), 'June 5, 2003, a historic decision by the EU council of transport ministers', unpublished document.

Wassenbergh, H. (2003b), 'International air transport: fair and equal opportunity to compete', unpublished document.

Weber, C.E. (1984), 'Strategic thinking: dealing with uncertainty', *Long Range Planning* 17:5, 60–70.

Weber, M. and Dinwoodie, J. (2000), 'Fifth freedoms and airline alliances: the role of fifth freedom traffic in an understanding of airline alliances', *Journal of Air Transport Management* 6:1, 51–60.

Wells, A. and Young, S.B. (2004), *Airport planning and management* (New York: McGraw-Hill).

Werson, M. and Burghouwt, G. (2006), 'Airport planning in free market regimes', German Aviation Research Society Conference, 29 June–1 July 2006, Amsterdam.

Westley, F. and Mintzberg, H. (1989), 'Visonary leadership and strategic management', *Strategic Management Journal* 10: Summer, 17–32.

Williams, G. (1994), *Airline industry and the impact of deregulation* (Cambridge: Cambridge University Press).

Williams, G. (2001), 'Will Europe's charter carriers be replaced by "no-frills" scheduled airlines?', *Journal of Air Transport Management* 7:5, 277–86.

Williams, G. (2002), *Airline competition: deregulation's mixed legacy* (Aldershot: Ashgate).

Williams, G. and Pagliari, R. (2004), 'A comparative analysis of the application and use of public service obligations in air transport within the EU', *Transport Policy* 11:1, 55–66.

Wilson, I. (1998), 'Strategic planning for the millennium: resolving the dilemma', *Long Range Planning* 31:4, 507–13.

Wodon, Q. and Yitzhaki, S. (2001), *The effect of using group data on the estimation of the Gini income elasticity* (Washington: World Bank).

Wodon, Q. and Yitzhaki, S. (2004), *Inequality and social welfare: poverty reduction strategy sourcebook* (Washington, DC: World Bank).

Wojahn, O.W. (2001), *Airline networks*, PhD Thesis (Frankfurt am Main: Peter Lang. Europäischer Verlag der Wissenschaften).

Worthington, J. and Briggs, G. (2000), 'Airport city: interchange, gateway and destination', in M. Collin (ed.), *Aeroports et dynamiques des territoires. Rapport du comité scientifique. Laboratoire théories des mutations urbaines*, MR CNSR 7543.

Yitzhaki, S. (2002), 'Do we need a separate poverty measurement?', *European Journal of Political Economy* 18:1, 61–85.

Zacher, M.W. and Sutton, C.J. (1996), *Governing global networks: international regimes for transportation and communication* (Cambridge: Cambridge University Press).

Zhang, A. (1996), 'An analysis of fortress hubs in airline networks', *Journal of Transport Economics and Policy* 30:3, 293–308.

Zhang, A. and Wei, X. (1993), 'Competition in airline networks: the case of elasticity demands', *Economic Letters* 42, 253–9.

Zhang, A. and Zhang, Y. (2001), 'Issues on liberalization of air cargo services in international aviation', ATRG Conference 2001, Seoul.

Index